Breaking the Land

Pete Daniel

Breaking the Land

The Transformation of Cotton, Tobacco, and Rice Cultures since 1880

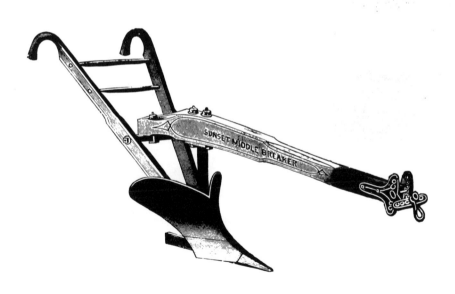

University of Illinois Press

Urbana and Chicago

Publication of this work was funded in part by a grant from the National Endowment for the Humanities, a federal agency that supports study in such fields as history, philosophy, literature, and languages.

This book is printed on acid-free paper.

Library of Congress Cataloging in Publication Data

Daniel, Pete.
   Breaking the land.

   Includes index.
   1. Cotton trade—Southern States—History.   2. Tobacco industry—Southern States—History.   3. Rice trade—Southern States—History.   I. Title.
HD9077.A13D36 1985   306'.3   84-197
ISBN 0-252-01147-3 (cloth)
ISBN 0-252-01391-3 (paper)

For Louis R. Harlan

Contents

Acknowledgments

The National Endowment for the Humanities supported this project with a fellowship for independent research and study in 1978–79, and I was a fellow at the Woodrow Wilson International Center for Scholars in 1981–82. I wish to thank Martha Loerke and Michael Machell for helping as research assistants at the Wilson Center, Eloise Doane, coordinator of typing services at the Center, and her staff, and Michael Lacy, secretary of the American Society and Politics Program. The archivists and staff of the National Archives provided not only guidance and encouragement in research but also a community of friends. Research assistance was provided by Helen Boyd, curator of the Arkansas County Agricultural Museum, the staffs of the Georgia Department of Archives and History, the Southwestern Archives and Manuscripts Collection, the Louisiana State University Archives, and the Prints and Photographs Division and the Manuscript Division of the Library of Congress.

I appreciate those who critically read drafts or portions of this manuscript: Gladys Baker, Mary O. Furner, Louis R. Harlan, Jack Temple Kirby, Wayne Rasmussen, David L. Smiley, Raymond W. Smock, John Thomas, David Whisnant, Harold D. Woodman, and Nan Woodruff. Robert B. Morgan and James P. Kelly, Jr., fellow Tarheels, gave special support. Susan J. Courter not only critically read the manuscript but also gave welcomed encouragement throughout the project. My daughters, Lisa and Laura, as always, pampered and encouraged me. The staff of the National Museum of American History, especially Arthur Molella, has encouraged me to complete this project. Ann Weir of the University of Illinois Press edited the manuscript with her usual thoroughness. Mentioning such support and encouragement in a list fails to transmit deeper appreciation that I feel.

Introduction

This book deals with work cycles and transformation in the cotton, flue-cured tobacco, and prairie rice cultures, with the daily and seasonal routines of farm families, the annual cycle of breaking the land, planting, cultivating, harvesting, and marketing. In a longer view it deals with the transformation forced, over time, by mechanization and government policy. The old Cotton Belt stretching from Virginia to Texas has dominated southern agriculture as well as southern history. This cotton crescent, at the turn of the century, was anchored at one end by tobacco growers and at the other by rice farmers; each end overlapped with the center, for many tobacco and rice farmers also grew cotton. Still, farmers customarily identified themselves with one crop and took pride in their ability to coax its seedlings from the ground and bring it to harvest. Each of these crop cultures underlined the diversity of the rural South and, as important, revealed how each culture's peculiarities reacted differently to the forces of modernization fed primarily by governmental policy and mechanization. The transformation of southern agriculture was part of an encompassing movement to substitute machines and capital for labor in all segments of the economy.

These three rural cultures were as distinct in origins as in their twentieth-century development. Commercial tobacco production, of course, dates to the Jamestown colony in the early seventeenth century, but cotton cultivation became important only after the invention of the cotton gin in 1793. Rice had been a staple of the Carolina and Georgia lowcountry since colonial times, but while rice planting faltered there after the Civil War, a highly mechanized rice culture sprang up on the Gulf Coast in the 1880s and quickly eclipsed Carolina and Mississippi River producers. Unlike tobacco and cotton, the prairie rice culture was unsouthern both in growers, mostly transplanted Midwesterners, and in modern machinery, modified wheat binders and steam threshers. At the turn of the twentieth century, each culture faced distinct problems that challenge the idea that southern agriculture presented a uniform set of maladies.

The commodity cultures discussed in this work vary in important ways and thus furnish three distinctive lenses for viewing rural life. Clearly each commodity has a different use. The cotton plant provides fiber for clothing and seeds that yield vegetable oil and other by-products. Tobacco is used for smoking and chewing, and rice is a basic food throughout the world. Each had a distinct labor requirement, and the scale of each commodity called for a different farm organization. While flue-cured tobacco families tilled three to eight acres and cotton farmers fifteen to twenty, a family in the rice area could manage two hundred acres with a hired hand and a large crew at harvest and threshing season. While the prairie rice culture quickly became highly mechanized, the traditional Carolina and Georgia rice culture had been extremely labor intensive; however, it faded into obscurity by the turn of the century.

Each culture utilized the common forms of southern tenure—own-ers, tenants, and sharecroppers. The forces set in motion by Civil War and emancipation established sharecropping in the cotton and tobacco areas of the South. Although arrangements varied, in most cases a landlord or credit merchant furnished housing, land, seed, fertilizer, and work stock for a half-share of the cash crop. Tenants and share-croppers could also fish the streams, plant gardens, hunt the woods, and cut firewood for their homes. The elements of paternalism that de-veloped during slavery persisted and increasingly crossed the color line. Rice tenants and sharecroppers were different, for most owned expensive machinery. Indeed, because of crop rotation practices, an owner might till his own land one year and then sharecrop with a neighbor the next. Most rice tenants were white. Farmers who culti-vated these crops ordered their lives in a routine that coincided with the crop cycle, and their family structure, recreation, and vocabulary —that is, the entire society—reflected the commodity that dictated their lives and once a year paid them a cash settlement.

Each of the three cultures mechanized at a different rate. Rice growers in the prairie adapted binders and threshers in the 1880s, in-stalled expensive irrigation networks by the 1890s, replaced mules with tractors during World War I, and turned to combines by 1945. Cotton farmers haltingly used tractors in the 1920s, increased their use greatly in the mid-1930s, and by the late 1940s invested in me-chanical cotton pickers and chemical weed killers that ended the need for seasonal labor. Only in the 1970s did harvesting machines and bulk curing significantly cut labor requirements in the tobacco culture. Internal dynamics and tenure systems also varied. The rice culture, restricted to a small area, by 1910 organized successful cooperatives that prevented the depressing surpluses that affected cotton and tobacco farmers whose cooperative attempts failed. It proved difficult to organize small-scale cotton and tobacco farmers—indeed, it took federal programs to curtail production. These and other variations offer contrasts in assessing how the transformation occurred and how each commodity culture evolved uniquely into agribusiness. Certainly other commodities such as sugar, peanuts, and soybeans offer different insights; still, cotton, tobacco, and rice offer a place to start in assessing the impact of government and machines on the South.

In many ways the South in 1900 was like an underdeveloped colony that looked north for credit and ideas, and northern investors eagerly extracted southern resources. While some boosters stressed industry and urbanization as the road to progress, others toured the countryside preaching scientific farming and mechanization. Of course, farming could never assume the efficiency of the business world, for the caprices of weather, the vast geographic distribution of producers, and fluctuating international demand preserved a certain sense of anarchy. Still, the southern commodity cultures of cotton, tobacco, and rice resembled industries as diverse as steel, meat packing, or petroleum in that each organized the work cycle in a distinct manner. Just as during the Progressive Era many industries called for order and advocated federal rules to rationalize enterprise, farmers by the end of the 1920s, after unsuccessful farm movements, cooperatives, and political lobbying, demanded that the federal government bring order to the chaos of rollercoaster prices that charted the peaks and valleys of supply and demand. The advocates of rural change reflected no more upon long-range human displacement than did the captains of industry; each wanted an efficient operation that depended more upon the regularity of machines and federal guidelines than on the whims of workers and the marketplace.

Although backward in many respects, the rural South was far from placid and stagnant. The expansion of the flue-cured tobacco culture into new growing areas, the emergence of the prairie rice industry, a dynamic shift in cotton production to western growing areas, the boll weevil, the rise of the federal Extension Service, war, migration, depression, and mechanization altered traditional rural life. The problems generated in the first part of the century led agricultural thinkers to draft plans in the 1920s that New Dealers wrote into the Agricultural Adjustment Act a decade later.

The new emphasis on scientific farming developed while the South made the transition from slave labor to sharecropping and as white yeomen lost their land and also joined the sharecropper ranks. In the three-quarters of a century after the Civil War the number of white landowners fell drastically, and while some blacks purchased land, most continued as landless tenants. These peasants fell into the cycle that crops and landlords dictated, and at the end of each year many moved to different farms hoping to improve their lives. While prairie rice growers established a highly mechanized crop culture, cotton and tobacco farmers continued to exploit family labor and use labor-intensive methods of cultivation. Such backward methods did not fit into the government's dream of progressive farmers.

As land-grant universities matured and expanded, as high schools and colleges educated not only prospective farmers but also a new generation of agricultural specialists, and as the Extension Service fattened on a budget to exterminate the boll weevil and encourage diversification, the long arm of government reached into the recesses of the southern hinterland. In many respects these government institutions encouraged social engineering as they wrenched farmers from dependence on a single poorly cultivated crop and led them into diversification and the utilization of machines, chemicals, and ledger books. While more affluent farmers welcomed changes that saved labor and produced better crops, others had neither the education nor the finances to take advantage of modern ways. Nor did the agricultural education complex or the United States Department of Agriculture devote much effort to uplifting sharecroppers and tenants.

By 1930 the numerous and eroded cotton and tobacco farms barely supported families and gave little hope to a new generation of prospective farmers. Rice producers held production steady and waited for higher prices. The agricultural depression during the 1920s, overproduction, the international financial collapse in 1929, and farmers' inability to act in concert led them to accept New Deal programs. At the same time, a host of new implements appealed to landowners who, with dependable parity prices and government payments, could afford them. As these forces coalesced in the 1930s, a revolution spread across the South, a gigantic yet muted transition from the old cultures to a more rationalized and businesslike way of farming.

Indeed, in the fifteen years after Franklin D. Roosevelt's inauguration in 1933, both cotton and rice growers adopted new machines that drastically cut labor requirements. By the 1960s tobacco farmers also began mechanization. Millions of farmers displaced from the land left quietly, many for cities and new opportunities. The struggle between landlord and tenant over provisions, government payments, and a just settlement, the planter's decision to evict certain workers and retain others, and the refugee's choice of destination encompassed the South, but such struggles were particularized. The spirited but unsuccessful protests that did emerge only underlined how quietly rural people melted away. The old labor-intensive and mobile culture that even in good years produced little cash gave way to agribusiness and a farm lobby that voiced new concerns about credit and government programs.

Fewer but more sophisticated farmers require more federal programs; still, thousands of farmers fail each year. Yet the rural traveler sees constant reminders of the agricultural system that once characterized the South—vacant and decaying tenant houses, sagging barns, and empty mule lots. These museum pieces stand juxtaposed with brick houses and mobile homes, bulk tobacco barns, irrigation equipment, tractors, and picking machines. The human relics, however, have migrated to cities where they try to preserve the heritage of rural life and to overcome their legacy of illiteracy and poverty.

This book makes no claim to be a definitive history of the transformation of southern agriculture, nor does it trace the paths of those who left the South. At several junctures in the research and writing it became apparent that only booklength studies could settle certain questions. For example, historians have not studied the crucial points of commodity exchange. Tobacco warehouses, cotton gins and buyers, and rice millers demand careful study, as does the cottonseed industry. Government payments to farmers or other landowners question the intention of federal policy and demand a complete analysis. The entire agricultural complex of research, extension, education, and policy needs a fresh historical approach, with an eye to resolving the contradictory policies in effect over the years. Because of the rural South's diversity, family, community, county, state, and sectional studies would answer questions about the peculiarities of changing farm life. To complete the picture of the farmstead, historians of material culture need to investigate the houses and tools that farmers used. Oral historians have time left to quiz farmers and former farmers on the old ways, and students of documentary photographs can analyze images from the past. While the old commodity cultures are fading into the mists of the past, they represent not only the southern heritage of hard work and tradition but that of conflict, exploitation, and failure as well. Much of what is contained in this book is written in the hope that themes treated briefly and incompletely here will stir additional interest.

A note on the photograph captions: they are standardized, beginning with the exact description found with the image, the photographer's name (if available), the photograph number, and the location. Any editorial material is placed within brackets.

Book One: Three Southern Commodity Cultures, 1880–1932

Thus saith the Lord: Stand ye in the ways, and see, and ask for the old paths, where is the good way, and walk therein, and ye shall find rest for your souls. But they said, "We will not walk therein."

—Jeremiah 6:16

Weighing cotton picked by hired pickers. This is a familiar scene in the South. The plantation owner weighs the cotton as often as the hampers are filled. It is frequently called the "weigh up." N.d. J. C. Coovert. (16-G-121-1-2, National Archives)

1

The Boll Weevil, the Government, and the Cotton Culture

If we win the cotton crop, the cooperative Demonstration work will be accepted as the most valuable work yet undertaken for the farmers. If we fail on the cotton crop, our work will stand condemned and be swallowed up by other agencies regardless of the great assistance we give in the development of other crops.
— *L. M. Calhoun, 1914*

For a century and a half cotton farming dominated the southern United States. Indeed, the invention of the cotton gin followed by only four years the establishment of the government; the cotton culture and the fledgling nation grew up together. Between 1793 and 1861 the cotton culture expanded from the Atlantic seaboard across the Mississippi River. The cotton gin was such a simple machine that it was endlessly replicated in each settlement as cotton marched west from county to county. A way of life moved across the land—a classbound society run by planters, acknowledged by white farmers, and fueled by slave labor. Dynamic and expansive, the short staple cotton culture literally burst upon South Carolina and paused only briefly to gather young sons and additional slaves before moving through the Black Belt of Georgia and Alabama and into Mississippi and Louisiana.

The peculiar needs of the crop dictated the way cotton farmers ordered their lives. Cotton had its cycle of land preparation, sowing, chopping, and harvest. After breaking the land in the late winter, rows were run and then the cotton was planted. After it sprouted, the workforce passed through the fields, thinning the plants and chopping out the weeds. Plowing alternated with chopping until around July, when workers laid the crop by—a term that simply meant they ended fieldwork. Then there was time for fishing, religious revivals, and leisure. In September or October the bolls filled out and burst into white puffs of lint, and then workers moved through the fields with sacks, picking out the cotton. As additional bolls burst, the task continued throughout the fall until the field had yielded its crop. The cotton gin separated the seeds from the lint, which was baled and sold. Until the 1880s seeds were discarded, except for enough to plant the next year. This annual work cycle persisted from the late eighteenth century well into the twentieth.

Although cultivation practices changed little for a century and a half, the end of slavery revolutionized tenure arrangements in the cotton culture. Most former slaves as well as increasing numbers of white yeomen became sharecroppers who worked on yearly contracts and received housing, food, fuel, and the right to hunt and fish in exchange for their labor. Much of the subsequent history of the rural South revolved around the localized relations between landlord and tenant. By the turn of the twentieth century the United States Department of Agriculture (USDA) attempted to reconfigure traditional tillage. While leading the fight against the boll weevil, the USDA also introduced the latest ideas on diversification and mechanization. Unless all aspects of cotton farming were mechanized, however, owners needed seasonal labor, so the old farming practices and sharecropping endured through the 1930s.

The evolution of the new tenure system, characterized by sharecropping and tenancy, spanned the thirty years after the Civil War and became an incredibly complex mixture of law and custom, freedom and slavery, prosperity and ruin. Throughout those years landownership became concentrated into fewer hands. As King Cotton reorganized his realm, merchants, landlords, banks, loan companies, and life insurance companies controlled increasing expanses of southern cotton land. Historians have not explored fully the dynamics of the vast shift in landownership, in which whites increasingly lost their land and joined blacks at the bottom of the agricultural ladder as sharecroppers.[1]

Historians have explored in great detail, and at times with vitriolic disagreement, the evolution of the labor system that emerged after the war. Like a patchwork quilt, the new labor system was a varied but unpatterned blend of illiteracy, law, contracts, and violence, confusing if not incomprehensible even to those closest to it. Blacks struggled to stay out of the quicksand of debt, and white yeomen fought to save their land as low cotton prices left less and less for taxes and food. The sharecropping arrangements varied—from state to state, crop to crop, county to county, and farm to farm—and changed with the passage of time and the passage, enforcement, and understanding of laws.[2]

The 1890s have often marked a symbolic historical turning point. The historian Frederick Jackson Turner proclaimed the significance of the vanished frontier line revealed in the 1890 census. The presidential election of 1896 symbolized the end of rural domination and the rise of business and urbanism as the controlling factors of American destiny. Other events pointed to major themes of southern history in general and of agricultural history in particular. The black educator Booker T. Washington became, by the mid-1890s, the leading spokesman for black Americans. His 1895 Atlanta Address, which accepted the tenets of segregation, found eager endorsement among whites. In many ways this speech, assuring whites that blacks accepted second-class citizenship, symbolized the end of the Reconstruction experiment. Although the dreams of property and equal rights had dimmed since the Civil War, Washington's address symbolically closed the door on an era; a year later in *Plessy* v. *Ferguson*, the Supreme Court concurred. Hope for reform through the Farmers' Alliance and Populist-Republican fusion faded after 1896. Instead of encouraging racial harmony, southern state legislatures established a legal system of segregation, political disfranchisement, and strict labor laws.[3]

Even as legislatures acted to disfranchise and segregate blacks, they also moved to extend landlords' control over agricultural laborers. It was as if the more pressure the modern world exerted on the South, the more stubbornly the South retreated into the past. Involuntary servitude has proven to be the inheritance of nearly every disintegrating slave system in the New World, so it was not unique to the southern United States.[4]

The rural labor system that evolved after the Civil War increasingly became codified in the statute books. Coercion that drove reluctant blacks and impoverished whites came from the law, which progressively tightened its grip on workers; from the contract, which became a year's sentence on a few acres; from violence, which gave object lessons to those who resisted the system; and from illiteracy, which placed the worker at the mercy of the literate elite and kept him from seeking jobs that required more skill than plowing, hoeing, and picking. In the moiling confusion of the post–Civil War South, debt visited most houses in the hinterland; it did not discriminate by race. Using debt as the fulcrum, planters increasingly found ways to force sharecroppers to remain on the land. Enticement laws, emigrant agent restrictions, contract laws, vagrancy statutes, the criminal-surety system, and convict labor laws snared many laborers. The laws and customs that covered the South gave landowners and merchants increasing control over rural workers.[5]

Even as the number of sharecroppers increased and proscriptive laws eroded their status, other harbingers of change in the 1890s suggested the development of southern agriculture in the next half-century. In 1894 the boll weevil crossed the Rio Grande and infested the cotton fields of Texas, beginning an invasion that would ultimately doom the old cotton kingdom. The federal government reported the progress of the weevil and educated farmers on how to combat it, but those efforts did not halt its thirty-year conquest of the Cotton South. The weevil not only ravaged the cotton fields but also set in motion a demonstration program and the federal Extension Service run by the U.S. Department of Agriculture. Extension agents educated farmers and, more important, stressed commercial farming with the latest machinery and methods. This well-intended government intrusion helped the more educated and aggressive farmers to survive, while those who were marginal gradually disappeared from the land.[6]

The primary tools of human displacement and transformation also appeared in the 1890s. In 1892 John Froehlich built the first successful gasoline tractor; though it would take more than a half-century for this implement to become more than a curiosity in the South, by the late 1930s it had begun to replace sharecroppers. More important, in 1895 Angus Campbell patented a spindle-type cotton picker. Again, it would be a half-century before the Rust brothers and then International Harvester would perfect the machine, but when it arrived commercially after World War II, the picker and the tractor joined with federal agricultural programs to push millions of sharecroppers, tenants, wagehands, and eventually small owners off the land.[7]

As mechanization continued, southern farmers eked out their livelihoods and confronted nature. There was something almost biblical in the way plagues invaded the South. Indeed, one could argue that the plagues that visited Egypt prior to the Exodus had a parallel in the South. In addition to the boll weevil, Mississippi River floods in 1912, 1913, 1922, and 1927 and the 1930 drought combined with the Great Depression to ruin the southern economy. The 1927 flood and the drought three years later introduced many rural Southerners to Red Cross relief, which not only dramatized the acute conditions of south-

A cotton picking machine mounted on a Beeman garden tractor, and the engine of the tractor operates the machinery which picks the cotton. Little Rock, Arkansas. December 1919. McNair. (83 F 7970, National Archives)

ern rural workers but also suggested a solution for the collapsing cotton culture.[8]

More than any other factor, however, the fight against the boll weevil heralded government intervention. It upset the traditional culture enough so that southern farmers were willing to look up from their almanacs and listen to agricultural experts. Ultimately the weevil would force cotton into western growing areas that were less vulnerable to the pest. In 1894 C. H. DeRyee of Corpus Christi, Texas, wrote to the USDA calling attention to a weevil that destroyed cotton bolls. The Agriculture Department assessed the situation, perceived grave problems, and suggested that the Texas legislature halt cotton planting for a year in the infested area. Failing to bring about legislative action, department entomologists suggested that farmers pick up and destroy the punctured squares, or young buds, that fell from the plant and served as nests for young weevils, and that they also use Paris Green as an insecticide. Experts later suggested that farmers destroy the cotton stalks immediately after picking and, during cultivation, that they use a plow with a crossbar that would knock the infested squares from the plant. As the weevil spread, some Texas farmers and businessmen put a bounty on the head of the boll weevil, from ten to twenty-five cents per hundred.[9]

When the insect neared the Mississippi River, alarmed farmers on the east side suggested a fifty-mile cotton-free zone along its banks. The USDA, unable to calculate how to reimburse farmers for their sacrifice, never made a decision on this plan. Failing to halt the spread of the weevil, the agency instead instructed farmers on how to cope with the insect. This plan was an outgrowth of farmers' institutes, correspondence courses, and other outreach plans that preceded it. In 1902 the Department of Agriculture hired Seaman A. Knapp as "Special Agent for the Promotion of Agriculture in the South." A year later, on the Walter C. Porter farm near Terrell, Texas, Knapp set up a demonstration farm to show farmers how to defeat the weevil with good cultivation practices. While restoring production, the new methods drove up the cost of cotton farming east of the Mississippi River and pushed cotton growing to less infested western areas.

A native of New York, Seaman A. Knapp had taught school until an accident to his leg spurred him to move to Big Grove, Iowa, where he operated a farm. He preached, served as superintendent of the state school for the blind, and edited the *Western Stock Journal and Farmer*. In 1879 he began another teaching career at Iowa State College, becoming its president in 1884. Ever restless, in 1885 he moved to Louisiana, where he helped inaugurate the prairie rice culture. Knapp hired twenty-three agents with his $40,000 share of the appropriation. They persuaded farmers to use their land for demonstration purposes so that neighboring farmers could observe their successful methods. The idea quickly caught on; Knapp estimated that 7,000 farmers adapted USDA advice, and others heard of the program at some 1,000 meetings.[10] The weevil outran the demonstrators, however, so Knapp inaugurated the county agent concept in 1906: county funds paid the salary of an agent who spread the USDA gospel.

By 1908 the boll weevil had eaten its way northward into Arkansas and leaped over the Mississippi River. Agents fanned out over the area, giving farmers basic training for combat. Some planters and sharecroppers adjusted to the emergency, but others moved from infested areas. Farmers in Concordia Parish, Louisiana, started growing rice in 1909, dismantled the old cotton gins and oil mills, and built a rice mill in Vidalia. After several years farmers discovered that, even with the weevil, it was more profitable to grow cotton, so the cotton culture re-emerged and the rice culture lapsed. Such shifts in crop cultures easily escaped censustakers. Yet the weevil did push some farmers toward diversification, and Louisiana farmers tried peanuts, truck crops, livestock, and dairy herds. In the decade following 1910, however, farmers increasingly turned back to cotton, learning from extension agents that they could cope with the weevil although they would have less production. In that sense the Extension Service stunted diversification by concentrating on maintaining cotton production. It would not be the last contradiction in government agricultural policy.[11]

As the weevil ate into Mississippi in 1908, many farmers in hill counties, alarmed at what the extension agents prophesied, moved to Oklahoma, Arkansas, and the Mississippi Delta. The black population of Quitman County, in the Delta where there was minimal weevil damage, increased between 1900 and 1910 from 1,785 to 4,687; that of Sunflower County increased from 5,220 to 11,211. Cotton production also increased dramatically there between 1909 and 1915 despite the weevil. The further away from the core Delta counties, the higher the infestation. By 1913 the Mississippi cotton crop had been reduced by 33 percent, and farmers outside the Delta increasingly turned to hogs and cattle. By 1916 the weevil was at the Georgia border.[12]

The boll weevil did not discriminate by the race of the farmer, and Seaman A. Knapp acted in conjunction with Booker T. Washington to aid black farmers. Washington, of course, attempted to educate not only those who wanted to farm scientifically but also traditional farmers who lived around Tuskegee Institute. In 1892 he inaugurated the Tuskegee Negro Conference, and he later sponsored farmers' institutes, short courses in agriculture, county fairs, a farm newspaper, and miscellaneous leaflets. In 1906, after securing backing from a New York banker named Morris K. Jesup and the John F. Slater Fund, Washington sent forth the "Jesup Agricultural Wagon" to tour the countryside near the school.

Despite his reluctance to engage black agricultural agents, Seaman Knapp realized that the wagon was the perfect vehicle to carry information to black farmers, and he cooperated with Washington. Thomas M. Campbell took over the mule team that pulled the wagon and drove off to begin a career that spanned a half-century. Tuskegee Institute's parent school, Hampton Institute, also sponsored an agent, John B. Pierce. At first restricted to Macon County, Alabama, and to

Norfolk County, Virginia, the agricultural wagon idea performed so well that Knapp hired additional black agents. Although never equal in number or funding to the whites, black agents by 1919 were in all southern extension programs. The Smith-Lever Act in 1914 encouraged the sponsorship of black agents, but these men and women were always closely supervised by whites.[13] Although most black agents were dedicated to their work, the task before them proved immense. Indeed, with their dependence upon the white agricultural complex for funds, they could never innovate plans to reform the sharecropping system.

From the beginning, black extension agents did not concentrate on helping the poor sharecroppers and marginal farmers who most needed instruction, but instead sought out more prosperous farmers. They had a delicate task. First they made peace with local white landlords and merchants; then they selected their clientele from among the most respectable black farmers. Black agents had no choice but to abide by the dictates of white administrators, but white agents also concentrated on the better class of farmers. Thus the bottom strata of both races faltered before the weevil, just as they had under other natural and manmade calamities.[14]

Not all Southerners acquiesced in even a token force of black agents. W. W. Long, the extension director in South Carolina, wrote to federal extension field agent H. E. Savely in January 1915, questioning the ability of black agents and claiming that landlords resented "negro agents interfering with their tenants." Savely reminded Long that there were seven black agents in Alabama, three in Mississippi, two in Georgia, and one in Florida. "We have never had any complaint from the white people in the territory where these negroes have been at work," he wrote. Savely further reminded Long that, in congressional debates over the Smith-Lever bill, northern congressmen wanted black agricultural colleges to receive half of the funds. "This was defeated," he reminded Long, "only by the promise and assurance of southern senators that if the white colleges were allowed to administer the work they would see to it that the negro had his just share of the instructions from the agents provided out of this fund." If voters elected a Republican-controlled Congress, he surmised, the Extension Service would be in "serious danger of having the Lever Bill so amended that the negro agricultural colleges of the south would get their share of these funds. "This," he stressed, "I hope, will never happen." He concluded that it was the wise policy to have a few excellent black

Negro county agent and district agent discussing the advantages of
proper fertilizing and poisoning for boll weevil control. J. W. Daniels,
Negro county agent, and A. H. Ward, district agent. Orangeburg
County, South Carolina, August 19, 1924. George W. Ackerman.
(16-G-77-3-535-26-C, National Archives)

agents and to treat them the same as white agents. Where there were
no black agents, the whites should spend "a reasonable amount" of
time instructing black farmers.[15]

The job proved difficult for even the most dedicated agent. Eugene A.
Williams wrote to Thomas M. Campbell in June 1916 of his work
among black farmers in Georgia. He had traveled 31,000 miles since
October 1914, he wrote, and he listed a staggering number of demonstrations and institutes that he had attended. Georgia had an exhibit
car, a "School on Wheels," he called it, and the best people of the state
had visited it and praised it—"lawyers, ministers, doctors, senators,
college presidents and professors, farm agents, agricultural experts of
railroads." At one point his life had been threatened, and at first he had
encountered opposition. He had overcome the "dark clouds of disappointment" and boasted that he had not a single enemy in the state. He
had not taken a day's vacation during the past year; he slept in his
clothes for five days at a stretch, and he worked at night. "I found
when I entered the work most of the negro farmers were discouraged,

and I have had to spend considerable time trying to convince a number that their white neighbor was his friend and desired to see him improve."[16]

By 1917 many southern whites realized the significance of the black exodus, and the Extension Service mobilized to pacify would-be immigrants. "Thousands of negroes have left this State and gone north during the past two months," the director of extension work in Mississippi complained. "The labor problem, I fear, will materially affect crop production in this State." The migration made planters more conscious of conditions among black sharecroppers. H. E. Savely attended the Delta Community Congress in Clarksdale in June 1917 and admitted that diseases such as tuberculosis, pellagra, malaria, and typhoid were widespread. He thought that, by bringing this out at the conference, public health work would be encouraged. "There was quite a sentiment in favor of a campaign to see that negroes were given a square deal, better living conditions provided for them, and other steps taken to make the negroes of that section more contented so that they would stop migrating to other sections." Many blacks had left the rural areas, he wrote, and he feared that not enough would remain to harvest the cotton crop.[17]

In 1923 the United States Department of Agriculture put out a bulletin on black extension work. After reviewing the history of the program, the pamphlet cited the lack of county funds as the main drawback to continuing the work. Blacks were eager to participate in the extension programs, and this was "the most significant of all signs of progress." The Extension Service pointed out the great exodus from the South, estimating that over 100,000 blacks had left since 1920. "It seemed to be generally considered that extension work offered the best means of overcoming the poverty, dissatisfaction, and unrest prevailing among negro farmers, and of thus checking the migration from the rural sections." By this time 294 blacks were working for the Extension Service as county agents, home demonstrators, and in boys' and girls' club work.[18] By advocating better living conditions and scientific farming methods, the Extension Service and its supporters hoped to prevent or at least delay black migration. Even as it advocated mechanization and diversification, the Extension Service attempted to stabilize the traditional sharecropping system.

As the Extension Service expanded in scope and in size, it faced problems of growth and also a problem in defining its role in the nation's agriculture. After all, it represented a sharp break with the old notions of agrarianism, and it threatened agriculture with disruptions similar to those that accompanied industrialization. While many southern farmers voiced ambivalence concerning modernization, Seaman A. Knapp believed that the benefits of science were positive. He had a dream for the South, which he knew had been blessed with "superb soil, abundant rainfall and a plenty of general sunshine." If the South would accept his advice, Knapp predicted that it "will in a few years become the richest part of the world, agriculturally considered."[19]

On the surface the county agent system that disseminated Knapp's ideas seemed a democratic and practical way to aid all farmers. Meetings were held and a farmers' organization was formed; needing someone to carry out projects, the organization usually raised money to pay for a county agent who worked closely with the state land-grant college and the USDA to spread the latest methods to farmers. Yet the local organization, by its very composition, represented the most successful farmers. Membership dues screened out the poorer members of rural society. County agents had to receive the approval of local farmers, and although the Extension Service desired to put graduates of the land-grant colleges in agent positions, many local farmers were suspicious of college-trained agents. Still, extension agents spread the latest ideas formulated in Washington or in agricultural schools.[20]

Increasingly, the county agent system invited political organization as well as agricultural instruction. By 1920 in many areas the Farm Bureau, growing out of the local organizations, became a driving force that defended the county agent system and moved into national politics. In the South, however, the Farmers' Union at first benefited from the local organizations. The national administrators of the Extension Service recognized that they could benefit from strong grassroots farm organizations.[21] In this sense the Extension Service began inaugurating modern farmer organizations that became increasingly important in the formation of agricultural policy.

Like other bureaucracies, the Extension Service jealously fought for its place in the USDA structure. In 1914 district agent L. M. Calhoun wrote from Gilbert, Louisiana, to Seaman Knapp's son and successor Bradford Knapp, complaining that other state and federal agencies were "specializing in everything to the neglect of cotton." Insisting that cotton was the only cash crop for the area, Calhoun believed that the Extension Service should concentrate on that crop. "If we win the cotton crop, the cooperative Demonstration work will be accepted as the most valuable work yet undertaken for the farmers. If we fail on the cotton crop, our work will stand condemned and be swallowed up by other agencies regardless of the great assistance we give in the development of other crops." Calhoun thought the Extension Service should cast its lot with the cash crop, insisting that Louisiana grew more cotton in 1913 with the weevil than in 1905 without it. He also revealed that the Extension Service had to compete for funds within the USDA bureaucracy. Saving cotton farmers seemed the best weapon to ensure funding.[22]

Southern farmers studied the boll weevil carefully. In *All God's Dangers: The Life of Nate Shaw*, Theodore Rosengarten transcribed the words of the real Ned Cobb as he described his personal study of the boll weevil. When the weevil first appeared, Cobb said, "these white folks down here told the colored people if you don't pick them cotton squares off the ground and destroy them boll weevils, we'll quit furnishin you. Told em that—putting the blame on the colored man for the boll weevil comin in this country." Cobb put his children into the fields picking up squares. "I was industrious enough to do somethin about the boll weevil without bein driven to it," he bragged. He did not believe that picking up the squares, as the Extension Service suggested, destroyed all the weevils. "You couldn't keep your fields clean —boll weevil schemin to eat your crop faster than you workin to get him out." It was the weevil that led Cobb to make the statement used in the title of his autobiography: "Yes, all God's dangers aint a white man."

The weevil laid eggs in the squares, and "in a few days, one weevil's got a court of young uns hatchin." Cobb carefully observed the life cycle of the insect. "I've pulled them squares open and caught em in all their stages of life: found the old egg in there, and I've found him just hatched out and he's right white like a worm, just a little spot in there, that's him; and if he's a little older he looks green-colored and sappy; and after he gets grown he's a old ashycolored rascal, his wings is gray like ash. I've known him from the first to the last. I've picked him up and looked at him close. He's just a insect, but really, he's unusual to me. I can't thoroughly understand the nature of a boll weevil." He grew to the size of a fly, Cobb revealed. "And he's a very creepin fellow, he gets about too; he'll ruin a stalk of cotton in a night's time." Cobb walked through his fields and knocked weevils off the plants when he saw them. "And he'll get up—he aint quick about it, but he'll get up from there and fly off, you looking at him."

Understanding the insect's habits and interrupting the life cycle by

Negro dusting cotton with bag. Clarke County, Georgia. July 1929. George W. Ackerman. (s-12473-c, National Archives)

destroying squares did not get rid of the weevil. "When I seed I couldn't defeat the boll weevil by pickin up squares, I carried poison out to the field and took me a crocus sack, one of these thin crocus sacks, put my poison in there enough to poison maybe four or five rows and just walk, walk, walk; shake that sack over the cotton when I'd look back, heap of times, that dust flyin every whichway and the breeze blowin, that cotton would be white with dust, behind me." He wore a cloth over his mouth; still the dust bothered him. If the weevil returned, Cobb would dust again until the boll got "too far advanced for him to handle it and that boll will open with healthy locks." He concluded that poison was "the only way to beat the devil, run him out the field." But the battle renewed every year. "Everything, every creature in God's world, understands how to try to protect itself. And I believe that scoundrel goes right into the forests and finds his appointed place to wait; spring of the year, he right back in the field, soon as your cotton comes up, he right back on it."[23]

There were larger implications for the old cotton-growing areas of the South. The center of cotton production would have shifted westward anyway, as it always had, but the weevil "accelerated the process." Texas and Oklahoma doubled their acreage from 1910 to 1930, and Mississippi, Arkansas, and Louisiana increased theirs by 40 percent. Alabama, Georgia, South and North Carolina only increased acreage by 5 percent.[24] Thus the weevil had set in motion a westward movement that would accelerate during the 1920s and the New Deal.

The boll weevil and the efforts to combat it had a tremendous effect on southern agriculture. Institutionalized by the Smith-Lever Act in 1914, the Extension Service grew into a bureaucracy that increasingly served commercial farmers who controlled agents on the local level.[25] Linked to land-grant universities and eager to encourage scientific farming and mechanization, the Extension Service became an agent of change in the rural South. Had its information been dispensed evenly, sharecroppers and small farmers could have developed a strategy to stay on the land. Yet such marginal farmers lacked the education or the credit to utilize many of the innovations that appeared on the market. Chained to the old cultural methods and the credit system, such farmers held on as long as they could. The thread supporting them had weakened by 1930, and the New Deal—by cutting acreage, ignoring tenure arrangements, and giving landlords most of the funds that came from the AAA—broke their tie to the land.

The Extension Service was drawn into better farming methods that included mechanization, for in most cases southern farmers were incredibly backward technologically. Sharecroppers especially worked with implements that had changed little in a hundred years, and implement dealers saw the potential of the southern market. In 1915 International Harvester moved into the South to demonstrate its products, and Bradford Knapp was drawn into a crisis over whether the Extension Service should cooperate closely with implement manufacturers. For three years Knapp attempted to set policy that would prevent county agents from becoming closely linked with business. The issue involved the Extension Service, International Harvester, chambers of commerce, local bankers, landlords, and farmers.

The impetus for "improved and modern machinery" came both from large implement companies and from local chambers of commerce. Bruce Kennedy, secretary of the Montgomery, Alabama, Chamber of Commerce, worked closely with International Harvester and local businessmen. His office coordinated seventeen counties, and chambers of commerce in Mobile and Birmingham also established organizations in neighboring counties. Bankers, hoping to finance the machinery, eagerly employed field agents. Kennedy praised the International Harvester operation: "They have the machinery, they employ scores of talented men and they have a method that can not be excelled."[26]

Knapp faced a dilemma. On one hand he agreed that diversification should be encouraged; on the other he feared International Harvester's influence in the movement and worried about his integrity as a federal employee. In October 1915, after a stormy meeting of state extension supervisors, bankers, and Harvester representatives, he instructed extension agents to withhold cooperation but at the same time "make it clear that we were not opposing the campaign." Knapp preferred that Harvester "confine their campaign to the towns and to an effort to convince business men and let the extension forces of the states carry the agricultural campaign to the rural districts." Some of the larger implement dealers, however, decided to extend the campaign into the countryside. Knapp feared that some county agents would find themselves in a dilemma, for "in some places our failure to cooperate will hurt the county agent with the business men and in some places the fact that we are not in on the campaign is going to injure the campaigns. We will have to run chance on that." [27]

Two months later Knapp believed that he had made the correct decision. The Harvester campaign caught on in the South, and this actually helped promote the Extension Service, which was, after all, the best agency to coordinate local farmers, bankers, and merchants. Having just returned from a meeting in New Orleans in early December, he observed that the Harvester people "were on the ground and exceedingly busy." Writing to the director of extension work in Georgia, Knapp encouraged him to move quickly to expand his operations. A number of factors converged to promote extension work: "With the war in Europe, the great spread of the boll weevil and the great increase in the appropriations from your legislature," Knapp advised, "you have a great opportunity in Georgia to extend the work over a considerable territory." [28]

Knapp continued to hold out against direct association with corporations. Writing to Andrew M. Soule at the University of Georgia, Knapp reiterated that he was "bound under the law to stand pat on one subject and this is cooperation with big corporations." He argued that it was "not only unwise but unlawful" for department employees to cooperate directly with businesses. "We can not cooperate with the International Harvester Co., the Southern Settlement and Development Association, the National Fertilizer Association, or any other associations of that kind. We can meet and talk matters over with them but as far as doing any cooperative work with them, the spirit as well as the letter of the law prohibits." By 1918 the Extension Service had become so closely connected with the marketing of implements that some firms wanted a mailing list of county agents "in order that these firms may send them price lists or samples of their wares." The department took the position that agents were public officials and that their addresses were public information.[29] Despite Knapp's policy, the line that divided federal employees and private enterprise became blurred.

County agents received the latest information on new farm implements, and they encouraged farmers to utilize it. The role of the Extension Service in moving southern farmers into diversification and mechanization had been firmly established. Knapp and his agents were trying to open a new market for implement manufacturers and to mechanize southern agriculture, yet most sharecroppers could not invest in such new machines. Although business and government were kept separate, the farming methods taught in the universities and disseminated through a new generation of commercial farmers and extension agents relied on machinery. The formal lines of separation between government and implement dealers could be maintained while, as Knapp admitted, the parties could "meet and talk matters over." Although the groundwork had been laid, the significant impact of technology on the Cotton South came only in the mid-1930s, when government programs helped remove sharecroppers and stabilized landlords' incomes.

By the end of World War I the tumult created by the boll weevil and the drive for mechanization receded in the face of concern over wild fluctuations in cotton prices. Cotton growers had weathered a panic in 1914, when the European war created low prices and a demand for acreage reduction. Farmers decreased acreage from 36.8 million in 1914 to 31.4 million a year later, but in 1920 the price of cotton plunged again after acreage expansion and unusually high wartime prices. After another cutback (of 5.4 million bales) in 1921, the price of cotton increased; though it declined over the next years, farmers continued to expand their acreages. In 1926 their record 47 million acres created a tremendous surplus. Much of the additional acreage came in Oklahoma, Texas, and Missouri, where the boll weevil was less destructive and production costs were lower.[30]

Farmers in 1926 realized that their problem eclipsed that of 1914 and 1920, for this time the surplus drove prices below the cost of production. A campaign began throughout the South to encourage acreage restriction. It started in Texas, and in mid-October seven hundred cotton planters and credit agents met in Memphis, Tennessee. The conven-

Farm accident, ca. 1920. The transition from ox and mule to tractor was not always an easy one. This farmer may in fact be awaiting the arrival of a team of mules to rescue his equipment, whose weight was clearly too much for the wooden bridge. Paulding County, Georgia. (Vanishing Georgia Collection, PLD-8. Courtesy of Georgia Department of Archives and History)

tion split over the old problem of enforcing reduction, with many representatives fearing that voluntary cutbacks would not work. The upper South opposed reduction, for it had raised less cotton in 1926 than in 1914. Texas and Oklahoma, which had expanded acreage during those years, advocated reduction. In the end the convention approved voluntary reduction and drafted ground rules to ensure compliance. The opinion-shaping media, credit agencies, planters, and the government joined together to push the campaign, hoping to cut production by 25 percent.[31]

One irony of the reduction movement lay in the fact that, despite boll weevil damage, there was a massive surplus of cotton. The Extension Service had, in one sense, been too successful in its campaign to outwit the weevil. Nor did the diversification campaign discourage cotton planting. Furthermore, upper South farmers had higher production costs than did farmers in western growing areas. The Department of Agriculture estimated that a Johnston County, North Carolina, farmer had three times the costs of a Texas farmer. While the upper South planted about the same amount of cotton in 1926 as in 1916,

Oklahoma had nearly doubled its production during the decade. Farmers did reduce acreage by 6 million acres in 1927, which resulted in a 12.4 percent drop in production. Yet such a reduction normally followed a bad price year. Oklahoma and Louisiana decreased plantings by 18 percent; Texas, by only 11 percent. As had always been the case, while some farmers cut their acreage, others planted more to take advantage of what they hoped would be high prices due to a smaller supply. The twenty-cent cotton of 1927 resulted in increased plantings the next year and held at about 40 million acres from 1928 to 1932. Despite falling prices and the onset of the Great Depression, cotton farmers continued planting large acreages, hoping to show a profit even with lower prices.[32] As with the tobacco farmers' attempt to set up cooperative marketing and acreage reduction at about the same time, cotton farmers were unsuccessful in voluntarily cutting acreage.

The crisis of 1926 did not discourage cotton production. In August 1931 when the Federal Crop Reporting Board announced that the South would harvest 15.5 million bales and that he annual carryover would reach 8.7 million bales, farmers knew that prices would fall even lower. Some planters in north Louisiana approached Governor Huey Long with a radical plan: drop the entire cotton crop in 1932. The simplicity of the plan and its obvious merit in getting rid of the surplus appealed to Long, who immediately invited the governors of the cotton-growing states to meet in Louisiana to discuss the measure. Only the governors of Arkansas and South Carolina attended the August 21 meeting; a few other states sent representatives. On August 29 the Louisiana legislature enacted the measure, and Long appealed to Texas Governor Ross Sterling, whose state grew one-fourth of the country's cotton, to support the idea.[33]

Other southern governors waited for action from Texas, which they knew held the key to a successful "drop-a-crop" campaign. Governor Theodore G. Bilbo of Mississippi, reacting with anger to Long's proposal, announced his own plan that would leave one-third of the cotton unpicked in 1931. He notified other southern governors of his plan and waited for their response. The Federal Farm Board supported a similar proposal, but under a Republican administration it hesitated to advocate that a federal agency administer it. Every cotton farmer and legislator realized that prudence required a cut in production, yet neither state nor federal governments acted to ensure compliance.[34]

The Texas legislature, meanwhile, defeated the Long proposal and instead approved an acreage reduction of 30 percent for the next two

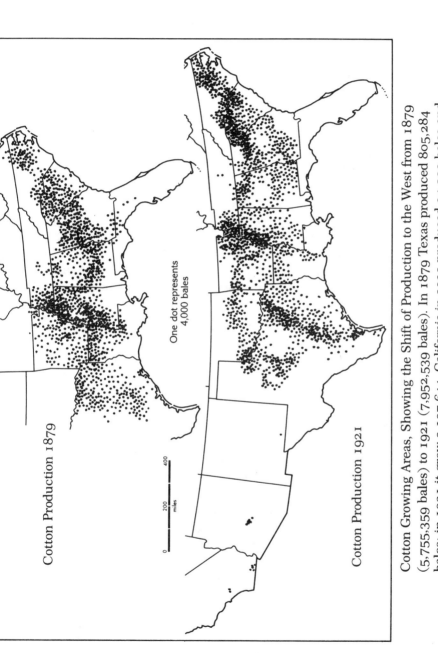

Cotton Production 1879

Cotton Production 1921

One dot represents
4,000 bales

0   200   400
      miles

Cotton Growing Areas, Showing the Shift of Production to the West from 1879 (5,755,359 bales) to 1921 (7,952,539 bales). In 1879 Texas produced 805,284 bales; in 1921 it grew 2,197,644. California in 1921 produced 34,109 bales and Arizona 45,323. From USDA, *Yearbook*, 1921.

years, hoping to cut production by 50 percent. Bilbo then called a special legislative session in Mississippi that followed the Texas example;
it voted for voluntarily acreage reduction and defeated the drop-a-crop
measure. The Long plan failed, and the results were predictable. Without a means of enforcement, some cotton growers cut acreage while
others planted more. Legislators and even cotton farmers knew that
only a reduction of the tremendous supply of cotton could force up
prices, but enforcement would await a federal program that, like the
Long idea, took bold action.[35] Long's drop-a-crop plan had the virtue
not only of drastic action but also of affecting all farmers equally. When
acreage reduction came in the 1930s, it hit small producers and stabilized larger growers.

It would take a federal program to stop cotton farmers from planting
all they could tend. Farmers bested the weevil, diversified, mechanized
to some extent, and even attempted cooperation in marketing their
cotton. But even if they fought a successful battle on all those fronts,
synthetics presented a new enemy that could not be exterminated or
voluntarily reduced. Foreign competition from India and Egypt also cut
into exports.[36] Yet for the old cotton-growing areas of the South, competition from the West presented the greatest challenge. In the eastern
Cotton Belt, plantings declined from 12 million acres in 1910–14 to
8.8 million by 1922 and remained at that figure in 1932. In the central
cotton-growing states along the Mississippi Delta, acreage rose from
6.6 million in 1921 to 11.1 million by 1930. The most dramatic change
appeared in the West—Oklahoma, Texas, New Mexico, Arizona, and
California. There acreage increased from 12.9 million in 1922 to 23.1
million in 1925. By 1932 it had slumped to 16.8 million acres, but the
shift still tilted cotton production dramatically westward. Low production costs and less weevil infestation contributed to this movement.
Thus, before the Depression and New Deal arrived in the old Cotton
Belt, a massive shift in production had already taken place.[37] Cotton
farmers entered the 1930s weary from fighting pestilence and oversupply, and they looked to Washington for help. The old cotton culture
of sharecroppers and planters, tenants and time merchants, mules and
primitive implements faced its ultimate crisis.

2

The Golden Leaf: Expansion of the Flue-Cured Tobacco Culture

It should be emphasized, too, that white tenants and some of the white farm owners are in equally as unfavorable a credit position as are the Negro farmers.
—*Roland B. Eustler, 1930*

The generations of Americans who cultivated tobacco, starting with John Rolfe in the Jamestown colony, have contributed a rich chapter to this country's rural history. Until New Deal acreage-control policies froze the geographical area where tobacco could be grown, the crop spread across the country with the ebb and flow of demand and changing tastes. At present there are twenty-one distinct types of tobacco grown in eighteen states, and each variety demands a different cultivation routine. Flue-cured or bright leaf tobacco, grown primarily in Virginia, the Carolinas, Georgia, and Florida, is the most important variety in terms of the number of growers and the cash returns. It is the progeny of John Rolfe's first efforts to produce a cash crop to save the faltering Jamestown colony. When smokers turned to cigarettes in the late nineteenth century, they created a demand for gold-colored tobacco, and this set in motion a dynamic expansion of the bright tobacco culture.

Virginia dominated tobacco culture into the mid-nineteenth century. North Carolina counties nestled near the Virginia border—Granville, Warren, Person, Caswell, and Stokes—were part of the Virginia culture. Maryland had grown tobacco since the 1660s, and Kentucky and Tennessee also had a thriving tobacco culture. All tobacco growers were part of the Atlantic trade pattern, and their fortunes rose and fell with the periods of oversupply and the disruption of trade caused by war. By the nineteenth century the tobacco culture had spread into South Carolina and Georgia, but then cotton became king and largely supplanted tobacco there for a century, until the boll weevil and low cotton prices reversed the trend.[1]

The quest for a light and aromatic leaf dominated the history of tobacco from John Rolfe's day until after the Civil War, when changes in curing, growing, and taste radically altered the bright tobacco culture. Over the years farmers learned that the best tobacco grew on thin soils, that starved leaf made the lightest and most aromatic tobacco, and that intense heat turned the leaves gold.[2]

While cotton farmers battled the boll weevil, expanded westward, and attempted diversification, tobacco farmers perfected a work routine that required some 370 hours of labor per acre to bring the crop to market. As remains the case in other tobacco areas today, farmers of bright tobacco used to cut the entire stalk and cure it. Fieldworkers severed the stalks and then impaled them on a stick and hung them in a barn for curing. By the 1880s farmers discovered that cigarette buyers demanded more uniformity in the cured leaf; this led them to prime the stalk three or four ripe leaves each week, moving from the bottom to the top. Handling the crop by loose leaves presented another problem. Farmers experimented by running a wire through the stem of each leaf, by attaching the leaves to sticks with rubber bands, and by sewing leaves to sticks with a needle and thread, but these methods were unsatisfactory.[3]

In the 1890s bright tobacco farmers learned of a method used by Connecticut tobacco farmers. It involved tying bundles of tobacco to the stick with string. Some resourceful farmers tried to patent this complex operation, but describing it in words proved impossible. There were subtle variations in such methods as tying, stringing, looping, or wrapping, and all quickly spread across the bright tobacco area. Despite articles on priming and stringing and the higher prices obtainable for tobacco barned and marketed this way, the old ways died hard. Some farmers in the Old Tobacco Belt of Virginia continued to cut the entire stalk into the 1930s; and burley and Maryland growers today still cut the entire plant and air dry their tobacco.[4]

The method of cultivating tobacco that evolved during the late nineteenth century endured with few changes into the 1950s. Curing barns, packhouses, and the slides that mules pulled through the fields at harvest time identified tobacco farms. As in the cotton culture, the entire family—men, women, and children—labored at cultivating the crop, yet the work was harder, dirtier, and in many ways more exacting than in any other commodity culture.

The season began in the winter, when the grower chose land for his plantbed, for the young seedlings needed special care until they were transplanted into the fields. Farmers mixed the tiny tobacco seed with ashes or sand in order to obtain a uniform stand of plants. Then they raked and packed the ground. By the 1890s farmers learned to place a cloth over the bed to keep out flea beetles. With typical inventiveness, other people found that the cloth plantbed covers could be used as underwear, and after a rash of stolen plantbed cloths, farmers put kerosene or some other agent on the cloth to make such use undesirable.[5]

Even as the seeds germinated, farmers continued cutting wood to use in the curing barns in July and August. As Luther Harris, a Martin County, North Carolina, tobacco grower remembered, "They would get together and have a wood cutting. One neighbor would help out another neighbor and several families would join in to cut wood: oak, sweetgum, poplar and different kinds of wood that would be good for fire wood log burning. They would cut wood just about like the ladies would get together and have quilting bees."[6]

As spring arrived, tobacco farmers harnessed the mules to break and harrow the land, and to plow rows. Until the 1940s and 1950s most tobacco farmers used mules, oxen, or horses on their farms. Mules also snaked logs from the woods, hauled split wood to the barn, and then pulled the plows that prepared the land. There existed a special relationship between mules and men. A farmer spent so much time with his mules that he came to look upon them as friends, and so there evolved a mule culture that existed side by side with other aspects of rural life.[7]

Henry Williams, a Georgia tobacco farmer, explained how he worked his mule. "I used to say 'Whoa,' 'Gee,' and 'Haw,' to my mules. Whoa means, 'stop,' Gee means, 'a little bit to the right,' and Haw means 'a little bit to the left.' If I said 'Git up!' they'd move on ahead. They were right considerate about doing what I told them." One farmer shared a chew of tobacco with his mule and insisted that this calmed the animal and made him work harder. Another man allowed his mule to have a Pepsi-Cola at break time. "The mule developed quite a taste for the soda pop and at the sound of a bottle top being removed from a bottle, he would pick up his ears like a radio antenna and walk right toward the person opening the drink!"[8]

After years of experience, growers became experts on soil types and selected their fields carefully. In the nineteenth century farmers hoed the soil into "hills," little mounds that gave the tobacco plant drainage and allowed soil aeration for the root system, and they placed fertilizer in each hill. Farmers often referred to the size of their crop by the number of hills planted. "My daddy always tended what we called 30,000 hills of tobacco," a Granville County native named Arthur Barnes remembered. "There's 4,000 hills of tobacco to the acre." By the 1880s farmers realized that they could greatly increase their yields by using commercial fertilizers instead of Peruvian guano. Other entrepreneurs followed the lead of the Southern Fertilizing Company of Richmond, setting up fertilizer plants and a distribution network centered in warehouses or with local merchants. While this increased the cost of tobacco farming, it also greatly increased the yield.[9]

Once the fields had been prepared, farmers transplanted the to-bacco. People used any sources at hand to carry the plants to the fields. "We took biscuit pans, wash pans, and all other pans on the planta-tion," Mary Ann Daniel of Martin County, North Carolina, remem-bered, "and with a spoon we dug the plants up and placed them in pans, carrying them in small numbers to the field." When the ground was moist, a simple foot-long sharpened peg opened the earth enough to drop a plant in, and then the farmer with his foot would press the soil against the plant. A mechanical development allowed a farmer to apply water as he dropped the plant, but this cumbersome cylindrical apparatus required constant trips to a water barrel. By 1910 many farmers relied on mechanical planters that allowed the workers to sit as they planted. After the plants set up root systems (usually in about ten days), farmers loosened the soil by plowing or hoeing, and this pro-cess was repeated three or four times before the plant matured. Farm-ers prided themselves not only on straight rows but also on keeping weeds out of the field.[10]

By midsummer a cotton farmer laid his crop by and went fishing, but a tobacco farmer continued to tend to the peculiar needs of his plants. As the weed matured, it sprouted a flowery top that, unless re-moved, sapped growth from the leaves. So farmers broke the tops off the tobacco stalks, judging carefully so as to allow the development of the desired number of leaves. Then the plant sprouted suckers, sec-ondary growths that appeared above the primary leaves and robbed them of nutrients. Farmers removed the tops and suckers by hand. Meanwhile, tobacco hornworms matured and began chewing the leaves. Many farmers simply threw the worms on the ground and

Mr. Jones, a tenant farmer, planting tobacco. Farrington (vicinity), North Carolina. May 1940. Jack Delano. (LC USF 34 40627-D, *Library of Congress*)

stomped them, while other farmers pinched them in two. Some farmers kept turkeys and guineas and turned them out into the fields to eat worms, which were especially active when the moon was bright.[11]

Like other crops, tobacco had its share of diseases and pests. By the turn of the twentieth century, Granville wilt, named for the North

*Children of the white owners and the Negro tenants, men and
women, working in the field together, topping and suckering tobacco.
Granville County, North Carolina. July 1939. Dorothea Lange.
(*LC USF *34 20048-c, Library of Congress)*

Carolina county where it was first discovered in 1881, had spread to
other areas. Danny Kelly, who grew up in Granville County, recalled in
1939 that "We've been dealing with that wilt for 45 years." He remembered the first patch that wilted: "When we first saw it we didn't know
what to think and didn't pay much attention, but when in three or four
years it began to spread we opened our eyes and paid attention." Other
diseases struck at random, including angular leaf spot, wildfire, mosaic,
black shank, blue mold, and frog eye. Experiment stations continually
sought to end these threats, and in 1944 E. G. Moss at the Oxford station found a wilt-resistant tobacco and dubbed it "Oxford 26."[12]

For the first half of the twentieth century most farmers followed a
basic routine at harvest time. In July the plant's bottom leaves would
start turning yellow, signaling the arrival of harvest. At that time the
entire family would begin the six-week process of barning the tobacco.
Men primed three or four ripe leaves from each stalk and put armloads
of leaves into a mule-drawn sled. The trucker, usually a young boy,
drove the mule to the scaffold, where women and young boys and girls

*Priming cash variety of tobacco. Farm of W. M. Zimmerman, David-
son County (Route 4), near Lexington, North Carolina. August 5,
1927. George W. Ackerman. (16-G-294-2-1, National Archives)*

handed the tobacco bundle by bundle to the stringer. The stringer took
each bundle of three or four leaves and tied it securely to the stick; if a
leaf or bundle fell off onto a hot flue, it could set the barn on fire. The
stringer, who was usually a woman, set a four-foot-long tobacco stick
on a horse (a U-shaped wooden frame with notches to hold the stick in
place) and took the bundles and tied them to the stick. When each
stick was filled, a stick boy put it in a rack or piled it on the ground.
The routine continued all day. The men in the fields primed the tobacco, the trucker took it to the scaffold, stringers took bundles from
handers, and a stick boy piled it to the side. It took about a dozen
people—four primers, a trucker, four handers, two stringers, and a
stick boy—to fill a barn in a day.

Workers stopped for morning and afternoon breaks for soft drinks
and Moon Pies. At the sound of the dinner bell, around noon, the primers left the field, joined with the scaffold help, and ate a large country dinner. Blacks and whites ate separately. After dinner, during the
hottest part of the day, the crew rested for an hour. Then the mules and
men headed for the field, and the women drifted to the scaffold as the

Tobacco barning in Nash County, North Carolina. 1926. (Courtesy of North Carolina Department of Archives and History)

first truck arrived. Often the woman of the house would work at the scaffold in the morning until an hour before dinner, prepare the meal, wash the dishes, and return to the scaffold.

At dusk, when the last sled led the men to the scaffold, they still faced the task of hanging some thousand to fifteen hundred tobacco-filled sticks in the barn. A tobacco barn customarily measured sixteen feet square, twenty feet high, and contained four sets of tier poles that ran from about six feet above ground up to the top of the barn, spaced about two feet apart. The columns of tier poles divided the barn into five rooms. Before the 1930s, most barns were constructed of notched logs that were daubed with clay or mortar. An A-shaped tin roof topped the structure, and usually a shed protected the furnace and whoever tended it during curing. Metal flues ran from the furnace along the barn floor and distributed heat.

Curing tobacco was an art, and tobacco farmers took pride in the skill required to turn the greenish-yellow weed into golden tobacco. By 1930 most farmers followed a three-step formula for curing tobacco. When the barn was fired up, the farmer held the heat at from 90 to 100 degrees for twenty-four to forty hours. When the leaf had been properly yellowed, he increased the heat to from 135 to 140 degrees, and this fixed the color. The barn ran at this temperature for thirty to thirty-six hours. Finally, to dry the stems, he increased the heat to 180 degrees and held it there for twenty-four hours. This rough formula in the hands of an experienced farmer would yield beautiful golden tobacco. Yet if the heat died out or was raised too quickly, the entire barn of tobacco could be either ruined or damaged. Curing proved the crucial element in the long progression from plantbed to market. As one farmer put it, "You have to be very careful with heat in curing tobacco; it's something like sitting up with a typhoid patient." After the tobacco had been cured, the barn door was left open so moisture would bring the leaves into order. Otherwise the brittle leaves would crumble when the sticks were transferred to the packhouse.[13]

When the harvest season ended, the entire family joined in to grade and tie the tobacco for market. Graders took each leaf and sorted it into a pile, setting aside the best grade for tie leaves. "The tobacco is in hands," observed Leonard Rapport, who spent a year interviewing people at tobacco warehouses, "sheaves of 20 to 30 leaves, wrapped with a leaf to the size of a half-dollar at the stem end, and hung on 4-foot, thumb-thick, sticks, about 25 hands to the stick." Throughout autumn and winter the family spent many days preparing the tobacco for market.[14]

Changing needs of the tobacco manufacturing industry altered the way that farmers marketed tobacco after the Civil War. Instead of prizing tobacco, packing it into hogsheads, farmers sold it in hands on warehouse floors. Auction selling probably began in Lynchburg, Virginia, in 1810, but it became institutionalized in Danville after the Panic of 1837, which destroyed the marketing system but allowed several factories to survive. Lacking any systematic way to sell their tobacco, farmers simply hauled it to town and sold it from their wagons in the street. A bugler signaled the arrival of a load, and buyers and a crier would conclude the sale. The buyer then took it to his factory, weighed it, and paid the farmer.[15]

During the 1890s, the bright tobacco culture spread from Virginia and North Carolina on into South Carolina and eventually into Georgia and Florida. The first expansion of tobacco into new areas coincided with the decline in cotton prices in the 1890s. When cotton fell below ten cents a pound, farmers turned to tobacco; they would persuade a farmer from the Old Belt, in Virginia or North Carolina, either to in-

struct them or to move into the community and let them learn by example. Anticipated prosperity attracted numerous people interested in
developing a tobacco culture, including those with undeveloped lands,
warehousemen, tinsmiths, bankers, and other businessmen. By 1890
Nash County, just southeast of the Old Belt, began cultivation; a warehouse opened at Battleboro. The county then served as a springboard
for further expansion southeastward. Between 1910 and 1920, tobacco
acreage in South Carolina increased from 25,000 to 98,000 acres. The
expansion also reached Georgia (along with the boll weevil), more
than tripling production between 1918 and 1919.[16]

Even as the growing area of bright tobacco spread, farm families
often lost the title to their land, for tenancy increased in the tobacco-
growing areas after the Civil War, as it did throughout the South.
Blacks who entered the free labor force from slavery and whites who
lost their land met on the common ground of tenancy. Landownership
concentrated into fewer hands, but because owners rented their property out in small parcels, the typical farm size remained small. Both
the old and the new bright leaf areas showed dramatic increases in
tenancy into the 1930s. For example, tenancy in Granville County in the
Old Belt rose from 44 percent in 1879 to 63 percent in 1929; in Nash
County, in the New Belt, it increased from 54 to 74 percent during the
same years.[17]

Three different kinds of contracts spelled out the mutual obligations
of landlord and tenant. In one arrangement the landowner furnished
the land, wood, buildings, and one-fourth of the fertilizer in exchange
for one-fourth of the crop. In another he furnished the land, wood,
buildings, feed, teams, tools, and one-half of the fertilizer and took half
the crop. In a third variation he provided the land, wood, seed, and all
the fertilizer and took half the crop. In most cases such contracts were
simply oral arrangements that also included an understanding that the
tenant could have a garden.[18] Thus tobacco sharecropping resembled
arrangements in cotton areas; both reflected the paternalism of the
antebellum days.

The system, of course, varied with what each farmer could bring to
the farming operation. Arthur Barnes, sharecropping in Granville
County, tried several types of tenancy. "I used his stock and he fed it,"
he explained of the arrangement with Robert Thompson. "I paid half
the fertilizer and we split what the crop brought." The next year, cropping with another man, he cleared $600 on a $2,000 crop. A year later
he rented a place for $100 a year, but wilt ruined his crop, and he lost

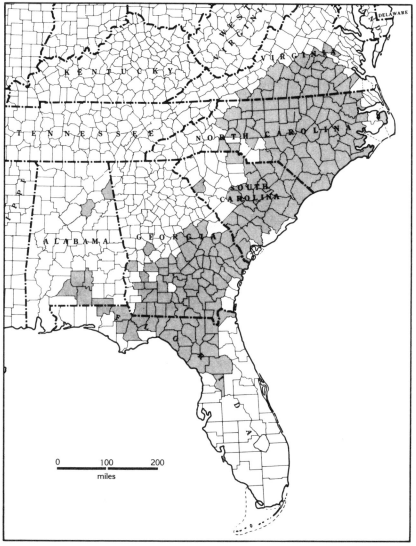

The Extent of the Flue-Cured Tobacco Growing Area, 1979. From
Tobacco Situation, ESCS, USDA, March 1979.

$600. Next he rented "for one-fourth of the crop and he paid a fourth of the fertilizer; I furnished and fed my own stock." Barnes continued his migratory life. "I was keeping on moving in just about a mile circle right back toward the McNeir plantation where I was raised." Danny Kelly, who grew up in Granville County, remembered that his father had sharecroppers, "and at planting and curing time we hired help and swapped work with our croppers." Landlord Sam Hobgood rented his farm to a tenant: "I furnish him everything but half the fertilizer, he has to pay for that, and we split what the crop brings." A farmer from near Bailey, North Carolina, had a simple arrangement: "I work on shares; live with my landlord and we split fifty-fifty." Tenancy permeated the tobacco culture, and many were black farmers. In Virginia 25.6 percent of the farmers were tenants in 1920, in North Carolina 43.5, in South Carolina 64.5, and in Georgia 66.6.[19]

Even as these developments occurred, farmers united to address low prices and challenge warehousemen, leaf buyers, and manufacturers. They insisted that the prodigious amount of work deserved higher prices, and they understood that only changes in the way tobacco entered the channels of commerce would guarantee them a fair return. They haltingly joined to buy fertilizer and implements cooperatively; they attempted to market, dry, and manufacture their own leaf; they hoped to raise prices by cutting production. In these reform efforts growers found rational approaches to their problems, but attempts to implement them failed, due in part to their lack of organization and dedication but also due to concerted attacks from the interests that profited most from bright tobacco. There was, in addition, a strong tradition of rural independence. Biblical injunctions on work and poverty, Jeffersonian ideas of rural life, distrust of most agents of finance, business, and government, and skepticism of organized protest inhibited farmers in uniting for reform.

The Grange led the first organized move for marketing and finance reform in the bright tobacco area. Chapters founded in Virginia and North Carolina in 1873 first attacked what they considered the monopolistic Danville Tobacco Association and then pressured warehousemen to reduce sale rates to 2.5 percent. Dissatisfaction with low prices in the early 1870s attracted farmers to the Grange, but the organization declined at the end of the decade as prices recovered.[20] The sudden rise and fall of the Grange presaged both the cycles of protest and the issues that would dominate the expanding bright tobacco area for the next half-century. Tobacco growers distrusted the auction system, with its incomprehensible pageantry and speculation, and they realized that those who bought and manufactured their tobacco prospered. The disparity between the farmers' sparse fortunes and the comparative opulence of the tobacco lords gave pause even to the most dedicated patron of husbandry.

Such dissatisfaction had little focus. Increasingly, though, the conventional wisdom of the tobacco country, as in other sections of rural America, suggested that low prices paid to farmers led to great profits for the middlemen—bankers, merchants, and manufacturers. From the formation of the Grange in the waning years of Reconstruction to the beginning of the New Deal over a half-century later, tobacco farmers attempted to alter the structure that kept them at the mercy of warehousemen, leaf buyers, and manufacturers. The Farmers' Alliance that swept through the South in the mid-1880s attracted farmers who saw in the cooperative program a way to improve their situation. They advocated that farmers market, process, and manufacture their own tobacco and reduce both the acreage and the use of fertilizer. Alliance popularity in rural areas prompted capitalists to use the name in their products: "Farmers' Alliance Tobacco," Alliance brand cigars, wagons, and plows.[21]

The breakup of the American Tobacco trust in 1911, the disruption of World War I, and increasing tobacco prices made 1911 to 1920 a golden decade for bright leaf growers. With continental agriculture disrupted and other supplies cut off, European and Oriental buyers turned to the United States for tobacco. Tobacco prices soared, farmers expanded production, and talk of exploitation faded. In 1919 tobacco prices rose to an average of over 86 cents a pound in Spring Hope, North Carolina, and the lowest market averaged 42 cents a pound.

In 1920 the price plummeted to 22 or 23 cents a pound.[22] A wave of anger and frustration swept across the tobacco belt and set the stage for a massive attempt to raise the price. "Violent hands were laid on some of the piles of weed sold in the beginning," an observer wrote from eastern North Carolina, and "the buyers were ordered to stop bidding, the houses were accused of stealing the crop and farmers were said to have been armed for any sort of fate." Fearing violence, several warehousemen closed their doors. Clarence Poe, the editor of the *Progressive Farmer*, advocated cooperative marketing and helped organize the Tri-State Tobacco Growers' Cooperative. By 1922 the over 32,000 members of the organization represented over half the tobacco production in the area. Warehousemen, leaf dealers, and several manufacturers opposed the organization, but most newspapers, two manufacturers, and most clergymen supported it.[23]

The cooperative cast a wide net in its effort to secure funds to operate warehouses. It obtained $30 million from the War Finance Corporation, additional funds at low interest from the National City Bank of New York, backing from 350 banks, endorsement of the American Bankers' Association, and the hope of more credit with the passage of the Agricultural Credits Act of 1923. By securing credit from outside local channels, the Tri-State Cooperative threatened the traditional and usually expensive sources of rural credit—small banks, landlords, time merchants (small store owners), warehousemen, and even mule dealers. With the battle lines drawn, the cooperative obtained the services of a Californian named Aaron Sapiro who had successfully organized West Coast farmers. With good leadership, they bought warehouses and redrying plants. Despite the promising start, the cooperative lasted only five years.[24]

Uneducated and suspicious, farmers often believed rumors and gossip spread about the organization, and warehousemen and leaf buyers were adept at spreading self-serving stories. Nonmember growers undermined the others, and not all members lived up to their contracts. When some cooperative leaders spent money on automobiles, drew large salaries, and overextended the organization, farmers began to doubt the movement. In some ways the failure of the Tri-State Cooperative paralleled the demise of the Alliance and other reform movements. When farmers tried to address their economic problems rationally, entrenched interests attempted to undermine them. In 1925, after a Federal Trade Commission investigation, the cooperative went into receivership even though it was still solvent. This set in motion a legal nightmare that resulted in many cooperative warehouses selling out to a new generation of aspiring warehousemen.[25]

The continuing decline in prices in the late 1920s spurred a final attempt to reduce acreage and market tobacco cooperatively. The Federal Farm Board, with the support of Clarence Poe, supported the effort of Dean I. O. Schaub, director of the Extension Service in North Carolina, and in March 1930 established the Interstate Flue-Cured Tobacco Committee. Like the efforts that preceded it, this organization failed to attract enough support to challenge the existing system. Addressing a meeting in Raleigh in September 1930, Congressman Lindsay C. Warren argued that "acreage curtailment will help and is about the only practical thing which can be suggested . . . you and I know that the farmers in eastern Carolina are not going to join a cooperative marketing association, so why strangle a movement in the very beginning by adding that to it."[26] Thus the Grange, the Alliance, strong-minded independents, the Farmers' Union, the Tri-State Cooperative, and the Federal Farm Board failed to break the grip of warehousemen, leaf buyers, and manufacturers.

The impact of the Depression and low prices, combined with the tax burden and mortgage payments, led to the forced sale of some 150,000 pieces of North Carolina farm property in 1930. There were in the state some 3,500 foreclosures. Farmers found it increasingly difficult to borrow money; ninety-three banks closed that year. This affected landowners and merchants who traditionally carried tenants through the crop year until the tobacco auctions of autumn. In 1932 landlords cut some 25 percent, or 15,000 to 20,000, of their tenants. Instead of increasing acreage, many farmers cut back on their traditional plantings for lack of money.[27]

The financial structure of agriculture in North Carolina during the Depression resembled the arrangements that had typified the tobacco culture for three-quarters of a century. Most landlords and time merchants obtained their money from banks or local lending agencies at the market rate. They, in turn, lent this money at a higher rate to furnish their tenants and sharecroppers for the year. In 1930 G. W. Forster of North Carolina State College conducted a study of 112 farms in Lenoir, Pitt, Edgecombe, and Wayne counties. Landlords paid an average of 6.5 percent interest for their money and 30 percent for fertilizer, but their sharecroppers paid an average of 44 percent interest for their furnish.[28]

Roland B. Eustler conducted a similar study of 588 black farmers, 313 of them owners, in twelve eastern North Carolina counties, including several that tobacco dominated. He observed that "the kind of tenant contract tends to be influenced by the kinds of crops planted," and in Pitt, Edgecombe, Wake, and Wayne counties he found the one-third share common. Cotton and tobacco mixed well, he found, since the commodities "do not materially conflict in their demands for labor during the crop and harvesting seasons." Tobacco farmers planted about 40 percent of their cropland to cotton. Tenants, encouraged to pay off their loans, concentrated more on cash crops than did owners. Most blacks did not understand how the credit system worked: "They know little more than that funds are needed, and without regard to costs and conditions which must be met, they turn in their ignorance and helplessness to the sources from which credit can be secured most easily." In the survey area Eustler found four types of loans—mortgages, short-term cash, fertilizer, and merchant. Fifty-one percent of the black farmers had mortgages on their land and paid an average interest of 6 percent on the loan. Forty-three percent borrowed cash for a short term, paying 16.8 percent. Fertilizer proved the most expensive credit, and three-quarters of the black farmers borrowed at a 37.2 percent interest rate. Some 52.4 percent turned to merchants for loans and paid 26 percent for this line of credit. The crop lien law required a farmer who mortgaged his crop to obtain all of his credit from the same source. Farmowners used banks, merchants, and individuals for their loans, while tenants were dependent upon landlords for their cash.[29]

"Despite all that can be said against merchant credit in the south," Eustler admitted, "it is often the only form of credit available." Tenants especially were at the mercy of merchants; 67 percent of the sample obtained credit from merchants, while only half as many owners did. Merchants usually ended up shouldering most of the financial risk of black tenant farmers. "They are in a vicious circle with poor farming methods, lack of knowledge and education, concentration of production on cash crops, and methods of living being partly responsible for the dependence upon and high charges of merchant credit; while, on the other hand, those charges are partly responsible for keeping them in that condition of life." The conditions Eustler found were not exclusively the domain of blacks: "It should be emphasized, too, that white tenants and some of the white farm owners are in equally as unfavorable a credit position as are the Negro farmers."[30]

The Great Depression brought into sharper focus the problems that plagued tobacco growers. Farmers and farm experts agreed that the cost of production for an acre of tobacco was from $94 to $125. An acre would produce about 670 to 700 pounds of tobacco. If a farmer had $100 in production costs, marketed 700 pounds of tobacco per acre, and received $12 per hundred pounds, he lost $16 per acre. This was the economic reality for most flue-cured tobacco farmers as the Depression began. They had failed to form a successful cooperative or to reduce acreage, and by 1933, like cotton farmers, they looked desperately to the federal government for aid.[31]

3

*Southwest Louisiana is a
paradise for the farmer, and its
people are growing wealthy
faster than any agricultural
people in the entire country.*
—*Sylvester L. Cary, 1901*

Providence:
Development of the
Prairie Rice Culture

During the antebellum, Civil War, and Reconstruction eras, the country's rice culture stretched along the coast of the Carolinas and Georgia and, in its labor-intensive cultivation, resembled other rice-growing areas of the world. The Civil War disrupted the rice coast with the destruction of dikes and, as important, with the emancipation of the slave labor force. As that culture faltered, Mississippi River planters competed with eastern growers using similar cultivation methods. In the early 1880s a land promotion campaign in the southwestern Louisiana prairie led to a revolution in rice cultivation. Midwestern farmers migrated to the rich prairie lands and quickly adapted the technology of the Midwest wheat culture to rice growing. Within a few years the highly mechanized Gulf Coast rice industry eclipsed the older areas of rice cultivation.[1]

From its inception, the prairie rice culture exhibited an unsouthern profile. While Cajuns who grew rice in the prairie depended on Providence for rainfall and used primitive implements that typified southern farming, Midwesterners introduced mechanical reapers with binder attachments, steam threshers, and irrigation networks. The heritage of slavery did not appear in the tenure system that developed, nor were farm plots as small as in most of the South. While tobacco factories and textile mills were usually far from the fields that produced these commodities, rice mills sprang up near the broad fields. The grain also entered the channels of trade differently. Still, the capital-intensive cultivation practices provided the most striking difference. Instead of the age-old cultivation methods that characterized much of the South, rice farmers from the beginning concentrated on mechanized and scientific farming. Relying so much on machines, they left behind little of the graphic detail of the work routine that survived in the cotton and tobacco areas.

The origin and development of the Gulf Coast rice culture furnishes a classic example of the interaction of transportation developments, land promotion, and modern agricultural practices. As high interest rates, unfavorable climate, and grasshoppers threatened their livelihood in the 1880s, midwestern wheat farmers looked for new lands to settle. Their migration and the subsequent rise of the prairie rice industry represents one of the most dynamic chapters in American agriculture.[2] In some ways it resembled the expansion of the flue-cured tobacco culture, and it contrasted sharply with the plague-ridden cotton culture. The development of the barren prairies and coastal marshes of Louisiana, inhabited mostly by Cajuns who fished, trapped, raised livestock, and grew subsistence crops, began in 1881 with the completion of the rail link between New Orleans and Houston. Louisiana commissioner of immigration William H. Harris and local businessmen promoted development of the area. In the early 1880s Sylvester L. Cary moved from Manchester, Iowa, settled in Jennings, Louisiana, and became the station agent for the Southern Pacific Railroad that had taken in the independent lines to form a transcontinental rail system. A railroad promotional bulletin described Cary's contribution. He served as station agent in Jennings for four years and put "all his spare time in advertising this country by sending letters, circulars and books to his Northern friends, and was so successful that the Southern Pacific Company promoted him to Northern Immigration Agent for the Company, with headquarters at Manchester, Iowa. He organized excursions and attracted so many settlers from Iowa that the area was called the 'Iowa colony.'" Cary became a revered figure along the Gulf Coast, and people there called him Father Cary.[3]

One large venture, the Louisiana Land Reclamation Company, failed in 1884 when the Mississippi River flooded its Terre Bonne Parish project. Meanwhile, Jabez B. Watkins, a Kansas banker, saw the possibilities of land promotion, and with English financial backing in 1882 he formed the North American Land and Timber Company, Ltd. A year later he bought some million and a half acres of prairie land in Cameron, Vermilion, Acadia, and Calcasieu parishes.[4]

At first Watkins and his associates inaugurated a plan to drain the marshland and set up an agricultural paradise in the lowlands. The engineering blueprint called for vast canals that would not only drain and irrigate the land, but also furnish transportation for harvested crops and machinery. Pulleys and cables working from barges would drive gigantic plows across the drained land, doing away with the need for draft animals. After starting the project, Watkins cast about for an agricultural expert to develop this mechanized promised land. He settled on Seaman A. Knapp, farmer, college president, preacher, and rural editor, and also a man who knew many midwestern farmers and would be adept at attracting them to the Gulf Coast. After a visit to the area, Knapp decided that his future lay not with academia but with Watkins's land promotion scheme. In 1885 he moved his family to Lake Charles, Louisiana.[5]

Even as the Watkins syndicate drained the marshes, it flooded the Midwest with pamphlets describing the opportunities in Louisiana, and Knapp shrewdly placed advertisements in farm journals and encouraged farmers to see for themselves the attractions of the prairie. At first the promoters thought in terms of a Garden of Eden with fruit, vegetables, cattle, and field crops. The first prospective settlers left disappointed, for they saw only barren prairie and marshland, and Cajuns informed them that nothing but cattle could thrive there. The ever resourceful Knapp then set up demonstration farms run by industrious Midwesterners. Though these farms graphically illustrated the possibilities of the area, settlers were still unaccustomed to the tropical climate that alternated flood with drought. They could neither make a success of the suggested crops nor transplant the cultivation of wheat and corn from their native Midwest.[6]

The immigrants quickly observed that Cajuns grew small plots of rice, so new settlers learned to cultivate rice by the "Providence" method that relied on rainfall instead of irrigation. They recognized the similarity between the rice plant and its cultivation and that of wheat; both were grains. Within a few years the migrants imported gang plows, disc harrows, and other implements from the Midwest and started growing rice in earnest. In 1884 Maurice Brien, an Iowa native who lived in Jennings, successfully adapted a Deering grain binder to handle the tougher rice stalks. In 1887 the Deering company shipped three hundred binders to Jefferson Davis Parish on a twenty-two-car train "gaily bedecked with flags and bunting." Almost magically, the prairies sprouted large fields of rice, and the horizon framed not cattle grazing but four-horse teams pulling gang plows or binders. For a decade these pioneers relied on Providence to supply irrigation, just as Cajuns had for years. With a cash crop, the prairie became more attractive to immigrants, and the entreaties of Cary, Watkins, and Knapp pulled ever more settlers into the area. Paradoxically, the Watkins syndicate's gigantic canals along the coastal marshes were abandoned, for the rich and firm prairie proved best suited for the cultivation of rice.[7]

Watkins and his associates spared no expense in advertising the area. When prospective settlers arrived, Watkins and other promoters took them in tow to the rice area. Many expected to find small plots of rice, and they were amazed to see farms with hundreds of acres under cultivation. The harvest and threshing routines seemed familiar to wheat farmers, who saw the sparsely settled prairie as a new frontier. The promotional network stretched from Louisiana to railroad stations and land offices in the Midwest, where agents encouraged exploratory tours. Prospects arrived in New Orleans, where often city fathers welcomed them. Advertisements and pamphlets praising the new farming country papered the Midwest.[8]

Gulf Coast promoters never tired of bragging about the mechanization of the rice culture and the economic potential of southwest Louisiana. "Southwest Louisiana is a paradise for the farmer," Sylvester L. Cary wrote, "and its people are growing wealthy faster than any agricultural people in the entire country." He boasted that relatively few rice farmers failed and that rice yielded more cash than either cotton or corn. Another article observed that "one man with a machine and four mules had the working power of forty with a sickle." Promoters stressed the large-scale machine-intensive cultivation routine familiar to wheat farmers. "One man and a team can handle one hundred acres of rice, except in harvest, one extra man is all that is required at that time," a promotional article reported.[9]

In the space of ten years the prairies of Louisiana had been transformed from barren land sparsely populated with Cajuns, their cattle, and Providence stands of rice into a booming and highly mechanized rice-growing area. The new culture contrasted sharply with the technologically backward methods in other commodity areas of the South. Four years after Maurice Brien adapted a binder to operate in rice fields, David Abbott, according to one account, figured out how to irrigate his crop and escape the whims of Providence. In 1888 he took a small engine from a steam launch, some chain, and buckets and con- structed an endless bucket chain to raise water from a bayou to his nineteen-acre rice field. The next year he improved the machinery and irrigated a hundred acres. In 1890 C. C. Duson used a vacuum pump to lift water from a bayou in Acadia Parish, and as drought brought crop failures in 1893 and 1894, more farmers turned to irrigation. By 1894 Acadia Parish had a canal network 15 miles long with 10 miles of laterals. Although the panic of 1893 slowed the development of the area and the Wilson-Gorman Tariff Act of 1894 lowered the rates on higher quality rice, by the turn of the century Acadia Parish had nine canals 115 miles long. "There are about 25 irrigating canals in Acadia, Calcasieu, Cameron, and Vermilion parishes," Seaman Knapp wrote in 1899, "with a total length of over 400 miles of mains and probably twice that extent of laterals, built at a total cost of about $1,500,000."[10]

Even as canal systems developed, farmers discovered a providential reservoir of underground water that could easily be tapped. "Scarcely had the surface canals been accepted as a success," Knapp reported, "when Southwestern Louisiana was startled by the announcement that there were strata of gravel at 125 to 200 feet under the surface of the entire section containing an unlimited supply of water which would, of its own pressure, come so near the surface that it could be readily pumped." Jean Costex of Mermantau constructed the first suc- cessful well using a windmill for power. Other farmers quickly sank wells with pipes from two to ten inches in diameter. "The water is soft," Knapp reported, "at a constant temperature of about 70 degrees, and absolutely free from injurious seeds or minerals." He revealed that a six-inch pipe could be sunk to 200 feet in fourteen hours, and a 200- acre farm could be irrigated with a pumping outfit that cost from $1,500 to $2,000.[11]

J. F. Wellington, in a promotional article entitled "A Model Planta- tion," described the move to irrigate rice fields. After drought stunted the 1897 Providence crop, he reported that "a stampede occurred to the pump lands" in Calcasieu Parish. In many cases large investors purchased vast areas of farmland and then hired tenants to work the crops. Wellington gave an example of how investors managed their properties. In the fall of 1897 two Jennings men purchased 4,000 acres of land near Lake Arthur and attracted three Iowa stockholders to help develop it with canals and a pumping station. By summer the investors had five miles of irrigation canals. They built thirteen new houses "containing from four to eight rooms each, for the use of the

*Canal and pumping plant in rice region of Louisiana. January 1906.
D.A.B. (83 F 4373, National Archives)*

tenants." Everything was new and well constructed. During the first
year the farm grew 3,000 acres of rice irrigated by water pumped into
the fields with steam power. The entire investment amounted to
$75,000.

Wellington also explained the tenure system on this plantation:
"Every tenant is an equal partner with his landlord. The company furnishes land, water, buildings, fence and seed. The tenant furnishes
the teams, machinery, feed, and labor. The crop is divided at the
threshing machine, each getting one-half." Such tenants, Wellington
argued, would make as much money as their midwestern counter-
parts. This tenure system, especially the fact that the tenant supplied
rather expensive machinery, would become an important factor in the
1930s, when the Agricultural Adjustment Administration assigned
acreage allotments in the rice area.[12]

By the turn of the century rice farmers had established an entirely
new culture in southwest Louisiana. Jennings had become, as a
Southern Pacific Railroad pamphlet aptly put it, "a Northern village on
Southern soil." There, it continued, "you can shake hands with people
from every and any state north of Mason and Dixon's line, and they
like to meet you, and are, if possible, more agreeably social since
breathing Southern air." All along the Southern Pacific tracks small

towns grew—Lake Charles, Welsh, Gueydan, and others. In 1900 one observer estimated that some 7,000 Northerners, mainly from Iowa, Illinois, and Nebraska, had settled in the area. After the binder had been adapted to rice, production increased from 2 million pounds in 1886 to over 200 million in 1892. By 1890 farmers utilized over 1,000 binders to harvest the crop; two years later they owned 3,000. Land values jumped from $.50 to $1 an acre and then rose to $10 within ten years. The boom fed upon itself as Watkins and his associates pulled ever more Midwesterners into the area. By 1899 Louisiana produced over 2.7 million barrels of rice, while areas using traditional methods produced just over 1 million.[13]

In 1897 Knapp began publishing *The Rice Journal and Gulf Coast Farmer*, which, after several name changes, still survives as *The Rice Journal*. He gave homespun advice to farmers and encouraged good cultivation practices. In the late 1880s Knapp had left the Watkins syndicate and, with English backing, formed a land company, the Louisiana and Southern States Real Estate and Mortgage Co., Ltd. The company had an American counterpart located in Vinton, Iowa, and Knapp was president of both. He bought for the companies some half-million acres of Louisiana prairie. It was from this tract that the towns of Vinton and Iowa sprang, two more indicators of the debt the development of the prairies owed to Iowa. In the late 1890s Knapp toured the Far East searching for a variety of rice that resisted breakage during milling. The varieties grown in the prairie cracked easily, and since up to 60 percent of the crop was damaged in milling, prices dropped drastically. Knapp returned with ten tons of Japanese Kiushu rice, and farmers discovered that this variety had 50 percent less breakage. Thus Knapp dabbled in real estate, milling, banking, editing, research, and promotion.[14]

The prairie did not stop at the Louisiana-Texas state line but curved along the Texas coast to the Mexican border. Prior to the introduction of rice in the 1860s, Texas prairie farmers grew cotton and sugar cane and raised cattle. When rice farmers started fencing off their fields, cattlemen bitterly complained that the enclosure threatened their livelihoods, but rice farmers persisted. Indeed, many of them raised both cattle and rice. The modern Texas rice industry began in Jefferson County in 1886 using Providence to provide irrigation. Like their Louisiana neighbors, Texans quickly exploited the rivers and streams of the area and discovered ground water near the surface. Even as farmers dug their wells and expanded the canal network, Anthony F. Lucas drilled for oil south of Beaumont, in the midst of the rice area. On January 10, 1901, Spindletop came in and transformed the prairie—especially Beaumont, which became a boom town. Cattle, rice, and oil all coexisted in the prairie.[15]

Cultivation practices followed those of Louisiana; Texans used drills, binders, steam tractors, and threshers. An agriculture bulletin revealed that one traction engine "with its plows running night and day can break 50 acres in 24 hours." The tenure pattern in Texas, like that in Louisiana, showed that in many cases large investment companies owned the land and sold or rented it to farmers. "The custom of renting," the bulletin observed, "is to charge 2 sacks per acre for water alone, and 2 additional sacks where the company rents the land, making a total of 4 sacks per acre where both land and water are rented." In 1900 Texas irrigated 8,700 acres of rice land; by 1909 the 1,088 rice farms reported 286,847 acres irrigated.[16]

Arkansas, like Texas and Louisiana, had prairie land suited for rice growing. In 1895 William H. Fuller, a native of Ohio who had farmed for twenty years in Nebraska, moved to a farm near Carlisle, Arkansas. A year later he loaded up a wagon and, with a neighbor named Hewit Puryear, headed to the Gulf of Mexico on a hunting trip. "When we got in about 8 miles of Crowley, La.," he wrote in 1909, "we came to the first rice either of us had ever seen grow, 8 of September, 1896, owned and operated by the Abbott boys of Crowley, La. We stopped there a half a day, viewing their rice fields and pumping plant." Intrigued, Fuller and Puryear talked to farmers for a few days, discovering all they could about the rice culture. "At that time," Fuller remembered, "there were no wells there, but they were talking of making wells, which gave me the idea of wells here." After the hunting trip they returned to Arkansas and began preparations for growing rice.

In the fall of 1896 Fuller put down two wells and obtained pumps. He planted three acres of rice in the spring of 1897, and the crop thrived "until I pulled my pump to pieces. Then I gave up for that year." Fuller realized that he did not fully understand rice cultivation, so he moved to Louisiana in 1898 and worked in the rice culture for four years. "I learned how to raise the rice, put down the wells, and how to manage it thoroughly." Meanwhile his brother-in-law, John Morris, tried to grow rice near Carlisle. When Fuller returned to Arkansas in 1903, he struck a bargain to grow seventy acres of rice and produce thirty-five bushels per acre. If successful, he would receive a $1,000 bonus. He bought the well machinery and seed in Loui-

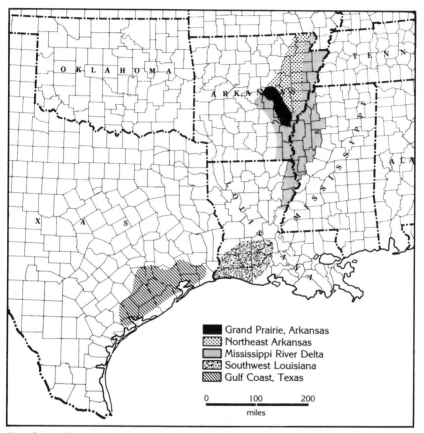

Southern Rice Growing Areas, 1979. From Shelby H. Holder, Jr., and Warren R. Grant, *U.S. Rice Industry*, ESCS, USDA, Agricultural Economics Report No. 433, 1979.

siana and returned to Lonoke County and planted the seventy acres in 1904, produced 5,225 bushels, and claimed the $1,000. "This crop is what started the rice business here and proved to the people there was a profit in raising it," he claimed five years later. The cost of putting down the well and cultivating the crop totaled $3,147.50.[17]

Emma Thompson Morris, a native of Nebraska, moved to Lonoke County in 1894, and it was her husband, John Morris, who experimented with rice in 1901. The crop failed due to "want of experience" in operating the pumps. A year later Morris planted five acres and produced 320 bushels. Encouraged, he went to Louisiana to gather more information, but while there he died. Emma Morris did not give up. She and her sons planted fifteen acres, managed to irrigate eight of them, and harvested 258 bushels from the ten acres that crabgrass did not devour. Both William H. Fuller and his sister-in-law, Emma Thompson Morris, claimed honor for introducing rice to Arkansas. During those years the University of Arkansas experiment station conducted rice experiments near Lonoke.[18]

Only two crop years passed after Fuller won his bet when George Sibly wrote to *The Rice Journal* that the rice culture was flourishing in Arkansas. Farmers still experimented and had occasional failures, but overall they were growing fifty-five to sixty bushels to the acre. In 1906 some farmers bought cheap pumps that failed, but others were improving their pumping plants as they gained experience. "Everybody," Sibly insisted, "is satisfied that the industry is profitable enough." In 1910, probably with some ambivalence at the new competition since *The Rice Journal* was published in Crowley, the journal carried an article, "The New Rice Eldorado," tracing the development of rice on the Arkansas prairie.[19]

William H. Fuller grew 75 acres of rice in 1904. By 1910 the acreage in Arkansas had increased to 55,000. "Prairies which were formerly idle," A. A. Kaiser boasted in 1909, "now send up smoke from almost countless chimneys and the exhaust from countless engines pumping water declare a new era." Six rice mills, two in Stuttgart and one each in DeWitt, Lonoke, Carlisle, and Wheatley, processed the crop. Prospective settlers arrived daily in Stuttgart, and G. W. Fagan observed that they were fortunate "to find a place to sleep" while "building a dwelling house." Stuttgart, he insisted, "is what Crowley was in 1900, what Bay City, Eagle Lake and El Campo were in 1902 and 1903." One measure of the town's prosperity—seventy automobiles—led Kaiser

Irrigation plant on rice farm at Lonoke, Arkansas. March 1906.
D.A.B. (83 F 4344, National Archives)

to conclude that "every farmer with 160 acres in rice has a perfect mint."[20]

According to G. W. Fagan, rice farming in Arkansas differed not only from the surrounding cotton culture but also from the tenure system in Louisiana. "The vicious tenant system does not prevail here," he wrote, and most farms contained about 100 acres. He thought it important to note that "the colored population is inconsiderable and the white population is made up of the best class of Americans." Farmers paid cash for their supplies, and he boasted that the advance system "which has proved the ruination of so many Southern agricultural communities, is practically unknown and is practiced not at all." H. S. McGavic, a statistician from Iowa, estimated that an investor could make 44 percent profit on a 160-acre rice farm "and does not put his hand to the plow." The work routine in Arkansas proved similar to that further south. "When teams were used for power on binders," the historian Florence L. Rosencrantz wrote, "neighbors exchanged work cutting the crop as well as threshing, and hauling to the mills or shipping points—as many as thirty wagons hauling for one farmer." Conscious of the woman's role, Rosencrantz observed, "Back in those days cooking for twenty or more men at threshing time was real work for the housewife."[21]

Yet, by the fall of 1910, Arkansas farmers experienced the same dis-illusionment that was spreading through Louisiana and Texas. Rice prices were lower than the year before, and one observer concluded, "The mill men seem to have an understanding among themselves and are buying it as cheaply as possible and grading it much closer than they have ever done heretofore." Low prices coupled with wet weather during harvest season discouraged Arkansas rice growers. The Arkansas rice boom tapered off as land sales declined.[22]

The problems that surfaced by 1910 in the prairie rice areas came not only from the oversupply of rice that flooded the national market and failed to find overseas buyers, but also from the struggle between growers and millers and even disputes within the millers' ranks. Prior to the development of the prairie rice culture, river rice, grown from one hundred miles north of New Orleans to as far south as the levees reached, moved to New Orleans through brokers for milling. By 1875 New Orleans boasted several mills that handled river rice, and by 1892, despite the presence of several mills in the prairie, most growers viewed the New Orleans millers as a trust.

Prairie businessmen had already responded and in 1886 built a mill in Rayne, the first in the prairie. In 1889 Seaman Knapp arranged credit to build the Lake Charles Rice Milling Company. Still, prairie millers sold the milled rice to New Orleans brokers who bought from millers' samples. "The moment rice leaves the farmer," Knapp wrote in 1903, "it undergoes a marvelous increment in price at the hands of every one that touches it, the miller, the transportation lines, the bro-ker, the wholesaler and the retailer, until the article that left the farmer as a staple food at moderate prices has by the time it is offered to the consumer become a luxury too costly for the masses."[23]

As acreage and production increased, millers relied on crop esti-mates to set prices; as prices dropped, farmers blamed large crop es-timates, or "bear" predictions. "The public has been afflicted with so many statements of the rice yield of last year," *The Rice Journal* re-ported in 1903, "that it has almost become a mark of ill breeding for anyone to mention the subject." It suggested that the U.S. Department of Agriculture furnish estimates.[24]

In 1908 James Ellis of Welsh expressed his disgust at millers' esti-mates. "We suppose that some infallible city smarty," he suggested, "has been through on the sleeper again and can tell us by this time just how many sacks of rice the crop of 1908 will count." It was a joke among rice farmers by then that most crop estimates were made by brokers or millers who boarded a train from New Orleans at dusk and, upon arrival at Lake Charles the next morning, called in the estimate based on a careful tour through the rice country. Though the USDA failed to establish rice crop estimates, in 1908 the Bureau of Plant Industry created a Rice Investigation Division. C. E. Chambliss, who headed the unit, stressed that he would concentrate on better growing practices and plant diseases. "I have found in the course of my investigations that the rice farms of Louisiana and Texas have badly deteriorated where they have been farmed by renters," he announced. "I attribute this not only to carelessness but to indifference and ignorance."[25] Evidently not all rice farmers matched the advertised product, and Chambliss set out to cure both plant and human deficiences.

Another issue emerged in 1909 as canal companies, many owning vast tracts of land, insisted on cash rent for water instead of one-fifth of the crop. By 1909 Louisiana and Texas had developed distinct arrangements for supplying water for rice crops. Over half of Louisiana growers supplied their own water from wells, but in Texas only one-third did so. All but a small percentage of Louisiana growers who relied on canal companies gave one-fifth of their crop for irrigation, whereas in Texas only 10 percent paid in a share of the crop. Most Texas growers paid either a fixed crop rental for water, usually two bags per acre, or a cash rental of from $6 to $9 per acre. In 1911 Louisiana canal companies struck a compromise with growers, providing that farmers whose crops graded high would be charged one-fifth of the crop, while those whose rice graded lower would pay $6 per acre for water.[26] This, they argued, would force renters to employ better farming methods and encourage them to pull up quality-spoiling red rice.

The water rate dispute led the Texas Rice Farmers' Association in its January 1908 meeting to call for a state commission to set rates. Association President E. G. Cloar of Matagorda argued that farmers needed consistent rates in order to arrange their production credit. The organization decided to hire legal counsel to draft bills and then lobby the legislature for a rate commission. "I realized the man who owned the water would be master of the situation," Cloar argued. F. V. Evans of the Farmers' Union addressed the meeting, and he put the question into perspective, charging that canal companies did not want to share the risk with growers. "They want to take no chances on the weather and cultivation, but want to fix themselves an assured income from the farm, whether the farm earns it or not." On November 2, 1908, the Association turned to the issue of crop estimates. "The fact of the matter is," Secretary A. E. Groves of Houston observed, "there has been for some time back a bear movement on the part of some mills and especially one mill man in New Orleans, and it has the effect to demoralize prices."[27]

Two weeks later, with Groves's aid, Louisiana growers organized the Louisiana Rice Growers' Association and elected W. B. Gabbert of Welsh as president. Forty-five farmers from Iowa, Kinder, Rice, Roanoke, Jennings, and Elton gathered at Crowley to hear speakers condemn a threatened tariff reduction on Philippine rice and plug cooperative marketing. Like Texas growers, those who met in Crowley argued that "certain interests" had circulated "false and misleading reports" to drive down prices. Growers quickly rallied, and the association held meetings throughout the Louisiana prairie; by mid-December over 150 farmers belonged to the organization. In February 1909 the two state organizations merged into the Texas-Louisiana Rice Farmers' Association and elected Hezekiah Winn of Lake Arthur as president. The group discussed advertising rice to increase the domestic demand, voted thanks to the banks and merchants "for their aid in holding this rice crop," and resolved that the USDA should provide crop statistics. The "important work of the meeting" began when growers discussed a plan to market rice. Milling and marketing had fallen into disarray, members charged. "Today," the Crowley newspaper argued, "you could not get two rice millers to agree on the time of day."[28]

The issues of water rights and the impending decline in the Philippine tariff dimmed before the issue of crop estimates. Gordon S. Orme, owner of the Empire Rice Mill in New Orleans, was singled out as the main bear in estimating crops. On March 8 he estimated the 1909 crop, as Hezekiah Winn charged, "months before the crop is put in and even before the ground for it has been broken." After asking where Orme got his information, Winn surmised, "Perhaps he got it from the tail end of an observation car." Orme had predicted a 20 percent increase in the 1909 crop over the previous year. The year before, Winn reminded farmers, Blair Campbell wrote a bear letter "which started a slump in rice that cost the farmers of the rice belt two million dollars."[29]

Despite growers' complaints, lower prices did reflect increasing supplies of rice. In 1905 Louisiana growers produced 3.7 million bags of rice and received $1.98 per hundred pounds. Production increased steadily and by 1910 had reached 5.9 million bags, while the price dropped steadily to $1.44 per hundred pounds. Production in Texas did not increase as much as in Louisiana, from 3 million bags to 3.6 million, but prices fell from $2.22 to $1.49 during the same years. Arkansas production, meanwhile, increased dramatically, from 14,000 bags in 1905 to 1.2 million five years later, while prices fell from $2.25 per hundred pounds to $1.51. No doubt the large increase in production in Arkansas flooded the domestic market, making the job of selling rice more difficult for millers and distributors.[30]

The crop estimate issue simmered for over a year before Gordon Orme on September 24, 1910, published yet another bear prediction. By this time growers openly scorned such estimates, referring to them as "The New Orleans Raffles" and labeling millers "thieves, pirates, and robbers." The prairie press bristled with attacks on Orme and his replies. The common enemy united farmers and led them in December to form the Southern Rice Growers' Association. They elected W. B. Dunlap, a rice farmer and banker, as president and vowed to fight the millers.[31]

A rice analyst named S. Locke Breaux, who regularly gave marketing reports in *The Rice Journal*, argued that the Southern Rice Growers' Association had a golden opportunity to end the marketing confusion. Yet he pointed out that only when rice manufacturers did a better job of advertising and distribution could millers sell the large supply of prairie rice. At that time the Rice Association of America, a promotional organization, was distributing "Creole Mammy Rice Recipes" to encourage domestic use of rice. The association justified the two-cent pamphlet by observing that "the old 'mammies' could turn out a dish of rice in such a delicate state of perfection that no French chef could approach them." Breaux also gave some sobering thoughts about the nature of the organization. "The Rice Growers' Association, though purporting to be an association of farmers, is, as a matter of fact, administered and controlled by bankers, millers, canal owners and men of large affairs, and it is up to that element in the association to take hold of the present problem and work it out." If the chaos continued, he warned, "then the blame should not rest upon the farmers, but upon that element within the Rice Growers' Association who, furnishing it with brains and administrative, controlled its destinies."[32]

Even as Texas and Louisiana growers organized, farmers in Arkansas addressed their problems. In 1909 growers united to gather statistics, give crop reports, conduct institutes, and cooperate with the rice experiment station. Its crop estimates, it boasted, were "more accurate in detail than of any other state in the rice territory." It also hired professor John S. Collier of the University of Chicago to investigate rice blight, maggots, and fertilization. Writing in *Farm and Ranch*, J. A. Kinney observed that usually farmer organizations "either dry up in summer or freeze out in winter." Conditions were changing, he stressed, "and the farmer is no longer the independent individual he formerly was." Farmers were the last class to unite, he concluded, "but they are gradually being forced to organize."[33] Ultimately, Arkansas growers joined with Texas and Louisiana farmers in the Rice Association of America. Prairie rice growers moved ahead of cotton and tobacco farmers in cooperation to rationalize their capital-intensive and geographically small industry.

By 1917 the Southern Rice Growers' Association had become a force in marketing rice throughout the Texas, Louisiana, and Arkansas prairies. W. B. Dunlap, a Texas rice farmer and banker, served as president. E. A. Eignus served as secretary, treasurer, and general manager and directed the daily operations of gathering statistics, organizing sales, and leading a campaign for more domestic consumption of rice. Each of the three states had a vice-president, giving the organization a broad base. The Association's headquarters in Beaumont, according to *The Rice Journal*, was "a beehive of activity, not only during the selling season, but throughout the entire year." The Association held sales and "great numbers of brokers and buyers for mills flock to Beaumont to place their bids and get their share of the rice offered." The cooperative held sales throughout the rice area, calculated statistics on prices and sales, and furnished crop estimates.[34]

Even as growers and millers bickered over crop estimates and organized to pursue their separate goals, thirty-one-year-old Frank A. Godchaux, a rice miller from Abbeville, Louisiana, organized twenty-eight mills and to a degree united the prairie and New Orleans millers. In 1911 the Louisiana State Rice Milling Company organized with capital stock of $9.5 million. Despite the fact that all the officers were from the prairie, *The Rice Journal* observed, "The incorporators are among the most prominent millers, land owners and rice growers in New Orleans and Southwest Louisiana." Godchaux argued in an interview that "production of rice the past year has increased beyond its consumption and no single mill has felt justified in undergoing the expense necessary for a general campaign to increase the consumption of rice and to instruct householders in the proper preparation of it." He promised that his mills would use the latest equipment and "pay to the farmers a higher price than he has been in the habit of obtaining for his rough product." He stressed that this would "inure not only to the benefit of those sections of the State engaged in producing rice but also to the city of New Orleans."[35] Even as growers and millers organized, Godchaux moved through economic means to centralize milling, utilize more systematic marketing, and unite the New Orleans and country millers through incorporation.

The milling industry had been loosely organized since 1902, when the Louisiana and Texas Rice Millers' and Distributors' Association was organized. For the first decade the group held irregular meetings and lacked a systematic program. In 1910, no doubt due to the threat of grower cooperatives and the controversy over crop estimates, it hired J. R. Leguenec as secretary and statistician. Formerly mayor of Abbeville, Louisiana, before working as a USDA statistician, Leguenec prepared monthly reports on acreage, production, and distribution. Largely due to his influence, by World War I the organization boasted that its figures were more reliable than those of the USDA, which by that time employed a rice expert. In 1914 the organization changed its name to the Rice Millers' Association and expanded to include millers, brokers, and wholesalers. "The purpose of this organization," *The Rice Journal* reported in 1917, "is to collect and disseminate reliable information bearing on all phases of the growing and marketing of rice, to the end that all information as to yields, acreage, percentage planted in the different varieties, crop prospects, amounts purchased by the mills each month, amount distributed, stocks on hand, the amount imported and exported, also foreign crop statistics having a bearing on the domestic market, in fact anything in the line of information that can benefit directly or indirectly any person interested in rice." In 1912 the Rice Millers' Association moved its offices from Crowley to Beaumont.

Charles J. Bier of Crowley first held the presidency. Joseph E. Broussard, who headed the Beaumont Rice Mill, took over in 1907 and held the office until 1919. The membership came from all of the prairie rice states as well as California. By 1917 fifteen mills in Texas, seven in Louisiana, five in Arkansas, and four in California belonged to the association, as did brokers, wholesalers, and distributors from all over the country. In 1923 the association limited membership to those active in the milling business. In 1919 J. A. Foster of Lake Charles became president, succeeding Broussard, and the association instituted an annual presidential rotation. Like the Southern Rice Growers' Association, the millers had vice-presidents from Arkansas, Texas, and Louisiana. In the fall of 1919 F. B. Wise, a former grain expert with the USDA, became secretary-treasurer. After several moves, the millers' association finally settled in New Orleans.

Both groups, growers and millers, reacted to the disorganization of the rice industry at the turn of the century by organizing. After steady expansion from 1884 to 1910, prairie growers saturated the U.S. rice market, and, lacking foreign markets of any size, the industry required more planning. Both organizations attempted to discover foreign markets, increase domestic demand, and lobby for a protective tariff.[36]

From 1910 to 1916 the price of rice gradually increased from $1.47 to $2.19 per hundred pounds. During these years Arkansas acreage increased from 60,000 to 125,000, while Louisiana and Texas acreage remained about the same. Since 1912 California had come on the rice market; by 1916 its growers harvested 59,000 acres. During the years when growers struggled with millers, formed cooperatives, and tried to bring order to marketing, they were also utilizing improved implements. The gasoline binder engines and utilization of tractors arrived almost simultaneously with World War I. Since rice proved a strategic crop, demand increased, and farmers expanded production. In Louisiana the acreage harvested increased from 385,000 in 1915 to 676,000 in 1920; Arkansas increased from 100,000 to 180,000; and while Texas acreage remained stable from 1915 to 1919, it jumped from 212,000 in 1919 to 281,000 in 1920. With increased foreign demand, prices rose from $1.86 in 1915 to $5.46 in 1919. Herbert Hoover, who was in charge of food distribution, coopted the Southern Rice Growers' Association and federalized it. Under its new guise, the Southern Rice Committee for the U.S. Food Administration, it regulated the price of rice and monitored production. Yet rice farmers were not immune to the collapse of farm prices in 1920. In an instant, it seemed, the $5.46 per hundred pounds sank to half that. Rice prices did not reach the $5.00 level again until after World War II.[37]

The collapse of demand in 1920 dramatized the fragile position of U.S. rice growers in international trade. Since the Civil War the United States had been a net importer of rice, and thus rice growers anxiously sought to protect themselves from foreign competition. Louisiana rice farmers found natural allies on the tariff issue among neighboring sugar planters. Even by using the most advanced machines, prairie rice farmers could not grow rice as cheaply as could labor-intensive farmers in other countries. The Spanish-American War opened new markets in Cuba, Puerto Rico, and the Philippines. Politically, southern growers and millers struggled with San Francisco and New York millers who cleaned the imported rice and thus favored a low tariff. Obviously, if the prairie rice industry was to continue to expand, it had to push for more domestic consumption and more exports. In 1911 rice exports began a steady increase that, fed by World War I demand, resulted in the United States becoming a net exporter in 1919. In the 1920s rice politicians managed to preserve tariff duties on imported rice. Despite their small political base, rice farmers managed to protect their industry from imports; in that sense they were quite different from most southern farmers, who traditionally opposed a high tariff.[38]

Most of the rice crop that left the United States went to Puerto Rico and Hawaii. During the 1920s exports to Europe, other North American countries, South America, and Japan fell drastically. In 1922 the United States exported over 507 million pounds, but by 1926 the figure had declined to a mere 27 million. Imports in 1926, on the other hand, amounted to over 92 million pounds of cleaned rice and 30.7 million pounds of uncleaned rice. The imports came primarily as a result of the poor growing season in 1925; a year later farmers expanded production, hoping that the previous year's shortage would raise prices. The larger supply drove prices lower, however, and they continued to fall until 1933.[39]

Faced with low prices and in many cases notes on new machinery and additional acreage, prairie rice farmers experienced hard times. By 1920 rice acreage in Texas, Louisiana, and Arkansas had reached a plateau that continued until World War II. The unity that had blossomed in 1910, as growers in all three states banded together, disappeared in the 1920s. In Louisiana and Texas, growers formed the American Rice Growers' Cooperative Association, the legatee of the former organization. Homer L. Brinkley and S. Arthur Knapp led the group. An export group headed by two millers had less success. Indeed, during the 1920s rice farmers seemed sapped of vitality. Farming innovations declined as rotation practices lapsed and acreage stabilized. In October 1925, for example, F. B. Wise, head of the Rice Millers' Association, toured the Texas and Louisiana rice area and found nearly 70,000 acres abandoned because of poor conditions and heavy rain. In 1920 (a year when growers expanded, hoping to take advantage of the higher war prices) Louisiana harvested 676,000 acres, but by 1932 (in the midst of the Depression) acreage had dropped to 415,000. Texas acreage over the same years fell from 281,000 to 186,000. Prices hung at around $2.00 per hundred pounds, rising to $3.30 in 1924 but falling to $.93 by 1932.[40]

Arkansas growers also decreased acreage in the 1920s, harvesting 180,000 acres in 1920 but only 163,000 in 1932. Because of low prices Arkansas growers united to form the Arkansas Rice Growers' Cooperative Association. Meeting in Little Rock on September 23, 1921, growers elected B. E. Chaney president and Charles G. Miller vice-president and general manager. Taking advantage of the Capper-Volstead Act of 1922, which protected cooperative farmer organizations, securing $4 million from the War Finance Corporation in 1921 and 1922, and arranging credit through federal intermediate credit banks, Arkansas growers managed to survive through the trying agricultural depression of the 1920s. The cooperative expanded vertically, largely due to rumors that private millers siphoned off some of their rice. (An employee of a DeWitt mill alleged that a chute there diverted from 2 to 4 percent of the rice into the miller's secret bin.) At first the cooperative leased mills, but in 1926 it bought the properties of the Stuttgart Rice Milling Company, which included two mills in Stuttgart and one in DeWitt. It also leased a mill in Wheatley. By this time the cooperative marketed 50 percent of the Arkansas crop. In 1929 it reorganized, and H. K. Smith became president and general manager.[41] In the flue-cured tobacco area, meanwhile, the Tri-State Cooperative unsuccessfully attempted the same strategy.

Even as prairie rice growers fought agricultural depression with reduced acreage and cooperative movements, the culture spread further north. In the spring of 1923, after losing three successive wheat crops to flooding, A. V. Rowe, who owned a farm near Elsberry, Missouri, planted sixty-five acres to rice. Since Rowe's neighbors had the same problem with their wheat, they also turned to rice. By 1926 the culture had spread to Kampville, Winfield, King's Lake, Kissinger, and other towns in the area, with Missouri farmers planting 10,000 acres in rice. They irrigated with water from the Mississippi River, having quickly discovered that well water there proved too cold to stimulate growth. In 1926 growers fought autumn rains that flooded the fields during harvest. Using tractors and binders equipped with power takeoffs and mudguards, they harvested the rice in up to six inches of water. Despite having to shock the grain in mud, growers reported that they had little loss. The new crop gave a boost to the local economy, and one implement dealer in Elsberry reported selling sixty-eight tractors in 1926.[42]

Even as the mechanized rice culture of the prairies spread north to Missouri, the rice growers along the Mississippi River in Louisiana clung to their age-old methods. River rice had traditionally been one of the highest grades of long-grain rice grown in the country. To irrigate the fields, planters siphoned or pumped water from the Mississippi River. Flumes cut through levees had been outlawed because they weakened the levees and could cause crevasses. By 1903 a mill in Donaldsville saved river growers from complete reliance on New Orleans millers. Workers still cut the rice with a scythe, let it lie in the stubble for twenty-four hours, and then tied it into bundles by hand before shocking it. Due to the soft ground in the growing area, the modern machines that typified prairie rice culture could not be used in the fields.[43]

The abrupt price decline in mid-1920 ended the boom period of prairie rice. The plight of overmortgaged growers bore little resemblance to the dreams stirred by promotional literature at the turn of the century. Still, compared to cotton sharecroppers, rice tenants lived in luxury. The Grand Prairie of Arkansas—Lonoke, Arkansas, Monroe, and Prairie counties—was surrounded by cotton farmers who eked out a bare living in conditions that resembled those of antebellum days. Grand Prairie rice farmers owned machinery valued at $2,281 per farm, while cotton farms possessed equipment worth only $137. Though rice farms were larger than most cotton farms, the average value of implements and machinery per acre favored the rice farmers, $6.54 per acre to $2.54.[44]

The postwar slump caught many Arkansas farmers overextended. During the 1920s the number of rice farms decreased while the amount of irrigated acreage increased, suggesting that farmers had bought adjoining farms during the boom years, hoping that demand and prices would remain high. Land and equipment purchases in flush times led to a high mortgage rate as prices fell. By 1930, 41.1 percent of Grand Prairie rice farms were mortgaged. Even that high rate was misleading in one respect: in one sample of 119 debt-free farms, 47 had no debt only because of recent foreclosures. In fact, nearly 65 percent of the farms in the Grand Prairie were or had been mortgaged during the 1920s. In addition to mortgages on the land, farmers also owed for machinery and production credit. Growers persisted, though, and many paid off equipment loans that had been contracted during the war or early 1920s.[45]

In Arkansas County, nonresidents owned nearly 30 percent of the farms, and 70 percent of these were acquired by foreclosure. The passing of farms from owners to nonresidents, in most cases corporate owners, changed the tenure pattern of the prairie. By 1930 the census reported that 44 percent of the irrigated farms in the Grand Prairie were tilled by tenants. Still, tenants kept their machinery, which gave them a better bargaining position with owners. Most tenants paid a share of the crop to the owner. The landlord furnished the land and pump, paid taxes, and divided the cost of seed; the tenant provided implements and labor and divided the crop equally. Other contracts stipulated that the tenant pay hauling expenses, cost of sacking, and other costs; in such cases he paid only one-fourth of the crop to the landlord.[46]

By the 1920s the water table under the Arkansas prairie had fallen. This made it difficult for farmers there to obtain federal production credit, and the problem alarmed many growers. Many farm units turned to streams to provide irrigation, while others constructed small reservoirs to store water. By the early 1930s there were plans to construct large reservoirs and sell the water. Very few farmers sank deep wells, for by 1930 there were only nine in the Grand Prairie. The drought in 1930 and 1931 aggravated the problem, but normal rainfall, farmers surmised, would raise the water table to normal.[47]

The situation in the Grand Prairie as the Great Depression began showed how farmers had weathered the hard times in the 1920s. Overextended when prices fell in 1920, many managed to hang onto their property; others lost their land but kept their machinery and continued as tenants. The growers' cooperative helped market the crop, prevented farmers from glutting the market at harvest time, and stabilized prices. As in other commodity areas of the South, rice farmers lost their land, which became increasingly concentrated in the hands of corporate owners. Nevertheless, in 1931 *The Rice Journal* boasted that rice farmers "have suffered less than any of the other American farmers from the drouth and business depression." It claimed that the American Rice Growers' Association had made this possible by the orderly marketing of the crop. It even praised millers who had shown restraint in not buying "for speculative purposes." Cooperation among rice growers saved them from the large surpluses that drove cotton and tobacco prices below the cost of production. Still, after another year of depression and prices that fell below $1 per hundred pounds, even rice growers looked longingly to the federal government to add stability to their way of life.[48]

Book Two: Federal and Technological Intrusion into Traditional Cultures, 1933–41

For whosoever hath, to him shall be given, and he shall have more abundance: but whosoever hath not, from him shall be taken away even that he hath.

—*Matthew 13:12*

F. W. Latham, Reform, Alabama, receiving benefit check from George Fluker. Carrollton, Alabama. March 23, 1939. O. S. Welsh. (16-G-151-2 ab, National Archives)

4

The Origins of Southern Relief

The shirt was taken from a colored client for display purposes, not because it was so badly worn but because of the infinite care that had been taken to keep it patched.
—*C. W. E. Pittman, 1934*

The southern newspaperman and author Virginius Dabney recalled that, during the first few years of the New Deal, a prominent friend "counted the number of separate Federal agencies which were trying to help the farmer in one Southern county, and reported finding no fewer than twenty-seven!" Dabney's exclamation point was well placed, for prior to the New Deal the South had repudiated federal intrusion, whether from lingering outrage over Reconstruction or from apprehension that outside intervention might alter its peculiar ways. To a people who still tasted defeat, dimly recalled a myth of a yeoman's paradise, and believed in the apocalypse, southern tenants welcomed the New Deal as the millennium—Franklin D. Roosevelt, many believed, rode a white horse and would judge landlords and merchants. In this new day of reckoning, tenants would cross the Jordan River to the Promised Land.[1]

Falling commodity prices in the 1920s, flood, drought, and finally economic depression not only appeared as divine signs but also broke the stubborn southern pride that had rejected aid. Hardship laid open the South for a federal invasion, and wave after wave of agency troops attacked, won some battles, and generated hope for liberation. In this moiling confusion, good ideas—unlike cream—did not rise to the top but were homogenized to better serve the common denominator. The New Deal campaign proved ambiguous, full of false starts, lost opportunities, small accomplishments, and great fanfare. Instead of reviving the old system, as it promised, the New Deal in many areas destroyed that system's remnants more thoroughly than Sherman's troops had wrecked antebellum dreams.

New Deal programs arrived in the South to offer, among other things, employment, relief, housing, and agricultural stabililty. In most rural areas planters and merchants had supplied jobs, housing, credit, and supervision to millions of tenants. First natural disasters and Red Cross aid undermined this role; then federal relief agencies progressively took over this responsibility. The federal government supplanted landlords and merchants with relief and, at the same time, with acreage allotments and benefit payments assumed direction over agriculture that had once belonged to the planter class. Changes in such responsibilities altered the relationship between landlord and tenant and created a different attitude toward relief. After initial opposition and enduring ambivalence, landlords and merchants abdicated their paternalistic role.

Until the second quarter of the twentieth century, state and local governments in the rural South had provided meager organized relief. Although there were people who lived on the edge of survival, southern communities informally looked after their own. In the premodern southern society, even uneducated and unskilled people could find enough work to put food on the table. The work ethic permeated the South; for those who did not work, the community had pillorying terms—lazy, good for nothing, no account, trash. Even the most dismal tenant farmer took pride in working, and his wife likely took pride in her kitchen, children, and chores. The South measured its men primarily by brawn, although the ability to tell stories and church attendance (or the lack of it) also figured.

Such a traditional society placed strong contempt, sometimes pity, on those who leaned on charity or ended up in the poorhouse. The economic proximity of many sharecroppers to the poorhouse made the institution even more threatening. The South had its share of poor white trash and shiftless blacks, but even they usually worked enough to avoid charity. Southern communities, being wary of outsiders, still found ways to care for their own people, and the unfortunate often discovered that they could obtain food and clothes when all their efforts at making a living failed. There existed a fragile balance between pride and humiliation, between independence and peonage. Those who accepted the gospel of hard work received community support even if they failed, but the community scorned the idle.

The Good Book, after all, encouraged extending a helping hand to those who faltered, for it observed that the poor would always be present. William Faulkner gave an example of a biblical lesson in *The Town*. Old Het, a beggarwoman, relied on the Scriptures for justifying her calling: "There's some folks thinks all I does, I tromps this town all day long from can-see to cant, with a hand full of gimme and a mouth full of much oblige. They're wrong. I serves Jefferson too. If it's more blessed to give than to receive like the Book say, this town is blessed to a fare-you-well because its steady full of folks willing to give anything from a nickel up to a old hat. But I'm the onliest one I knows that steady receives. So how is Jefferson going to be steady blessed without me steady willing from dust-dawn to dust-dark, rain or snow or sun, to say much oblige?"[2]

While the more successful people might hold their noses and give alms, little has been written about the attitude of those who received. Old Het was a fictional character, but Harry Crews, a writer who grew up in rural Bacon County, Georgia, made observations that go against the prevailing wisdom on the subject. Sometimes, he noted, people received charity from organizations including the church; they welcomed it. "That may seem strange to those who have a singularly distorted understanding of the rural Southerner's attitude toward charity," he explained. "The people in the South I come from, those who knew what it meant to be forever on the edge of starvation, took whatever they could get and made whatever accommodations they had to make in their heads and hearts to do it." In the country there was no organized relief when he was growing up. Neighbors gave things like meat that might go bad if not eaten or goods they could not sell. "But nothing was made out of giving or receiving. It was never called charity or even a gift," Crews wrote. "It was just the natural order of things for people whose essential problem, first and last, was survival."[3]

If a man worked hard and still failed, the community understood and helped out. If a man was lazy, people had little use for him and consigned him to the poorhouse. Farmers were judged not just by their work but by how well they did it. "For reasons I never knew, perhaps it was nothing more complicated than pride of workmanship, farmers always associated crooked rows with sorry people," Crews observed about plowing.[4] Agriculture pitted man against nature, and anyone could lose. So farmers kept score on how well one played the game, not on winning and losing.

The agricultural system of the South, which stressed the one-crop cultivation of tobacco or cotton, relied on hand labor It took very little in the way of implements to farm. The landlord made provision for credit and furnished for sharecroppers the house, fertilizer, mules, plows, and other necessities. As Ned Cobb showed in *All God's Dangers*, one could supplement farming with odd jobs—in his case, hauling logs for a sawmill with his prize mules.[5] Other farmers worked at cotton gins in season, at sawmills, or at other tasks to supplement the wages that came at settling time from the main crop. Yet subsistence farmers ordered their lives very carefully, and as Crews noted, "The world that circumscribed the people I come from had so little margin for error, for bad luck, that when something went wrong, it almost always brought something else down with it. It was a world in which survival depended on raw courage, a courage born out of desperation and sustained by a lack of alternatives."[6]

Low agricultural prices during the 1920s and the more widespread depression in 1929 upset the balance of this fragile world. Odd jobs practically ended as businesses went broke. Many sawmills had closed already as the timber had been cut over, and the unemployed townsfolk joined hungry farmers. Communities that had before 1930 been able to cope with an occasional disaster and give alms to those who fell victim to the system lacked the resources to help out. Because the community had always found quiet ways to aid the indigent, the interpretation that people put on their hardship changed. Instead of seeing depression and drought as the causes of their misfortune, they blamed themselves for failing. As the Depression deepened and survival became ever more precarious, local, state, and federal governments searched for ways to relieve rural people.

Disaster Relief

Although Southerners had nearly always relied on local resources, two notable disasters had set precedents for relief—the Mississippi River flood of 1927 and the drought of 1930–31. In 1927 the Mississippi River and its tributaries roared across 170 counties, covering over 16 million acres and disrupting the lives of a million people. Because of the magnitude of this disaster, Secretary of Commerce Herbert Hoover led the rescue and relief effort. The Red Cross set up 154 camps that cared for over 325,000 people; another 300,000 people survived on

Red Cross rations, while hundreds of thousands of others searched out relatives on high ground.[7]

Both planters and farm laborers drew lessons from the flood experience. Planters feared that, if the Red Cross treated workers too well, they would become discontented with the parsimonious furnishing system. Still, the Red Cross insisted that people have adequate lodging as well as food, recreation, and health care. Many agricultural workers discovered that they were better cared for in the relief camps than on farms. Despite their uneasiness at being in a large tent colony with what amounted to urban problems at a time when they would usually be plowing the fields, they realized that the flood had a providential aspect. Planters and credit merchants were alarmed lest dissatisfaction with the sharecropping system lead to migration. In some cases planters kept close watch on their workers and insisted that the camps be patrolled by the National Guard to prevent blacks from leaving. They were horrified at the spectacle of blacks watching movies, playing games, receiving a balanced diet and medical care. Although camp life presented many new problems, movies, sports, and abundant food certainly opened the eyes of many croppers who had lived off fatback, cornbread, and molasses in the unhealthy and isolated backwaters of the river.[8] Planters grumbled about how the Red Cross had upset their laborers with idle dreams that were (according to planters) impossible to realize. Years later they would charge that the Red Cross and its relief efforts had started the plantation system on its decline.

Yet, in this case, the issue remained clear. A mammoth disaster clearly required Red Cross aid. That the organization did not cater to the whims of the planters in all cases proved that it had a certain immunity to local pressure. In other ways—by allowing discrimination, ignoring a venereal disease epidemic, and tolerating National Guardsmen's mistreatment of blacks—it yielded to local pressure. The effort also taught poor farmers that, when times were extremely hard, they could look not to the planters but to an outside agency for relief. It was the first faint sign of a weaning of sharecroppers from planter control.[9]

Discerning the difference between a disaster and a depression became a crucial problem in 1930, when a drought spread across the South. Whereas the 1927 flood had been sudden, devastating, and concentrated, the drought came slowly as hot winds dried out the soil and no rain fell. Although people ran out of food and a disaster certainly existed, the Red Cross held back relief—partly because it was not sure that massive relief was needed, but also because local planters did not want relief before cotton-picking season. While the Red Cross argued that local efforts should be able to meet the crisis and President Herbert Hoover insisted that local resources be exhausted before any national relief would be given, planters played down the seriousness of the drought. Because it was difficult without intense investigation to determine if people were starving, the press and community and state leaders insisted that those who needed food could earn it.[10]

Instituting relief hinged not on people's need but on whether it would disrupt labor during the cotton-picking season. Dr. William De-Kleine, a Red Cross officer, visited Arkansas and talked to planters and community leaders. He concluded that "the croppers would not work if they expected to be fed later by the Red Cross. Apparently the only way to get negroes to exert themselves as much as they should is to let them feel that they will not receive any help." Blacks did not accept the local incentive program quietly. A local white man wrote to the Red Cross, complaining that blacks had been holding meetings, "and I am sure they have written everybody from Hoover down. They are not in as good humor as I would like to see them. They do not like to pick cotton at 50¢." When blacks and poor whites refused to pick cotton, local Red Cross workers took the names of those who refused to work so they could be denied any Red Cross aid that did materialize.[11]

Obviously many people wanted to work for their food, for they understood the premium placed on labor. It was one thing to depend on the Red Cross when a flood overtly threatened life, but to watch crops die, credit vanish, and any opportunity for work disappear undermined farmers' confidence. Too many things were going wrong at once, as if God were rewriting the book of Job.[12] To ask for help, in the minds of the farmers, put them in the same class as trash or those consigned to the poor farm. "The small farmer does not want the government nor anyone else to GIVE him anything," wrote a man from Mississippi in August 1930. "All he wants is some assistance until he can have a chance to COME BACK."[13]

Community charity dispersed occasionally did not threaten the economic structure, but comprehensive Red Cross aid posed a challenge to planter control. In late September, as picking season neared, the Red Cross chairman in Pulaski County, Arkansas, wrote to Red Cross headquarters and warned that a feeding program "at this time is, I think, not to be considered; would be extremely harmful to the participants, and disturb economic conditions. Such a program is a constant fear in the minds of many of our people. Of that we speak advisedly." Ultimately such advice prevailed, and no relief came from the Red Cross before picking time. Hungry farmers picked cotton in most cases for $.50 per hundred pounds and spent their paltry earnings on food. During the picking season planters insisted that the old system worked well enough and that workers should exert themselves and earn their rations. When the cotton had been picked, however, planters encouraged relief efforts, for these also relieved them of having to furnish food for tenants.[14]

President Herbert Hoover, of course, firmly believed that the federal government had no role in providing relief. His ideology in many ways paralleled that of Southerners, who did not want to rely on relief. Concerned over the drought victims, Congress began an extended debate over relief in December 1930. The crucial bills would allow the secretary of agriculture the discretion of loaning money to people, although such loans would probably not be collectable. Secretary of Agriculture Arthur Hyde observed that from "a national point of view this latter class of loans approached perilously near the dole system and would be a move in the wrong direction." In early December the Senate passed such a bill, and Hoover severely criticized it. The debate pitted ideology against starvation.[15]

A crucial question had been raised: Should the federal government give funds directly to people? While some congressmen feared that government relief would set a terrible precedent, others demanded that needy people receive help. Congress at last acted in mid-February 1931 with a $20 million farm production and rehabilitation bill which would strengthen the credit structure of the South but avoid the controversial question of food. Farmers could secure food loans only if they had collateral. If landlords would waive the liens customarily taken on tenants' crops, poor farmers could obtain federal loans. This, of course, threatened the traditional credit arrangements of the South. Due to the inflexible requirements, in Arkansas only 22 of 5,500 farmers who applied secured loans. The remainder, who had to pay a processing fee that ranged from fifty cents to several dollars, experienced their first frustrations in dealing with government programs.[16]

To people who read their Bibles, the hard times suggested some divine retribution. They could not figure out what awful sins had been committed for them to be called upon to suffer so much. The drought caught Southerners at a time when neither planters, local leaders, nor state or federal governments were willing to take responsibility for unprecedented problems caused by depression and drought. Such a combination of economic and climatic disasters had never before coincided, and the remedy was beyond the means of local efforts, a strain on state governments, and ideologically repugnant to the Republican-dominated federal government.

It was as if the old culture had run down like a clock, and farmers who had never needed government aid furtively looked to Washington to repair it and wind it up. When the federal government set up work and relief programs that substituted for sharecropping or community alms, most recipients were elated. Such aid did not, at least at first, have the debilitating effect of the English Poor Laws a century before. Government jobs in many cases paid more than rural people had ever earned. When it began, federal intrusion challenged landlords by undermining the furnish system, but they quickly learned to manipulate programs. Combined with payments for cooperating with acreage reduction programs, the work and relief programs stabilized landlords with higher commodity prices and payments and allowed them to dump onto the government the paternalistic remnants of the tenure system. So long as federal relief policy did not disperse the seasonal work force or drive wages too high, planters accepted it.

Federal Relief

The New Deal championed the idea that the federal government had a responsibility to rebuild the broken economy. Franklin D. Roosevelt instinctively knew that depression had sapped the nation's morale and that most people desired action of any kind— not the tired excuses and self-help preaching of the Hoover administration. Only two months after taking office, Roosevelt created the Federal Emergency Relief Administration (FERA) and appointed Harry L. Hopkins to spend the $500 million authorized. Unlike the Reconstruction Finance Corporation under the Hoover administration, states received federal grants instead of loans. In June 1933 the Public Works Administration (PWA) began awarding grants to state and local governments for projects that would improve communities. At about the same time, the Civilian

Conservation Corps (CCC) inducted young men and sent them off to do conservation work. As winter approached, the Civil Works Administration (CWA) furnished jobs to many people, giving them support during the cold months. The Agricultural Adjustment Administration (AAA) meanwhile set up commodity programs that reduced acreage and raised prices toward the parity goal.[17]

Concerned that relief would "pauperize" recipients, the FERA conducted a sweeping survey of sample counties in six rural problem areas of the country—the Appalachian-Ozark, the Lake States cutover, the short grass wheat (spring wheat and winter wheat areas), the eastern Cotton Belt, and the western Cotton Belt.[18] The examination of four problem counties in the eastern Cotton Belt reveals elements of southern diversity and uniformity. In each county the federal government had become, in the space of a year, a major force of innovation. Accustomed to discussing crops, religion, and the weather, rural people quickly mastered a host of acronyms—CCC, AAA, WPA, TVA, FERA. Every county suffered high unemployment; most had bank failures; poor schools, meager libraries, collapsing housing, and inadequate health care were universal. The success or failure of federal programs ultimately rested with local administrators, and many were ambivalent about the role of the federal government. It was in local federal offices that the principles of local government came into conflict with federal programs.

The FERA reports on these four Cotton Belt counties provide a window upon the ravages of depression in the rural South. Franklin County, located in northeastern North Carolina, grew both tobacco and cotton, and its FERA administrators boldly challenged unemployment. Meriwether County, Georgia, contained a unique sharecropping arrangement that New Deal agricultural policies destroyed. Dallas County, in southern Alabama, lay in the heart of the Black Belt, where the boll weevil had taken a heavy toll. Leflore County, Mississippi, in the rich Delta area, had undergone several population shifts in the early twentieth century and was adjusting again to the forces of agricultural depression. Significantly, no rice county appeared as a problem area. The impact of federal relief and work programs had a significant impact on the old culture and, combined with federal agricultural programs, set in motion changes that would revolutionize the old traditions of rural life.

Franklin County, North Carolina

Franklin County lay in the heart of the flue-cured tobacco area in north-central North Carolina. Farmers had grown tobacco there since Reconstruction days; as the demand for leaf increased, production rose from 58,932 pounds in 1879 to 8.8 million in 1934. The FERA report primarily documented the problems of the relief population, but many of these families had only a few years earlier been involved in the tobacco culture.[19]

Founded in 1779, the county had a population of 29,456 in 1930 and remained primarily rural. Fifty-six percent of its 29,456 inhabitants were white. In 1934 there were five incorporated and twenty-four unincorporated towns. Louisburg, the largest and the county seat, had a population of 2,182, Franklinton 1,320, and Youngsville 395. A railroad ran through the three towns, and all boasted tobacco warehouses, cotton gins, and general stores. Bunn, on the other hand, had "burned up" but still had 243 residents, and Wood was "dead," due in part to the playing out of old gold mines in the area. Of the five incorporated towns, the report listed two at a standstill, one declining, one burned up, and another dead. Most of the twenty-four crossroads settlements also experienced hard times. Edward Best, for example, had "lost out in depression," and it was filled with "drunkards" and "bad business." Pearce, on the other hand, was "thriving" due to "bootlegging" and the fact that it was a "good tobacco section." Seven Paths and Alert were "dead," Centerville was "thriving," and Mapleville "declining" as "farmers lost out in depression."[20]

Of the 4,205 farms in the county in 1934, 2,980 grew tobacco and all but 250 of them were operated by tenants. Despite the ravages of the boll weevil, 3,469 of these farmers grew cotton. Indeed, farmers planted 38,957 acres of cotton in 1929, compared to 16,393 acres of tobacco; but tobacco returned $2.3 million, and cotton $1.8 million. Farming provided work for 79 percent of the whites and 74 percent of the blacks.[21] As had been the trend since Reconstruction, an increasing number of farmers did not own land. Sharecroppers in the black farm population increased from 38.3 percent in 1900 to 57.8 percent by 1930, while white sharecroppers during the same years remained steady at 27.7 percent. Two-thirds of the farmers had no stake in ownership—a factor that became increasingly important as New Deal agricultural policies began.[22] Of the 14,171 people employed in the county, 10,487 worked in agriculture, 686 at sawmills and planing mills, and 310 in cotton mills; others toiled at gins, the building trade, railroads, automobile repair shops, and other jobs.[23]

Like most southern counties, Franklin provided sparse aid to its residents and reflected the prevailing racial discrimination of the section. It had primitive health care for the poor—one health officer, one nurse, and one clerk. There were twenty-one licensed midwives, all but one black. They charged $5.00 per case and, the report noted, were "fairly efficient." For sixteen years prior to the New Deal there had been a meager appropriation for indigent relief starting at about $100 a year and by 1934–35 budgeted at $3,500. A county home provided shelter and food for thirty people, and various fraternal orders gave sporadic aid. Black lodges, with the exception of the American Legion, had "become defunct when the banks closed."

Eleven elementary and six high schools served whites, and there were thirty-eight elementary schools and one high school for blacks. The white schools were consolidated, and the children rode in "trucks." The county spent $23.53 for the education of each white pupil and $8.12 for each black, and 5.2 percent of the whites and 18.6 percent of the black population was illiterate.[24] Ashamed of their ragged clothes, poor children often stayed out of school unless the PTA or Red Cross found them castoff shoes and clothing. The school term ran for eight months, but often parents held children out of school during planting and harvest seasons. Lacking a public library, residents relied upon the 2,139 books in white schools and the 579 in black schools for reading material. Underlining the illiteracy and isolation, only 5.53 percent of the inhabitants subscribed to a daily newspaper.[25]

In 1934 only one bank remained open in Franklin County. Two banks collapsed in 1930, one in 1932, and another in 1933, and although one had paid its depositors 85 percent on their deposits, another had managed to pay only 10 percent. During the 1920s farmowners reporting mortgage debt increased from 11 to 33 percent, and the bank failures "left no means by which landlords could secure financial aid to make a crop or supply their tenants." While idle sawmills and textile factories contributed, the report concluded that the "basic factor producing the relief situation is the depression in agriculture, the landlord-tenant system having proved inadequate to the task of carrying the labor supply over the present period of restricted production."[26]

Despite the economic blight, only 349 of the county's 5,831 families were on relief at the time of the report. Although most relief clients blamed scarce jobs and insufficient income for their predicament, the Agricultural Adjustment Administration acreage reduction program displaced 9 percent of the blacks and 8 percent of the whites. Cutbacks and closings at lumber mills, planing mills, and textile factories accounted for other relief cases, and many people were simply unable to find work.[27]

Franklin County experienced a situation that Lorena Hickok, investigating conditions throughout the country for WPA director Harry Hopkins, noted in her 1934 reports from the South. Writing from Birmingham, Alabama, in April 1934, Hickok noted that unemployed middle-class workers sought relief jobs. What they feared most, she explained, was losing their homes: "I honestly believe that, if we force them to give that up, we shall in many, many instances, either break their morale completely or make Communist leaders out of them."[28]

In Franklin County, the FERA reported with some alarm, "The so called upper class is being pauperized." This class insisted on relief though they "really could get along without it." When relief workers denied requests, they "attempt to bring various sorts of pressure to bear on the officials." These upper-class paupers increasingly argued that the government owed them a living, but relief workers reminded them that they would be taking food from starving people. By contrast, the poorer people eagerly tried to get off the relief rolls. "They are thankful for the help they get but are continually trying to get outside jobs so that they get off 'relief' instead of trying to get on as is the case with a considerable number of the white collar class. The abuse of relief comes not from the lower but from the upper classes."[29]

In 1934 the FERA relief and rehabilitation program in Franklin County increased when the Civil Works Administration phased out in March after spending $52,000 and employing 253 men; 807 families faced unemployment.[30] Because so few jobs existed outside agriculture even in good times, FERA administrator C. W. E. Pittman searched for farms. Four hundred relief families secured tenant positions, and one hundred village people sought work relief and odd jobs. Another hundred clients were unemployable and went on direct relief. The other two hundred families could work, but depression shut them out of the traditional farming culture. There was plenty of land available but not enough work stock or tobacco and cotton allotments. The state Emergency Relief Administration furnished the county seventeen mules; more than any other single factor, this raised the hopes of people on relief.

The FERA staff called a meeting with an advisory group composed of the county farm agent, agriculture teachers, federal and private lending representatives, and the farm managers from two life insurance companies; each of these brought a landowner to the meeting. All sympathized with the program and offered suggestions. A sharecropping arrangement seemed familiar and promising, so the agency tried to place the two hundred families "on such terms as would permit them to produce more corn, vegetables, peas and sorghum than they could consume" and barter the surplus "for items they could not produce, namely, meat, flour, and clothing."

The relief families got nowhere with the suspicious landlords, for although the government promised support, landowners feared they would end up furnishing the relief clients. So caseworkers and clients together visited landlords, and, despite the scarcity of work stock, placed all the families. It became impossible, however, to furnish both fertilizer and supervision, so many clients worked independently. The tenure arrangements varied: 15 clients farmed their own land, 19 paid no rent, 2 cleared land for its use, 2 others worked for the landlord, and 169 sharecropped for one-fourth of the corn and sorghum. Thirty-six families shared government mules, 18 used their own, 98 gave one-fourth of the corn and sorghum for teams, 53 exchanged a day's work for the landlord for a day with the mule, and 2 used teams rented by the FERA. "The fact that six oxen are being used successfully by clients is of interest," the report observed. "That one of these oxen was broken by two of our women this year and is producing a good crop for them is even more interesting." The clients had 1,782 acres under cultivation, primarily in corn, vegetables, potatoes, sorghum, field peas, and forage. There were 16 acres in tobacco and 31 in cotton, farmed on allotments that belonged to landowning clients.

These arrangements produced an average return of $133.23, which, the report argued, "seems a small return for the efforts of six months until it is considered relatively." Had these clients not worked, they would have had no income, but with this stake and the food they raised, many could barter for other supplies and survive without government aid. "Most people are deeply ingrained with the instinct to exalt work," the report stressed. By requiring work the program had stifled criticism that originated when the federal government began relief work. The report concluded optimistically that the success "prepares the way for future progress of these people."

The FERA boasted that the program salvaged the pride of poor people. Although they were inadequately housed, fed, and doctored, the government program had given them hope. From the material standpoint the relief work had been successful, but "from a spiritual standpoint it has yielded a rich harvest in increased hope, self reliance and confidence." A symbol of this attitude hung in Pittman's office, for he had obtained a client's patched shirt. "The shirt was taken from a colored client for display purposes," the report noted, "not because it was so badly worn but because of the infinite care that had been taken to keep it patched." In many ways the shirt exemplified the dynamic change in the area. Tenants had kept the old plantation system patched up for years, taking their advances from the landlords and using local credit and the furnish system to survive. The New Deal was replacing that patched-up system by taking over the task of the furnishing agent. The government was making a patched-shirt rural existence impossible; increasingly the federal programs favored efficient people who did not sew patches but purchased machines and could understand and utilize government programs.[31]

The patched shirt probably belonged to a client named Pete Bobbitt, who had been living in a three-room house with his family of eight and his brother's family of eleven. Bobbitt worked at odd jobs to earn food. When the FERA rehabilitation program started, he found an empty house that the landlord rented for one-fourth of the corn crop. He shared a mule with another client, but because funds ran out, the FERA could not give him food or clothes. "Buying clothes was simply out of the question," the FERA admitted. "Pete was wearing his one shirt, a very clean, blue shirt with the back and half the sleeves made of many different kinds of shirting neatly pieced together by hand. Half naked and half starved, he cheerfully worked his crop." He also took great pride in making $133.44 off corn, sweet potatoes, cane, peas, fodder, and shucks, and the family had thirty-seven quarts of vegetables that had been put up at the cannery. Bobbitt, like other farmers who had been dispossessed by the Depression, discovered that he could survive off subsistence farming. While tobacco and cotton produced more cash, hard work and good management achieved a living, and in the mid-1930s that seemed providential.[32]

The Franklin County program revealed how little experienced farmers needed to succeed in the country. Without growing cotton or tobacco, most of these families came out ahead primarily because the rehabilitation program gave them hope, and it supervised them as much as funds permitted. The government in these cases simply replaced the traditional furnishing system with impartial and honest government oversight. That these unlikely candidates succeeded raises questions about the structure of the old sharecropping system and the exploitation that characterized it, for, even growing cash crops, few tenants broke even at settlement time. Of all the workers in problem counties, Franklin FERA workers approached relief with the most imaginative and successful program. C. W. E. Pittman preserved the work ethic and demonstrated the agency's interest in individual families. His staff had, in effect, become overseers of the two hundred families and, despite a tight budget, led them out of debt. It took little to survive in depressed Franklin County, but to break out of the bonds of dependence it did take opportunity. That the FERA could produce such results raises serious questions about the effectiveness of the Extension Service and, later, of the Resettlement Administration and Farm Security Administration, among other agencies.

Meriwether County, Georgia

The South contained tremendous diversity, yet common problems encompassed the old cotton-growing areas. Of the fourteen problem counties studied, Meriwether County, Georgia, contained elements that showed how similar and how diverse the cotton culture could be. Southwest of Atlanta and only a county away from the Alabama border, Meriwether County in 1930 had a population of 22,437, a little over half of which was black. In August 1934 there were 2,385 people on relief, 10.6 percent of the population. The county had lost nearly 4,000 residents since 1920, primarily due to the black exodus. It was overwhelmingly rural until the twentieth century, when several towns emerged. In 1930 Manchester, the largest, boasted a population of 3,716.[33]

Warm Springs, the most famous part of the county, had developed into a rehabilitation center for polio victims. Franklin D. Roosevelt often visited, attracted by the soothing water that he hoped would restore his legs to full strength. He ultimately invested a large part of his personal fortune in the center and set up the Warm Springs Foundation. He enjoyed meeting people in the community and often drove his specially equipped automobile throughout the countryside, stopping to drink moonshine, watch coon hunts, and discuss everyday problems. He owned a farm in the county and raised livestock and grew some crops. He often described himself as a farmer, both because of the Georgia farm and because of his upbringing in bucolic Hyde Park. If there was one part of rural America that Roosevelt knew, it was Meriwether County, Georgia. Whether he ever measured his New Deal policies by that county remains problematical, but if he did observe the forces flowing from government programs, they must have given him pause.[34]

The old tenure arrangments that stressed raising a cash crop faltered during the Depression. "The principal factors producing this situation," the FERA report noted, "are drought, low cotton prices, and decreased cotton yields which, when combined with the consequences of poor and short-sighted farming methods have resulted in many Meriwether farm families—especially farm tenant families—being caught without even the barest necessities of living." Like many southern counties, Meriwether had little relief experience. Churches gave some relief "on the appropriate Christian holidays," and the Red Cross chapter collected about $200 a year which went for emergency medical cases. When the FERA began in April 1933, it took over nearly all relief duties. The county continued to support people not eligible for FERA relief and to pay utilities and rent for the FERA offices.

The relief recipients came primarily from the rural areas, and most were sharecroppers. As the report observed, "the Negroes are strikingly underrepresented on the relief rolls, for while they constitute 52 percent of the total population, they account for but 28 percent of the relief population."[35] Blacks applied for relief but did not receive it as often as whites. In June 1934, for example, there were 84 applications from blacks and 49 from whites. The FERA accepted 24 applications, all white. The report concluded that "while Negroes are applying for relief in much larger numbers, the whites are being accepted in a ratio all out of proportion to the applications." Whites also received higher rates: "The average total relief for whites was $19.51 and for Negroes, $15.17. The average work relief was $29.86 and $19.23, respectively." The differential between whites and blacks appeared throughout the South, and the general statement ran that blacks could survive on less.[36]

Agriculture suffered, the report concluded, because of "land exhaustion brought about by careless farming methods the chief of which are lack of rotation of crops and failure to provide adequate fertilizer." It was as if some pride and competence had leaked out of the farmers. "It is partly tradition, perhaps, like the planting of cotton, but it is also partly a dull, unplanning, dilatory sort of lethargy somewhat akin to the unkept, exhausted, barren aspects of the country itself." While a few exceptional farmers built up their land and rotated crops, most grew primarily cotton, moved often, and ruined the land. "Part of Meriwether's agricultural problems can indeed be traced to the landlord-tenant system,—but the blame cannot be placed on the tenant entirely; the landlord is party to the condition even more than the tenant," the report charged. "It is his business to provide some cover crop for his fallow land. He has evaded that responsibility."[37]

Farm tenants comprised 75 percent of the 2,430 farm operators. Of these, 7.7 percent were cash tenants, 45.5 croppers, and 21.8 percent "other tenants."[38] The census categories did not reveal a unique rental plan that characterized the county. Hidden among "other tenants" and even sharecroppers and renters, a substantial number of farmers paid a bale of cotton per plow in rent. Censustakers did not record this class separately, but FERA officials estimated that from one-third to two-thirds of all farm tenants were bale-per-plow renters.

Before the boll weevil arrived, most farmers paid one and a half bales per plow rent, but with reduced output landlords settled for one bale. "From the landlord's point of view, the bale of cotton is easier to collect from tenants than cash; and from the viewpoint of the tenant, this arrangement gives him a higher legal status in landlord-tenant relations than does share-cropping." While a sharecropper gave a lien on his crop and worked under careful scrutiny from the landlord, a bale-per-plow tenant could sign his own cotton reduction contract and manage the farm as he pleased. The system encouraged initiative, for, except the one bale for rent, the cotton stayed with the renter. "These bale-per-plow renters furnish their own seed, fertilizer, mule, and perhaps implements as well," the report observed. Obviously these renters had more capital than did sharecroppers who only furnished their labor. Landlords to some extent shared in the risks of farming, for the price they received for rent depended on world market prices. In another way the plan simplified the landlord's work, for settlement with even the illiterate farmer proved easy.

Bale-per-plow renters cultivated about ten acres per plow and produced four to five bales of cotton. One bale paid for fertilizer, one went to the landlord, and the two or three remaining plus the seed went to the renter. While the 40 percent acreage reduction affected most tenants in the cotton South, it devastated the bale-per-plow arrangement in Meriwether County. Under the AAA, one plow only turned five or six acres, producing about two and a half bales of cotton. After paying the landlord and settling for fertilizer, the renter would only have a half-bale left for his profit. He would have been better off without a New Deal.

The FERA report thoroughly explored the economics of acreage reduction on the bale-per-plow farmers. When cotton sold for 8 cents a pound, a farmer stood to make $80 to $120 on his two or three bales, and he also received about $75 seed money from five bales. Thus a renter would earn from $155 to $195 a year under the old plan. With one-half bale that sold for 12 cents, he earned $30 for the lint and $45 from the seed from two and a half bales. His yearly earnings came to $75. Of course, he received $4 to $5 per acre for renting the other land to the government, but his yearly earnings did not reach $100. Even if the price of cotton had fallen to 6 cents a pound, the renter would have earned from $135 to $165 under the old plan. Although his rent had not increased in absolute terms—he still paid only a bale of cotton— the renter paid 40 percent of his earnings for rent, while in the past it had been only 25 percent.

Of course, the report continued, landlords had their side of the question, and they were unlikely to reduce the rent to less than one bale. County landlords believed "that now they are getting their 'break'; they feel that they deserve it, and they will not be enthusiastic toward any suggestion that they give up any part of their present rental." The report concluded that the entire burden of the acreage reduction had fallen on the renter class.[39]

Because tenant farmers moved often, they saw little reason to plant cover crops that would benefit the next tenant. Instead they poured fertilizer onto the land. The average farmer spent $80 for fertilizer in 1909, $222 in 1919, $141 in 1924, and an estimated $150 in 1929. Cover crops that enriched the soil would have reduced the fertilizer bill, but many landlords did not care about cover crops so long as they received their annual bale of cotton. FERA officials suggested that landlords either lower their rent or share the cost of fertilizer and other farm expenses. Tenants should plant gardens and raise hogs and cattle; otherwise many of the bale-per-plow farmers would end up on relief, using government jobs to supplement their incomes.[40]

Most families lacked "modern conveniences." Of 2,430 farm operators in the county in 1930, almost a third owned an automobile and 4.3 percent had trucks, but only 2.6 percent had tractors. Only 4.16 percent had telephones, and 3.5 percent had electricity in their homes. Nor had running water and indoor toilets made many inroads: only 3.1 percent of the farm homes had water piped into the house; 2.3 percent had water piped into a bathroom.[41]

Some 80 percent of the farms were mortgaged, and the economic distress had been heightened by the failure of four banks, two in Warm Springs, one in Manchester, and one in Greenville. Few jobs existed outside the agricultural sector. The county's 218 retail stores employed 250 people, suggesting that most were probably crossroads stores owned and managed by one person. A pepper plant employed 400 seasonal workers, and cotton gins also gave seasonal employment. The AAA had infused $151,000 into the county in acreage reduction payments, the Civil Works Administration had spent $81,000, and 10 men had worked on a Public Works Administration project. The Civilian Conservation Corps had taken 85 white boys and 6 blacks, which represented the usual racial differential throughout the South.[42]

If the county was to recover, it would be not because of industrialization but because of adjustments in the agricultural sector. Most people were unskilled and had only rudimentary educations. Whites had benefited more from education than had blacks, for only 1.7 percent of the whites were illiterate, compared to 15.1 percent of the blacks.[43] One community, "The Cove," never had schools that went above the seventh grade. "Women and children have spent all their lives in 'The Cove,' never having been for a single day outside of its confines." Blacks had not lived there until 1933, when one family moved in. The area was a bootlegging center until federal raids dried it up.[44]

Lacking the imagination of Franklin County administrators, the FERA staff did not know how to revive the old system or rehabilitate those who had fallen by the wayside. It stressed that any rehabilitation would come from "the rebuilding of the fundamental land resources." The land had not been eroded; it had simply fallen into poor cultivation, and the recovery would come when "the existing land resources can be brought back to the peak of their productive capacity." Yet the report offered no structural suggestions for meeting rural problems. In addition to restoring the soil to better productivity by "an intensive campaign to introduce leguminous crops," it suggested home gardens and canning projects—something that the Extension Service had been advocating for two decades.[45]

Diversification had not taken hold in Meriwether County. The investigators found "an astonishing deficiency of dairy cows, hogs, poultry," and other items that would lead to self-sufficiency. The proof that livestock played a small part in the county could be seen in the fact that "little of the county is fenced." Since the state still had open ranges, farmers fenced in their crops to keep livestock out. Despite their self-sufficiency in earlier days, people were either buying pork or receiving it in surplus commodities.[46]

The county's depressed economy showed little hope of revitalization even with government aid. While the CWA, PWA, and federal credit schemes attempted to prop up the old system, the AAA set in motion contradictory restrictions that would doom it. The poverty in goods, collapsing housing, illiteracy, and other problems raised the question of how the people had survived in the cotton culture as long as they had. While the statistics and observations of the relief staff furnished insight into the problems, the case studies, accompanied by photographs, reiterated the conditions and revealed assumptions of the relief staff.

Dallas County, Alabama

Dallas County, located in the Black Belt of Alabama and drained by the Alabama River, had a black population of nearly 75 percent. Selma, the county seat, contained 18,012 people in 1930, about a third of the county population. Selma also had the bulk of relief cases, which were expected to grow from 1,341 families in June to over 1,500 by August. "The major factors contributing to the relief load," the report concluded, "are the decline in the value of the cotton crop, the dislocation of manufacturing industries processing cotton, and the interrelationships of these factors." Although agriculture supported the county's economy, 84 percent of the relief families lived in Selma.[47]

The FERA staff gave a succinct account of the county's history by first observing that it developed in the slave and cotton South and that farmers shipped cotton down the Alabama River. After the Civil War planters used tenants to till the land, "and in 1930, 87.8 per cent of the farms were operated by tenants, nearly all of whom were colored." The boll weevil hit especially hard, for the soil did not warm up quickly in spring, delaying planting and intensifying weevil damage. Diversification made some impact after the weevil arrived, but the low price of cotton and debts contracted during the war boom period "seriously injured the cotton farmer and with him the whole county, and the cotton states for that matter." Sharing the natural calamities with other southern states, Dallas County suffered from the drought in 1930, floods in 1919 and 1928, and a windstorm in 1932. The Red Cross had given relief during these emergencies, although the county had its own relief association. There had been only one bank failure, but it affected a quarter of the county. The disaster toll mounted —the boll weevil, postwar depression, floods, drought, and finally economic depression.

The report gave a vivid insight into the operations of the sharecropping system and how it reacted to relief from the federal government. Of the relief sample, 65 percent were black, although the county's rural population was about 80 percent black. This, the report stressed, did not happen because blacks were better off; rather, there was a widespread belief that blacks did not need relief. "Speaking of this matter a member of the county board of revenues stated that the county would be 'better off' if no Federal relief had come in." This man had numerous tenants and shared the prevailing view that "relief to the Negro farmer demoralizes him and makes him less valuable as a farm worker. The general philosophy back of this is that all the Negro should have is bare subsistence." This same landlord stated that no black had ever starved to death; he alleged that giving blacks "articles of diet to which they were unaccustomed" made them aware of "new wants" and was "decidedly unwise." He thought it "preposterous" that blacks should have a choice of "eight different kinds of food to eat." Given that set of ideas, the report noted, "it is not to be wondered that relief to them is held to a minimum." Planters feared that blacks would indeed become aware of a better life. Like victims of the 1927 Mississippi River flood, sharecroppers, according to the report, "have gotten their first view of some of the so-called better things of life from their contact with the relief agency. This is precisely what the landowner quoted above calls 'demoralizing.'" The prevailing racism could be seen in the relief differential: blacks received $5.07 per household and whites $15.50. The report explained that such ratios were established in part by investigating the former level of living. "The difference in amount of allowance seems to be not so much a matter of overt discrimination as a feeling in general that the Negro does not 'need' so much as the white. This is a direct outgrowth of the widely accepted belief in racial superiority," it added. The county did have one black FERA worker who was "well respected and efficient," yet she "naturally has little voice in the policies of the office."[48]

Relief in Dallas County had been riddled with politics. The rector of the Selma Episcopal Church complained that some aid went to fictitious people and that racial discrimination was widespread. He pointed out that whites were often given work near their homes, while blacks were transported daily in "CWA trucks owned by politicians." Workers paid for transportation, "and in some cases the weekly transportation charges amounted to as much as the weekly wage earned." Faced with this impossible situation, some blacks refused to work. (A local administrator argued that "those niggers will go to work again in a few days when they get hungry.") The report stated that the blacks were not asking for higher wages exactly but struck "to get what they think they should have in comparison with white workers."

Certainly Dallas County blacks had pride that conflicted with the relief program. One case supervisor noted that a half-dozen blacks "voluntarily came to her in the last several weeks stating that they could get along without relief now and did not wish to receive it longer." Another group of blacks refused to pick up their relief checks "because they did not feel that they deserved them since it had rained a great deal and they were unable to work." Addressing the primary question, the effect of relief upon rural people, the FERA report concluded that "the recipients of relief are not being pauperized thereby to any great extent. It appears that in many respects, governmental relief is less pauperizing than the cotton furnishing system of farming to which most of these people are accustomed."[49] Relief in Dallas County almost bypassed the sharecropping class, for planters did not want to disturb their labor supply. Rehabilitation plans called for the usual diversification and subsistence farming, but landlords opposed that also. "This baron class is too much interested in keeping an available labor supply on hand," the report concluded, to offer rent waivers to those who might be rehabilitated.[50]

Leflore County, Mississippi

Leflore County, located in the Mississippi Delta on the Yazoo River, had a population of 55,506, 76 percent black. In January 1934, 9,066 people were receiving relief; in June 3,524 were. The staff expected that in the winter months the load would increase again by 1,500 families. The county had extensive experience with relief. In 1900 the Kings Daughters had been organized; the group dispersed relief until it disbanded in 1930. The 1927 Mississippi River flood pushed high water in the county, and in 1932 another flood displaced 27,808 people, nearly half of the population. The Red Cross responded to both calamities. In 1930 the drought affected over a thousand families.[51]

The planter class saw in the federal programs an opportunity to consolidate its power. Until World War I most sharecroppers had been black, but many migrated thereafter. Although whites from the hills moved into the county to replace the fleeing blacks, landlords never liked to deal with whites. As blacks filtered back to the county, planters attempted to get rid of the whites. "The white croppers and tenants were too shrewd traders and bargainers to suit the planters and they always had arguments over their 'trades' and accounts." When the AAA reached the county, landlords released white sharecroppers and retained blacks. The report quoted one landlord as saying, "I won't have any G—damned white cropper on my place. Get off and stay off. All I want to work are niggers who will do what I tell them to." Another observer noted that "the use of firearms by the white tenants in dealing with their landlords is by no means uncommon." Landlords also received $390,504 in AAA benefits in 1933 and expected over $437,000 in 1934.[52]

Many of the relief cases came from the ranks of the white dispossessed and aging blacks. Planters furnished black households but would not give rations to those who could not work. Planters had formerly allowed old blacks to remain on the plantations and had furnished a cabin, a garden, and some food. Most blacks in the county sample were such old folks, for the report showed that over half of the blacks in the relief sample were over sixty years old. The report linked such dependence to slavery days, when a landlord "made ample provisions for his slaves the year around as a healthy slave was an asset much the same as a good mule." The sharecropping system had picked up many of the obligations of the slave system, but it was breaking down. Increasingly, "the farm laborer, cropper and tenant are now thrown on the relief agencies for support between cropping seasons."[53]

When the cotton economy failed, satellite businesses suffered also. Of the 65 businesses in the county, 50 were linked to cotton—"cottonseed oil mills, cotton compresses, cotton gins." There were a few lumber mills, bakeries, ice plants, and dairies, and two railroads crossed the county. The CWA employed 4,714 men and disbursed $147,145; the PWA employed people from 100 families. All 54 CCC boys were white. Of the eight banks operating in the county in 1930, only two remained open in 1934. Rehabilitation plans centered on getting unemployed people back on the land. The staff observed that in many ways its role resembled the old furnishing system; they put out money for crops and hoped they would recover it.[54]

One FERA worker who tried to return people to the land wrote to Governor M. S. Connor in August 1933. The FERA report withheld his name, fearing that the entire FERA staff would be dismissed in retaliation. Obviously the writer knew Leflore County well. He observed that there were two classes of landlords: those who did well by their tenants, and those who would furnish them until the crop was laid by and then dismiss them. Although this had not developed into a "general practice," the letter noted that many tenants made nothing, and planters would not allow them to see their accounts. These dispossessed people fled the land and attempted to get through the winter, but they usually did not have enough confidence to obtain furnish for the next season. Hundreds of families in the Delta lacked "sheets, pillow cases, towels, etc." Quilts had been used until they were "in shreds." Nor did the people have underwear, "and many times they have only one piece, the outer garment." When the FERA tried to help, planters objected that relief was "ruining these people."

When the correspondent tried to tempt planters to hire whites, one refused "because they were white people." When he asked planters what they intended to do about such whites, "invariably the answer is 'Starve them out. They are not worth feeding. We do not want them in our county.'" The FERA board felt selfish pressure from planters to end relief. Their intent "is to gather this crop with pickers who are acceptable and to force, through a process of starvation, those who will not be acceptable out of the locality or out of existence." When the cotton-picking season ended, he argued, the same planters would appear at the FERA office, seeking relief for their hands to get through the winter. The relief staff experienced tremendous pressure from such landlords, while other planters were "some of the finest men in this state."[55]

By 1934 the South was experiencing the initial break from the old plantation system of furnishing by the landlord to the new system of displacement, rehabilitation, and federal intrusion. In these first months of the New Deal, it seemed possible that new programs could usher in reform, or at least perform some holding action until prosperous times returned. The FERA reports also showed that even the good times on the plantation were not equal to the bounties of relief, even when so discriminatingly disbursed. The forces of change were upon the land, and as the New Deal ground on other factors in the acreage reduction plan would more radically change the nature of southern farming.

One theme emerged time and again in the FERA reports, a theme that had been augured during the 1927 Mississippi River flood and the 1930 drought. Many rural people had never been far from their homes, and they had relied on their communities in hard times. Natural disasters and the Depression had shuffled people around and drawn outside help into isolated communities. Rural people welcomed the attention that they received from Red Cross and government workers. Finally someone had taken notice and encouraged them. "A lot of these people who used to look up that way to their paternalistic landlords and employers have now switched to the President and Mrs. Roosevelt!" Lorena Hickok wrote to Harry Hopkins in April 1934. "They just expect them to take care of them."[56] The old plantation system relied on stasis, subsistence, and community aid. Planters encouraged their workers to become dependent, continuing the paternalism that had characterized slavery times. While planters feared the invasion of relief in any form, the recipients saw vividly that, though they had been shortchanged, there was hope for a better life.

Yet even as the agencies of relief and rehabilitation moved into the South, they were countered by a collapsing agricultural system. Without a massive transfusion of expertise, credit, and education, the old farming ways were doomed there, along with the marginal families. Even as some New Deal policies propped up the old system with relief, the AAA undermined small-scale agriculture with policies that benefited primarily landowners. The optimism that characterized the inception of the New Deal gave way to despair, especially in the old cotton country, for the cotton culture had metamorphosed. Its new form would rely more upon capital, government programs, technology, and science than upon sharecroppers, tenants, and the community.

5

*The self-appointed, so-called
farm leaders never mention these
basic agricultural ills, but only
howl for crack remedies, price-
fixing, inflation, subsidies, and
the like.*

—D. S. Wheatley, 1933

"Crack Remedies":
The Federal Cotton
Program

The transformation of the cotton culture evolved in a series of changes
beginning with the invasion of the boll weevil and extending through
depression, federal relief and farm programs, increasing utilization of
tractors, and the successful development of the cotton-picking machine. Mechanization emancipated millions of fieldworkers, but it was
a dubious freedom for people anchored in the soil and neither prepared
nor eager for urban life. A traditional way of life that contained elements of paternalism and tyranny, community and independence, illiteracy and folk wisdom, faith and fatalism, and that relied on months of
subsidization and an annual cash settlement faded away. Yet the forces
of change did not coalesce until the Great Depression in 1929 undermined the tenure system and the tenuous credit system that fueled it.
At this point the emergence of relief and Agricultural Adjustment Administration acreage reduction coincided, easing the transition into
commercial farming for landlords but disrupting traditional tenure arrangements. During the transition the federal government increasingly replaced landlords and merchants as the furnishing agent for
rural laborers. As landowners received cash for their cooperation in
government programs, they bought machinery and dismissed more
croppers.

The cotton situation in the spring of 1933 derived from earlier production shifts and the forces of depression. The year before the stock
market crash, cotton farmers had earned $1.5 billion, but in 1932 they
only received $0.5 million. Both the Depression and the annual carry-

over that rose from 4.5 million bales in 1929 to 13 million bales by 1932 affected prices. During the World War I era, prices rose to an average of 35.2 cents per pound, but prices twisted downward in the 1920s and hit bottom at 4.6 cents per pound in June 1932.

New Deal agricultural economists calculated that cotton should bring 12.7 cents per pound to reach parity. Yet farmers hoped to gain in increased plantings what they would lose in lower prices, and in 1933 they planted 41 million acres that would have produced some 14 million bales and a carryover of 12.5 million bales. Despite a consistent demand for cotton throughout the world, it would have taken four years to reduce such a carryover to the 1929 level of 4.5 million bales. Faced with this situation, the Agricultural Adjustment Administration consulted with cotton growers, manufacturers, and handlers; all concurred that some action should be taken to reduce the cotton supply. After meetings in Memphis and Washington, the Cotton Section of the AAA set up a program to reduce the 1933 crop, which in most areas of the South had already been planted.

The AAA and the Extension Service directed some 22,000 workers and set the machinery in motion. To attract the cooperation of cotton farmers, the AAA presented two plans. Farmers could take land out of production and receive a payment based on its historic production. This payment varied from $7 for an acre that produced from 100 to 124 pounds to $20 for land that produced 275 pounds or more. The other plan resembled the first in that farmers received cash for reducing acreage, but it gave them another option. For 6 cents per pound they could purchase surplus cotton equal to the amount taken out of production and resell it at the market price. The reduction payments in this plan varied from $6 per acre for producers of 100 to 124 pounds to $12 for land that produced over 275 pounds. The supply of surplus cotton came from the holdings of the Farm Board and the Stabilization Corporation.

The scheme presented the AAA with an organizational nightmare. It had to inform each farmer of the program, furnish a contract, have it checked, calculate the payment due, and mail the check. The entire plan was voluntary, so farmers who did not cooperate could possibly profit from the higher price that acreage reduction would bring. The administration proved remarkably efficient, and contracts quickly reached the country's 800 cotton-growing counties. County committees and the county agent reviewed each contract and inspected each farm. Since cotton was already growing, farmers had to plow it up. On

July 12, 1933, the date of the final extension, the AAA concluded that enough farmers had agreed to cooperate with the program to make it a success. Cully A. Cobb, a former farm editor, headed the AAA Cotton Section. He proved especially successful in gaining widespread support for the government program and convinced several opposition newspapers to join in the effort.[1]

Overproduction, low prices, and the tireless work of the AAA led southern farmers to cooperate with the reduction program, although the rate of cooperation varied among the states. North Carolina, for example, only put 50.5 percent of its acreage under contract, while the next lowest was Tennessee, with 68.2 percent. All of the major southern cotton-growing states put at least 70 percent under contract, and Louisiana led with 79.5 percent. Further west, New Mexico signed up 65.2 percent of its acreage, Arizona 45.8 percent, and California followed all states with 20.7.[2] The AAA in 1933 had no power to force growers to cooperate or to penalize them if they did not. In that respect the government reduction program suffered from the same problem that had crippled earlier cooperative plans.

S. Peirson of Enfield, North Carolina, explained why so few Tarheel farmers signed contracts. In his county the two largest landlords had refused to cooperate. "A large majority of the individual farmers are heartily in favor of cooperating with the government to the fullest extent, but those controlling a majority of the cotton acreage are opposed to the program, or to come right down to brass tacks they are not opposed, but are hopeful that the little farmer will put the program across and that they will reap the benefit of the high price caused by the reduction." He heartily supported the program and thought Roosevelt was "the greatest President this country ever had." Yet he constantly heard people asking why they should reduce acreage when their neighbors did not. Such farmers wanted a guarantee that they would come out better than those who did not cooperate. Peirson favored a tax on noncooperators.[3]

Rumors reached the AAA that the plan was not foolproof. One of the most pervasive complaints came from people who thought some farmers were adding fertilizer to the crops to boost production.[4] Others griped that farmers were plowing up their worst cotton; thus the program would not have the proposed impact on total production. Jonathan H. Johnston of Searcy, Arkansas, frankly admitted that he would destroy cotton on his worst land. "In my case," he wrote, "I have land in different Counties, some that is not good, this I will plow up, but any land located in localities that has been producing from three to six hundred pounds per acre I will leave as it is." He complained that the $20 top price for reducing acreage worked against those in fertile growing areas. Although local committees were charged with policing the plowups, complaints revealed that some farmers cheated. G. W. Pearrow wrote from Bald Knob, Arkansas, that "a lot of crooked work had been done in Phillips and Desha counties." Some farmers plowed up weeds. "The negroes are made to do this, they are hardly to blame, the higher ups are the ones that should be prosecuted."[5]

Nick Tosches, in his biography of Jerry Lee Lewis, recorded what may well be an apocryphal story of how the New Deal program was received in Ferriday, Louisiana. A local landowner and relative who rented to Lewis's father, Elmo, told him "to pay no mind to that damnfool New Deal cripple talking at people from out of a damn-fool radio. He told him that Franklin D. Roosevelt had taken us off the gold standard, and that was bad enough, but now the fireside-talking fool had gone too far, trying to take us off the dirt standard." So Elmo Lewis did not plow up any cotton. He then took the earnings, Tosches wrote, and bought every Jimmie Rodgers record ever made, got drunk, and sang along with the records. It took standardization with teeth to tame such a spirit.[6]

Most complaints, however, arose in the relations between landlords and tenants. The AAA in 1934 and 1935 insisted that its acreage-reduction program displaced few tenants, and it minimized persistent complaints in 1933 that landlords did not share government payments with tenants. Yet in 1933 many tenants did not benefit from the plowup provisions as the law stated. According to the provisions of the contracts, the tenant was to share the plowup payment in proportion to his interests in the crop, usually a 50–50 or 75–25 split.[7]

Several of the Rural Problem Areas reports mentioned abuses. The Marlboro County, South Carolina, report observed that the AAA payments were of "great direct benefit" to farmers but added that "croppers have not received an equitable share of the benefits from this program, and interviews with other responsible persons in the community support the validity of this contention." The Limestone County, Alabama, report stated the problem more explicitly: "Most of the money went to the landlords for, as the investigator points out, the contract was so written that this group could reap all the advantages and did so. In 1934 the effect of this operation was somewhat better since the contracts were revised but . . . the displaced croppers and tenants obviously did not reap any benefits." Most of the tenants in Limestone County were white. Arthur F. Raper and Ira De A. Reid, in *Sharecrop- pers All*, observed that in some cases planters took the money to cover tenants' back debts. They added that "some planters got the whole check by saying they took out the 'option' and the tenant had nothing to do with it."[8]

The customary sharing arrangement in the Arkansas Delta was halves. E. D. Hartsell wrote from Marked Tree that landlords were ask- ing sharecroppers to settle for a third of the government payment due them. Cully Cobb replied that tenants who had an interest in the crop had a right to part of the check, but he added that "the government did not dictate how landlords split the proceeds." Yet, as David Conrad re- vealed in *The Forgotten Farmers*, "A tenant was lucky if he received any cash from the 1933 plowup."[9]

Fearing that a reduced crop would lead to cutbacks in harvest work and ginning, Dawson Kea of Adrian, Georgia, wrote a reasoned letter suggesting that the government burn or dump in the ocean the cotton already on hand. "By paying for and destroying cotton already on hand, instead of that in the fields, you would reduce the crop just as much, but leave a great amount of money to be paid for laborers who need it, and would earn it by picking, ginning, hauling, etc." Kea continued, "When a government lends a man money to grow a crop, then pays him to plow under that same crop before he gathers it, if that is states- manship then Thomas Jefferson was a weak-minded amateur." Cully Cobb did not deal with the implications of Kea's suggestions but an- swered that farmers would turn to other crops. C. O. Maddox, cashier of the Peoples Bank in Winder, Georgia, agreed with Kea. He thought the government should have taken "one or two million bales of dog-tail cotton now in existence and had it destroyed as it has no value and the cotton gamblers of this country are using it as a shield in case their hand is called on deliveries."[10]

Some landlords reflected the general uneasiness of their class over the emerging relationship between the government and tenants. A law firm representing a mercantile company that financed tenants in Car- tersville, Georgia, asked about the "waiver of consent to be signed by the lien holder that the Department of Agriculture deal directly with the producer with reference to the terms of the contract and as we take it authorizing the Government to pay to the producer the money for the acreage taken out of production." The firm asked if the Depart- ment of Agriculture could send the money directly to the lien holder, that is, the merchant or landlord. Cobb replied that the checks would "be payable jointly to the producer and the undersigned lien holders."[11] W. D. Haas of Bunkie, Louisiana, complained more stridently of having the government pay money "to one who has no right or title whatever to the rent." He paid the taxes and kept up the land, Haas pointed out, but "my tenant will collect from the Government the rent due me." He observed that his taxes were higher than ever, yet his commodities were selling below the cost of production. "I do not hesitate to tell you that the man carrying the load in the South today is the land owner," he concluded.[12] Such landlords feared the shift of control from their ledger books to government records. They doubted that a tenant would pay to the landlord the money he owed. Under the old system a landlord took his share before settling with a tenant; the AAA reversed the formula.

As the summer passed, some farmers asked the AAA whether natural disasters and accidents would serve the same purpose as plowups. R. V. Kerr, superintendent of schools in Benton, Louisiana, wrote to Eleanor Roosevelt asking that 50 percent credit be given to farmers for flood damage, the same as if they had plowed up their crops. Kerr explained that water still covered the land and that the Red Cross had to evacuate and feed the refugees. "The Negroes are in destitute circumstances. These people have lost not only their cotton crop and gardens but in a great many instances their livestock has been drowned." He concluded, "Surely an act of God should be worth as much as an act of the Government."[13] J. R. Lowery of Salisbury, North Carolina, reported to Wallace that he had stored seventy-four bales of cotton, his production for the last two years, and that it had burned. "As this took that much off the market it looks as though I should get some pay for it, about what we would get for plowing cotton up." He explained that the cotton belonged to his tenants. Cobb had no sympathy in this case; he wrote to Lowery that, if he did not have insurance on the cotton, "certainly you are the only one to blame for the loss due to fire." Another farmer from South Carolina asked if cotton destroyed by hail could be used to obtain credit for government payments; he was also refused.[14]

Not all farmers took their grievances to the government. "On Sunday morning, August 27," wrote O. L. Warr from Timmonsville, South Carolina, "I found over two acres of my cotton pulled up, and a sign in the field reading: 'Pick this and we will pull up more.'" Several of his neighbors, he explained, "have been served in a similar fashion." He had not cooperated in the plowup campaign. "I believed, and still believe, that, in the long run, the public welfare will be more harmed than helped by the adoption of this policy." Had there been no AAA plowup campaign "these fields would not have been laid waste," and he asked Wallace for credit as if his two acres had been plowed up. "This simple act upon your part would not only effect justice, but would in some degree assuage the bitterness which cannot but pervade the feelings of men who have viewed the efforts of these cowardly mobs." Cobb explained that there was no provision under law to accommodate Warr.[15]

Finally, there was concern that in the future landlords might reduce the number of tenants because their acreage had been cut. Because crops had already been set out when the plowup started, little displacement occurred in 1933. D. S. Wheatley of Greenwood, Mississippi, wrote to Wallace in November arguing that the future for sharecroppers was grim. "In my opinion," he wrote, "one of your most serious problems in the acreage reduction plan is the surplus tenant farmer who will be left without a farm to farm." He recommended adding a clause to future reduction contracts that would protect the tenants. "The tenant farmers, white and black, have been worse used than any other class in our country." He thought that their lot would worsen. "The self-appointed, so-called farm leaders never mention these basic agricultural ills, but only howl for crack remedies, price-fixing, inflation, subsidies, and the like." Paul Appleby replied to Wheatley, assuring him that the contract did have such a provision: "He shall effect the acreage reduction as nearly ratably as practicable among tenants on this farm; shall, insofar as possible, maintain on this farm the normal number of tenants and other employees."[16] This vague provision would ultimately become the most controversial part of the AAA cotton program.

Any number of analogies come to mind when thinking of the relationship between landlord and sharecropper. In some ways it was like a marriage, a very personal arrangement that differed with each set of participants. Many landlords regarded themselves as father figures, paternalists, who cared for their cropper children as best they could. Prodigals left, the inept lingered on under the wing of the father, and good children received better land and honest settlements. In other respects the system resembled a penal colony—the landlord or his overseer constantly supervised sharecroppers and controlled them by threats, rations, and settlement. Southern sharecropping was exceedingly complex, and though the traditional settlement may have been halves, variations clouded the arrangements. Given such a fluid system, planters could easily manipulate sharecroppers and siphon off federal money.

The Agricultural Adjustment Administration's Cotton Section realized that acreage reduction and government money would present temptations to landlords and problems for tenants. In the 1934 and 1935 contracts the section inserted provisions that protected sharecroppers and other plantation residents. Not only was a landlord bound to distribute acreage reduction equally among his tenants, but also he was to allow other farmers who customarily lived on the plantation "to continue in the occupancy of their houses on this farm, rent free, for the years 1934 and 1935, respectively (unless any such tenant shall so conduct himself as to become a nuisance or a menace to the welfare of the producer)." All residents could cut firewood, grow food and feed crops, and pasture their livestock without charge.[17] In this way the AAA hoped to preserve a semblance of paternalism.

If destitute farmers could squat on plantations and use existing housing and fuel while raising part of their food, the relief situation would be simplified. The seasonal labor would also be on hand at plowing, chopping, and picking seasons. Certainly many landlords complied with so familiar an arrangement. After all, if the planter owed no obligation to squatters in the way of furnish and did not share any federal money with them, he stood to benefit from their occasional labor. The FERA would basically furnish the squatter, while the landlord got the labor in season. This was a variation of the successful Franklin County, North Carolina, FERA experiment, but the AAA placed larger responsibility upon landlords and offered no supervision to squatters.

Despite guarantees written into contracts, a reduction in the number of tenants seemed inevitable. As Fred C. Frey and T. Lynn Smith, two Louisiana State University sociologists, wrote in 1936, "There are few people gullible enough to believe that the acreage devoted to cotton can be reduced one-third without an accompanying decrease in the laborers engaged in its production."[18] Yet the displacement of agricultural laborers during the first two or three years of the New Deal presents a complex puzzle; the 30 to 50 percent acreage reduction did not lead to a parallel tenant reduction. The clearest case of displacement came from the Arkansas Delta and involved the Southern Tenant Farmers Union and its fight to end evictions. Of the 1,457 complaints of eviction the AAA received by September 7, 1934, 477 came from Arkansas. Only 11 Arkansas cases—21 in the entire cotton program—

A plantation owner near Clarksdale, Mississippi, in the Delta area. June 1936. Dorothea Lange. (LC USF 34 9699-C, Library of Congress). [On the extreme left is the profile of Paul S. Taylor, Lange's husband and expert on rural labor.]

led to recommendations for cancelled contracts. In most cases the complaints went before county committees composed of landlords or to county agents who sided with landlords. The complaint machinery fed the victim to his oppressor. Indeed, in one Arkansas case the planter named in a complaint served on the county committee that investigated abuses.[19]

While the AAA attempted to muffle complaints, it consistently maintained that the acreage-reduction program did not displace tenants. "There has been no wholesale displacement of tenants or sharecroppers due to the operation of the cotton and other adjustment programs in the South," a report by J. Phil Campbell concluded. In rare cases, the report admitted, landlords evicted tenants, but they always had "some good reason for doing so." Clearly the AAA Cotton Section put its investigations in the best light possible, for the conditions in the Arkansas Delta were like the early skirmishes of war.[20]

The exact nature of rural change during the first three years of active federal participation in farming remains unclear. When depression struck in 1929, scores of urban unemployed headed to rural areas where many had come from, working with relatives or squatting wherever they could find shelter. This glut of rural laborers put another strain on the old plantation system, for planters realized that a large pool of desperate workers was available for seasonal work. Frey and Smith, in a survey of 170 sample counties in the Cotton Belt, found a decrease of only 1.1 percent in the total number of tenants from 1930 to 1935 but a 12 percent decline in sharecroppers. Tenancy decreased in such areas as the rich delta lands but increased in new ground and hill areas where many urban refugees settled. The increase in tenancy, according to this study, came from people not usually engaged in agriculture, primarily whites; there was an overall gain of 15 percent in white tenancy. Black tenancy during the same five-year period dropped by 19 percent across the South. Sharecropping decreased for both races, by 18 percent for whites and 8 percent for blacks.

The authors found that the displacement of wagehands "appears to have been very great, far greater than that of tenants or even croppers." They maintained that many planters had cotton fields that were usually worked by wagehands and that they preferred to keep the cropper cotton and plow up the other. Thus, wagehands found themselves unemployed immediately.[21] No doubt the forces that would ultimately drive millions of farmers from the land started at the bottom of the legendary agricultural ladder, first culling the weakest. As landlords surveyed the situation, they must have asked whether it was necessary to continue paternalism. There was plenty of labor, the federal government cared for those who were without work or food, and the agricultural program favored landlords. With a few adjustments, a landlord could change the status of his sharecroppers and tenants, keep nearly all of the government money, transfer the furnish to the government, and save money toward a tractor. County agents, farm magazines, and farm radio programs all stressed diversification and mechanization. The winds of change blew ever stronger in the rural South.

The Cotton Section received numerous complaints from farmers about the administration of the cotton program, and the agency conducted investigations and made adjustments in the contracts. The section also carefully conducted public relations work to show that the program worked well for all tenure classes. As AAA head Chester C.

Davis wrote, "the impression must not be created that there has been widespread effort to 'Chisel,' cheat, or be unfair." He suggested that most landlords had cooperated and "have shown a desire and a willingness to be entirely fair and unselfish in connection with the cotton adjustment program." Some, he noted, had even given tenants a larger share than required under law.

Five primary complaints came from the cotton-producing areas. First, many tenants complained that landlords had evicted them. Some landlords dismissed a tenant family and replaced it with a smaller family to till the reduced acreage; others, in violation of the contract, would not allow unemployed workers to stay in the empty plantation houses. Second, to obtain more of the federal money, some landlords changed the status of tenants. Third, planters often withheld money from the government or inserted clauses into their contracts stipulating that all federal money go to the landlord. Given the power relationship and the depressed conditions of rural areas, sharecroppers and other tenants were in a poor bargaining position and would agree to almost any arrangement in order to remain on the land. Fourth, managing-share tenants, who simply rented acreage and furnished all the stock and fertilizer, found it increasingly difficult to rent a farm, for landlords could simply change the contract and demote the managing-share tenant to another type tenure that would deny him federal money. Finally, some landlords changed the customary division of the crops to give themselves a larger share of the payments.[22]

Although the federal government had responsibility for this program, Chester Davis claimed that he did not want the government to intrude into social problems: "To undertake to tie up the solution to a deep-seated social problem with the Agricultural Adjustment program would probably make it impossible to carry out these emergency programs successfully." He admitted that some of the conditions were "regrettable and undesirable," but by simply executing the AAA program he hoped to avoid the issue. Davis did not admit that the AAA program itself intensified such problems and even laid the basis for restructuring the plantation system along different lines. Yet the AAA program inserted the elements of revolutionary change into the landlord-tenant relationship, and, with his attitude that the federal government had no role in the change, Davis allowed landlords to shape the new structure in the way they desired.[23]

To present an image of evenhandedness, the Cotton Section conducted several investigations throughout the South and also investigated the complaints that poured in. The agency's files bulge with memorandums and reports that put a good light on the AAA cotton program. In September 1935, for example, W. J. Green, who investigated contract violations, submitted a report showing "little, if any, relationship" between the AAA reduction program and the number of tenants on relief.[24] This report raised even more questions in the AAA administrative offices than it solved, and William T. Ham in the Labor Relations unit analyzed it. He concluded that the report "will be satisfactory to no one who is inclined to be critical of tenancy aspects of the cotton program." He set out six major faults in the report, concluding that, because of its narrow focus on displacement and methodological clumsiness, the "report will be described as side-stepping the chief points in controversy." It dealt only with displacement and not with other issues, such as croppers not receiving their share of the payments. Ham's critique dramatized how eager the AAA Cotton Section was to present its work as beneficial, as well as revealing splits in the AAA staff.[25]

W. J. Green headed a staff of seven former extension agents who investigated contract violations. In December 1934, D. P. Trent, assistant director of the commodities division of the AAA, submitted a report on Green's work. While top AAA administrators praised Green's work, Trent raised questions about the unit's effectiveness. In September 1934 he confided to Jerome Frank, a lawyer in the Cotton Section legal staff, that "we have been too much inclined to pussy-foot and dodge responsibility" concerning tenant problems. In many cases, he concluded, "we have dismissed each complaint by simply writing a reply instructing the complaining tenant that he should see his county agent and county committee."[26] The report showed that the Cotton Section had investigated 2,098 complaints. Of those, 1,512 had "no basis for complaint," 347 were adjusted by county committees, 215 were settled by field investigators, and 24 contracts were cancelled.

During the settlement season in the fall of 1934, Trent reported a flood of letters complaining about the distribution of parity payments. As new arrangements were being negotiated among landlords and tenants for the 1935 crop year, he indicated that "a rather large number of tenants and share-croppers have, during the past few weeks, received written notice that they must seek other locations for the coming year and that the landlord or landowner plans to operate the land himself or operate it through the employment of hired labor." Such problems were not local—"this practice is rather general throughout the cottonbelt." Despite investigations and contract guarantees, landlords were making drastic changes in traditional tenure arrangements. Some landlords were charging a bonus in addition to the usual split of the crop in the "form of a charge for the use of houses, barns, gardens and other equipment on the farm." Such landlord evasions were an "indirect means of changing the status of tenants, increasing the rate of rent or securing a larger share of benefit payments than the landowner would be entitled to under the contract and the regulations." The problems had not been solved, Trent observed, for "the difficulties which lie ahead are just as serious as those which have occurred in the past and the need for definitive, positive, prompt action is just as great as ever." He concluded by observing that most landlords had complied with the regulation.[27]

The reduction in tenants in the cotton South proceeded unevenly, and sources do not reveal the extent of displacement. An example of the inner dynamics of the change has been shown above, in the displacement of white tenants by blacks in Leflore County, Mississippi. The same trend occurred in Arkansas on a plantation surveyed by the AAA in 1935. This plantation, one of three studied, was not identified by name but was described only as Plantation One. From 1930 to 1935 cropland increased from 3,600 to 5,650 acres, the overall tenant population grew from 156 to 249, and the number of white croppers fell from 77 to 48. Plantation Two had no white sharecroppers, and the number of black croppers dropped from 114 in 1930 to 109 in 1935, while wagehands rose from none to 15. With 10 more farmers than in 1930, the acreage cultivated increased from 2,482 to 2,543 acres. Plantation Three held its share tenants at about 20, reduced black sharecroppers from 132 to 82, and the one white cropper who left in 1930 was not replaced. Significantly, the number of wagehands increased from 36 to 66 over those years. Thus there were 21 fewer farmers of all classes tilling the same acreage in 1935.[28] These three plantations shuffled the tenure cards differently as each looked for the high cards to win the AAA game.

The report revealed that sharecroppers were able to pay off their debts by 1934, crediting this fact to the benefits of the AAA. Yet the AAA had an even greater impact on the income of the landlord on Plantation One. While the tenants' share of cotton lint rose from $16,128 in 1932 to $17,308 in 1934, the landlord's share rose from $38,677 to $77,162. Tenants did share more returns from cottonseed over the three years, increasing from $2,688 to $5,192, but the land-

lord's share rose from $7,282 to $19,619. From all products sold from
the plantation, the tenants' share rose from $21,960 to $29,842, while
the landlord's share rose from $51,554 to $102,202.[29] Obviously, the
AAA program rewarded landlords handsomely for their cooperation.

The problems that New Deal agricultural policy generated in rural
areas forced conflict in the offices of the Agricultural Adjustment Administration. The U.S. Department of Agriculture had, for most of its
history, encouraged scientific farming, expanded use of implements
and chemicals, and crop diversification. The alliance between land-
grant universities, the Extension Service, the Farm Bureau, the Department of Agriculture, and southern politicians encouraged commercial
farmers at the expense of the tenant class. In the AAA, administrator
Chester Davis and Cotton Section head Cully A. Cobb personified the
established agricultural complex. They defended the AAA as an emergency agency, not one that should delve into customary arrangements
between landlord and tenant.

While the policy flowing through these channels was portrayed as
conservative and impartial, it embodied the elements of radical change.
If offered an opportunity to bury the decaying sharecropping system
and, by stabilizing landowners, to build a capitalist farm structure
more like that of the business world. Acreage reduction, government
payments to landlords, and mechanization pushed increasing numbers of poor farmers into a life elsewhere. On the other side were a
small band of visionaries—Rexford G. Tugwell, Lee Pressman, Jerome
Frank, Alger Hiss, Gardner Jackson, and Frederick C. Howe—who insisted that sharecroppers not be displaced and that they receive a fair
share of government money. These so-called radicals, in effect, were
trying to preserve and reform the old structure and stood in the way
of forces that represented modernization, rationality, and emerging
capital-intensive southern farming.

The conflict between these groups came to a head over the eviction
of tenants in Arkansas. Immediately after the AAA legal section ruled
that the AAA require landlords to keep the same tenants (not just the
same number of tenants) on their plantations, Chester Davis sided
with Cobb and convinced Secretary Wallace that the "radicals" should
leave the agency. Wallace had been under tremendous pressure during
this struggle, and at a press conference in February 1935 he agreed
with Davis, who stated that, for the good of the AAA, "I think it is important to have in the key positions in the Triple-A men who have some
familiarity with farm problems and who have a farm background." It is

surprising that the small group without "a farm background" came so close to winning a fight that pitted them against the entire commercial agriculture complex and southern politicians.[30] If planters were looking for a signal from Washington, the purge blazed as a beacon.

Yet in the old cotton-growing areas accumulating problems, government payments, and mechanization would have altered the tenure structure whether or not the AAA persisted with this ruling. The Department of Agriculture realized that tenure arrangements were undergoing a revolutionary change, and though they came up with ideas that could have relieved some of the distress, there were dynamics that defied stopgap measures. The old structure was crumbling, and the design of the new structure became the issue. Would the tenant class find a savior, or would it be the sacrifice to the god of agribusiness? Every indicator since Seaman Knapp set up his experiment stations pointed to the answer. The AAA program was but the most recent catalyst that agitated the rural South.

Even as the old tenure system deteriorated, liberal New Dealers tried to patch it up. Within the USDA the Bureau of Agricultural Economics conducted extensive investigations into the possibilities of transforming tenancy into a more just system based on that of other countries. The tenant aid programs of the Resettlement Administration (later the Farm Security Administration) encouraged farmers who had managerial and farming skills to buy farms or to keep the ones they had. In 1937 the Bankhead Act provided additional support for small farmers and tenants, and the President's report on tenancy pointed out grave problems in the hinterland. Yet the forces of change had already run past these liberal efforts to maintain the old structure. It was too late even in 1937.[31]

The old tenure system in the Cotton South had no more chance of survival than did the radical group purged from the Cotton Section. Both stood in the way of the USDA dream of progress. New Deal agricultural policy in every commodity program favored landowners or those who had significant capital, such as rice tenants. Paul Appleby, Secretary of Agriculture Henry A. Wallace's chief aide, remembered in the early 1950s that his millionaire farmer boss preferred the label *conservative* to *liberal*. The AAA, Appleby insisted, was "militantly for the larger farmers and was much less interested in the lower economic level farmers and very little interested in farm tenants and farm laborers and so on. It was an organization whose function had to do with the more successful farmers by and large." Likewise, Calvin Hoover, who served as an economic advisor to the AAA, quickly comprehended by early 1935 that the AAA program "has been of little net benefit to the tenants, share croppers and laborers in the South." He argued, however, that the situation would have been even worse had there been no AAA. "Nevertheless," he concluded, "the facts remain that the net advantages of the program have been primarily to landowners and not to other classes of farmers." [32]

Mordecai Ezekiel, another economic advisor in the USDA, agreed with Appleby and Hoover, adding that "the farm owners, constituting less than half of those engaged in agriculture, have been the dominant element in the preparation and administration of AAA programs heretofore. In certain commodities, notably cotton, this has resulted in their receiving the lion's share of the benefits resulting from the program." In February 1936, a month after the Supreme Court held the AAA unconstitutional, Ezekiel predicted that under the new soil conservation approach it would be "even more difficult to maintain equity in the treatment of these weaker groups in farming than it has been in the past." He suggested that more tenants be placed on local committees and that the department face tenant problems, not avoid them. [33] The AAA program proved conservative in that it stabilized large farmers and radical in that it transformed the tenure system and displaced sharecroppers. Most important, it gave landlords the power to alter the mode of production by manipulating federal policy and restructuring tenure.

The Department of Agriculture continued to duck the issue of tenant displacement, often blaming it on mechanization and not on AAA policies. In late 1939 Will Alexander, head of the FSA, commented on a draft letter from Wallace to Senator Hattie Caraway of Arkansas, arguing that it was less than honest in claiming that the AAA and the Farm Security Administration were solving the problems created by mechanization when department policies led to much of the disruption. The FSA had recently set up a cooperative in Arkansas that would take care of 285 displaced families, but there were 400 applications for the positions. Instead of solving displacement problems, Alexander wrote, "The trend is much greater in the opposite direction." Displaced tenants simply could not obtain land to farm, and the FSA did not have the resources to care for them. To pacify Caraway, Wallace cited the AAA rule that forbade landlords from displacing tenants. The senator had passed to Wallace a constituent's complaint that his neighbors displaced tenants. Wallace concluded that this farmer's problem

A Farm Security Administration project. Picking cotton near Lake Dick, Phillips County, Arkansas. September 1938. Russell Lee. (LC USF 33 11671-M2, *Library of Congress*)

came from using mules while his neighbors used tractors, adding that the department was not attempting to stifle progress. The draft letter to Caraway epitomized the USDA attitude—it was innocent of displacing tenants, it favored programs that displaced tenants, and it washed its hands of the conflicting results.[34]

A BAE study reinforced Will Alexander's concern, noting that by 1940 increasing numbers of prospective FSA clients could not find land to farm. "The question has been raised," the report observed, "as to whether this displacement is a sign that all present programs of the Department designed to perpetuate the small independent farmer are in the long run doomed to failure." The trend toward concentration of landholdings was not bad in itself, it pointed out. "It is when these forces tend to concentrate production in agriculture in large commercial types of farms at the expense of the family sized farm that these forces come into conflict with the above-stated policies of the Department."[35]

As late as June 1941 the department struggled with the problem of displaced tenants and the AAA's obligation to enforce contract provisions. When CIO organizer Lucy Randolph Mason wrote to the department complaining about the tenant problem, Paul Appleby asked for a ruling from the Solicitor's office. "As you are aware," the reply

Group receiving checks. Brookhaven, Mississippi. September 26,
1940. Harmon. (AAA-6200, *Box 151, National Archives*)

stated, no government agency had power to dictate "the settlements
which landlords make with their tenants, sharecroppers, or wagehands in connection with their farming operations." Farmers who par-
ticipated in the commodity programs, however, fell under provisions of
the Soil Conservation and Domestic Allotment Act, and the department "shall, in every practicable manner, protect the interests of the
small producers." In his reply to Mason, Appleby observed that the
AAA program and other factors were changing the structure of American agriculture. "About all the Triple-A program can do is to attempt to
govern that process of change in an orderly way," he replied.[36] The
dreams of the early New Deal were dissipating into the reality of what
the AAA cotton program had wrought.

Paradoxically, as the mood of the country became more conservative,
rural disruption entered another phase due to mechanization. Even as
the President's tenancy committee, the FSA, the BAE, and.other agencies studied rural problems and offered suggestions to solve them, the
mechanical forces that would eliminate sharecroppers were chugging
across the fields.

The historical verdict on the Agricultural Adjustment Administration, if it is ever rendered, will be filled with qualifications and equivocations, for policies varied from state to state and commodity to commodity. The AAA acreage and parity program stabilized both tobacco and rice cultures with little disruption of traditional tenure arrangements. With cotton, however, the program proved a threat to tenants and a boon to landlords. The government program that put money in the hands of landowners and increasingly moved the government into the furnishing business through relief and unemployment programs cannot be separated from other simultaneously operating forces. The structure of landownership, the AAA bias of payments to larger landowners, the credit structure of the South, ideas on how to combat the problem of tenancy, and increasing mechanization all figured into the equation of change during the New Deal.

Some historians have concentrated upon the first Roosevelt administration and upon the forces of change in the Arkansas Delta connected with the Southern Tenant Farmers Union. While this struggle proved important in showing the AAA at its most biased, there were other significant elements of agricultural change. By the time the first AAA had been held unconstitutional in January 1936, structural changes had begun that would ultimately lead to capital-intensive agriculture. Their effects would be as significant as the enclosure movement that revolutionized the Old World.

6

The Federal Tobacco

Patent Medicine

*I believe it would be just to allow
a tennant to carry his allotment
with him from farm to farm and
require Land lords to reduce
their planting in acordance with
the total indicated allotment
allowed them and their tennants.*
—*Maynard P. West, 1933*

Though tobacco farmers did not achieve the structural changes in marketing and processing that they pursued prior to 1933, they survived and prospered under federal control for thirty-five more years, until congressional changes in the allotment and marketing laws in the 1960s unleashed mechanization that decimated the ranks of sharecroppers and small owners and further consolidated landownership. Despite their mutual hostility for half a century, farmers, warehousemen, and manufacturers cooperated with each other and with the federal government to stabilize the traditional tobacco culture during the Great Depression. When the government entered the bright-leaf area of the South in the fall of 1933, it came not as an intrusive agent but as an invited guest, after all other efforts to stabilize the industry had failed.

During the summer of 1933, as tobacco grew to maturity, farmers looked apprehensively toward the marketing season. The Agricultural Adjustment Act passed on May 12 set up machinery that could bring supply and demand into harmony by reducing tobacco acreage and implementing a processing tax to finance payments to farmers. The act sought "to establish and maintain such balance between the production and consumption of agricultural commodities . . . as will re-establish prices to farmers at a level that will give agricultural commodities a purchasing power with respect to articles that farmers buy, equivalent to the purchasing power of agricultural commodities in the base period." In other words, by cooperating with government programs, farmers would receive a parity price. While other commodities took the 1909 to 1914 years as the base, tobacco farmers used the 1919

to 1929 period, which increased the parity price by 17 percent. Tobacco politicians successfully argued that the economics of burley tobacco had changed dramatically since 1914 as burley growers had
turned to a thinner leaf for use in cigarettes, altering both prices and
cost of production. Flue-cured growers, although they had not
changed production patterns since the turn of the century, shared the
windfall.[1]

Tobacco interests proved formidable politically, and apparently no
objections emerged to tobacco's inclusion as a basic commodity. Obviously tobacco farmers held a key economic position in the nation's
farm structure and, if omitted from the agricultural recovery plan,
would have suffered severe hardship. Yet tobacco was not food or fiber,
as were the other six commodities—wheat, cotton, field corn, hogs,
rice, and milk. No doubt tobacco's economic importance assured its inclusion, for omitting tobacco would have jeopardized rural recovery.[2]

As tobacco matured and farmers moved through the fields crushing
worms, topping, and suckering, their uncertainty increased. The conventional wisdom held that manufacturers had not suffered from the
Depression, and farmers resented those profits compared to their own
paltry income. "How can we live under such conditions?" a woman
asked President Franklin D. Roosevelt. The "big tobacco cos," she argued on the day when the Agricultural Adjustment Act passed, "are
getting richer year by year at the hands of poor old farmers. Can't you
in the name of suffering humanity help the poor farmers by giving
them a better price this fall for their tobacco." She feared that the big
companies had sent representatives to Washington to "fight against
our getting a better price for our tobacco," and she urged him to ignore
them "as they have had us working for them long enough and we need
help and need it right now."[3]

Farmers insisted that the federal government intervene to secure
higher prices for their tobacco, although this contradicted the old tradition of independent farmers going it alone. Yet across the country
farmers willingly cooperated with the government, and, given the failures to alter the marketing and processing structure over the years,
tobacco farmers encouraged the government to establish a program.
The Depression had created an experimental mood among many
Americans, and ideas about independence and government intervention changed, at least for a while. The farm editor Clarence Poe, who
had unsuccessfully advocated the Tri-State Tobacco Growers' Cooperative and the later crop control efforts of the Federal Farm Board, sup-

ported government intervention. In the *Progressive Farmer* he argued that the times demanded "planning for an entire industry or industrial group." Individuals should not be allowed to harm society at large. He argued that there was a crucial difference between socialism and social planning. "Within limits, however, social planning is actually a safeguard against extreme socialism," he explained. In this analysis Poe foreshadowed the main thrust of the New Deal—government intervention to forestall an assault on private enterprise.[4]

At the Farmers' Week celebration held in Raleigh in late July, forty-year-old John B. Hutson, chief of the Tobacco Section of the AAA, urged cooperation between government and growers. Hutson, who had worked in tobacco economics for the USDA for eleven years and was the only department career worker to head a commodity program, knew at first hand how farmers reacted to low prices. He had been born in Murray County, Kentucky, and grew up on a tobacco farm and was a youngster during the violent Black Patch War in the century's first decade.[5]

Farmers realized that the crisis situation favored reform, and a mood of expectation and ferment gripped growers. They no longer confined their complaints to neighbors at the crossroads but addressed New Deal officials in Washington. Growers from Halifax County, Virginia, sent a petition to Secretary of Agriculture Henry A. Wallace outlining their problems. Drought had combined with low tobacco prices to cause "destitution" there: "During the past winter practically eighty per cent of our tobacco farmers were dependent upon the work relief program of the Reconstruction Finance Cooperation [*sic*] to provide food for their families." Many had mortgaged to the point where they were about to lose their farms. These farmers, the petition argued, were eager to cooperate with the government to achieve higher prices.[6]

When the Georgia tobacco markets opened on August 1, tobacco farmers realized their worst fears. "The farmers are being paid ruinous prices for tobacco and the market is lower than last year, considering the quality of tobacco," Coffee County growers complained to Secretary Wallace, "and bankruptcy, starvation and ruin face the tobacco farmers of South Georgia unless tobacco prices are put on a parity for the period between 1919 and 1929 as established by the Agricultural Department of the United States of America." Secretary Wallace asked for suggestions from growers on how to reduce the supply of tobacco and raise prices.[7] Although Governor Eugene Talmadge of Georgia had no suggestions to offer, he observed that "there is something wrong when five big companies get rich off of tobacco, and the growers have to sell it at below cost." The unrest intensified in Coffee County, and a few days later 700 farmers met and complained again. They agreed that Washington should listen to their delegates and take immediate action. Since some tobacco had already been marketed, farmers feared that the entire 1933 crop would be sold at low prices before the government acted. "The situation is almost desperate here," the petition ended.[8]

The dread of low prices spread quickly to eastern North Carolina, where farmers met in some twenty communities and demanded action from the Department of Agriculture. Meeting in Stantonsburg on August 10, for example, farmers sent a petition outlining prices for the past three years and the current low prices in Georgia. Unless some action raised prices, the result would be the "deprivation, hardship, ruin and consequent dispossession of the tobacco farmers."[9]

Sensing the feeling of hopelessness and outrage, on August 10 *News and Observer* editor Jonathan Daniels wrote to Wallace privately. "Rightly or wrongly, these planters believe that they are completely at the mercy of the few big tobacco companies which are the only buyers and that these companies agree among themselves upon the lowest price at which they can secure tobacco." On August 22 Daniels editorialized that everyone who "touches tobacco from the buyer through the manufacturer prospers out of tobacco except the man who tends it from virgin bed through the most careful curing of the crop." Two weeks later he prodded Wallace, observing that manufacturers would not raise prices "of their own volition." Most of the large fortunes of the state, he pointed out, came from the manufacture of tobacco. "Yet I do not think that in the whole of America you will find any men engaged in the production of a crop which requires as much intelligence and care as tobacco who are so generally denied the decent living standards which all of us today hope for in America."[10]

The mood swung from disappointment to outrage when the Border Belt markets of North and South Carolina opened in early August. L. T. Townsend visited the markets in Fairmont and Lumberton and complained of extremely low prices. Unless something happened to offset the low prices, he predicted that "pretty soon our people will not be any higher in their aspirations than Russian peasants." When the major markets opened in the Eastern Belt on August 29, the situation became more desperate. Cash-hungry farmers flocked to warehouses and blocked the markets in Wilson with some three million pounds of leaf. Prices averaged 11 cents a pound, and many farmers, even though eager for cash, turned their tags, indicating that they did not accept the bid. Some 10,000 angry farmers milled about the town. The central markets furnished a natural rallying place for discontent.[11]

Anticipating low prices, growers had arranged a meeting in Raleigh on August 31, two days after the eastern belt markets opened. There farmers demanded that all markets close immediately and that the government and manufacturers meet and decide how to raise prices to a 20-cent average. They sent a resolution to North Carolina Governor John Christoph Blucher Ehringhaus asking him to close the markets. A lawyer and former state representative, Ehringhaus responded with a proclamation for a "voluntary marketing holiday" until the federal government and the manufacturers agreed on a formula to raise prices.[12] Most Tarheel farmers supported his move to close the markets.

Ehringhaus knew that manufacturers and government representatives had been meeting in Washington for a month but had made little progress in resolving the problem of low prices. During the Labor Day vacation, the governor traveled to Washington to expedite the negotiations, heading a delegation that included representatives from Virginia and South Carolina, where the tobacco markets were also closed. The problem centered around obtaining growers' cooperation to cut future acreage in exchange for immediate price increases, for manufacturers refused to buy the large 1933 crop without a guarantee of future production control. Congressman Lindsay C. Warren from Washington, North Carolina, suggested that growers sign a tentative contract that would show their willingness to reduce acreage. Having worked out the details, delegates rushed home to a meeting in Raleigh on September 6. Farmers overwhelmingly supported the plan, and Ehringhaus asked that mass meetings be held throughout the Tobacco Belt. A week later he reported that farmers representing 95 to 98 percent of the state's tobacco acreage had agreed to reduce their plantings in 1934.[13]

Still Ehringhaus refused to reopen the markets, for manufacturers had not agreed to raise prices. With farmers still angry and desperately needing cash, the Winston-Salem *Journal* observed that by keeping the markets closed Ehringhaus was using a form of blackmail against the manufacturers. When he set the opening for September 25, the governor indeed put pressure on the manufacturers to come to terms. Hoping to resolve the crisis, he returned to Washington on September 22 for another meeting. There he engaged in a heated discussion with manufacturers' representative Clay Williams, president of R. J. Reynolds Tobacco Company. Williams offered a 17 cent per pound average for as much tobacco as had been marketed in 1932 but not for all of the larger 1933 crop. Ehringhaus reminded Williams that manufacturers had "lived sumptuously and made fine profits," but tobacco growers had "not received anything but wages of a peon and slave."[14] The discussions continued.

Low prices and the marketing holiday fanned the flames of resentment in the tobacco country. On September 14, H. Kemper Cooke of Galivants Ferry, South Carolina, vividly portrayed the conditions among tobacco farmers. "I have seen mothers go from the curing barns late in the night, worn out and exhausted," he wrote to Wallace, "their small children sleepy and pitiful, and crying like hungry pigs following the sow. I have seen men, strong men, bow down between the tobacco rows, like an inverted V, cropping in the August sun with not a dry thread on them. I have seen them faint from overheat and dragged from the field on a tobacco drag." He had seen them work seven days a week, stay up with the curing barns all week, and still not receive much pay because the landlords did not have money to pay them with.

Cooke contrasted this work routine with the wages that R. J. Reynolds Tobacco Company paid and the changes that the National Recovery Administration (NRA) codes would effect. If the government could raise the wages of laborers who toiled for R. J. Reynolds, he asked, "why can't you do something for his slaves all over Virginia, the Carolinas, and Georgia, who toil in the hot sun for him from daylight til dawn, and who produce the product on which the very life of his industry depends?" If the New Deal really stood for "a more equitable distribution of wealth," he asked, how could he allow manufacturers to "add to their fabulous fortunes, increase the centralization of wealth, and cast a shadow of of gloom and despair over the hearts of millions of men, women and children?" Other letters eloquently called for higher prices.[15]

When the markets reopened on September 25, prices increased only a few cents per pound and hovered at 12 to 13 cents. J. Y. Joyner, who had been an advocate for higher prices and marketing reform, wrote to Ehringhaus from Greenville on September 27 that the markets there were blocked and that prices remained low. He saw "dissatisfaction among farmers," "wild talk," and "danger of violence." Two days before, dissatisfaction had already caused alarm in the village of Wendell, near Raleigh. Outraged at low prices, farmers swarmed into the Star Warehouse, halting sales. That night a farmer named Lonnie M. Knott addressed a crowd of 250 growers, telling them to insist on a guarantee of higher prices or to keep the market closed. He asked all who agreed with him to raise their hands and yell. When pressed to give a vote to those who wanted to keep the markets open, he asked anyone who wanted "to continue giving away tobacco" to raise his hand. The head of the local tobacco board had some words with Knott, and a scuffle broke out. The mayor stepped in and restored order.[16]

Two weeks after the markets opened the government and manufacturers reached terms on a marketing agreement. After threatening manufacturers with a mandatory licensing agreement, on October 12 the government accepted a compromise. Domestic buyers would purchase as much tobacco as they had a year before at an average of 17 cents a pound, and foreign firms agreed to abide by the spirit of the agreement. The government won the right to inspect manufacturers' financial books, one of the most bitterly contested points of the negotiations.[17]

Immediately after the agreement, prices rose quickly to the promised 17 cents, and buyers purchased the remainder of the crop at that average. The 1934 reduction plan contained a provision to raise the average price to 17 cents for farmers who had sold their crops before the agreement. As Anthony Badger makes clear in his recent study, the economic impact was electric: "In the Christmas shopping spree, used car lots were cleared for the first time in a decade. Railroad traffic increased, bank deposits in some areas doubled, and taxes were being paid three times as fast as in earlier years. The Regional Agricultural Credit Corporation reported a 99 percent collection of loans due on the year's crop—the best record of any region in the country." The 1933 price for flue-cured tobacco averaged 15.3 cents per pound, compared to 11.6 and 8.4 cents in the two preceding years. "In no other major commodity were the benefits of the New Deal in terms of prices and cash receipts for the crop seen so tangibly or so quickly," Badger concluded.[18]

Although bright-leaf tobacco farmers sighed with relief after prices rose in the fall of 1933, they had already anticipated problems with the allotment program that would reduce acreage in 1934. In an extremely perceptive letter, Maynard P. West of Axton, Virginia, wrote to his congressman not only outlining some of his community's problems but also proposing a solution. He had attended a meeting in Martinsville a few days before, he wrote on September 13. Many farmers, he observed, would gladly reduce not only their tobacco acreage but the number of tenants as well. He proposed a plan to protect such tenants. "I believe it would be just to allow a tennant to carry his allotment with him from farm to farm," he wrote with unsure spelling, "and require Land lords to reduce their planting in acordance with the total indicated allotment allowed them and their tennants." By assigning allotments to tenants, a landlord could bargain with them and set up an operation that suited his farm. Unless tenants received some protection, West feared their dispossession. "I heard one land lord say yesterday that he was giving his tennant orders to move, so he could increase his production for him self. I think that tennant is entitled to carry his allotment with him. For unless some credit is given a tennant we may find our selves confronted with the problem of a lot of homeless folk who are victim of circumstances."

West saw another tenant class that would suffer, that of the standing renter. A landlord signed a preliminary agreement, and the farmer who rented from him "was told that he had no allotment." Without some allotment the standing renter had no way to secure a farm to work. West hoped that the men in the Tobacco Section would see the logic of his suggestion. "My only aprehension about this," he concluded, "is that theory will triumph over experience and sound judgement."[19]

His congressman passed the letter to the Tobacco Section for comment, and J. B. Hutson replied. "After considering different agreements for production adjustment," Hutson wrote, "we decided that it would be necessary to contract with the owners or responsible operators of land if we were to be assured of any control of production." To give the allotments to the tenants, he suggested, "would cause the landlords to bid for these tenants in order to increase the acreage of tobacco on their particular farm." He concluded that this would put the landlord "in an even worse position than he would be with a production allotment for his farm." True to the spirit of the AAA, Hutson sided with landlords in this matter. Ironically, at the same time that Huston rejected this option, southern rice growers—not landlords—received allotments. West's suggestion would have given to the people who had grown tobacco the right to continue growing it, and, more importantly, award to tenants and sharecroppers a bargaining tool to secure better terms from landlords. West furnished one of the few original ideas that could have protected small growers.[20]

Hutson dismissed outright the problem that West suggested would affect standing renters, yet on September 15, 1933, Thomas R. Buckman of Clover, Virginia, complained of just such a situation. He was a tenant farmer, he wrote, and had been growing ten acres of tobacco with two workers. For the approaching 1934 crop, he had rented a farm that had a smaller allotment. He asked if he would be bound by the owner's allotment or his own historical production. Hutson's reply was curt; the allotment went with the land. When a small farmer from Warsaw, North Carolina, asked for protection under the reduction formula, Hutson replied that the program required all farmers to cut their acreage. "This program offers the same advantage to the small farmer that it offers to the larger farmer," he replied to Farmer H. Jones.[21]

R. S. Hazelwood of Vernon Hill, Virginia, feared that landlords would receive all the benefits from the program. Landlords, he wrote, did not even want tenants to attend the meetings that explained the program. "They tried to slick around as if they had something up their sleeve, and it is causing wide spread alarm," he cautioned. "Land owners in this section has gone so far as to count up how mutch money will be returned to them, and has in many cases decided, in stead of reducing each man's crop on their farm they will raise the required amount with less help and make the other men move. So you see instead of helping all the people it will put thousands of men out of homes." He had no confidence in landlords. "If the renters and share croppers are left to the mercy of the land owners they will fare worse than the Belgians did when invaded by the German Army," he concluded.[22]

Landlords also resented government intrusion into their farm operations. "I have 40 families looking to me for food," wrote Selma A. Katzenstein of Warren Plains, North Carolina, in February 1934. "They are halfshare tenants." People in the community had coerced him to sign the reduction agreement "by the threat of salting seed beds." The AAA reduction would mean that each tenant family would have only a three-acre allotment. "They can't live on it," he observed, "yet I did not want to start a civil war." The Civil Works Administration paid $1.80 a day, he argued, so he wondered if tenants would till three acres of tobacco when they could earn more from the government. "All the world is not made in one pattern," he pointed out. He argued that the program did not work for a man who had tenants. Obviously, Katzenstein wanted to keep all his tenants. "Please leave us free to just dodge the sheriff," he concluded, "please let us alone."[23]

Although most studies minimize the disruption of the labor force in the tobacco country during the New Deal, Lorena Hickok, who toured the country for Harry Hopkins in 1934, reported that both the Depression and the AAA swept people from the land. Writing from Raleigh, North Carolina, in February 1934, she estimated that 10,000 former farmers had no place to till. "The number has been increasing for some years, owing to a reduction in acreage forced by the depression," she explained. Some farmers had not been on the land for six years. She also admitted that no matter what landlords said about keeping their tenants, towns were filling up with rural people. In Wilson, North Carolina, she discovered that 300 former farmers had moved into the town of 13,000 people. In fifty cases, she wrote, their landlords moved them and paid their first week's rent. Three-quarters of them were black, and nearly all were illiterate and sick. Those left on the land were not doing well either, and she described a family that lived in a tobacco barn. There were two daughters, sixteen and eighteen, and the younger one had won her heart. "Rather slight, with fair hair and the kind of blue eyes that look right into your own, this girl wore over her thin dress a pair of overalls, worn but recently washed. And pinned on her bosom, as one wears a brooch, was a campaign button of 1932 —a profile of the President."[24]

Hickok's impressionistic findings paralleled those of Gordon W. Blackwell and a team of researchers from the University of North Carolina and the Tennessee Valley Authority who studied displaced tenants on relief in North Carolina's Greene, Nash, and Wilson counties. Blackwell estimated that "approximately ten per cent of the tenant farm families in counties having a tenancy rate above 60 per cent have been displaced in the past five years and have become partially dependent upon government relief." Blacks displaced from the land outnumbered whites by 15 percent to 6 percent. Blackwell estimated that there were "between 8,000 and 11,000 farmer families who do not have a crop for 1934," and three-quarters of them were on relief.

The rural tenure situation had begun to deteriorate in the 1920s, and by 1932 "many landlords were unable to furnish tenants for another year." Even before the AAA reduction plan, "thousands of tenants were set adrift each year." Instead of setting up tenants, many landlords in the North Carolina tobacco and cotton area hired wagehands. And the AAA took its toll. Blackwell estimated that, due to acreage reduction, there were several thousand fewer sharecroppers in 1934 than the previous year. Many of the displaced families, as

Hickok suggested, ended up in small towns, hoping to obtain work in tobacco warehouses or with the government. "Higher prices for cotton and tobacco," he concluded, "do not benefit the farmer who has no land to tend."[25]

As the tobacco program matured, Hutson addressed the problems of small growers and tenants who had not been displaced. He reduced the rental payment to landlords and increased the benefit payment, awarding tenants a greater share of government money. Under the orginal AAA, Hutson increased the benefit payments to those who had been allotted fewer than four acres. Under the Kerr Tobacco Act in 1934, 6 percent of the county allotments could be used to supplement those who did not have an equitable 1934 allotment, so long as two-thirds went to growers who produced under 1,500 pounds. In 1935 the provision allowed a farmer with a base acreage of under 3.2 acres to plant up to three acres despite the reduction formula. In 1938 it protected growers with a base poundage of at least 3,200 pounds. In 1939 small farmers whose allotments had been decreased over time could increase them by 20 percent, as long as they did not produce more than 3,200 pounds of tobacco.[26]

While small growers pondered the effect of acreage reduction, large owners, life insurance companies among them, offered cooperation with the AAA. Arthur M. Collens, vice-president of the Phoenix Mutual Life Insurance Company, wrote to Hutson in September 1933 asking for some clarifications. The county agent of Appling County, Georgia, had sent him a contract. "As we interpret the contract," he wrote, "by signing said contract, we agree that the reduction in production will be carried out on every farm which we own in this particular county." Although he wanted to cooperate and had urged all tenants to sign, "cooperation on our part on any blanket basis presents tremendous difficulties from the standpoint of administration." The large holdings made it "very difficult" to control "a large number of separate properties upon any of which tobacco may be grown by the tenant." If some tenants refused, he queried, would it jeopardize others? Collens did not believe that he could force any tenant to sign against his will, but he wondered if "we assume full liability for the tenants's nonconformance."[27]

In January 1934 Glen E. Rogers, manager of farm properties for the Metropolitan Life Insurance Company, wrote to Hutson outlining how his company handled the government program. He also gave an indication of how life insurance companies handled sharecroppers. His company would sign the contracts as producer and furnish its share of fertilizer, although he did not reveal the share. Even though the contracts did not specify this, the tenant would share the rental payments on a 50–50 basis. The company also bought fertilizer in large lots, allowing tenants to share in the reduced price but also giving the company a say in its application.

Like a traditional landlord, the Metropolitan furnished supervision of sharecroppers with "well trained farm supervisors." These agents would do all the paperwork for the tenants and save local committees the trouble. "We find," Rogers explained, "that tenants do not fully understand all of the provisions and clauses of the contract sufficiently to make them up themselves and most of them are totally confused over the making up of plats and maps and accurately showing the rented acres set aside." He asked if Hutson accepted this interpretation. Hutson wrote that he was satisfied with the arrangement: "Since the contract provides that all of the rental payment be paid to the landowner or other person who has complete control over the land for 1934 and 1935, any arrangement which you may make with your tenants regarding the distribution of this payment should be satisfactory to the Secretary."[28]

As tobacco prices rose to the 17-cent parity price, farmers decided that they liked the taste of the government patent medicine. As odd as it seemed, they were promised more money for raising less tobacco—something that had not sunk into their consciousness in all the years of volunteer marketing plans. The contracts arrived in December, and agricultural extension agents distributed them to tobacco-growing counties for signing. Throughout the month signed contracts trickled in, and farmers discussed the merits of the program. Governor Ehringhaus again urged cooperation, and the *Progressive Farmer*, the Bible of many tobacco farmers, put the issue simply and forcefully: "Everybody who prefers 20-cent tobacco to 10-cent tobacco should sign!" By January 21, 1934, some 95 percent of North Carolina's tobacco farmers had signed.[29]

While it was difficult to police the accuracy of every reduction contract, complaints about noncooperating growers spurred action. Since the origin of cooperative marketing ideas, possible holdouts threatened every effort. In 1933 and 1934 farmers looked to the government to punish neighbors who did not cooperate. Again, relying on a federal policeman must have created ambivalence, for it conflicted with the stubbornness and independence that typified farmers. Yet they also wanted to be free of debt, and only through high prices could they achieve that. At any rate, in June 1934 the Kerr Tobacco Act plugged this loophole. Sponsored by Congressman John H. Kerr of Warrenton, North Carolina, and Senator Ellison D. Smith of South Carolina, the act prevented noncooperating growers from profiting from higher prices by placing a tax on all tobacco sold at the markets. Growers who signed government contracts received tax-payment warrants that covered their tax. Nonsigners had to pay a 33.3 percent tax on the tobacco they marketed. Small growers who marketed 1,500 pounds or less could also benefit from any excess in poundage that came about in the county. By hitting noncooperating growers with a tax and providing relief for small growers, Congress further sweetened the government tonic. Even growers who had refused to sign in the winter got another chance to farm with Uncle Sam.[30]

The government money that flowed into the tobacco areas raised questions about the traditional arrangements between landlords and tenants. The payments that arrived in the summer of 1934, equalizing the price of 1933 tobacco sold before prices rose, tempted landlords. The checks were made out to the tobacco growers—not to landlords. Although incoming letters do not survive, the replies from the Tobacco Section reveal what planters had on their minds. "A payment by the government to a person can not be assigned, pledged, hypothecated, or mortgaged by the person to whom the payment is to be made," J. Con Lanier wrote to a South Carolinian. The government made the payment to the person who earned it. "If, thereafter, he wishes to apply it to a debt or an obligation it is perfectly proper that he do so." Lanier, a native of Pitt County, North Carolina, played a key role as contact for flue-cured tobacco politicians, warehousemen, and farmers, but he also made it clear in this case that tenants had rights to federal money. Ever since the sharecropping and tenancy system emerged after the Civil War, landlords had controlled nearly all money flowing to tenants. It was difficult to accept the new ways of the government master.[31] Yet the AAA Tobacco Section, unlike the Cotton Section, insisted that landlords abide by the letter of the law.

As summer work continued in 1934, farmers cast an anxious eye toward Washington, where the government and the manufacturers wrangled over a marketing agreement. Again Governor Ehringhaus and Clay Williams had words as negotiations faltered. Williams held his ground, and ultimately the talks broke off, as he claimed that there was no reason for an agreement; prices that autumn would be so high that a set scale would actually discourage bidding. Skeptical growers interpreted Williams's statement to mean low prices; they waited. The *Progressive Farmer* observed that the farmers had done their part and have "turned the spotlight on the buying interests. Now it's up to them to deliver."[32]

When tobacco markets had opened in 1933, farmers had angrily denounced buyers and talked of ruin. In 1934 there was even more excitement, but the noise came from "jubilant whoops," not angry outrage. The Border Belt had followed the Georgia Belt in sales that ranged from 22 to 32 cents per pound. When the Eastern Belt opened in late August, Rocky Mount sales averaged $27.82 per hundred pounds, up from $11.22 a year before. Wilson averaged only 54 cents less, and Winston-Salem claimed "a new 1934 opening day record for the South"—$30.20 per hundred pounds.[33] Farmers looked at sales tickets with disbelief. After five years of official depression and almost fifteen years of dragging prices, they thought that the millennium had arrived. Ed Long of Rougemont, North Carolina, a black farmer, furnished Anthony Badger with an example of the AAA tobacco program: "In 1932 five acres of tobacco had brought him $11.30. In 1933 five acres of equal-quality tobacco had yielded $480.00, but in 1934, even with his acreage cut, he received $1,472.00."[34]

The welcomed transfusion of cash into the bright-leaf Tobacco Belt attracted an even larger than usual number of people who leached off tobacco farmers. Market days had always been scenes of farmers with cash burning holes in their pockets and a sideshow of people ready to take it from them. From pinhookers who speculated on tobacco to con artists who tried to pick cash from farmers' pockets, markets furnished a carnival atmosphere. Merchants obviously enjoyed the infusion of money, and for once farmers did not seem shy about spending it. The Winston-Salem *Journal* reported that, in the eastern part of the state, farmers who a few months earlier "were grinning philosophically from their Hoovercarts" were now buying second-hand automobiles. The *Journal* reported the story of a black farmer who met one of his white friends while on the way to market with his tobacco. After exchanging pleasantries, the white man began asking about the crop, and the black man found it increasingly difficult to continue his deference. Impatient, he finally said, "Boss, I must get moving along because I want to be sho and sell this tobacco while them buyers are drunk."[35]

In early 1934, Representative John W. Flanagan, Jr., of Virginia's 9th District worked with the Tobacco Section to draft a bill that would re-

Farmers listening to the sales talk of a patent medicine vendor during a tobacco auction in a warehouse. Durham, North Carolina. November 1939. Marion Post Wolcott. (LC USF 34 52783-D, Library of Congress)

form problems in warehouses and the auction system. Farmers had complained about many of these abuses for years, the Bristol congressman observed. The bill would license warehousemen and weighmen, inspect scales (which were often off by several pounds), control the opening date of markets, and set other regulations. The bill also called for government grading. While none of these measures challenged their business structure, warehousemen reacted with characteristic paranoia. Congressman Lindsay Warren, receiving word of the bill from Con Lanier in the Tobacco Section, warned warehousemen and urged them to oppose the bill. Warren, in a strange twist of logic, interpreted the bill as an attempt to "destroy the auction system." [36]

While warehousemen denounced the reform proposals at congressional hearings, the NRA warehouse negotiations reached a conclusion, and warehousmen, perhaps to minimize the need for a law, did accept some changes. They agreed to sell no more than 375 lots of tobacco an hour, and a grower would have fifteen minutes to decide whether or not to accept his bid. Weighmen were licensed, and a string of abuses was made illegal. Nothing in the NRA code threatened warehousemen. It did not mention government grading. More important, warehousemen obtained all they could have wanted, for the voting members of the code authority, as Badger explained, "were to be elected by the warehousemen's associations, and the first administrator was to be Con Lanier, who had done so much to secure agreement on the code and who was well known as a friend of the warehousemen."[37]

Warehousemen were illogical on the government grading issue. Even after a law passed that set up limited grading, they opposed implementation at the local level. In 1936 four North Carolina markets voted on government grading, and only one refused—Smithfield. Con Lanier and the warehousemen continued to fight government grading, but ultimately it spread through the flue-cured area.[38]

As the new grading requirements and other government reforms took hold, warehousemen invented strategies of protest against the government. Like other businessmen who resented extra paperwork, they projected every problem onto the government. In the Georgia-Florida belt in 1938 a number of complaints revealed this attack at work. In Vidalia, Georgia, a concerned farmer who had somehow lost his pile of tobacco approached the warehouseman, who replied that the government had him "tied up with office work." The farmer would have to return later. "A number of warehousemen allow their office help to continually fuss and complain to farmers about the government 'interfering in their business and delaying the issuing of checks to farmers,'" an AAA memorandum noted. One warehouse employee told an irate farmer whose bill had been incorrectly tallied that the "government representative could not even add much less get anything else correct. The pounds on the warehouse bill," the memo revealed, "had been added by an employee of the warehouse." The larger the government role grew in the tobacco culture, the more handy it became as a scapegoat.[39]

At every level during the New Deal the federal government's involvement became more obvious. From rural areas farmers looked with awe to Washington and with respect bordering on worship to Franklin D. Roosevelt. They had seen the AAA tobacco program bring them more money than at any time since the boom days during World War I. When neighbors failed at farming, they could often find work with the CWA or the WPA and send their children to CCC camps. The money that they earned returned to the local economy, spreading prosperity to merchants and bankers. While warehousemen fought off every threat to their lucrative position as the trade center for growers and buyers, they were reaping greater profits, for they also shared in the farmers' prosperity. Tobacco companies, although they paid more for leaf under the AAA marketing agreements, were almost immune to the Depression.

Of all these groups, manufacturers opposed the New Deal most vehemently. They especially opposed the processing tax, and in 1935 they lobbied against amendments to continue the licensing and taxing powers of the Secretary of Agriculture. Clay Williams, who did most of the government relations work for the tobacco industry, denounced the "revolutionary character" of the processing tax. From his testimony before congressional committees Williams implied that the manufacturers were undergoing extreme hardship because of the tax.[40]

The Bureau of Agricultural Economics in the Department of Agriculture, however, conducted a confidential study which revealed that manufacturers passed the tax on to consumers and did not bear it themselves. The BAE study revealed that in nearly every case the processors of commodities either passed the tax backward to growers by offering lower prices or forward to consumers through higher prices. The tobacco processing tax went into effect on October 1, 1933, and lasted until the *Hoosac Mills* decision on January 6, 1936. Tobacco presented BAE statisticians with the complex problem of evaluating the various types of tobacco, the many different manufactured products, the mix of tobaccos in each item, demand elasticities, and margins. Ironically, by raising prices the processing tax proved a bonanza to the major brands. "The taxes made it more difficult for some of the price-cutting units of the industry to operate, thus permitting the rise in price." Taking all these factors into consideration, the report concluded that "it appears probable that tobacco processors as a group not only could but actually did pass on to consumers a large part if not all of the processing taxes."

The major manufacturers not only passed on the processing tax to consumers but also received the additional benefit of hurting the sales of ten-cent brands. Despite all this, Clay Williams attempted to defeat the processing tax time and again. Perhaps he reasoned that government intervention in the tobacco industry presented a greater threat than competition among manufacturers. At any rate, the manufacturing industry, especially the cigarette industry, actually prospered from the processing tax. By 1934 cigarette production had returned to pre-Depression figures.[41]

*A country store located on a dirt road. A gasoline pump is on the right and a kerosene pump is on the left of the door. Negro men are sitting on the porch. Gordonton, North Carolina. July 1939. Dorothea Lange. (*LC USF *34 19911-E, Library of Congress)*

Tobacco farmers' reaction to the 1935 AAA program illustrated how quickly they had become addicted to the acreage reduction potion, for they predicted that, by planting 85 percent of their base acreage, prices would fall. When the markets opened and prices hovered at 15 to 16 cents per pound, farmers attempted to reenact the 1933 scenario and called for a marketing holiday. Hutson and the Tobacco Section resisted this pressure, insisting that prices were at or above parity. As the AAA stalled, prices rose and in 1935 averaged 20 cents per pound, compared with 27.3 cents the year before. The larger crop, however, brought in $10.5 million more to growers.[42]

When the markets closed after the 1935 season, tobacco farmers could look back over the past three years with satisfaction. Prices had risen from 10 cents per pound to more than double that. At last many farmers could lift their heads and walk with dignity; they could buy clothes for their wives and children; and they could look forward to the future with some degree of confidence. The years of indifference to the federal government had ended—the New Deal had won a rural constituency in the South. When the Supreme Court, in the *Hoosac Mills* case in January 1936, ruled the Agricultural Adjustment Administration unconstitutional, a wave of nausea spread through the Tobacco Belt. Legislators promised aid, farm groups invented plans, and tobacco farmers girded for a fight to preserve the program that had redeemed them from poverty.[43]

With uncharacteristic haste, Congress passed the Soil Conservation and Domestic Allotment Act a month and a half after the Supreme Court decision. Farmers could secure payments for reducing soil-depleting crops and for planting more soil-building crops. In practice, then, tobacco acreage could be reduced just as it had been under the AAA, keeping supply and demand balanced.[44]

Ultimately Congress passed a revised Agricultural Adjustment Act in 1938 that established a new legislative program for crop control and parity prices. Tobacco, as usual, presented a special case. More than any other farmers, tobacco growers insisted on tight production controls. As legislators who supported other commodity programs worked for compromise, tobacco representatives wrote their own bill. The urgency that had characterized 1933 activities had dissipated, as prices for the 1937 crop proved excellent even without compulsory control.[45]

The tobacco title of the bill assured tight crop control. The Secretary of Agriculture, after considering the year's carryover of tobacco, could recommend marketing quotas, and then farmers would vote on the program. Small growers who produced less than 3,200 pounds received protection, and a 50 percent tax punished farmers who did not cooperate. Immediately tobacco growers in North Carolina approved quotas for 1938.[46]

Throughout the tobacco-growing areas an army of enthusiastic drummers peddled the new AAA program. When Farm Bureau and AAA spokesmen could not reach every county, Con Lanier appealed to his warehouse friends in Greenville and Rocky Mount to sign resolutions and buy radio time. A warehouseman named Bill Fenner of Rocky Mount, who toured eastern North Carolina plugging control, admitted his motivation: "I was working for Bill Fenner because the more the farmer gets for his tobacco the more I get for selling it from the warehouse." Not only warehousemen but also the Farm Bureau, which primarily represented large growers, as well as bankers and merchants, knew that prosperous farmers meant better earnings throughout the economy. The campaign stressed that a vote against control could mean the return of depression; it was enough to get the attention of tobacco farmers. Despite some farmers who saw in the new AAA visions of socialism and oppressive government control, the 1938 referendum carried, with 86.2 percent of the growers who voted approving control.[47]

The new program got off to a rocky start. Many farmers had already planted their crops before they received an allotment. More important, farmers would not market their acreage allotment, for in the summer they would receive a poundage quota. This seemed an unnecessary complication, and many farmers did not understand the distinctions in this formula. First the AAA explained the acreage allotment scheme. "Acreage allotments of tobacco under the program are determined on the basis of past acreage of tobacco," W. A. Minor explained to Eugenia Boone of Castalia, North Carolina. The formula considered "land, labor and equipment available for the production of tobacco; crop rotation practices; and the soil and other physical factors affecting the production of tobacco. Special consideration is given farms for which the acreage allotments are small."[48]

As the summer months passed, farmers became apprehensive over the coming announcement of poundage quotas. Many feared they had planted acreage that would yield more pounds than their quota. Attorney Warren R. Mixon of Ocilla, Georgia, complained to Senator Richard B. Russell that farmers were in an uproar over this problem. "Now, this county has already been cut to the bone on the acreage allotments to tobacco, and to now take another thrashing in the poundage allotments is more than our folks will stand for without a rebellion against the entire program." Georgia, he suggested, did not receive fair treatment on allotments. The county agent had been trying to keep farmers "sort of content and quieted off" until county poundage quotas were announced. "The farmers," he revealed, "are mad under their skin, and it keeps him busy talking with them and trying to get them to hold themselves and trust that the whole thing will come out better than they are apprehensive at present."[49]

The AAA patiently tried to interpret the 1938 program to growers, yet the more it explained, the less farmers understood. They knew neither how much they could plant nor how much they could market. As Badger pointed out, county agents did not generally explain (as the Franklin County, North Carolina, agent did) that growers could ignore the allotments as long as they kept within the poundage quotas.[50]

Landlords also continued to have problems adjusting to farming with the government. Newton Watkins, superintendent of the Ben

Hill, Georgia, public schools, owned a 650-acre farm and ran two tenants and one wagehand. He had cooperated with the AAA all along, he stressed, and in 1938 had planted 18.5 acres of cotton, 9.1 acres of peanuts, and 2.5 acres of tobacco. "The reason I have tobacco this year," he explained, "is two of my tenants farmed last year in Coffee County and planted tobacco and their landlord replaced them with wage hands and they had to move." Although he had planted tobacco before 1933, the county agent told him that he would be a new grower. When he went to sign his farm worksheet, the county agent told him that there would be no poundage allotment for his tobacco. His tenants were entitled to a fair deal, he insisted. "They were turned out by Mr. A. R. Royal last year for wage hands this year and now they have made a crop within the required demands of the farm program and can not sell the products of their labor without a penalty." Unless some adjustment was approved, he wrote, "I will be compelled to pass them on another year and do as Royal did, work my land with wage hands and let these families go on the relief." The Tobacco Section suggested that Watkins return to the county office and ask for "a tobacco marketing quota for your farm." From the information included in his letter, "it appears that the farm will be entitled to a small quota."[51]

When the markets opened in 1938, prices averaged less than a cent below the 1937 figure, yet the total income to tobacco growers fell because of the smaller crop. After growers received their poundage quotas, they explored the flexibility built into the marketing scheme. B. B. Sugg, co-owner of the New Star Warehouse in Greenville, North Carolina, warned J. B. Hutson of rumored fraudulent schemes to obtain extra poundage allotments, and he reported rumors that growers in Georgia and Florida were attempting to circumvent poundage quotas by posing as both sellers and buyers. There were also widespread reports of farmers illegally exchanging and altering marketing quota cards. Newton H. Eildon of Madison, North Carolina, wrote to Senator Robert R. Reynolds, revealing that a leading citizen had observed some marketing cards that "showed only half as many pounds sold as the tobacco sales slip" revealed. He was not sure that this was true, but he warned that such collusion could undermine the AAA program and reduce the price of tobacco. At least one grower speculated on marketing quotas, buying up extra pounds from growers who did not market their full quota.[52]

By the fall of 1938 confusion and anger ruled the tobacco belt. The complexity of the new AAA program alienated many farmers, and prices did not please them. Charges of altered marketing cards and speculation only added to the fury. While many tobacco farmers talked about the coming December referendum for the 1939 growing year, merchants, warehousemen, the Farm Bureau, extension agents, and AAA administrators launched a campaign to secure a marketing agreement for the coming year. To head off the confusion that reigned in 1938, E. Y. Floyd, who ran the AAA in North Carolina, got the marketing quotas to the farmers by December 1. Unless the quotas were adopted, advocates warned, cotton growers in Georgia, Alabama, Florida, and South Carolina would switch to tobacco, increase the supply, and drive down prices.

Throughout the tobacco area farm leaders, bankers, warehousemen, the Farm Bureau, and, in the case of North Carolina, Governor Clyde Hoey and editor Clarence Poe all backed the government plan. This campaign did not convince tobacco farmers. Flue-cured farmers voted only 56.8 percent for the 1939 program, less than the two-thirds needed for approval.[53] No doubt many tobacco growers, accustomed to a more simple way of life, voted against the program simply because they saw it assuming unnecessary complexity. They did not mind government intrusion but objected to total federal immersion.

The defeat of acreage control for 1939 did not end the federal tobacco program. As the markets opened in 1939, Congress passed amendments to the tobacco program, making it more attractive to growers. Legislators felt more confident after the Supreme Court, in April 1939, upheld the constitutionality of the 1938 Agricultural Adjustment Act. Attempting to simplify the tobacco program and also to help small growers, Congress levied a ten-cent per pound penalty tax instead of the 50 percent figure and granted a 20 percent greater allotment for farmers who grew less than 3,200 pounds to help them reach that magic figure. To give farmers and buyers a better idea of the next year's program, the Secretary of Agriculture could announce the quota at any time from when the markets opened until December 1.[54]

When the markets opened in Georgia in 1939, prices were low. While some farmers were content and blamed this on the low quality of leaf, others met to demand government intervention in the markets. Meanwhile, the AAA, Farm Bureau, and other control advocates lobbied for a referendum on a new program. Throughout August farmers attended meetings, heard various programs suggested, and wondered about tobacco prices. When war broke out in Europe on September 1, farmers did not have long to speculate on the effect. Eight days later the Imperial Tobacco Company pulled its buyers off the markets. The result dwarfed the 1933 emergency, for the Imperial customarily bought one-third of the best grades of the flue-cured crop. The next day the markets closed. The Middle Belt opening was set for September 11, a Monday, and before the announcement by Imperial many farmers had arrived at the Durham market. Warehouses sold off all the tobacco already on the warehouse floors—1,258,000 pounds—and then closed.[55]

As had happened in 1933, representatives of the tobacco industry met in Washington to make marketing plans for the 1939 crop and to set a referendum. With such a large volume of tobacco awaiting auction, the representatives knew that the government could take no action until future production had been decided. After considering several options, the government decided to purchase the Imperial's share using British buyers and Commodity Credit Corporation funds. This would place money directly in the hands of the growers, and the Imperial could buy the tobacco at any time before July 1941.[56]

With this agreement in hand, the proponents of the federal program flooded the tobacco country with literature supporting control. The entire government and financial structure of the Tobacco Belt mobilized —AAA spokesmen, farm organizations, politicians, warehousemen, bankers, and merchants. All of these groups saw their interests linked with those of the growers. Control opponents were buried beneath this propaganda barrage. When the votes were tallied after the October 7 deadline, 89.9 percent of the voting growers approved. The markets reopened, and prices averaged 14.9 cents per pound. The larger volume put almost as much money into the growers' pockets as had the higher prices a year before.[57]

To further stabilize growers, Congress provided for a vote on a three-year control package, and in July 1940 growers overwhelmingly approved. The government continued to buy tobacco for the British without assurances that the weed would ever be delivered. Prices for the 1940 crop averaged 16.4 cents per pound, but the reduced supply made it a bad year for farmers. Even as tobacco was being auctioned off in the fall of 1940, tobacco politicians in Washington again changed the base period for parity prices, moving it from 1919–29 to August 1934–July 1939. This raised the parity price even higher.[58]

The emergency created by war in Europe led to massive and precedent-setting changes in the tobacco program. Through all these changes, the structure remained basically the same, with owners and tenants tilling small three- to six-acre tobacco patches using the same implements current at the turn of the century. The lack of mechanization preserved the old work culture, and this sharply contrasted with the dynamic changes in the cotton culture in the late 1930s.

7

*As far as the rice milling
agreement is concerned, it is the
biggest mess I have ever seen in
my life.*
—*Frank A. Godchaux, Sr., 1934*

"Struggling on
Promises": The
Federal Rice
Program

While the Tobacco and Cotton AAA Sections forcefully carried out government policy, the Rice Section proved weak and inept. During the 1930s it experimented, equivocated, faltered, and in the end neither contributed stability nor spurred mechanization. It created more problems than it solved and entangled rice farmers and millers with the federal government. Despite its shaky administration, the Rice Section imaginatively assigned allotments to producers, regardless of tenure—not to landlords, as had the Tobacco and Cotton Sections. This innovation contained broad implications, for with other commodities tenants and sharecroppers could only continue on the land at the invitation of landlords. Producer allotments offered an alternative, a road not taken with other commodities and one that could have avoided the worst abuses threatening landless farmers.

Unlike cotton and tobacco growers, rice farmers had adjusted to market forces and balanced production with demand after the World War I boom collapsed. Although the Depression drove prices even lower, rice's inclusion as a basic commodity in the Agricultural Adjustment Act and its relationship to other commodities such as wheat and corn had an almost magic effect as prices quickly climbed to parity level. This proved fortuitous, for in many ways the AAA rice program was mismanaged in 1933 and 1934. The highly mechanized state of rice farming protected growers against such major adjustments as beset the cotton culture during the 1930s, just as the intense hand labor of tobacco farmers protected them from massive displacement. The AAA rice program reiterates the immense differences in southern agriculture as well as the independent approaches of AAA commodity sections.

Throughout the winter and spring of 1933, anxious millers journeyed to Washington and attempted to influence government rice policy. Long before the Agricultural Adjustment Act passed on May 12, Rice Millers' Association newsletters reported that the Roosevelt administration wanted to reduce acreage and institute a processing tax. William McMillan Reid, executive vice-president of the Rice Millers' Association, occasionally visited Washington along with leading millers, and he reported on the progress of rice legislation—and on rumors. Reid began his career with the Orange Rice Mill in Orange, Texas, spent several years in the San Juan, Puerto Rico, offices of the Rice Millers' Association, and then moved to take control of the daily business of the organization. He predicted in late April that "unsettled financial conditions" would keep acreage down by 15 to 20 percent. Of course, any acreage reduction would also cut the supply of rice going to the mills. Neither the the association nor large interests (such as Frank Godchaux's Louisiana State Rice Milling Company) could control contentious and single-minded millers, especially those in Louisiana.[1]

Prices increased even as farmers, millers, and administration spokesmen discussed a potential program for rice in the spring and summer of 1933. On May 30 Frank A. Godchaux, one of the most prestigious leaders of the rice industry, asked Secretary Henry A. Wallace to move cautiously in setting up a rice program. "Prices to farmer on rough rice have already increased more than 100% in the last sixty days," he observed. Suspecting that the 1933 crop would be relatively small, he correctly prophesied that "the natural law of supply and demand will accomplish what the bill is designed to do withot the expense of applying the measures authorized in the bill." Godchaux also saw an opportunity to stabilize the rice industry, which he argued had "not yet entirely 'found itself.'" Explaining to Wallace that some of the larger millers, by using name brands and good advertising, were creating a domestic demand for their product, he denounced "one stand" mills that sold for low prices and neglected promotion. Godchaux insisted that he spoke not only for the large millers but also for small farmers;

he had investments in rice land, canal companies, and mills. He promised Wallace full cooperation in making the New Deal rice program work.[2]

Throughout the summer and early fall of 1933 growers, millers, and the AAA debated a plan to increase prices, reduce acreage, and provide for orderly marketing. Growers petitioned for higher prices, and when Rice Section head A. J. S. Weaver announced a parity price of $3.00 per barrel, they sought congressional aid in raising prices higher. As the debate continued throughout September, Louisiana farmers marketed practically the entire Early Prolific crop at below the parity price. On October 13 the conflicting parties finally accepted a plan which in some regards resembled the tobacco program. Some 98 percent of the millers agreed to pay the parity price for rice. Distinct varieties were pegged at different levels. There was, however, no processing tax on rice. Millers also agreed to a fixed resale price for their product which included the cost of processing, packaging, and expenses of operation. Mills paid $.10 per barrel of rough rice into a marketing fund to encourage domestic consumption. The combination of market forces and the government program pushed prices up from as low as $.42 per hundred pounds in 1932 to $1.73 in 1933.[3]

Despite the agreement and the rise in price, when rice reached the market in the fall of 1933 not all millers complied with the marketing agreement. To deal with problems the AAA set up the Control Committee for the Southern Rice Milling Industry and called the organizational meeting for October 27, 1933. Millers from Texas, Louisiana, and Arkansas attended, as did Rice Section head Weaver and Charles G. Miller, who had worked for the growers' cooperative in Arkansas before joining the Rice Section as an expert in production, processing, and marketing. In order to reduce the surplus, millers suggested that Harry Hopkins could use rice "in feeding the starving people of the country." A few weeks later a major problem emerged. Neither Frank A. Godchaux's Louisiana State Rice Milling Company nor F. A. Farda's Standard Rice Company of Houston was paying on the agreed scale. Although both men were members, the committee recommended that these firms and other noncooperating millers be fined twice the amount of underpayment.[4]

On December 4 the Control Committee informed Secretary of Agriculture Wallace that it could not function with Farda and Godchaux on the committee. Godchaux argued that his firm had paid within 1/2 to 1 percent of the parity price and insisted that he would comply only if no fine were assessed. By December the problem had been reconciled: under pressure, Farda and Godchaux signed. Meanwhile, millers were upset with Weaver, who seemed incapable of interpreting policy, enforcing the marketing agreement, or influencing the administration. Reid both defended and disparaged the administrator, asserting that "you will find that there is a large amount of turmoil going on in Washington and he is just a cog in the wheel." Godchaux and Farda relentlessly criticized Weaver's vacillation. The confusion in 1933 was a portent of what would happen a year later.[5]

A miller could bypass the marketing agreement in any number of ways. William M. Reid suspected that some millers bought rough rice for cash to avoid keeping a record of it and later blended it with legitimate stock. Others, he suggested, used rebates. Such a miller, Reid charged, "has the mentality of a thief, and actually is a thief, because he is defrauding his competition." He called for strict enforcement of the agreement.[6]

Throughout the fall and winter of 1933 and 1934, growers and the Rice Section worked out details for an acreage reduction and allotment program for 1934. The Rice Section ruled that Arkansas and Louisiana growers should cut production by 20 percent, using the past five years' average, and Texas growers should cut by 22 percent, using the past three years as the base period. Louisiana growers complained that the base years and calculations for allotments were unfair, and some growers suspected that noncooperating farmers and millers would defeat the program. To ensure compliance, each county or parish had a chairman and three elected members, as well as an executive committee that reviewed applications; a state committee, composed of county chairmen, answered to the chief of the Rice Section and to the secretary of agriculture.[7]

Allotments went to producers—not to landlords, as in the other commodity programs. Two reasons emerged for creating this unique system. First, rice was a highly mechanized commodity requiring a large investment in binders, tractors, wells, and threshers. Tenants as well as landlords owned expensive equipment, and thus the Rice Section acknowledged that a rice farmer, no matter what his tenure, had a sizeable investment to protect and should receive the allotment. It was a guarantee that his capital could be utilized. Second, crop rotation practices encouraged producer allotments, for rice farmers moved crops from one part of a farm to the other and in many cases from farm to farm. A man might farm his own land one year and become a tenant the next, for growers along a canal network cooperated with each other to make the most economical use of their land.[8] In essence, each rice grower had enough equipment to cultivate a certain amount of rice, and the producer allotment guaranteed that he could take this "hip pocket" allotment and farm a suitable acreage. Had the AAA awarded producer allotments to tobacco and cotton farmers, the entire structural change in southern agriculture would have developed differently.

After southern millers signed the 1934 marketing agreement to enforce the AAA plan, federal machinery started moving in the rice program. The plan called for each mill to pay to the grower 60 percent of the secretary's price, or parity price, at the time of purchase. The remaining 40 percent went to an AAA trust fund that would be dispersed to cooperating producers, while farmers who refused to cooperate would not receive the additional 40 percent. As Rice Section chief A. J. S. Weaver summarized, "In effect this is the voluntary domestic allotment plan, virtually, the only difference being that the necessary funds are secured through a marketing agreement instead of through a processing tax."[9]

Millers as well as growers had reservations about the 1934 plan. In early May 1934 William M. Reid traveled to Washington to air his concerns about the 60/40 plan, and he immediately discovered that the Rice Section was in turmoil. When he arrived at the Agriculture Department, he learned that a Mr. Dickey had replaced Weaver as head of the Rice Section. After talking to Dickey about the 60/40 plan, he discovered that Dickey had been replaced by Charles G. Miller. He then pressed Miller on the plan, arguing that he saw a problem "between a non-signatory licensee and a signatory licensee." When the plan went into effect on July 1, he expected confusion and trouble.

Uncertainty over the obligations of cooperating millers continued throughout the summer, and on August 15 the Rice Section chief explained the rice program to the Millers' Advisory Committee in Beaumont. "It is my understanding," Miller began unsurely, "that the non-signatory mill does not have to make 60/40 check off and does not have to pay the voluntary 5¢ into the Marketing Fund." As millers attempted to digest the implications of that revelation, he continued, "Otherwise, he is in the same boat. He pays the Administration Fee and has to buy rice and pay the Secretary's price." Charles Miller did not understand, as did growers and millers, the potential for evasion, fraud, and confusion. Unperturbed, Miller averred that "the first Marketing Agreement we had was full of holes; as leaky as it could be," but he insisted that the new agreement was sound and would be enforced.[10]

Despite Miller's optimism, the 60/40 plan eroded, and by October millers demanded enforcement or abandonment. Charles G. Miller attended a meeting of the newly organized Millers' Advisory Council on October 4 and, before a hostile audience, defended the enforcement machinery. Frank A. Godchaux, Jr., charged that the Rice Section had not enforced the plan, and F. J. Jumonville asked that the section police huller mills and leave cooperating mills alone. "As far as the rice milling agreement is concerned," Frank Godchaux, Sr., declared, "it is the biggest mess I have ever seen in my life." Most violations occurred in Louisiana, although F. A. Farda admitted that Texas also had problems. George Smith of Arkansas, on the other hand, revealed that millers in his state experienced no problems with the 60/40 plan. When millers asked Reid again to travel to Washington, he showed the strain of dealing with the USDA bureaucracy. He could speak with individuals, he complained, but he could never get a group of them together for a decision. They only met in a group when they had the answer to a question. The meeting not only aired the shortcomings of the 60/40 plan but also condemned the irresolute Charles G. Miller. By December the plan had deteriorated to the point that it had to be abandoned.[11]

Some millers refused to cooperate, and when the enforcement machinery broke down, the resulting chaos destroyed the 60/40 plan. As John Wesley Bateman, the director of agricultural extension in Louisiana, explained, a small percentage of the large mills and nearly all of the plantation or huller mills refused to sign the agreement, and "it was possible for non-signatory and huller mills to purchase rice from non-cooperating growers and non-complying growers, paying therefore one hundred percent of the value of the crop." In effect, rice growers gained nothing by cooperating with the federal rice program. The problems were even more complex, for the 40 percent submitted to the Secretary was part of the value of the rice, "and before the mills could make the 40 percent check-off into the Trust Fund, consent had to be obtained from lienholders." When lienholders refused to waive their interest in the crop, mills could not check off the 40 percent, adding another burden to the program.[12]

Bateman complained that the rice acreage control program had also been poorly administered. Trouble began in January 1934, when the rice section sent out applications to growers for quotas, but calculations were not completed until June. "Every grower in Louisiana,"

Bateman noted, "had completed planting before he knew what his allotment and quota was." It was harvest time before the section mailed contracts to farmers for formal acceptance. "These intention to Plant forms (contracts) were just six months behind time," he charged. Bateman estimated that 40 percent of the 1934 crop remained unsold, and growers were unable to arrange credit for the 1935 crop. "As a result of these conditions and circumstances," Bateman concluded, "there are approximately 16,000 families in Louisiana paralyzed in their efforts and plans for the production of this years crop and it is imperative that the Administration take definite action immediately." Growers who had sold to cooperating mills and were promised payment within thirty days did not receive the supplemental 40 percent in price from the Secretary, while those farmers who sold to noncooperating mills received full market price. The situation affected not only Louisiana but also Arkansas and Texas.[13]

The program had been so ill administered that the potentially most controversial aspect, producer allotments, generated little opposition. Those who did complain naturally argued that landowners should receive a larger share of the allotments. A banker named Allen Dezauche from Opelousas, Louisiana, pointed out to Secretary Wallace that tenants tilled many rice plantations. A rice tenant, he complained, "carries with him a production average of four-fifths or three-fourths of his five-year average as the case may be, leaving for the landlord a production average of only one-fifth or one-fourth as the case may be." Dezauche proposed that tenants take only half a farm's allotment. Indebted landowners, he argued, would be unable to pay their taxes "while the tenant farmer who has no obligations in this respect will have a premium placed upon his qualifications to cultivate rice under the code."[14]

C. N. Taylor, secretary-treasurer of the Jennings National Farm Loan Association, complained to Weaver in January 1934. Like Dezauche, he urged that landowners receive larger allotments, for many were heavily in debt and some had lost their farms. He acknowledged that the Federal Land Bank, life insurance companies, loan companies, and wealthy landlords "are the owners of vast quantities of lands in the rice territory." This situation had come about "not by the exercise of the heartless methods usually attributed to the holder of the mortgage on the old farm, but has come about by reason of the drop in land values and the practical abandonment of the lands to these agencies." He feared that producer allotments would aggravate the trend, for the policy helped "a restricted class of individuals; that is, tenants and farmers who work their own land." Finally, he asserted, tenants whom he talked to did not favor the plan.[15] Predictably, no tenant letters complaining of producer allotments survive in the AAA records.

R. A. Wasson, who worked under extension director J. W. Bateman in Louisiana, raised another problem with producer allotments. Writing in February 1934, he encouraged section head Weaver to preserve state quotas and also allotments. Wasson warned that "there are emissaries and agents of large Texas interests busy at work here in Louisiana trying to take from us as many of our tenants with allotments as possible." Wasson revealed that Texans were asking, "Why stay here in Louisiana where your average production is only about ten barrels per acre when you can come to Texas and make twenty?" If a producer could take his allotment from state to state, Wasson concluded, it "would be just plain rice suicide for Louisiana." Texas and Arkansas agents argued self-servingly that little tenant bootlegging would result if the quota system were abolished, "but if their statement is true," Wasson observed, "then they have a much higher type citizenship growing rice than we have." Six weeks later the Rice Section replied, observing that the problem "will more or less take care of itself on account of the limitation placed upon each of the states by the crop control plan."[16] Some tenants did cross state lines, but they had little impact on the program. In the short run the quota system preserved the relative position of Louisiana growers, but during World War II and in the 1970s the rice culture expanded dynamically into new areas of Arkansas, Texas, and Mississippi while the Louisiana position deteriorated.

Although the AAA rice files, unlike the tobacco and cotton files, are notably bare of letters from tenants, W. J. Lowe of Iowa, Louisiana, wrote to Secretary Wallace in May 1935 explaining the views of a small landowner. The letter had been spurred by a remark that Lowe heard from a rice farmer who planted 600 acres yet complained about tenants receiving allotments. "He said they ought to go to Red Russia where they divide up everything," Lowe recounted. This set Lowe to thinking about the program and provoked several letters to Wallace and Charles G. Miller.

He had not grown up on the sidewalks of a great city, the fifty-three-year-old Lowe explained, "but I am from the sidewalks of a rice field levee on the prairies of Louisiana on the banks of the old Calcasieu." He had grown thirty-nine crops in his lifetime, and they had ranged from 200 to 1,000 acres. "I have always been a hard working, temperamental and conservative man with modern machinery to do my work with." He owned an 800-acre farm which he mortgaged during World War I. He had barely hung on through the Hoover years and was "still struggling on promises." Lowe had ambivalent feelings about the government program, and he wondered if in a free country the government should have so much control over the way people farmed. He doubted that he could pay off his debts with only a 270-acre allotment, and he insisted that farmers be allowed to raise rice for seed and table use without cutting into allotments.

Lowe envisioned a model rice farm. "My conception and experience of a real prosperous and economical rice farm is one section of land six hundred and forty acres with a fence around the outside and one through the middle, three hundred acres of rice on one side and two hundred head of cattle on the other side; worked visa versa every year." The 300-acre tract, he argued, "will fit one irrigation well, one tractor, six mules, one drill, one binder, one thrashing machine and a regular hired man." Lowe suggested that the AAA should balance rice farms so that each farmer could have such a unit. To achieve this, he suggested that every farmer who had over a 300-acre allotment should be cut 40 percent each year until the allotment reached 300 acres. A farmer who had less than 60 acres should not be cut at all. Eventually, by awarding acreage taken from large farmers to small producers, each farmer would have a 300-acre unit of production. A person who wanted to enter rice farming, who "has become of age, married, or has a dependent to take care of, that has worked on a farm for the last three years and not anywhere else and is experienced in farming rice," should get a 40-acre allotment that could be increased each year until he achieved the 300-acre unit. "It is no worse for the big farmer to come down to three hundred acres than it is to hold the little farmer in bondage so that he cannot rise to a profitable basis."

Unless small farmers could raise rice for their tables and for seed and unless large farmers cut back on acreage, Lowe feared that the entire program would "go up in smoke." He argued that the government program would hurt small farmers by taking away their freedom, while at the same time he urged the government to reduce large landlords' allotments. The contradiction sprang from his dislike of rich men owning land and "raising rice with cheap hired help." He distrusted government programs drafted "by high powered politicians that probably never wore overalls or tilled the soil; especially when they are a thousand miles away running the farmers' business, and whom they have never met personally and discussed their views with." While complaining about how farmers had been "planned, checked, inspected, mortgaged, charged, taxed, denied and red-taped," he suggested a program that would further regiment rice farmers by governmental planning.

Lowe personified in many ways the dilemma that the AAA presented to southern farmers. It held out the promise of higher prices, but the cost was increased federal intervention in farming. Although Lowe wanted justice for small farmers, he suspected that the AAA would come down on the side of the large farmer who had provoked his letter.[17]

Despite the irresolute and abortive 60/40 program in 1934, the Rice Section strictly enforced producer allotments. Landowners who inquired received replies that outlined how they could secure tenants to match the farm's allotment. Frank C. Middleton, who wrote from Casey, Illinois, about his rice land in Arkansas, received word that the program was meant to aid the rice producer who had farmed rice in the past five years. "This means that tenants who have farmed on a share basis are entitled to allotments proportionate to their shares and that cash tenants receive allotments proportioned to the total acreage which they have cultivated." Middleton should be able to find suitable tenants, the reply observed, for he had rented to tenants successfully in the past. Replying to J. G. McDaniel's inquiry from Weiner, Arkansas, the Rice Section insisted that no allotment transfers could be made between landlord and tenant. If McDaniel wanted to set up a 50–50 operation, he would have to find a tenant who had equal acreage, for "a landlord who has no allotment cannot himself grow rice under the program." Still, the landlord could secure a lien on the crop if he furnished credit. Growers could not raise separate patches of rice for home consumption or for seed.[18]

When the 1934 program failed so miserably, no doubt both tenants and landlords became embittered at the Rice Section's ineptitude. At least rice tenants had the satisfaction of knowing that the AAA had attempted to protect their interests by granting them allotments. On the other hand, by 1934 cotton sharecroppers faced displacement as acreage reduction cut them from the land with no allotment to protect them. Though tobacco farmers fared better after the first year of the AAA, tenants and sharecroppers could farm only at the invitation of a landlord. Producer allotments were in many ways like a form of property that could be used to bargain with landlords. In tobacco and rice areas, many farmers had gone out of business during the 1920s or early years of the Depression, and a lack of production history froze them out of farming. In this sense, an adjustment had already been made in these commodities which resulted in the remaining farmers being stabilized by allotments.

The Rice Section, having failed with the marketing agreement in the southern rice-growing area, decided to push for a processing tax for the 1935 growing season. Both technical and marketing problems stood in the way of such a program. Because of chaos in the rice markets, the Rice Section hoped to implement the program in the spring to encourage rice movement from growers to millers. Millers were hesitant to purchase rough rice, for if a processing tax went into effect, they would have to pay tax not only on the rice they bought but also on floor stocks awaiting sale. "Millers maintain that they have full Secretary's price, which is in an amount as nearly approaching parity as demand conditions will allow," J. W. Bateman explained, "and that it would be unfair and unwise to apply the floor-stocks tax in addition to the price which had been paid for rough rice, claiming that it would virtually mean double taxation." To counter this threat, millers had stopped buying rough rice and were selling off their floor stocks. "The natural consequences of this action is that the producers will be forced to hold their rice and upon August 1, instead of a normal situation where all the stocks of rice in the South are in the hands of millers, we will find all of it in the hands of producers." Farmers were in a bind, for they had to sell their rough rice to finance the 1935 crop.[19]

Congressman Rene L. De Rouen from Ville Platte, Louisiana, sponsored a bill signed on March 18 to initiate a processing tax of one cent per pound to go into effect on April 1, 1935, four months before the official AAA marketing year began. For rice products exported, millers and other dealers received a refund of the processing tax, and remaining stocks of rough rice covered under the government program received tax payment warrants. Thus the rice program shifted from a marketing agreement between the Secretary and the cooperating millers to a statutory obligation for millers to pay a processing tax.

By opening the program to all farmers and millers, the Rice Section avoided penalizing growers or millers who had not cooperated in 1933 and 1934. At last the Rice Section had drafted a workable program. Before the final plan was approved, state extension workers set preliminary allotments. As R. A. Wasson revealed, extension workers "gained through many devious and unofficial channels" a working knowledge "as to what the official program would be in its final analysis."[20] Indeed, J. W. Bateman set up the entire allotment program before the lethargic Rice Section issued rules.

On March 19, 1935, the Rice Section announced the final program for converting from marketing agreements to a processing tax. The allotment for southern ricegrowers was reduced 20 percent from the base years. The section set allotments based on acres and quotas in barrels produced. Actually, plantings in 1935 were about the same as in 1934. "The objectives of the new program," the AAA announced, "are to insure that growers will continue to receive an income from the market price and adjustment payments in the neighborhood of last year's income; that the surplus from the 1934 crop will be moved into trade channels; and that production in 1936 will equal normal domestic and export requirements."

The rice program proved more complex than the cotton and tobacco commodity programs. Growers received adjustment payments on 85 percent of their crop, for "no processing tax income is derived from the 15 percent which ordinarily is used for seed or exported." If a grower planted from 85 to 100 percent of his allotment, he would receive adjustment payments on 85 percent of his quota; those who planted less than 85 percent received "proportionately smaller payments." Farmers would receive two payments, one as soon after August 1 as possible and the other after December 1. Many southwestern Louisiana rice farmers objected to the processing tax and signed petitions stating that it operated "against the Farmers and not the consumers" and would "mean the ruination of the Rice Industry."[21]

The De Rouen Amendment and the timely processing tax on rice solved the problems created by earlier mismanagement. As late as January 1935 southern growers still held 3.4 million barrels of rice. Millers began buying aggressively as soon as they learned that the new processing tax would not apply to unsold floor stocks. By April 1 there remained only a little over a thousand barrels of rice in the hands of growers, and most of that was sold by July, leaving only 420,000 barrels of southern rice as carryover. "This relatively small carryover," Charles Howe concluded, "indicated that the stocks which had accumulated during the period 1930–1934 finally had been moved into consuming channels." Overall, Louisiana farmers received $1.82 per hundred pounds for their 1934–35 crop, $1.73 for the 1933–34 crop, and $.96 for the 1932–33 crop. Despite poor management in 1933 and 1934, the price increased, and the processing tax further helped the southern rice industry. The export refund also encouraged foreign trade. Only 362,560 pockets of the 1934 rice crop had been shipped before April 1935, but from April to August 810,480 pockets were exported. Howe estimated that refunds on exported rice came to $1.7 million, and he concluded that the De Rouen Amendment allowed millers "a substantial profit."[22]

The processing tax, De Rouen Amendment, export refunds, and acreage control all benefited rice farmers and millers in 1935. Each rice state received a quota and acreage allotment, and practically all growers cooperated with the program. Farmers stayed within 3 percent of the assigned allotment, and production in 1935 was kept almost to the 1934 figure. Charles Howe, no doubt stung by the previous year's ineptness, eagerly pointed out that payments to farmers due in August and December 1935 had been paid promptly. By January 1936 there were fewer than 150 contracts unpaid, and most of those were being held until proof of compliance could be determined. U.S. rice farmers received payments totaling $9.4 million under the processing tax, and prices remained high for them in 1935. Preliminary figures showed that rice sold for $2.35 per barrel; the processing tax added about $.92 more per barrel, which gave a return some $.30 higher than the year before. Millers, on the other hand, who had expected rice to mature early and had sold short, were caught with contracts priced optimistically low. The export business in 1935–36, Howe predicted, would bring substantial losses to millers.[23]

There was no problem between landlord and tenant concerning a division of federal money in the rice area. For the first two years the AAA program operated under a marketing agreement; in 1935, under the processing tax, proceeds went directly to the grower, whether landlord or tenant. As the Senate investigation on AAA payments to large producers noted, "the landlord and the tenant each had a separate rice contract, covering their own interest in the operations." Most tenants farmed two-thirds of the land on a unit of production and thus took that fraction of federal money. Of course, landowners who had numerous tenants received large sums.

In the three southern rice-growing states, Arkansas had four contracts in the $10,000-and-above category that yielded a total of $69,483; Louisiana had twenty-five that paid $484,151; Texas had eighteen for $411,574. California's thirty-one contracts paid $564,905. Altogether rice growers received $9.4 million for cooperating with the 1935 program. Southern growers in the $10,000-and-over category received about 10 percent of the federal support money based on $1.22 per barrel produced.

Large recipients varied from landlords and millers to banks and canal companies. In Lonoke County, Arkansas, for example, the Winooski Savings Bank received $18,338 from an allotment of 1,210 acres. The largest recipient in the state, L. A. Black of Arkansas County, received $28,261 for his 2,205-acre allotment. In Louisiana the Calcasieu National Bank took $24,705 for its holdings in Calcasieu and Acadia parishes. The Acadia Vermilion Rice Irrigation Company received $64,800 and had contracts on 6,428 acres. Millers also had ties to the land, for the Louisiana Irrigation and Mill Company received $73,659 for its 5,804 acres in Acadia and Jefferson Davis parishes, the largest amount in the state. No Texas banks showed up on the chart, but canal and irrigation companies, along with farmers, shared the proceeds. William K. Lehrer of Colorado County received $51,014 for 3,584 acres, and the largest, the Richmond Rice Company, took $45,561 for its 3,368 acres. Much of the early landholding structure remained intact into the 1930s, for from the beginning large holdings had been common. Unfortunately, the chart did not distinguish between landowner and tenant, but most tenants' acreages would probably have been too small to reach the $10,000 level. On the other hand, the listed acreage of the large landowners applied only to the land that they had under contract, an amount about one-third of the total acreage they controlled.[24]

When the Bureau of Agricultural Economics analyzed the processing tax on rice, it discovered that millers passed most of it back to growers in the form of lower prices. "The rice millers," it concluded, "apparently did not bear any large portion of the tax." Nor did they pass it on to consumers. "It follows," the report concluded, "that a large part of the tax represented in effect a deduction from the price which otherwise would have been received by producers."[25] Rice growers were paying themselves for cooperating with the 1935 government program.

Still, millers objected to the tax and claimed it was unconstitutional. After securing opinions from the AAA, the Treasury Department, and the Justice Department that the tax had to be paid, millers brought suit. At an October 11, 1935, meeting, the Rice Millers' Association sought an injunction to restrain payments. On January 13, a week after the *Hoosac Mills* decision ended the AAA, the Supreme Court ruled that the funds should be repaid to the millers.[26] The millers thus collected the amount paid in processing taxes and also paid less to farmers on account of it.

The *Hoosac Mills* decision struck down the processing tax on January 6, 1936, and the Rice Section subsequently set up a new program under the Soil Conservation and Domestic Allotment Act passed on February 29, 1936. Administered on a regional basis, the new program operated much like the earlier AAA. State committees drew up lists of producers and their base acreages using the 1929–33 base period for Louisiana and Arkansas and the 1931–33 period for Texas. In 1936 the allotment was cut 25 percent from the base years. The grower's quota was 96.73 percent of his base allotment. "This percentage was determined by the Agricultural Adjustment Administration to be that percentage of the rice produced in 1936 and 1937 in the United States which was needed for domestic consumption," an administrator explained.

Producers who did not use their allotments for reasons other than crop rotation lost them for that year. Also, new growers could receive an allotment in 1936, but a year later the Rice Section limited new allotments to growers who secured machinery from farmers who did not have a base acreage in 1936 or who went out of the rice business. Again, capital became an important measure in the rice program. The new plan included the provision that a grower plant between 85 and 100 percent of his allotment, but it added that he must plant acreage at least equal to a fourth of his rice allotment in soil-conserving crops. Rice growers could simply leave part of their rice land fallow and it would qualify for soil conservation crops. The program penalized growers who overplanted allotments or did not plant soil-conserving crops.[27]

Despite inducements to reduce acreage, rice growers increased production in 1936 to 935,000 acres (46,883,000 bushels) compared to 816,000 acres (38,784,000 bushels) the year before. Although early prices in 1936 were high, the Rice Section, fearing that they would fall, set up a plan to furnish rice for cattle feed in the drought area and also to use it for relief distribution. The government had purchased about 50 million pounds for relief in 1934. Rice growers simply had a small export market, and unless domestic demand grew or some outlet for exports could be found, they would be forced to keep acreage down or receive lower prices.[28]

On February 16, 1938, Congress passed the Agricultural Adjustment Act, establishing loans, support, and adjustment programs based on the soil conservation concept of the earlier program. This legislation became the basis for federal agricultural programs from that day to the present. As I. W. Duggan, director of the southern rice division explained, "The Agricultural Adjustment Act of 1938, as it applies to rice, has as its objective the production of rice supplies sufficient to meet the needs of domestic consumption, normal exports, and carry-over without the creation of a price-depressing surplus." The act provided for marketing quotas when the supply "exceeds the normal supply by more than 10 percent." There were no marketing quotas for the 1938 crop, but if oversupply became a problem in the future, the Secretary of Agriculture could set up an allotment program based on the past five years' rice production among the states.[29]

Yet rice farmers, eager to expand production, largely ignored the soil conservation program. T. B. King of the AAA marketing section wrote to W. A. Mayfield, manager of the American Rice Growers' Cooperative Association in Stuttgart, Arkansas, analyzing the carryover problem. "We have tried to assist in removal of the surplus by purchases of rice through the Federal Surplus Commodities Corporation for relief distribution," he wrote, "and will continue to make purchases on a moderate scale, at least for the present." King was upset by reports that rice acreage was increasing in 1938, especially in Texas and Louisiana. He warned that prices would decline to export levels if this trend continued. "Farmers have been urged to cooperate in the agricultural conservation programs of 1936, 1937 and 1938, but instead of reducing they have increased the acreage planted." This, he feared, would increase the carryover for 1938. King did not want to employ export subsidies, for he concluded that foreign countries saw them "as a means of economic warfare and most foreign countries are in a position to apply anti-dumping or countervailing duties to offset any export subsidy this country might grant." The USDA was attempting "to reopen world markets through the reduction of trade barriers," and if this could be accomplished, "the gains to American agriculture will far outweigh the benefits which could be anticipated from an export subsidy program."[30]

During the 1930s Texas growers fared better than their Arkansas and Louisiana neighbors. Looking at the twelve years from 1928, the last normal year before the Depression, to 1940, a year before wartime demand led to increased production and higher prices, Texas growers increased their harvested acreage from 162,000 acres to 291,000 and

A street dance at the National Rice Festival. Crowley, Louisiana.
October 1938. Russell Lee. (LC USF 33 11741-M4, Library of
Congress)

improved on yield per acre from 2,254 to 2,574 pounds. Although the
price per hundred pounds declined from $2.02 to $1.87 due to expanded production, the value of the crop rose from $7.3 million to
$13.9 million. During the same years the Arkansas harvested acreage
rose from 173,000 to 191,000, yield increased from 2,156 to 2,259
pounds per acre, the price per hundred pounds remained within nine
cents, and the value of production grew from from $7 million to $7.7
million. Louisiana growers actually harvested less acreage, the figure
dropping from 495,000 acres in 1928 to 469,000 in 1940. Yield per
acre only rose by 85 pounds, prices were still twenty cents per hundred pounds lower, and the value of production dropped from $17.7 to
$15.9 million. Although these broad statistics do not reveal annual
fluctuations in acreage and price, they do show that the southern rice
culture remained stable during the New Deal years.[31]

Despite confusion and poor administration in the AAA rice program
during the 1930s, the rice culture weathered the decade with few
changes. No doubt production remained consistent because the expense of entering rice production and federal allotments kept out potential new growers. Producer allotments guarded against the landlord

abuses which characterized the cotton program. Since rice was already highly mechanized, the adjustments that were sweeping the cotton culture in the late 1930s bypassed the rice area. Yet rice and cotton were poised on the brink of mechanical changes that would alter both cultures. The rice and tobacco cultures continued as they had in the past, for AAA programs limited new growers and stabilized old ones. While it took mechanization another twenty years to reach the tobacco culture and displace sharecroppers, the rice industry was already mechanized and stable. The cotton culture, at the intersection of mechanization and feudalism, paid a high cost in human terms for modernization.

Book Three: Persistence and Change in Rural Work and Tenure

The harvest is past, the summer is ended, and we are not saved.
—Jeremiah 8 : 20

A sharecropper's grave in Hale County, Alabama. 1936. Walker Evans. (LC USF 342 8175-A, Library of Congress)

8

The Southern
Enclosure

*It seems to me it is only through
such a complex of meanings that
a tenant can feel, toward that
crop, toward each plant in it,
toward all that work, what he
and all grown women too appear
to feel, a particular automatism,
a quiet, apathetic, and
inarticulate yet deeply
vindicative hatred, and at the
same time utter hopelessness,
and the deepest of their anxieties
and of their hopes: as if the plant
stood enormous in the unsteady
sky fastened above them in all
they do like the eyes of an
overseer.*

—James Agee, 1941

The southern tenure system as well as the way farmers cultivated
their cotton have often been portrayed as static from the Civil War
through the New Deal. Whether one reads descriptions from Freed-
men's Bureau agents, Booker T. Washington, Ned Cobb, WPA interviews, or James Agee, cotton farmers seem frozen in time, transfixed.
Indeed, for most tenants and small farm owners, implements and work
cycles changed little over those years. A few plows, a team of mules,
harnesses, plowlines, a wagon, hoes, some sacks for picking time,
scales to weigh up, and (by the turn of the century) a mechanical
planter and a stalk cutter identified the typical cotton farm. Some
farmers owned part or all of this equipment; others accepted it from
their landlords and worked on shares. Despite the universality of such
primitive implements, the relations of farmers to the land changed
dramatically over the three-quarters of a century after the Civil War,
for increasing numbers lost their land, stock, and implements, and
thus they lost control over the kinds and acreage of crops they grew.
The boll weevil forced a more expensive planting and cultivation cycle;
as the weevil moved toward the east coast, cotton cultivation moved

west to less infested areas, where farmers utilized modern machinery in areas free from the heritage of slavery and less rooted in the tradition of sharecropping.

Such changes rolled slowly over the South and varied with the voracity of the weevil's appetite for cotton and the landlord's for land. The revolutionary changes in the southern cotton culture, however, appeared with the advent of the Depression and the inception of the New Deal. While the tobacco and rice cultures experienced little structural change in the 1930s—for quite different reasons—the old cotton culture caved in, crushed by the untimely confluence of government intrusion and mechanization.

The Old Culture

Cotton farmers lived in a fragile balance with nature. They constantly studied such variables as soil, insects, climate, and seasons and cultivated their crops with individual flourishes. There were almost as many nuances in growing a crop as there were cotton farmers. They watched the sky and the earth and moved in harmony with nature and in accordance with the collected wisdom of their forebears. Whether tenant or owner, each cotton farmer had certain tasks that were tied to the pages of an almanac, to experience, and to the weather. "He identifies himself with a spot of ground," John Crowe Ransom wrote in *I'll Take My Stand* in 1930, "and this ground carries a good deal of meaning; it defines itself for him as nature. He would till it not too hurriedly and not too mechanically to observe in it the contingency and the infinitude of nature; and so his life acquires its philosophical and even its cosmic consciousness." [1]

Ransom admitted that his language was not in the "vernacular" of most farmers, but Ned Cobb spoke the language of farmers—in particular, of the Alabama Black Belt farmer at the turn of the century. His words capture both the spirit and the routine of cotton farming. If new ground had to be cleared of trees, the job should be done before Christmas, he began, so this was the first task of the new season. Immediately after Christmas he cut cotton stalks that had been left standing in the field from the previous crop. He sometimes knocked them down with a stick, a "seasoned hickory stick or seasoned oak stick, somethin stout that won't break easy." He preferred a mechanical stalk cutter with a seat, drawn by a pair of mules. Next he cut wood for the cook-stove, completing this task before the labor-intensive plowing, plant-ing, and cultivation seasons arrived.

Then he broke the land. "Catch a seasonable time when the ground's in good shape to plow, as early as you can—don't plow it wet." Cobb prepared for planting in April. "Your last preparin before your plantin come along is this," he related, "you take a middle-bustin plow—that land broke, in good shape—that's a plow that carries two wings, throwin dirt each way, makes you a nice bed." After running the rows, "You take a guano distributor that you walk behind, just like a plow stock only it's got a big box to it, and get on that bed with one mule and put out your guano before you put down your seed." He then ran a har-row lightly over the field. Using a rake planter or a one-armed planter, he planted the cotton seed. "That rake planter," he explained, "has a spoon bout as wide as my two fingers that runs into the ground just ahead of them seeds and them seeds feedin out right behind that spoon." He did not let it "wiggle or woggle every sort of way," for he prided himself on straight rows.

Cobb then waited for nature to bring the seed to life. "If the weath-er's just right, you can plant the first days of the week and by the middle of the next week, you got a pretty stand of cotton all over your field." But weeds came up with the cotton, he warned, and "the weeds beats the cotton growin." After plowing with a cultivator, he thinned the young plants, spacing them ten inches apart. Timing was essen-tial: "If you chop it too early, decidin wrong about what the weather's goin to do, you go out there and thin out your crop, that bad weather come and get the balance of it." Indeed, Cobb, like most farmers, was preoccupied with the weather. If plentiful rain came in the spring, the crop did not require much in the summer. He sometimes had cotton that "growed so high until it was just a stalk, not many bolls I'd get off it." In other seasons he would have short cotton "no more than three foot high, just layin down with bolls."

The cotton took several more plowings and hoeings before it ma-tured. "Owin to when it was planted, if it was planted any time after the first days of April on up until the middle of April, that cotton will be bloomin, if you treat it right, the last of May." As the plant matured, "them branches will just roll off with squares. And as them squares grow they'll bloom; keep a growin just a short period of time, it won't be many days after that square comes out that it's bloomin." The blooms only lasted a few days. "When the bloom falls the boll is right

Hoe culture. Near Eutaw, Alabama. July 1936. Dorothea Lange.
(LC USF 34 9539-C, *Library of Congress*)

behind," he said, "and that little boll aint a bit bigger than the tip of your little finger." Sometimes a stalk would produce a hundred bolls. "It'd be so heavy with bolls until it couldn't stand up."[2]

At this stage, in the middle of the summer, farmers laid by the crop and allowed nature to bring it to harvest. By the latter part of August or the first of September, the straining lint would burst the bolls. It was during this season that the novelist William Faulkner had his character V. K. Ratliff ride past some Mississippi cotton fields on his way to Frenchman's Bend. "It was now September. The cotton was open and spilling into the fields; the very air smelled of it. In field after field as he passed along the pickers, arrested in stooping attitudes, seemed fixed amid the constant surf of bursting bolls like piles in surf, the long, partly-filled sacks streaming away behind them like rigid frozen flags. The air was hot, vivid and breathless—a final fierce concentration of the doomed and dying summer."[3]

Ned Cobb had started picking cotton when he was a child and insisted that a five-year-old could do good work. The entire family—men, women, and children—headed for the field at picking time. As a child Cobb had picked up to a hundred pounds a day, in his maturity three hundred pounds, and as an old man he had slipped back to a hundred. "The Bible says, once a man and twice a child—well, it's that way pickin cotton. I picked at the end of my cotton pickin days how much I picked at the start." He put the lint into a long sack that dragged behind him; when it got heavy he poured it into a basket,

Cotton being suctioned into a gin near Tuskegee, Alabama. 1902.
Frances Benjamin Johnston. (LC J694 244, *Library of Congress*)

weighed it, and dumped it into a wagon. His wife figured how much it took to make a bale, and he stored it in a cotton house.

Twelve to fourteen hundred pounds of seed cotton produced a bale of lint cotton. "Come time to make a bale," Cobb related, "I'd drive my wagon up to the door of that house and load it all out, take it to the gin." During picking time farmers clogged the roads to the gin. If the line at the gin was long, Cobb would confer with the ginner, and "he'd tell me about when my time would come." Then he would take his mules out of the traces, go home, and return later. "They observed your turn strictly, for white and colored," he testified. "It was mighty seldom that anybody would go ahead of your wagon." While waiting, black and white farmers talked about crops, weather, and prices.

When his turn came, Cobb drove the wagon under a large suction pipe that lifted the seed cotton into the building where the gin separated seed from lint. The lint was baled and returned to him; he sold some of the seed but always kept enough for his next crop. "Some-times I'd sell the seeds to the ginner and the seed out of one bale of cotton would pay for ginnin two bales." The seed money was the first cash of the crop year.

He took his bale home and later sold it at the area trading center. A prospective buyer took a sample from the bale and made an offer based on the grade. "Much of it is a humbug, just like everything else, this gradin business," Cobb complained. If he did not like one estimate, he tried another buyer. Occasionally a white friend offered to take his sample and try to get a higher price. Cobb drew a lesson from this: "Colored man's cotton weren't worth as much as a white man's cotton less'n it come to the buyer in a white man's hands." Yet a black man's labor "was worth more to the white man than the labor of his own color because it cost him less and he got just as much for his money." Many white men worked hard, he noticed, and the poorer ones worked as hard as blacks. "But ones that didn't care so much about stoopin down and pickin cotton" would hire black children at picking time.

This annual routine took place in the context of an economic system that relied on credit for food, implements, and fertilizer. Ned Cobb worked as a sharecropper, a cash tenant, and a farmowner. His autobiography is filled with his observations on the various types of tenure in rural Alabama. He and other farmers settled their debts after selling the cotton. In his early years as a sharecropper, Cobb sometimes failed to make enough to pay off his debts. As he explained, "if you don't make enough to have some left you aint done nothin, except givin the other fellow your labor." Cobb farmed in 1907 and 1908 with one man on shares and "made nothin"; he tried another landlord in 1909 and 1910 "and made nothin there." But in 1911 he moved to a farm and paid cash rent—"I come up from the bottom then."[4] Cobb's determination, his shrewdness and deference, his work at logging in the slack season, and his wife's ability to figure pulled him out of the ranks of sharecroppers. He was, in this sense, an unusual man, for all around him his neighbors were caught in the cycle of debt.

Cobb lived only a county away from Tuskegee Institute. He had seen its president, Booker T. Washington, at farmers' conferences, and he questioned both the educator's association with whites and his concern for poor blacks. At times, however, Washington showed remarkable insight into the problems of the rural South. Less than candid about many aspects of race relations, Washington spoke in 1888 before the Boston Unitarian Club and revealed why his fledgling school needed support to educate black youth. Describing life in the hinterland, and especially the crop lien system, he explained, "This is a curse

Square crowded with people on market day. Many of them brought their cotton to town. Part of the business district seen in the background. Note the Confederate Monument, the types of wagons bringing cotton to town, the period automobiles in the foreground, and the wagon in the center of the photograph near the monument. The wagon may have been an early form of concession stand. The photograph was taken looking north. Carrollton, Georgia. 1913. O. V. Fowler. (Vanishing Georgia Collection, CAR-114, *Courtesy of Georgia Department of Archives and History)*

of the Negro. It is the mortgage system which binds him, robs him of independence, allures him and winds him deeper and deeper in its meshes each year till he is lost and bewildered." The merchant took a lien on the crop and furnished provisions at high interest rates. At the end of the year, the farmer "finds hanging over him a debt which he cannot pay. The second year he tries again to free himself, but in addition to the burden of the second year, he finds the first year's debt saddled on to him and thus from year to year many of them struggle." In a letter to the novelist George Washington Cable a year later, Washington revealed that in many cases a black sharecropper might be cleaned out at the end of the year. The lienholder "takes every thing, mules, cows, plows, chickens fodder—every thing except wife and children." Although some blacks escaped from this cycle, Washington estimated that four-fifths of the farms in Alabama had "fences tumbling down, animals poorly cared for, and the land growing poorer every year."[5]

At the turn of the century Congress expressed interest in the southern tenure system. As the Industrial Commission held hearings throughout the region, Southerners talked complacently about the crop-lien system and how it operated, but a sense of decay crept into the testimony. It was obvious that whites as well as blacks were failing. Testifying before the commission in March 1901, O. B. Stevens, the Georgia Commissioner of Agriculture, described a typical sharecropping agreement but warned that this formula would "vary with individuals." In most cases, Stevens declared, "the tenant pays a large and exorbitant rate of interest on the supplies or advances which he receives on time." It not only applied to blacks, he concluded, "but it is the rule with the whites." Stevens admitted that the crop-lien system drove many farm laborers to work year after year with no hope of getting ahead.[6]

A week later Robert Ransom Poole, the Alabama Commissioner of Agriculture, stressed the nascent mechanization growing in the rural areas of his state. He observed that farmers used mechanical cotton planters and stalk cutters. "We have dreamed of a cotton picker, but so far we have not been able to obtain anything that is a success," he mused. Pitt Dillingham, principal of the Calhoun Colored School in Calhoun, Alabama, mixed optimistic remarks with examples of the ravages of the crop-lien system. He, too, observed that the credit system oppressed both races. "The small white farmers are in the same boat with the colored farmers, so far as the crop-mortgage and the credit-price system go, and their effect on land and people."[7]

In South Carolina, L. W. Youmans, who owned a plantation working 300 to 400 blacks (he was not sure exactly how many), expressed satisfaction with black workers. He thought, however, that whites were being run out of farming: "They have the title deeds yet, but they are mortgaged. The small farmers are being crowded out. The mortgages have eaten them up. They get in debt, increase the mortgage, and every year it takes a little more, and finally they have to give up the deeds. I think it is only a question of time until most of them will be drawn into town." Merchants were also absorbing plantations, and small banks were closing. Youmans had isolated two of the main trends in the rural South—the increasing concentration of land, and white farmers being drawn into the cycle of debt and dispossession.[8]

The boll weevil invasion further undermined the precarious economic situation of southern farmers by destroying part of the crop, increasing the cost of production, and making cotton farming more attractive to growers in western areas. Economic forces ground on, and whites and blacks fell into the pattern that characterized landless rural Southerners. According to President Franklin D. Roosevelt's commission on tenancy, in the South "there was a 69 percent increase in the number of white croppers between 1920 and 1930." Sharecroppers moved often, as the tenancy committee put it, "with the propertyless pioneer's hope of finding a better farm and a better deal with the new landlord." As a Georgia farmer described such moves, "it is a Right sad sight to see wagon loaded with house hold stuff and mother and little children on top going probly to an old shake some Where." The cotton frontier had moved west, leaving behind a tenant system that disintegrated during the 1930s.[9]

Cotton farmers did not understand the forces that were moving across the land. In April 1935 Books Hays, who was working on labor and resettlement issues for the government, toured eastern Arkansas, picked up hitchhikers, and talked to them about their problems. One man "longed for the 'good old days' when a man would have the landowner, credit man and merchant 'pattin' him on the back' and offering him everything if only he would work his land and buy his goods from him. 'There was plenty of work and what I don't understand is why it ain't that way now, 'cause the land is still here.'" Nonresident ownership was increasing, and Hays had heard of large tracts in Cross County being taken over by mortgage companies. "Several plantations in that vicinity are owned by residents of Memphis," he heard.

An older man made a statement "full of pathetic irony," Hays related. "I helped clear up all this country and now I can't get a foot of it." A young farmer wanted to join the Southern Tenant Farmers Union but gave up the idea after a shooting incident. Hays talked to a lawyer who had helped defend some union members. There had been a 40 percent displacement of labor in the area, the lawyer argued, and many workers fled to Memphis to seek employment or relief. "The County Agent had been of little assistance, since he apparently was under control of politicians and landowners." The good land was owned by "a few individuals and corporations." Hays also picked up stories of landlords cheating tenants out of AAA money.[10]

The problems that Hays witnessed in Arkansas typified the South and revealed the upheaval that swept through the cotton culture. The Depression first sent shock waves through the area and disrupted traditional patterns of farming. Acreage reduction further altered the relations between tenants and landlords, and gradually mechanization threatened the system with a permanent alteration. Brooks Hays hoped that the old system of farming could be salvaged by encouraging tenants to buy land, or by colonies of sharecroppers on federal projects, or by other reforms. Meanwhile, farmers became ever more confused over the contradictions between what federal programs were supposed to do and what they actually did.

Those who had radios listened to farm programs, to government leaders, to President Roosevelt, and heard promises that old abuses would end and people would share equally in the new system. "I cannot guarantee the success of this nationwide plan," Roosevelt said in his July 24, 1933, fireside chat, "but the people of this country can guarantee its success." If the New Deal failed, he seemed to imply, it would not be because a brave and honest president had failed but because people had refused to follow him. Roosevelt threw out the lifeline, but drowning people had to swim a few strokes to grab it. Even as the country was entering an era of great upheaval, Roosevelt suggested that the New Deal would stabilize the old ways—not usher in a modern world.[11]

Nearly every government agency used the radio to explain New Deal programs. In October 1933 Frank Mullen, director of agriculture for NBC, warned his superiors, "We are rapidly approaching a situation in which we can almost be regarded as an administration publicity organ." The president's wife and two of his children had their own programs, cabinet members spoke once a week, and each agency explained its programs. The administration often used movie stars and other celebrities to give testimonials. Washington had never appeared so near or so friendly, and such voices offered hope that a new day was dawning.[12] No matter how desperate rural conditions became, administration radio voices promised better times.

Despite all the New Deal programs that provided work and relief, the AAA disrupted the very agricultural system that poor farmers wanted to see reformed. Government broadcasts (as well as escapist soap operas) diverted attention from the reality of the rural revolution that enriched landowners and displaced farm workers. The radio, in this sense, was an instrument of consensus.

Colie Smith, youngest son of Lemuel Smith, a Farm Security Administration borrower. Carroll County, Georgia. April 1941. Jack Delano. (LC USF 34 44054-D, *Library of Congress*)

Even after three years of government intrusion, when James Agee and Walker Evans found the three Alabama sharecropper families that formed the focus of *Let Us Now Praise Famous Men*, living conditions were primitive, and the implements were as basic in Hale County in

*Fred Garvrin Ricketts (Frank Tengle), "a two-mule tenant farmer,
aged fifty-four"; Thomas Gallatin Woods (Bud Fields), "a one-mule
tenant farmer, aged fifty-nine"; George Gudger (Floyd Burroughs),
"a one-mule half-cropper, aged thirty-one." [The names in paren-
theses are the actual names of the farmers; the descriptions come
from the text of Agee and Evans,* Let Us Now Praise Famous Men,
*xxi.] Walker Evans. (*LC USF *33 31313, frame 24, Library of
Congress)*

1936 as they had been as on Ned Cobb's farm thirty years earlier.
The three neighboring families farmed under different arrangements.
"Gudger has no home, no land, no mule; none of the more important
farming implements," Agee wrote. These he obtained from the landlord, and the Gudgers paid him back with both their labor and half the
corn, cotton, and cottonseed. "Out of his own half of these crops he
also pays him back the rations money, plus interest, and his share of
the fertilizer, plus interest, and such other debts, plus interest, as he
may have incurred." If Gudger owed anybody else, he paid that, too;
what was left constituted his annual earnings. "Gudger," Agee stated,
"is a straight half-cropper, or sharecropper."

The two other families had a different arrangement. "Woods and
Ricketts own no home and no land, but Woods owns one mule and
Ricketts owns two, and they have their farming implements." These
farmers gave the landlord a third of the cotton and a fourth of the corn.

Bud Woods (Bud Fields) and his family at their home in Hale
County, Alabama. 1936. Walker Evans. (LC USF 342 8147-A, Library
of Congress)

"Out of their own part of the crop, however, they owe him the price of
two thirds of their cotton fertilizer and three fourths of their corn fertilizer, plus interest; and, plus interest, the same debts on rations money."
These families, Agee summed up, "are tenants: they work on third and
fourth."

These families, and by extension all cotton sharecroppers and tenants, harbored contradictory feelings about rural life, as did Agee.
"They live on land, and in houses, and under skies and seasons, which
all happen to seem to me beautiful beyond almost anything else I
know," Agee wrote, "and they themselves and the clothes they wear,
and their motions, and their speech, are beautiful in the same intense
and final commonness and purity." Parallel with the beauty and simplicity of farm life, Agee observed bitterness and frustration. "It seems
to me it is only through such a complex of meanings that a tenant can
feel, toward that crop, toward each plant in it, toward all that work,
what he and all grown women too appear to feel, a particular automatism, a quiet, apathetic, and inarticulate yet deeply vindictive ha-

tred, and at the same time utter hopelessness, and the deepest of their anxieties and of their hopes: as if the plant stood enormous in the unsteady sky fastened above them in all they do like the eyes of an overseer."

The culture of tenancy and sharecropping, still so vivid in 1936 when Agee and Evans visited Alabama, was beginning to disintegrate. The Gudgers, Woodses, and Rickettses were the last generation of cotton sharecroppers and tenants.[13]

The Southern Enclosure

Just as in the Old World enclosing common pastureland and abridging other traditional rights had forced farmers off the land and into cities, so the forces of government intrusion and mechanization transformed the rural South. The traditional furnishing system, housing, hunting and fishing rights, and free fuel from the forests became transmogrified during the New Deal Era. Depression and federal agricultural programs drove workers from the land, while federal relief agencies supplied work and food for some of the refugees. The federal and mechanical enclosure in the South isolated farmers from their customary means of livelihood, closing off the old avenues of subsistence. While disruption persisted, the federal government attempted to ameliorate human costs with imaginative programs, but only a fraction of rural folk benefited from subsistence homes, farm security, and work projects. The government stabilized some farmers but destabilized the traditional tenure system; it guaranteed parity prices but allowed eviction; it paid farmers to grow less but encouraged mechanization. Ironically, tenant farmers fought to preserve the tenure system that they had so often cursed. Even more than to receive justice and prosperity, it seemed, they wanted to remain on the land.

As testimony before the Industrial Commission suggested, the pattern of landownership had changed drastically by the turn of the century, and concentration continued thereafter. Many farmers who expanded acreage and secured loans during World War I.could not pay off their loans; their creditors foreclosed. Charles S. Johnson, Edwin R. Embree, and Will W. Alexander estimated in *The Collapse of Cotton Tenancy* that life insurance companies and banks owned 30 percent of all southern cotton land in 1934. A Bureau of Agricultural Economics report supplied additional insights into the pattern of landholding in the South. No class of farmers had much equity in the land: "In addition to the tenant class, who have no equity in the farms they operate, owner-operators have no equity in the land which they rent, and due to heavy mortgage indebtedness, only partial equity in the land they own." Increasingly, financial institutions took over southern farmland. "In all seven of that block of Cotton Belt States that included South Carolina, Georgia, Alabama, Mississippi, Arkansas, Louisiana, and Texas between 60 and 70 percent of the value of the farm real estate belonged to persons or agencies other than the farm operator," the report concluded.[14]

Using a Works Progress Administration survey of 246 southern plantations, the BAE determined that from 1934 to 1937 the size of farms increased. The average plantation increased from 955 acres to 1,014 acres, and cotton acreage increased from 178 to 230 per unit. At the same time, wage laborers supplanted other tenure classes, and tractors increased from 1.8 to 2.3 per thousand acres of cropland. Resident families per thousand acres fell from 37 in 1934 to 34 in 1937. "These trends in the plantation organization certainly explain in part, at least, the present widespread unemployment in the rural South and the persistence of relief needs."

The report analyzed the trends in several states. In South Carolina almost 3 percent of the farms were 500 acres or more in size; these farms contained 28 percent of all farm acreage, whereas the 50 percent of small farms contained only 9 percent of the total acreage. "The average size of properties held by individuals was 102 acres, banks 153 acres, insurance companies 259 acres, and the average size of holdings held by other corporations was 457 acres." An Alabama report showed a similar profile. "This trend in Alabama," the report observed, "appears pronounced when it is considered that in 1935 12,000 fewer owners than in 1900 owned 6,000,000 acres more land." The number of nonresident owners had tripled between 1900 and 1935, when some 15 percent of the land was held by nonresidents. The report observed that "more than 84 percent of the land in the old plantation Piedmont section of Georgia is owned by credit companies, banks, and mortgage corporations."

The significance of increasing land concentration lay as much in the changing organization as in size. As the report noted, "If these changes mean that the typical plantation is eventually going to be highly commercialized with all the workers reduced to the lowest possible economic position of wage laborers, the continuance, let alone the increase in number and size of plantations, is in direct conflict with the stated policy of the Department in achieving for all those engaged in agriculture a reasonable level of living." Such a trend, the report correctly concluded, would mean that New Deal plans for converting sharecroppers and tenants to owners would never come to fruition. The report predicted that as commercial agriculture increased and migratory wage laborers did seasonal work, local economies would be disrupted, small towns would disappear, and social stratification and unrest would increase.[15]

The AAA payment schedule accelerated the increasing concentration of land. Payments went mostly to landlords for cooperation in the acreage-reduction program. Obviously, large landowners reaped most of the federal money. The bias in payments attracted the interest of a Senate committee in 1936. Between 1933 and 1935 the Delta and Pine Land Company received over $318,000 in federal funds. Such large payments to landlords—especially in this case, to an English firm managed by the man who drew up the AAA payment schedule—provoked the Senate to conduct a study of large AAA recipients. The study only listed those who received $10,000 or more from the government or firms that had 150 or more farms under contract. It only revealed the top of landowner pyramid.[16]

Despite its limited nature, the report did show large payments going to some landlords. In Leflore County, Mississippi, one of the rural problem areas discussed above, two plantations received nearly $23,000 in 1934. The FERA report recorded that county farmers had received $262,200 in AAA payments, so these two plantations garnered almost 9 percent of the money. Oscar F. Bledsoe, a planter who bragged about his innovative farm operation, received from 1933 to 1935 over $44,000 in AAA payments. Bledsoe wrote to the USDA saying that he shared his money with his tenants, as the contract stipulated.[17]

From listings in the Senate report it is not possible to determine how much money went to tenants and how much was retained by landlords. In the case of the Mississippi State Penitentiary in Sunflower County, no doubt the state retained all $155,000 received over the three-year period. In Washington County the listings showed ten plantations receiving $148,022 in 1933, five plantations taking $86,707 in 1934, and four receiving $68,202 in 1935. By 1934, obviously, some plantations had reorganized or made applications that did not reflect the same acreage as in 1933. Eugene H. Fisher, for example, received

$24,800 in 1933 but did not appear on the other yearly lists. It is unlikely that his government payments fell below $10,000, for payments to the Delta and Pine Land Company, which held land in the county, only fell from $16,208 in 1933 to $11,368 a year later.

Only one insurance company appeared on the schedule of owners receiving $10,000 or more, yet these companies dominated the list of multiple landowners that reported 150 or more farms under AAA contracts. Connecticut General Life Insurance Company did not appear on the 1933 Washington County list, but in 1934 it received $35,022 and in 1935 $31,679. The firm had 179 cotton farms under AAA contract in 1934 or 1935, yet it was not the largest holder of cotton farms. John Hancock Mutual Life Insurance Company, for example, listed 1,580 farms under cotton contracts; Metropolitan Life had 1,141, Prudential 999, Aetna 705, Travelers 636, Union Central, 609, General American 602, and several other companies had hundreds of farms. In all, fifty-five multiple landowners who reported 150 or more AAA contracts owned 10,858 cotton farms. Either these companies spread their holdings evenly over many counties or the payments were reported under other names, for only one appeared in the $10,000 list.[18]

Arthur F. Raper in *Preface to Peasantry: A Tale of Two Black Belt Counties* compiled data on how much farm real estate was owned by insurance companies in Greene and Macon counties in Georgia. In Greene County, John Hancock Life Insurance Company owned 5,842 acres, Metropolitan Life owned 3,063 acres, and Penn Mutual Life held a smaller acreage. Other large landholders included the Scottish American Mortgage Company with 2,305 acres, the Federal Land Bank with 1,117 acres, and smaller acreages held by the Canadian-American Mortgage Company, the Federal Intermediate Credit Bank, the Citizens and Southern National Bank, and the Federal Reserve Bank.

In Macon County, Metropolitan Life held 7,335 acres, John Hancock 1,884 acres, and Penn Mutual, Equitable, and Penn Life held smaller acreages. The Atlantic Joint Land Bank held 4,152 acres, the First Joint Stock Land Bank 2,662 acres, and the Federal Land Bank 1,041 acres. By 1932, Raper pointed out, farmers had lost to loan companies 17,000 acres in Greene County and over 20,000 acres in Macon County.[19] If these two counties were representative of the old cotton-growing area, life insurance companies had spread their investments widely. Still, the Senate report should have picked up such holdings, unless the contracts were entered under other names.

Although AAA files do not reveal the extent of federal payments to life insurance companies, in July 1933 C. G. Wosham, Connecticut General's supervisor of farm mortgage loans in Memphis, wrote to Cotton Section head Cully Cobb informing him that Connecticut General intended to reduce its cotton acreage. The company, he wrote, "approves secretary Wallace's cotton acreage reduction program and are cooperating in every way by agreeing to reduce by approximately eight thousand of our twenty four thousand acres in cotton." In 1934 the company received $35,021 from the AAA for taking 3,680 acres out of production in Washington County. If the other land had approximately the same yield, the company received over $76,000 from the government in 1934. It was not clear whether Worsham was managing all or a part of the company's southern cotton land. Kenyon B. Zahner, manager of Union Central Life Insurance Company's Atlanta office, instructed his field representatives to cooperate with the AAA program. The company took out the acreage it thought proper and allowed tenants to sign separate contracts.[20]

Life insurance companies had invested in land or foreclosed on mortgages throughout the early years of the Depression, and they held this land until the late 1930s before selling. Data on twenty-six large companies showed that most of the $535 million of farm real estate held in 1938 had been acquired during the Depression. Harsh rural economic conditions had obviously enlarged the landholdings of insurance companies, and estimates ran that the asset value of land held in 1938 was nine times that of 1929 and three times that of 1933.[21]

The Senate report revealed that, after the 1933 cotton plowup campaign, all states experienced a drop in federal money paid to large growers. Indeed, North Carolina and Georgia appeared only on the 1933 list; the Tarheel state had only had one grower who received $11,381, while seven Georgia landlords received $81,873. South Carolina did not have a planter who qualified for the list, and Louisiana remained on it for two years and received $413,298. Alabama planters only got $129,879 over the three years, but Mississippi planters received $2.5 million, Arkansas $2.1 million, and Texas $1.2 million.[22] Significantly, mechanization increased most rapidly in the states that received the bulk of federal money.

Whether the progressive reductions came from a different reporting system that allowed separate contracts under different managers, from less acreage and thus smaller payments, or from a significant number of marginal $10,000 payments falling out of that category is not clear.

The Senate report only revealed landlords that fell into its narrow categories, ignoring the larger bias of government payments. For example, it remains impossible to discover the amount of AAA money that life insurance companies and other large landowners received from their 10,858 cotton farms, 39,907 corn and hog farms, or 1,045 tobacco farms. Perhaps the most significant aspect of the report was the revelation that some $7 million of AAA money went not to struggling farmers but to large corporations and landlords. In this respect the New Deal propped up business interests and commercial farmers. A thorough analysis of the division of AAA payments would be a significant contribution to the economic history of the New Deal.

The Bureau of Agricultural Economics furnished broad statistics on AAA programs for 1939, and it showed that 43,454 payees received $1,000 or more under the Agricultural Conservation and Price Adjustment Program. "The number receiving $1,000 or more in 1939 represents 0.8 percent of the 5,776,240 payees," it concluded. Most farmers received less than $200. In 1939 Congress limited the amount for a soil conservation payment to $10,000, and the report observed that before the cap had been put on the program there were farms or firms receiving "well over $100,000." Not until 1970 did Congress place a $55,000 ceiling on cotton price adjustment payments.[23] Thus the cotton program served the large landowners well—as had been intended.

In addition to its studies of changing farm structure, the Bureau of Agricultural Economics conducted a confidential study of the processing tax. Processors paid the tax, but, after calculating mill margins and wages, the BAE estimated "that from the standpoint of the cotton-textile industry as a whole very little of the tax was borne by manufacturers as a group in the form of lower mill margins." Distributors also increased their prices "more than enough to take care of the processing tax." The study concluded that "the processing tax in large part was passed on to consumers in the form of higher prices for cotton goods or passed back to the producers in the form of lower prices for their raw cotton."[24] In effect, consumers—and to a lesser extent farmers, who were also consumers—paid the processing tax. These same groups, then, were taxed to support the large landholding interests that reaped government payments. Ironically, processors fought the tax, even though it had been passed on to other groups. Cottonseed processors, who crushed the seeds to obtain the lucrative oil and by-products, evidently escaped paying a processing tax.

Even as landlords consolidated their position in rural areas with

New Deal programs, private credit agencies revived from the dark days of the early 1930s. Although New Deal lending programs helped small farmers hold their land with government credit, the beneficiaries of this situation included not only farmers but also traditional credit institutions. The redistribution of farm credit between 1929 and 1934 shows a radical shift from the private to the public sector. In 1929 individuals held 44 percent of new mortgages; in 1934, they held only 14 percent. Insurance companies held 14 percent in 1929 and 3 percent five years later; banks dropped from 23 percent to 8 percent. Federal land banks, in contrast, increased new mortgages from 5 percent in 1929 to 68 percent five years later.[25]

This drastic redistribution of farm credit did not destroy private lending agencies—indeed, the opposite was true. As a study by the Farm Credit Administration showed, land banks filled the credit vacuum left by private lending sources. From 1933 to 1939 federal land banks lent $2.5 billion, 71 percent of which went to refinance mortgages originally held by private credit agencies, particularly banks and insurance companies. "In addition to strengthening the assets of banks and insurance companies," the report concluded, "this government lending had the effect of easing the breakdown in the private credit structure and restraining demands for its reconstruction."[26] Thus federal lending programs saved the private lending agencies and strengthened them through the worst of the Depression. Fortunately, the credit also allowed many struggling owners to hold onto their land.

After weathering the worst of the Depression, private agencies again asserted themselves. By 1939 new mortgages by federal land banks had fallen to 11 percent, while mortgages of individuals advanced from the 1934 figure of 14 percent to 31 percent, insurance companies from 3 to 19, and banks from 8 to 30 percent. In effect, the federal loan program had financed not farmers so much as private lending agencies.[27]

This readjustment was more subtle than the statistics reveal. Insurance companies, for example, had foreclosed on many mortgages and taken control of the land. They often rented to tenants and, as discussed above, complied with AAA programs taking the landlord's share of payments. By the mid-1930s they began selling land, again taking mortgages on it. A study by the BAE Land Tenure Section showed that farmers who bought land found themselves again owing payments to insurance companies. Such companies profited either way. If debtors borrowed from the federal government, the companies got paid; if the mortgages failed, they got the land, and when they rented it they got federal payments. The Depression, then, destroyed the assets of millions of indebted farmers while enriching their creditors. In 1932, for example, the twenty-six largest insurance companies acquired almost 15,000 farm properties.[28] In benefit payments and rural credit, the thrust of New Deal policy aided not so much the forgotten man (the announced beneficiary) as the landed interests. It helped clear the way for the rural transformation to capital-intensive farming.

Of all the elements of transformation, mechanization proves the most elusive to chart. In a sense, it was like a wave that had gained momentum since the turn of the century and was about to break over the rural South. International Harvester's promotional efforts during World War I had introduced many farmers to the new implements. Still, the old ways persisted in most areas where sharecroppers still followed mules and plows.

Mechanization in the Cotton Belt actually started in the western growing areas and spread east. Oklahoma, Texas, and the Mississippi River Delta mechanized first. The change from mules to tractors proceeded gradually. Large farmers bought tractors to replace old mules, and tractors and mules coexisted. In the late 1930s James Hand, an implement dealer in Rolling Fork, Mississippi, took trades of mules for credit on tractors. Farmers tilling only a few acres did not profit from tractors at first, for their scale was too small to recover investment costs. Even on large plantations tractors only met one part of the labor demand. After the tractor broke and tilled the land, hand laborers still chopped out the weeds and picked lint in the autumn. During the 1930s surplus farmers throughout the South made it easy for planters to obtain cheap hand labor.[29]

Still, many commercial farmers took the first step toward mechanization in the 1930s, and they often used government money to purchase tractors. With an assured parity price, they could invest with some certainty of paying off debts. According to one study, each tractor displaced several families, and the 111,399 tractors introduced into cotton-growing states in the 1930s displaced from 100,000 to 500,000 families or from a half-million to two million people. Of the 148,096 fewer farm operators over the 1930s, mechanization displaced from one-fifth to two-fifths, and AAA acreage reduction accounted for much of the remainder.[30]

The South lagged behind other areas in tractor purchases; in 1930 only 3.9 percent of southern farmers owned tractors, compared with 13.5 percent for the country at large. Over the next fifteen years the

South increased its share in the eight cotton states, to 9.3 in 1940 and 13.2 percent in 1945. Still, the South was fifteen years behind. The largest increase in tractor ownership in the 1930s took place in Oklahoma (22.9 percent increase), Texas (20.6 percent increase), and Florida (10.2 percent increase). The other cotton-growing states were closely grouped, from Virginia with a 6.2 percent increase to Mississippi with 2.7 percent. Significantly, mechanization spread from the area less encumbered with the legacy of plantation agriculture and sharecropping into the old Cotton Belt.[31]

The combination of New Deal acreage reduction and increasing mechanization during the 1930s started a significant shift in southern farm organization. Two studies, one of Georgia and the other of several Arkansas counties, show how traditonal tenure arrangements shifted due to the introduction of tractors. To better answer questions of farmers who wanted to know how tractor farming changed tenure arrangements, the Georgia experiment station and the Bureau of Agricultural Economics cooperated in the Georgia study. Completed in April 1942, "Farm Rental Arrangements in Georgia" showed that mechanization had altered traditional tenure arrangements. "With the rapid increase during the past few years of the use of mechanical equipment on Georgia farms," the report began, "complications have developed in the customary rental arrangements between landlords and tenants." The study concentrated solely upon the changing relationship between landlord and sharecropper, obviously the most significant sphere of tenure adjustment. As the report observed, the percentage of croppers dropped 39.6 percent during the 1930s, and the dynamics of mechanization pushed off more sharecroppers than had the earlier acreage reduction policies of the AAA.

The report began with the example of a farmer in the Georgia Black Belt who customarily ran ten tenant families and twelve mules. "He bought a tractor and tractor equipment for cultivating, displaced all 10 cropper families and sold 8 of his mules." He kept two mules to use in small fields, retained two of the families as wagehands, and did all the tractor work himself. In other cases landlords continued using sharecroppers for cash crops but utilized tractors to till "conservation crops" and hay for livestock. Most owners charged sharecroppers for tractor work, such as breaking land and running rows. The cost varied; some landlords charged for the labor of the tractor driver, others for driver costs, fuel, and depreciation, and a few simply charged a flat fee per acre. As the report noted, the families retained either as croppers or wagehands were the more able farmers. When landowners changed to tractor power, they usually expanded the amount of acreage tilled by the wagehands or sharecroppers.

Other cases from throughout the state illustrated changes in tenure. One landlord furnished the tractor, equipment, fuel, and half the seed and fertilizer and divided the crop equally with a sharecropper. Before the tractor purchase, the landlord had used three cropper families and farmed with mules. The tractor plan had been working for three years, and the plantation owner stated that the farm was in better shape than formerly. Both landlord and sharecropper "are well pleased with the change," the study concluded. Most examples showed a basic pattern as landlords displaced tenants, bought tractors, and increased the acreage tilled by the remaining croppers. In some instances the cropper's status had been eroded with wage work. On one farm a man worked 85 acres as a cropper and 65 acres for wages. On another, "The cropper is cultivating 160 acres of cropland with the tractor which was previously worked with 5 mules and 5 wage families." In another case the owner supplied the tractor and also allowed the cropper to do custom work in the community and paid him wages for the work.

The shift from mules to tractors did not require a large amount of capital. The study focused on a Newton County farm to illustrate the point. The landlord displaced two of his three cropper families, sold three of his four mules for $600 and part of his mule-drawn implements for $100. He purchased a tractor for $630 and equipment including a "disc plow, section harrow, planter, distributor, and cultivator equipment for $387." After selling off the mules and equipment, it cost the owner $317 to make the shift. He continued to plant the same number of acres but used one cropper and a tractor. As the report showed, "If, by using a tractor, the cropper is able to prepare the land better than with mule power, and if he is better able to seed crops at the desired time, income to the farm should be increased." Since the split was halves, "both will benefit from the change if net farm income increases." Obviously, landlords retained the more able tenants. "Most landlords," the study observed, "report that only a small proportion of their present sharecroppers are capable of operating a farm with a tractor." Also, the need for seasonal wagehands would increase, for such labor was still needed to chop and pick the crops. Finally, remaining sharecroppers would probably stay on the farms and give up the migratory pattern that had characterized southern agriculture.[32] The report neither questioned mechanization nor speculated on the fate of dispossessed sharecroppers.

A 1938 study conducted jointly by the USDA and the Arkansas Agricultural Experiment Station showed the impact of tractors on rich land in the Arkansas, Red, and Mississippi river bottoms in Jefferson, Miller, and Phillips counties. Using interviews with planters, sharecroppers, and wagehands plus AAA data, the report covered 89 plantation operators and 423 sharecroppers and wagehands. Unlike the Georgia study, which had included small units and the entire state, the Arkansas study measured plantations that averaged over 1,000 acres with over two-thirds of the land in cultivation, mostly in cotton. The study pointed out several new trends in farm organization traceable to government programs and mechanization. Tenant displacement took place in two periods: "from 1933 to 1934, when cotton acreage declined for the second successive year; and from 1936 to 1937, when there was a marked increase in the number of tractors used on the plantations."

Not only did some croppers leave farming, but landlords also changed the tenure pattern, assigning remaining croppers "nominal cotton acreages" and paying them extra for wage work. Data from two additional Mississippi River counties, Chicot and Mississippi, being studied separately, paralleled that from the other three. These two counties had a 12 percent displacement of resident families from 1932 to 1938, "a major part of the displacement occurring from 1937 to 1938 when a sharp reduction was made in cotton acreage."[33] Both counties were shifting from sharecroppers to wage labor. "The number of tractors employed on the plantations in these two counties," the report added, "has increased at a more rapid rate than the number used on the plantations in Jefferson, Miller and Phillips Counties."

Yet the change to tractors progressed unevenly in the rich Arkansas cotton area. In 1937 only fifty-six of the eighty-nine plantations used tractors, and thirty-six of these had been using them since 1932. Only three had used tractors before 1926. Most landowners used tractors for breaking land and for seedbed preparation, and they increasingly used them for hay crops. On traditional mule plantations, the number of "resident families" remained stable, but on tractor plantations they decreased by 9 percent from 1931 to 1937. Families remaining on mechanized plantations became wagehands or sharecropped reduced acreages. Further displacement, the report noted, had been "held in check by the inability, thus far, of plantation operators to mechanize the operations of cotton chopping and picking." Most planters kept resident families for these chores, but the report predicted that the successful development of a cotton picker "will pave the way for further displacement of resident families."

Unlike on the Georgia plantations, where those who remained on the land shared more income, in Arkansas the sharecroppers lingered on as wagehands and earned less than before. Some families had members who drove tractors, a skilled job that paid better than regular farm work. Planters charged croppers from $12 to $15 for custom tractor work. When asked whether they preferred to work as sharecroppers or as wagehands, a majority preferred cropper status. The report concluded that the "economic displacement" due to changes in status was "as important as the physical displacement of families previously noted."[34]

Donald Alexander's study, *The Arkansas Plantation, 1920–1942*, agreed with the plantation survey done by the BAE and the Arkansas experiment station. By 1940 farmers in Jefferson County, Arkansas, owned 395 tractors; 11 of these were on the Willey Planting Company plantation that had, in 1933, received $14,949 in AAA payments. While small owners continued profitable operations with workstock, AAA policies and mechanization displaced tenants from larger units. In Arkansas County, for example, there was a 20 percent decline "in the number of resident families per 10,000 acres of cropland from 1932 to 1938." Day labor fit better with tractor farms. Displaced tenants faced several options, none of them appealing—"migration, subsistence farming, part-time farming, wage labor, and relief."[35]

While plantations in the new cotton-growing areas of Oklahoma and Texas as well as in the Mississippi and Arkansas Deltas used tractors in large-scale operations, southern farmers on smaller farms used them for a wide variety of reasons. With the exception of those in Florida, Virginia farmers utilized tractors in higher percentages than other southern farmers east of the Mississippi River. In 1930, 5.4 percent of Virginia farmers reported tractors, and this increased in 1940 to 6.2 percent and in 1945 to 8.4 percent.[36]

In many cases farmers bought tractors not because they were a rational purchase for a small acreage but instead to escape drudgery. Many tractors were not used to full capacity. One study noted that by 1945 a tractor saved a cotton farmer about 8 percent in costs. Also, farmers reported that tractors proved more efficient and more dependable than workstock, and those who adopted tractor power found it necessary to restructure their farm operation, especially if they used sharecropper labor.[37]

Two North Carolina studies explored in depth the problems connected with partial mechanization that came from using tractors while still relying upon hand labor for chopping and picking. In a 1949 study Herman B. James found that tractors reduced per-acre operating expenses from $97.80 with mule power to $80.21 with a tractor. The northern tidewater had few cotton farms, but James found that it took a tractor 11.1 hours per acre in seedbed preparation, planting, cultivation, and harvesting cotton, while mule power required 43.1 hours. "Not until satisfactory harvesting equipment is developed for these crops will the farmer be able to obtain the full economy offered by mechanization," he predicted. James did not doubt that full mechanization was a good thing, and, with the war experience behind him, he observed that many former farmers had been trained successfully as defense industry workers or soldiers. "Many of these workers," he concluded, "have not returned and will not return to the farm."[38]

Charles B. Ratchford in 1951 conducted a massive study of Coastal Plain North Carolina, where farmers grew tobacco, peanuts, cotton, corn, and hay. As Ratchford observed, "the most significant development in crop production since 1890 is the tremendous increase in tobacco and peanut acreages." Cotton acreage had increased until the 1920s but then declined, probably due to the boll weevil. In the twenty-county area the number of tractors increased from 1,151 in 1925 to 2,576 in 1940. By the end of World War II the area boasted 7,543 tractors. The mule population rose steadily from 105,195 in 1925 to 125,608 in 1940, but by 1945 it had declined to 122,425. By then the number of horses had also fallen, to half the 22,000 counted in 1925.[39]

Ratchford gathered his data in 1949 from 216 farms in eight of the Coastal Plain counties. He found, among other factors, that tractor farms were larger, had more land in pasture, grew more soybeans and small grains, had better equipment, and even had more workstock than nontractor farms. No blacks surveyed owned tractors. Nine of the farms were classified as cotton farms, 73 as general farms, and 134 as tobacco farms. None of the renters in his survey owned tractors, but 45 percent of the part owners and 37.4 percent of the full owners did. Predictably, the larger units had the most tractors. Sharecroppers who used tractors had larger farms than those who lacked access to them.

As in other areas of the mechanizing South, various arrangements were made to collect costs from sharecroppers who benefited from tractor power.[40]

Paul S. Taylor, who toured the country with his wife, photographer Dorothea Lange, observed the changes taking place in the southern cotton culture. Taylor, who taught at the University of California, specialized in rural labor problems, and he testified before Congress and before the Temporary National Economic Committee that studied the concentration of economic power in the country. Before a special Senate committee studying unemployment and relief, he observed in 1938 that former cotton sharecroppers and wagehands were increasingly ending up on relief rolls. Many had been displaced by tractors. "A planter in the Mississippi Delta, to cite an outstanding example," he testified, "purchased 22 tractors and 13 four-row cultivators, let go 130 out of his 160 cropper families, and retained only 30 for day labor." Senator James F. Byrnes, skeptical at this example, asked for the name of the planter, and Taylor replied that it was J. H. Aldridge, who farmed near Greenville, Mississippi. Most of the displacement came in the flat and relatively boll weevil free states of Texas, Oklahoma, and the Mississippi and Arkansas Delta areas, where farmers could easily utilize machinery and profit from a lower cost of production.[41]

Displaced laborers, Taylor observed, "are forced into the towns in large numbers and drawn back onto the farms only for short seasonal employment at chopping and picking time." In June 1937 he had watched trucks roll into Memphis and take from 1,000 to 1,500 laborers to chop cotton in the nearby Delta area. Most, he observed, were former sharecroppers. "The burden grows of relief of unemployed farm laborers congregated in the towns and cities of the South."[42] It became increasingly obvious that the combination of acreage reduction and mechanization was changing the face of southern agriculture.

The utilization of tractors introduced shifts in farm structure. Farmers who grew crops dictated by the conservation policies of the AAA discovered that tractors could perform most of the work, and many a small farmer used a tractor as he would a handyman, to escape drudgery and increase efficiency. In plantation areas, mechanization led to displaced tenants and a change in the status of those remaining. Planters who depended on extra laborers to chop and pick their cotton did not want to drive off all labor and so kept wage laborers and reduced sharecroppers. The tractor did not solve the problem of mechanization for cotton farmers, since they relied on hand labor for seasonal work.

A tractor on the Aldridge Plantation. One man and a four row cultivator can do as much work as eight men and eight mules under the old system. Leland (vicinity), Mississippi, in the Delta area. June 1937. Dorothea Lange. (LC USF 34 17099-C, *Library of Congress*)

Yet partial mechanization with tractors began a structural shift that would be consummated with the perfection of the cotton-picking machine. By World War II the last piece of the mechanization puzzle was almost ready to be put in place.

The impact of New Deal policies in the rural South proved complex, contradictory, and revolutionary. The AAA and federal credit measures aided landowners more than tenants, traditional lending agencies more than borrowers. As the problem of human displacement intensified, New Dealers listened to the voices from the countryside and realized to some extent the turmoil that existed there. It was only in the fall of 1936 that Roosevelt and Wallace acknowledged the upheaval in the rural South. At that time the Southern Tenant Farmers Union had gained national attention, and documentary photographs and other evidence had been accumulated to show rural conditions.[43]

After years of promotion by implement companies and boostering by the Extension Service, by the mid-1930s southern farmers turned increasingly to machines. Despite the surplus labor clogging the byways of the region, landlords invested their government money in machines and looked with satisfaction at the stable prices produced by government programs. Increasingly the rural cycle, previously attuned to nature, became warped. Tractors prepared seedbeds, planted, and plowed the cotton land, while wagehands poured in to chop out weeds and then to pick the lint. The human contribution in crop production became fragmented. Many Southerners, black and white, hesitantly left the countryside, paused in nearby towns and cities, and moved on out of the South, never to return. They took little in the way of earthly goods, but they transferred a rich cultural heritage.[44]

The forces that had begun working at the turn of the century at last triumphed, and the South experienced its own enclosure movement. Neither those who left nor their neighbors who stayed behind shared the traditional relations with landlords that had typified southern rural life since Reconstruction. The custom or contract of landlord supplying housing, food, wood, pasture, and hunting and fishing rights receded into memory, and the government, to some extent, took up the role of paternalistic provider. Many of the rural exiles found work in defense industries or in the armed forces during World War II. The war rescued many victims of AAA programs and mechanization, in addition to those who had been displaced by other forces. The war gave them a purpose. It also became a great divide. Fifteen years of war and depression sapped vitality, and spiritual reserves were low afterward. It would be another generation before Americans could look back with nostalgia to the 1930s.

9

The Persistence of the Old Tobacco Culture

In tobacco the big gambler is the farmer himself. He has no guarantee of anything. He takes a chance on raising his crop and then when he gets it raised he doesn't know what it will bring. It's a ninety day crop growing but, as the farmers say, with the curing it takes thirteen months a year.

—Sam Hobgood, 1938

It was more than a clever saying that it took thirteen months to cultivate a tobacco crop. The daily cycle of work that coiled into a yearly routine remained static and unmechanized during the 1930s, but government programs as well as automobiles and radios altered rural life. The tension created by the collision of the old culture and the new manifested itself in many ways, yet the life of a tobacco farmer continued in a familiar daily and yearly routine that demanded hard work and afforded few pleasures. Most farmers had dreams of a better life that included literacy for their children, health care, and respectability, but these could only be realized if the tobacco crop sold well at auction. The warehouses embodied a distinct culture, one that owed much of its spirit and personnel to the surrounding rural culture. Despite a farmer's distrust of the auction process, he nevertheless relished the trip to market, for it was a break in the routine of farm life, a time to fraternize with other farmers, perhaps drink with them, and buy necessities and frills for the family. Neither the warehouse culture nor farming techniques changed radically as a result of the New Deal. Tobacco farmers and warehousemen continued in the traditional ways that had evolved since the 1880s.

The Tobacco Culture

Offering a description of a typical tobacco farmer presents the same danger as claiming typicality in any kind of employment; every worker is unique and looks at work through different eyes. The life story of John and Sarah Easton of Wilson County, North Carolina, however, captures the reality and dreams of tobacco sharecroppers. When WPA interviewers Mary A. Hicks and Willis S. Harrison found them, the Eastons were living in a converted one-room filling station near Wilson, one of the largest tobacco markets in the world. Twin sixteen-year-old girls still lived at home; there were two older daughters, Lucy and Macy, and a son, Jack. The filling station, Sarah Easton insisted, was "the worst we've stayed in since we was married thirty-two years ago."

Their one-room habitation was clean but cluttered. "It contained two beds, one iron and one wooden. One was painted sky blue, the other walnut. In the room also was a walnut dresser with a cracked mirror, a scarred white washstand with a dull mirror, two brown trunks which were new in 1880, an old sewing machine with a broken pedal, a small wood range, a cracked wood heater, a wobbly-legged dining table with a frayed white oilcloth, two long unpainted benches, a small table, and about ten straight chairs." Sarah Easton longed for some lace curtains for the windows.

The Eastons descended from tenant farmers. "If you know anything about tenant farming," Sarah Easton told the interviewers, "you know they do without everything all the year hoping to have something in the fall." Their fortune had fluctuated with the price of tobacco and the luck of the growing season. Children came along fast, she admitted. The hard times and extra mouths to feed had driven John to drink. "He'd always drunk some," Sarah admitted, "but now he was like a hog in a bucket of slops." When Sarah became pregnant with a third child, she used home remedies to abort it. "There was a old granny woman in our neighborhood—she's dead now—and she told me to drink cotton root tea. She swore that that would knock it up, and it did but I liked to of died." She finally told John about it, "and he cried and said that it was his sin instead of mine." The next child was a boy, and John liked that. He stopped drinking—until the last load of tobacco showed that he was not going to make any money, and "so he spent it all on a drunk and let the bills go to the Old Henry." When he got home at midnight, "drunk as a dog and as broke as a beggar," Sarah lost her temper and beat him with a barrel stave. It didn't cure him of drinking.

The twins came two years after the boy, and the bills increased. The doctors charged double, "and from that minute on ever' bill has doubled it seems like." A short time later Sarah had appendicitis, and "when the doctor operated he tied my tubes so I couldn't have no more." They still owed the doctor. The Eastons bragged that the federal government had benefited them. Sarah's health had been good, except for the appendectomy and the abortion. Most of her children had been healthy except for routine childhood diseases, but Amy, one of the twins, was born with a crooked leg. "God bless the government—it had Amy's crooked leg operated on two years ago and it's as good as Joyce's now," Sarah said.

They had been working for wages instead of sharecropping, but Sarah admitted that there was little work available. They owned a 1924 Dodge that John had bought new. "He was drunk when he bought it and he bent a fender before he got it home," she said, adding some credibility to a similar story that Erskine Caldwell related in *Tobacco Road*. They had not been able to afford a radio, pay for electric lights, or install indoor plumbing. Sarah did not go to church. "I used to belong to the Baptist Church but I've always been used to cussing, drinking, and working on Sunday." The main reason she stopped attending services, she admitted, was that she "didn't have nothing to wear for me nor them."

John Easton then walked into the house. "He is extremely stout and low and has a round jolly face," the interviewers noted. He had almost white hair but did not look his fifty-three years. "Taken all in all, he reminds one of a fat and mischievous elf." John had completely swallowed the New Deal tonic. When he met the WPA interviewers, he gave a little speech. "I'm a Democrat; I stand for the New Deal and Roosevelt. I am for the WPA, the NYA, the NRA, the AAA, the FHA, and crop control. I'm going to vote for control in December." He had not gotten much government money, he admitted, "but I'm still saying that the WPA, CCC, and all the rest is shore doing a big part for North Carolina. The government shore give us enough when it paid for Amy's leg operation."

He immediately began talking about tobacco farming, bragging that he was one of the best farmers in the county. The Depression had caused some new ways of looking at life, the couple revealed. They had come to play a game at mealtime. "You see," he explained, "when rations gits slim we just have two meals a day or maybe we'll just have a cup of coffee for breakfast. While we drink the coffee we poke the fun at rich people and pretend that we are having just what we want. We ask each other polite-like to have toast and jelly and bacon and eggs and it shore helps." When they did have meat for breakfast, they skipped dinner and then ate supper in the early afternoon. "As we set down to the table we play like all of us had been to dinner with friends. We ask each other what he had and we all make out we had turkey, chicken, cake, pie, and a heap of other fancy stuff. Sometimes when one's telling what he had somebody will say, 'That's funny, I had the same thing.' You'd be surprised how much that helps out."

The fabricated meals helped the Eastons through hard times, but the most obvious manifestation of the Depression turned out to be the New Deal. "There ain't no other nation in the world," John Easton insisted, "that would have sense enough to think of WPA and all the other A's." Yet the New Deal had not brought prosperity to bottom-rung farmers. Tenants, he argued, "work like niggers all the year" while the landlord "gits rich." Croppers seldom made enough to get through the winter. "I've had some pretty good landlords and some pretty bad ones but I reckon that I'll have to put up with them all my life. I hate the thieving rogues anyhow, good or bad." But the dream and reality intersected at Sarah's dream of lace curtains. "You're gonna have lace curtains someday, Sarah," he said. "Just as shore as God spares my life for a little while longer you're gonna have them lace curtains."[1]

The Eastons shared a work routine, hard times, and dreams with many families throughout the bright tobacco country. In many respects the old culture endured, yet changes altered the way people looked at their work, at the government, at the world. As when any traditional people face change, individual farmers reacted quite differently to the strains of adjustment. In many ways the bright tobacco belt remained premodern, conservative, and poor, but in other ways people heard of new inventions and styles, of government programs, and of hope. Tobacco farmers lived at the interface of two worlds.

Rural housing and furnishings had changed little since the Civil War, although an occasional radio or Victrola served as a reminder of changing times.[2] Two WPA interviewers found Thomas Doyle's eastern North Carolina house crowded. Like many other black families, the Doyles cared for people other than immediate family. At the time of the interview, probably in 1938, Doyle's eighty-year-old uncle was living with him. "He's the third old pusson I'se taken care of," Doyle said. He picked up the most treasured item in the house when he went to New York—a color picture of Joe Louis. Otherwise the furnishings were spare. "There was a carpet on the floor and a two-piece living room set, upholstered chair and sofa. Several assorted chairs were in the room. There was a battery radio and a winder phonograph. On the side table were a few china figures of the kind given away as pitchpenny prizes at the fair."[3]

Sam Bowers, a black farmowner, resided near the Cape Fear River, probably in Harnett County, North Carolina. He lived in an unpainted frame house with four rooms and a leaky roof. Margaret Jarman Hagood, who spent sixteen months in 1937 and 1938 talking to white tenant farmer women to obtain data for her excellent study, *Mothers of the South: Portraiture of the White Tenant Farm Woman*, found a white family of twelve in the tobacco country that shared two rooms and four beds. They ate in a lean-to kitchen and passed the time of day "on a rotting porch flush with the ground and half covered with mud washed on it from the slope up to the road."[4] Another black tenant family near Greenville, North Carolina, occupied a four-room house. "In one corner of the living room was a sewing machine, a double bed of strong iron frame, a dresser, and a broken-down phonograph. Two rockers and three straight chairs completed the furniture in the room." In many cases the amount of furniture was a function of the mobile life of sharecroppers. A wagonload of belongings constituted the outer limit of possessions—that and poverty. Sarah Carson, who lived near Smithfield, North Carolina, detested poverty and yearly moves: "We make mighty little after working ourselves near 'bout to death and we move just about every year."[5]

Like the Carsons, many families moved at the end of the year. During the holiday season landlords and tenants bargained over the next year's arrangement, and the old year's dissatisfactions and settlement and the new year's hopes led to a search for something better. "The folks before us didn't do anything either," a tenant woman complained, "and that's why we want to go somewhere else—the land's got so bad you can't make anything off'n it. Renters don't take care of the land because it ain't theirs and they don't know when they'll be leaving; and landlords don't fix up the inside of the house because they don't have to live there and nobody sees it."[6] Conditions were often so bad that sharecroppers believed that moving would surely make things better, although they were moving in behind people who had identical ambitions. They listened to neighbors talk about their landlords and took the best place offered. They moved often but rarely out of the county or to cities—unless there was no option.

When farmers did move off the land, they left something behind that defied description. The novelist Harry Crews, who moved from rural Bacon County, Georgia, observed the difficult adjustment to urban living. His mother moved to the Springfield section of Jacksonville, Florida, "where all of us from Bacon County went, when we had to go, when our people and our place could no longer sustain us." Rural people were not accustomed to houses packed so closely together, where a person could stand on the front porch and talk to his neighbor. "They felt like animals in a pen. It was, they said, no way for a man to live. But that was not the worst part of the city. In a way that was beyond saying, what they missed the most was their county's old, familiar smell: pine sap rising in trees, the tassels of corn topping out, the hard, clean bite of frost on dead and broken cotton stalks."[7] Most croppers moved in their little circles as long as they could, trying to avoid the tangent that led to the city.

Rural families were usually large, in part because people did not practice birth control but also because they took pride in large families that, of course, added to the labor force. Talking about the past to a WPA interviewer, John Sylvester Hinson, a landowner who lived in northeastern North Carolina, observed that "most couples had big families then. They knew nothin' about birth control, an' they had 'em like rabbits. It wuz nothin' to see a poor renter livin' in a one-room house with a fambly of ten or twelve children an' sometimes more." When the winters were bad and there was a lot of snow that kept the men inside, he said, "Most every woman in the neighborhood would get bigged and there'd be the biggest crop of young babies you ever saw in a year's time." Hinson believed in birth control but surmised that "single women will be affected by it as they will shore learn the trick an' half the girls has stayed ladies 'cause they wuz 'fraid of gettin' bigged, I reckon."[8]

Midwives, often called granny women, delivered most rural children. Thomas Doyle remembered that a "midwoman" delivered his wives' children. "Midwomen only charged five dollars and the doctor would'a charged twenty-five dollars." His first wife had two children, both delivered by a midwife. After the second child his wife went back to the fields too soon, took sick, and died. "She weren't but twenty-two year old. I didn't think nobody that young could die." After settlement he did not have enough to pay the doctor, so he went to work at a sawmill. He later remarried, and his second wife had a boy. "We used a midwoman," he said. "I alus' uses a midwoman." To avoid paying doctor's bills, many people used home remedies.[9]

Women took pride in being able to bear children and recover quickly. Sarah Carson boasted that she "was up cooking and washing dishes the third day" after her first child, "and with the last one I milked the cow on the third day." She admitted that she felt "pretty fainty, but there won't nobody else to do it." She had a doctor for both children, "and that's the only times we've had a doctor in eight years."[10] Margaret Hagood found a family suffering from pellagra. "They were fed— although undernourishment might be guessed from the fact that the twenty-one-year-old girl looked fourteen, the fourteen-year-old boy ten, the ten-year-old girl six, and so on all the way down."[11] Most farm families called for doctors only as a last resort.

People would endure their aches and pains a long while, as Harry Crews remembered. His mother hired a man named Mr. Willis, who suffered from a constant toothache, and his wails often kept the family awake at night. "What was happening," Crews related, "was only necessary. The dentist lived ten miles away, and Mr. Willis didn't have money to pay him." One cold night the young Crews heard Mr. Willis kick open the door. Crews followed him into the yard and saw "the craziness in his eyes, the same craziness you see in the eyes of a trapped fox." Willis drew some cold water from the well, held it his mouth a while, took out a pair of pliers, and pulled the tooth. He held up the tooth between them. "He looked at the tooth and said in his old, calm, recognizable voice: 'Hurt now, you sumbitch!'"[12]

Country doctors, of course, had a difficult time caring for the health of a community. Their practice was largely devoted to diseases that had progressed so far that about all they could do was give a fatal verdict. They knew that there might be no pay for treatment; though sometimes they took food to satisfy the bills, often they received nothing.[13]

Hard drinking and alcoholism proved common traits along tobacco road. John Sylvester Hinson did not deny his love for liquor. "Sometimes I have a party an' drink a little, 'fact is, I get drunk now an' then. The boys used to git a lot of cider or corn whiskey an' then steal a lot of chickens an' have a big party. We called 'em 'functums.'" John Carson did not hide his drinking, either, but it took a toll on his wife. "I married when I was sixteen and didn't care a snap that John drunk and fought and had been in jail a time or two," she said. "I thought he'd stop it when I married him, but he got worse. He kept drinkin' and stayed away two or three days and nights at a time." He even did it during curing time, and she had to tend the barns. When he returned, "he tells me it's none of my damn business, and that's all I ever know about it. He keeps his jug of liquor in the kitchen and drinks when he pleases."[14]

Jack Webster, who was a tenant farmer like his parents, told what was probably an apocryphal story on himself. He returned home drunk on a cold night, and the family was in bed. He went to the fireplace and blew on the coals. "I blowed and blowed, but nothin' happened. Then I seen I was just blowin' at a patch o' moonlight that come through the window and fell on the ashes." He then tried to go to bed, "but the bed was goin' round and round, and I couldn't catch up with it. So I just stood by the door and waited for it to come around to me. Every time the bed would come around I'd make a jump for it, and every time I jumped I'd hit the floor, kerplunk. Sally woke up and got me into the bed and took off my shoes and covered me up. This oughta broke me from drinkin', but it didn't."[15]

Just as people drank hard, they often worshipped hard. Most share-croppers and rural folk belonged to fundamentalist churches, and they enjoyed the singing and the preaching. Jack Webster remembered the simplicity of it all. "People know'd how to sing in them days, and the preacher know'd how to preach. He showed us hell on one side and heaven on the other, and there warn't no middle ground. We had to make up our minds, one way or the other." Sam Bowers, a black farmer, admitted that he felt the same way about religion as he did about politics; a person should be free to make up his own mind. "I thinks a person otta find de chu'ch he wants to jine no matter 'bout de 'nomination. Me an' my wife b'longs to de original Free Will Baptist Chu'ch. Pa an' Ma b'longed to it, too. I don't mean de Holy Rollers either." He noted that, since World War I, church attendance had fallen off. It was a strict and sometimes joyless world, and some of the strictest families condemned dancing, drinking, card playing, and the movies.[16]

In many cases, however, the church was the center of the community. Picnics and Sunday services broke up the week and allowed rural families to meet and enjoy fellowship. It was, for many, their only recreation. Children liked playing with neighbors, and young people paired off and courted. Revivals and creek baptizings were important and festive events. The Bible, after all, gave hope for eternal happiness to people who had few worldly joys. It also gave blessings for the poor, for they would ultimately inherit the earth. Religion justified the poverty of the rural South by furnishing beatitudes that praised the lowly. It forced people to look inward for strength, for material rewards did not seem to interest the God of the southland. Many people, no doubt, identified with Job and wondered how far God would go in testing them with afflictions. It was almost as if the Old Testament with its trials, plagues, and lean years ruled the work week, while the hope and promises of New Testament redemption dominated Sunday.

The average southern farmer probably spent more time in church than in school. A fundamentalist religion and fundamental education went hand in hand. John Easton did not attend church often, he admitted, but he wanted his family to attend. "I ain't tried to teach them no Bible 'cause if I can't read how am I gonna know that what I hear is in the Bible?"[17] His remark showed not only a healthy skepticism but the vulnerability and defensiveness of an uneducated man. Many rural families did not see the value of education or were content that their children learn basic reading, writing, and arithmetic.

Thomas Doyle recounted what was probably typical of black farmers in the Tobacco Belt. "My mother didn't have no education and my father had a common one. He went up to the third grade in school and got to be a deacon. My gran'daddy was a tenant and he didn't have no education neither. Hit was funny 'bout him, he couldn't read his name if hit was writ a foot high 'gainst the side of the house but he could figger as good as the next man." It was an almost Emersonian remark, suggesting that though his folks did not get an education, they had strengths that allowed them to do well at their chosen work. He hoped that his children would all achieve a high school education. One daughter finished high school and had a job "doing housework in New York." Doyle believed that "they ought to know enough to look after their interests, to 'figger' and keep accounts so nobody can take advantage of them." Sam Bowers agreed, and he took his ideas from his father, who "wanted all his chillun to have a fair eddication," but he thought "a colored chile otta go to work an' quit school atter dey learned to read an' write an' figger enough so people couldn't beat 'em out of what dey made." Yet Bowers was obviously proud of his learning, and his wife taught school.[18]

John Sylvester Hinson said that his "parents done all they could to educate us. All of us could read an' write an' figger good enough to do business." Margaret Hagood linked poor education with tenants' vulnerability. "Lack of education explains some of the ignorance and susceptibility to exploitation," she wrote of one family. "Neither mother nor father ever attended a day of school and neither can read or write. Of their twelve children only two have gotten so far as 'stopping out in the fourth.'" She found that superstition often outweighed education.[19]

Color also played a significant part in the culture of the rural South.

A tobacco field early in the morning. A white sharecropper and wage laborer are priming tobacco. Granville County, North Carolina. July 1939. Dorothea Lange. (LC USF 34 20015-E, *Library of Congress*)

In its most vicious manifestations, racism led to lynching, whitecapping, and peonage and created a feeling of dread among blacks and (at times) guilt among whites. Blacks and whites coexisted in an uneasy truce. While the law separated the races in many ways, it did not prohibit significant contacts. Some blacks managed to farm better than whites, and while this sometimes produced tension, it also broke down the conventional wisdom about black inferiority. Both black and white tenants worked under the same lien laws, and all farmers performed the same work routine and sold their crops at the same markets. By the 1930s blacks were voting on the AAA acreage reduction program

—another example of how the federal government forced change. In work relations blacks and whites primed tobacco together in the fields and mixed at the scaffold, and in both places they shared soft drinks and snacks. But they did not sit down together to eat the noon meal. Farmers of both races earned community respect for their ability to work. And every rural community kept up with its people, white and black; both races kept a ledger book on human credits and debits. Racial customs in the South, of course, were intricate, filled with ambivalence and contradictions. Yet most people, black and white, knew the boundaries and enforced them.

Tobacco, growing and using it, became an obsession for many farmers. Lee Johnson, who owned a small tobacco farm in eastern North Carolina, described his affection for the tobacco culture. "I love tobacco," he admitted. "I love to fool with it and get the gum on my hands and clothes. I love to sell it and I love to chew it and smoke it. Annie dips. She tried to get modern and smoke, but she got sick on it and went back to her snuffbox." He planted other crops too, "but nothing gives me pleasure like tobacco. I have never raised anything that I like to raise half so well." He traced tobacco farming in his family back before the Civil War. "Tobacco farmers are like gold miners," he concluded, "always hoping to strike it rich."[20]

Throughout the WPA interviews and other sources, automobiles and radios seemed to have the greatest impact on the old culture. The automobile or truck seemed a most important acquisition. The high 1934 tobacco prices allowed Thomas Doyle to buy a new V-8 automobile. He cleared $1,000 and spent $650 of it for the car. His son owned a Model A. Sam Bowers remembered that, when he got married, he first wanted a house and then a car. "I saved up money an' bought one. I paid cash fur it. It wuz a model T Ford. I kep' savin' an' when I could I traded fur a Buick car, de one I has now." Such extravagance often led to deprivation in other areas. Sarah Carson revealed that her husband had bought a used Model A the year before, leaving no money to buy her winter clothes. "We've still got the old car, but we ain't had no money to buy license plates this year. When John goes to town he catches a ride." Lee Johnson cleared $2,000 on his 1938 crop and quickly invested part of it in a truck. Margaret Hagood noted that automobiles were more common in the Piedmont than in the lower South, and she credited it to "one good tobacco year within the past decade, whereas cotton farmers have not been so fortunate." Many of the cars sat idle, she observed, for people were too poor to buy inexpensive license plates.[21] Automobiles gave rural people mobility and increasingly linked them to towns and to modern needs such as tires, gasoline, and the burgeoning filling-station culture.

The radio expanded the farmer's horizon further than the automobile. Even if a farm family could not buy a car, it might be able to afford a radio. After the price of tobacco rose in the mid-1930s, more rural families could purchase radios and learn about the New Deal, soap operas, music, and things to buy. They could hear directly from far-off places. A couple identified in *These Are Our Lives* as Morrison and Irma described themselves as "hard luck renters." She welcomed the WPA interviewers, admitting that she liked to have someone to talk to. "I used to tell Morrison our lives would make a good true story—like you read in the magazines and hear on the radio—Ma Perkins and the others. Oh, yes! We got a radio—a battery set. You see, we ain't got no electric power. We listen to all the good stories and string music. Sometimes we buy things they sell on the radio . . . medicine and other things."[22]

The radio opened a world that fascinated people who were largely illiterate and accustomed to isolation. Millions, of course, listened to Franklin D. Roosevelt's fireside chats. His optimism and good cheer raised the spirits of farm people, and certainly in the tobacco area the New Deal gospel seemed the way to salvation. When Roosevelt told the farmers in October 1933 that "during the last six months we have made more rapid progress than any Nation has ever made in a like period of time," tobacco farmers, who were watching prices rise, agreed. John Sylvester Hinson also obtained useful information on farming. "The county agent's an' farm talks over the radio helps me. They know more 'bout farmin' than I do, so I follow what they say. It shore has helped me to make more an' take care of my place better."[23] Still, sharecroppers who needed help most were the least likely to be able to afford a radio.

Much of radio programming in the the 1930s was beamed toward rural audiences. Since 1928 NBC had carried the "National Farm and Home Hour" six days a week. The U.S. Department of Agriculture prepared the programs for five days, and Saturdays were divided among national farm organizations, 4-H clubs, and vocational agriculture. "Uncle Sam's Forest Rangers," a feature within the program, ran from 1932 to 1943. Sharecroppers must have had ambivalent feelings about such programs, for they learned—in addition to some useful hints on farming—that in order to survive they had to modernize. The USDA-

*Network radio reached large farm audiences with "The National
Farm and Home Hour" from 1928 to 1960. (Courtesy of* Extension
Service Review)

prepared programs painted visions of tractors, implements, improved
seeds, and other capital-intensive goods. Such programs failed to deal
with those who could not modernize for lack of money.[24]

Hoke and Bennie Bradlee lived near Durham, North Carolina. "We
listen to the radio a lot," Bennie explained. "Hoke likes to listen to them
big fellers make speeches at Washington. He says they're the only 'uns
that talk for the little man and don't sound like a pack of liars, that the
forgotten man is bein' remembered by them that runs the government." Her interests proved different and give insight into how rural
people responded to the radio. "Me and the children like to listen to the
barn dance programs, the hillbilly cowboys and the rest. The plays are
good too—Ma Perkins and Uncle Ezra. Seems like they're folks just
like us."[25] Many rural people perhaps made the same connection between the radio promised land and their present reality that they made
between the pearly gates of heaven and present hardship. The goods
advertised on the radio were as remote as heaven's golden streets.

Whether talking about acreage control, county agents, government loans, or national politics, rural people had become vividly aware that government had reached the hinterland. Johnny Polk, a black tenant, told the WPA interviewer, "I didn't git no allotment for tobacco; they let me have four acres of corn and two acres of cotton." Still, if he had had the franchise (which he did not), "I'd vote for Roosevelt. I don't care if he is a Democrat, he helps the poor man and the farmer." Then, using the vivid imagery of the rural South, he explained why: "Ever since the war, the colored folks has looked on the elephant as the animal that helps 'em. But I'm coming to believe that the elephant may be all right in Africa but the American niggers had better stay close to the American mule." Sam Bowers agreed in part. He and his wife were Republicans, but he did not care much about politics. Not clarifying whether or not he had the franchise, he said, "I think Mr. Roosevelt sho' knows his bizness. He's done mo' good dan any of de rest of 'em but Pa wuz a Republican, so I is too."[26]

Bennie Bradlee, who prefered talking to listening to the radio, credited the government with improved prices. Since the government got into agriculture, "it seems prices ain't as low as they used to be. I remember when them buyers at the market didn't give us enough to pay the fertilizer bill. Now we got a radio and a old car." A sharecropper named Jimmy Cane grew six acres of tobacco. Times were hard, he said, but there were things that helped out. "I got a little parity money," he revealed, "and then there are the other things like vegetables and hogs." He thought that the county agents "do a lot of good, and so would the crop control if it was done right."[27] As much as any other factor, government intrusion had altered the rural culture in the tobacco region.

Government credit helped some farmers survive, but others objected to red tape. One farm woman admitted that "her husband would never again borrow from the government because they kept on sending him letters 'six feet long and three feet wide,' which he couldn't read, and kept him in a sweat." Most farmers who secured government loans thought the low interest rates were to their advantage, but rural people were of different minds about the accompanying oversight. One woman preferred government credit, Hagood noted, "because she is quite isolated and enjoys the home supervisor's visits while another has stopped using it because she didn't want anyone telling her what to do." Lee Johnson proved to be one of the few tobacco farmers who objected to the government. "I don't think we'd ought to have crop control; I think the government ought to leave us farmers alone. We don't mind our crops selling for nothing if we can get our food, clothes, and fertilizer for nothing, too. We want an even break, and it seems to me like the government could force down other prices easier than it can raise the prices of farm products. All we expect is a living and a little over."[28]

Rural women shared in the life and labor of their husbands to a great degree. Margaret Hagood discovered that many rural women knew all about crops and local credit arrangements. Although some women yielded to their husbands on farm matters, others spoke up on how they took part in the daily operation of the farm. "Their knowledge of farming matters is surprising and pertains not only to the immediate condition of the current crop but to details of renting, credit, the sequence of operations, and to the basic data for making an estimate of how they will 'come out this year,'" Haygood noted. Most women in the tobacco section worked in the fields until poor health or grown children relieved them, and they also ran the tobacco grading rooms. "Men ain't no good in 'bacca," one woman complained. "They can't set still and work steady. They's always got to be goin' outdoors to see about somp'n—even if they ain't got no excuse better'n the dog." Seven-eighths of the women preferred fieldwork to housework, saying such things as "I was brought up to it" and "I've always done it." They had worked beside men all their lives and were proud of it. "My papa said he lost his best hand when I got married," one boasted. Even when they were too old or ill to work, they talked about their earlier prowess.[29]

Women enjoyed the fellowship at the scaffold and in the grading room. Cotton farmers did not have such an opportunity for socializing, even though they usually chopped and picked in groups. Women, like men, loved the tobacco culture thoroughly. "Just smell it and you'll see why all my children except the two who stay in the house chew—boys and girls," explained one woman.[30]

Some women managed their own farms. Lillie Tart of eastern North Carolina boasted that she and her two sisters had managed a farm since 1937. "We did all the work," she said. "Sometimes we'd swap with the neighbors, maybe work on ourn one day and theirn the next." She plowed with her mules, Mag and Kate. "They were smart mules," she said, "until we got so old and feeble we couldn't do nothing with them, and then they'd run away!" She tended tobacco into the 1970s, and though the mules had disappeared, her love for the tobacco markets persisted: "You know, I love to go to the market!"[31]

The Titus Oakley family stripping, tying, and grading tobacco in their bedroom. Granville County, North Carolina. November 1939. Marion Post Wolcott. (LC USF 34 52628-D, Library of Congress)

The grinding poverty and hard work took its toll. Though some women might well know all about the work culture and enjoy it, others endured it as best they could. Sarah Carson had to leave her nine-month-old baby in the house while she worked at the scaffold. She justified it by noting, "Everybody else leaves their younguns at the houses. Mrs. Barham ties her baby to the table leg with a hemp rope because she's scared it'll get into mischief or swallow something that'll choke it." She left her child in the yard one time, she said, but it started eating "sand, chicken manure, and strings, so I decided to leave her in the house and take a chance on her eating buttons." Anyway, she admitted, if she left the scaffold often to care for her child, "John would raise the devil."

As they fell behind emptying a slide, John came in from the fields. "Damn it," he shouted, "what have you been doing that you can't keep trucks in the field? I told Ben that if it was his fault I'd skin his god damned hide. If you damned women wouldn't jabber so much you'd git done sometime." He grabbed Sarah by the collar and threatened to hit her with a tobacco stick.

At eleven o'clock she went to the house. "She ran in, lifted the baby, and hugged it. It was dirty and wet, but she had no time to change it." The house was a mess, unmade beds and clothing tossed all about. "After Sarah had suckled the baby she built a fire in the stove and warmed up the pots of beans, potatoes, and tomatoes that she had cooked before daylight." She then made a pot of coffee and sliced a cake for dessert. John washed up and rushed in and began eating before the other men. Sarah was embarrassed, but John retorted, "Ain't a man got a right to set down at his own table when he pleases?" The women ate after the men finished and then helped with the dishes.

Sarah Carson admitted that she was tired and that she hated barn-ing tobacco. "We're off till two o'clock, though, to let the mules rest. Thank God for the mules—John takes right good care o' *them*." She told the interviewer that she had worked hard all her life and couldn't understand why she was so tired. "I'll tell you what's so: tenant farm-ing ain't no pleasure at all." Her family had been tenant farmers, and they hardly ever made any money and moved nearly every year. "I've heard folks say that there was good landlords and bad ones. I ain't never seen no good ones. They're all alike, looking for every cent they can get, and landlords was all born without hearts." She admitted that she hardly ever left the farm. "I don't go to church, and I don't go to town once in six months. I ain't got no near neighbors and I don't care a straw about visiting nohow." All she did was work and rest. She and many women who slaved away at the tobacco culture presented a vul-nerable face to the world. If John had gone to jail again or left her for any reason, she could not have managed the farm alone. The options open to such women were simple—remarry, go back to parents, or take a factory job.[32]

Sarah Carson probably stayed home more than most farmers, but the rural South offered few opportunities for recreation other than church services, revivals, occasional farm organization meetings, and trips to town on Saturdays. Occasionally a carnival or tent show passed through a community, giving a welcomed break from the work rou-tine. Not all people engaged in the few sources of entertainment that were available, for fundamentalist religion had sucked the joy of life from many families. Thomas Doyle took his religion seriously. He was a deacon and treasurer of his church, and he did not drink, did not even know how to gamble, did not attend movies or allow his children to, and did not dance or even sing reels, which the church objected to. The WPA interviewer concluded, "He isn't interested in amusements."

But he did occasionally go "down the highway and hang around the filling station for a while."[33]

John Sylvester Hinson, who admitted that he drank and attended parties, made some observations about the changes he had witnessed. "When I wuz a boy people courted at home; now young people court in automobiles." He also noted that people did not visit each other like they used to, nor did they attend church services as regularly. "Movin' pictures, dance halls, an' jest ridin' 'round in automobiles is where you'll find most of the young folks. The old folks stays home, listens to the radio, an' talks. Times has shore changed." Hinson had not seen an outhouse or pump until 1897, when he was seventeen years old. "I wuz a full grown man 'fore I tasted ice cream or Coca-Cola," he admitted.[34]

No matter what the older generation thought, the younger folks in the rural tobacco area welcomed a break from the confining isolation of the farms. They rode around in cars and pushed out the horizon. They listened to the radio, heard famous people, and learned about things they could do and buy. For many people of the tobacco belt, the outside world made its first appearance.

But no matter what the people did for recreation, they were all tied to the autumn rite of selling tobacco and settling accounts. Nearly any sharecropper could recount a story of bad landlords. They all dreamed of good crops and generous settlements, but their lives were ruled by the caprices of weather and the unpredictability of landlords. They became fatalistic in some ways but still salvaged as much of their dream as possible.

A sharecropper named Jack Webster had hoped to buy a farmhouse when he started farming, but he gave that up. "My next aim was to have a good pack o' hounds and some good guns. I have them. Best of all, I've raised my children to be respectable. I've got ten, which is one short of what my daddy done, but Sally says she don't care if it is. Her health ain't what it once was, and she has to take medicine for female trouble. But we have a happy home, plenty of dogs, stock, and farming tools, and we are satisfied and happy."[35]

Thomas Doyle readily admitted that his dream was almost a reality. "What does I want? I got a option on a farm now. I'm hopin' the government's gonna help me get it." He had made arrangements for the payment. "I want 'bout a hundred acre of cleared land, 'nough for me and all these chillun of mine to work on. I want it good land and I want a good lil' house on it." Just as Doyle hoped that the government would

make the proper arrangements, Morrison and Irma also tied their
dream to the New Deal. "Some day we hope to own our own land as
well as the house," Irma said. "It might be a long time, but with the
grace of God we'll get there. It seems like that man in Washington has
got a real love for the people in his heart, and I believe it's due to him
and his helpers that the poor renters are goin' to get a chance. We've
got more hope now than we ever had before."[36]

Farmers feared most of all the day when they would not be able to
farm anymore. Even though the government had wound up the clock
that ran the old tobacco culture, it too could run down; or it might simply be ticking off the time until the new forces it had set in motion
would mature. Johnny and Leah Polk meditated upon time and motion
in 1939, as they watched the world from their rural North Carolina
haven. They knew the world could wind down. "The time will come,
though when you cain't travel," Leah Polk observed. "Maybe we'll jist
drop dead, and maybe we'll go slower and slower until we cain't travel
no mo'." Despite the vigor of the old tobacco culture in 1939, the clock
ticked slower and marked time until a new culture would arise, a machine and chemical-based culture fueled by capital.[37]

The Warehouse Culture

Although tobacco markets were in many ways alien to farmers, many
of the warehouse workers, auctioneers, buyers, speculators, and owners had grown up on tobacco farms. Though a farmer might resent the
buyer's bid and the warehouse's charges, he held a grudging admira-
tion for such successful former tobacco farmers. Shared experiences
eased the wounds of class. Before James B. Duke and R. J. Reynolds
became manufacturing giants, they and many other small manufacturers grew tobacco, manufactured plug, and peddled it throughout
the surrounding country. Local people continued to run the tobacco
industry from top to bottom, and many of them had started out dropping plants at transplanting time when they were children.

Railroads opened up areas and created marketing centers. The tobacco families from Granville County were responsible for much of the
expansion at the turn of the century and later, and they set in motion
what can best be described as Granville County imperialism.[38] By the
turn of the century, tobacco warehouses had followed planters and rail-

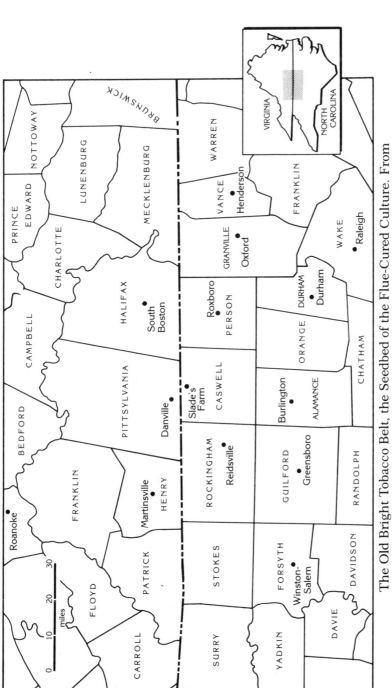

The Old Bright Tobacco Belt, the Seedbed of the Flue-Cured Culture. From Nannie May Tilley, *The Bright-Tobacco Industry, 1860–1929.*

roads, creating throughout the area an autumn festival at selling time. Not only did farmers like the almost instant cash, they also liked the break in farm routine and the exchange of talk.

The trip to market in the old days broke up the farm routine and often provided an adventure. Dixon Kavanaugh, who grew up seventeen miles from Durham, remembered that it took eight hours to haul tobacco to the market. "Several wagons would go together and when one would get mired or stuck on a hill the others would unhitch and fasten a pair of stretchers, like are used in snaking logs, to hook in the tongue of the stuck wagon and the teams would pull it out." The trip took two days when a Granville County native named Clyde Singleton was a youth. "We'd leave home one morning, spend the night on the road, and get into Durham the next afternoon." He sold at Parrish's warehouse. "When we'd get close to town on what was then the Roxboro Road but what's now Roxboro Street he'd have a pair of big mules waiting to hitch on and haul us in to the warehouse. The mud in the streets sometimes would be kneedeep to a mule." Otis Rucker remembered that tobacco arrived in Lynchburg "in schooner wagons drawn by maybe six horses and with three thousand or thirty-five hundred pounds and a gallon jug of corn liquor inside."[39]

Warehouseman Roy Pearce gave a vivid description of the old days. "We'd get there, put the animals in the stable under the warehouse, then go upstairs to what was called the camp room. The warehouse would have big pots of coffee there. We'd stand around them and talk and carry on till late at night. Had a great time! In the morning we'd unload the tobacco." Clyde Singleton remembered the camp rooms also. The Parrish warehouse in Durham had stalls for the horses and mules, and farmers would congregate in the camp room. "Everybody brought their provisions and cooked their victuals." There was no hurry in those days. "A farmer would wait around maybe a couple of days to sell," Otis Rucker recalled. Pearce bought a warehouse in 1936 and obviously enjoyed the market days. "Course, the farmers don't stay overnight anymore," he said, "because they come in trucks." Most people who frequented the markets as warehouse owners or managers, buyers, pinhookers, and wage hands, like Pearce, Singleton, and Rucker, had grown up on tobacco farms.[40]

Growers chose their warehouses with care, and experience dictated their loyalty. Warehousemen used any method to attract growers and keep them loyal. "Extending various courtesies to prospective patrons, hiring 'drummers,' spreading damaging rumors about other markets, advancing credit to patrons, and giving rebates to a few farmers," Nannie May Tilley wrote, "constituted some of the outstanding methods used by warehousemen to obtain the opportunity of selling the farmers' tobacco." Danny Kelly had spent many summers as a "trade man." He visited farmers in his home community and inquired about their crops and urged them to sell at a particular warehouse. Warehouse employees fanned out in all directions, inquiring about the crops, passing the time of day, and urging farmers to sell with them. Warehousemen favored respected farmers who could attract other growers. Sam Hobgood, whose father ran a warehouse in Oxford, North Carolina, started drumming when he was nineteen years old. "Sometimes you might go to a barn and meet half a dozen men there from Henderson, Creedmore, Durham, Oxford, all trying to get the farmer to bring his tobacco to their warehouse." Occasionally Hobgood would buy a farmer's tobacco as it hung in the barn. A North Carolina farmer named Richard Cornwall recalled that drumming ended around the turn of the century.[41]

In 1938 Leonard Rapport, a Works Progress Administration historian, interviewed warehouse people in Durham. By that time the flue-cured tobacco culture, because of the federal allotment system, had reached the limits of its expansion. Tobacco farmers, like smokers, became addicted, first to the culture and then to the federal program. Rapport joked that Durham thrived on addictive commodities— tobacco, BC and Goody's headache powders, and corn liquor.[42] As warehouse people related their life histories, they revealed significant aspects of the culture—its dynamic expansion, the role of auctioneers, buyers, and laborers, and a love for their work.

Warehouse people maintained a sense of place and history as they left the farms to handle the already cured tobacco. "Parson" Arthur Barnes, who worked in the Leaf Warehouse in Durham, bragged on his home county. "The best wrappers— the real number-one wrappers—come out of Granville County. They're just about the best the companies can get." His father had moved from Vance to Granville County because the soil was better for tobacco, at least until the wilt struck. D. W. Daniels, a tobacco buyer, remembered that his father's farm bordered on Caswell, Orange, and Granville counties. "He raised tobacco and his father before him, and the place is still being farmed in tobacco with a better yield than ever." Danny Kelly boasted that Granville County used to be "one of the wealthiest counties in the State," but he noted that the wilt had damaged production. Policeman Clyde

Roberts and cafe manager Claude King both came from Granville County and remembered their formative years working in tobacco.[43]

Leaf buyer Frank Tillman was born in Durham, but his father grew up in Person County on a plantation that was still in the family. As a youth Tillman had spent his summers working on the farm. Some buyers and auctioneers entered the business with no tobacco experience. "In my case, though, there was plenty of tobacco behind me," Tillman related. "My father started in the tobacco business when he left a tobacco farm to come to Durham and go into warehousing with old Captain Parrish as a bookman; on the sale he could carry either the book or clip." His father later bought for American Tobacco Company and retired as head of American's southern leaf department. Tillman had started out working for American but in 1938 bought for Apex Leaf Tobacco Company.[44]

Sam Hobgood, who managed a processing factory for the Imperial Tobacco Company, was born on a farm in Granville County, but his family moved to Oxford when he was two years old. "In tobacco the big gambler is the farmer himself," he remembered. "He has no guarantee of anything. He takes a chance on raising his crop and then when he gets it raised he doesn't know what it will bring. It's a ninety day crop growing but, as the farmers say, with the curing it takes thirteen months a year."[45]

The flue-cured culture spread partly because of promotion from railroads and warehousemen. Clyde Roberts, who was a policeman in Durham in 1939, had gone to Georgia in 1919 when he was twenty years old. He had heard of a job demonstrating for a railroad, and he got $50 a month from the railroad and another $150 from a warehouse to show Georgians how to grow tobacco. He went from farm to farm. "I coached them all the way from the seedbed through curing," he said, and he found many North Carolinians there. The boll weevil had hit Georgia, he remembered, driving cotton production down, and in 1919, with extremely high tobacco prices, farmers had eagerly switched to tobacco.[46] Increased production, of course, helped drive down prices. Buyers, auctioneers, and some of the warehouse workers moved in a large crescent that started in Georgia in July or August, moved through South and North Carolina and Virginia, and ended in the burley country of Kentucky and Tennessee in the winter. The way the belt selling of tobacco worked, the Georgia markets opened first and quickly sold off the untied tobacco. This freed buyers, auctioneers, and warehouse workers to move north as markets opened in the Carolinas and Virginia. No matter where a farmer sold his tobacco, he mixed not only with other growers but also with men who had left farming to enter warehouse work. They all shared a love of the tobacco culture, and from the poorest grower to the most arrogant buyer there was a bond and a tension when they met.

The night before a sale farmers milled about, some searching for bootleg liquor, others for women, while still others slept in their cars or in the segregated camp rooms. Some tried their hand at the shooting galleries or other games set up near the warehouses; a few would buy snake oil or be taken in by a scam, but most came only to sell their tobacco and get some cash. "On a market generally the average good-thinking man never gets in trouble or robbed," Parson Barnes remembered; "he might get tackled sometimes. I've had 'em try me. If you'll just keep out of the bootleg joints you're all right." Barnes, when he was farming, got good prices for his tobacco. "I never had any trouble about it on account of being colored," he said.[47]

According to a peddler named Josiah Roberts, Durham was dull compared to the carnival atmosphere of Winston-Salem. About two weeks after the markets opened there, he said, "heaven knows, if there was ever a medicine racket it's operated there. You can learn more about rackets and pitching on Trade Street in two days than you can in two months in Durham. The people have money and are in a carnival mood, buying and spending; all a man has to do to get started is to shake a cowbell and ballyhoo." Roberts knew the rackets and merchandise—girlie pictures, watches, "rattlesnake oil that never gets nearer a rattle-snake than oil of mustard," blood purifiers, and laxatives. "If it wasn't for constipation medical doctors wouldn't have a leg to stand on," he argued. "It's the only thing they can really treat for except something like broken bones." He went on with his medical lecture, arguing that city people took more BC powders than country people because "farmers aren't as constipated and therefore don't have as many headaches."[48]

The drinking, amusements, and talk served as preliminaries to the auction. A farmer with his tobacco sitting on the floor knew that his trip to town was focused on the few seconds when a buyer offered a bid. Farmers emerged from the camp rooms or from cars or hotels, and as the sun came streaming through the skylights and the tobacco reflected its golden color, the saleshouses came alive.

The auctioneer dominated the floor with his voice and humor, and he controlled the cadence of the sale. Colonel Chiswell Dabney Lan-

A tobacco auctioneer [Roy Daniel?] (wearing white gloves) and tobacco buyers at an auction sale which is being held in a tobacco warehouse. Mebane, North Carolina. November 1939. Marion Post Wolcott. (LC USF 34 52841-D, Library of Congress)

ghorne of Danville became the archetypical auctioneer, the model for numerous men who followed the profession. "Herbert Baker was the best auctioneer I ever heard," Durham auctioneer Earl Brady remembered. "He had the prettiest, softest voice, clear as a bell, and his lower jaw would be going like a sewing machine. When he came out on the floor his clothes were pressed smooth as if he was going to preach, and he wore a high starched collar with the tie tight at the top. People would come a long way just to hear him; from a voice standpoint he was considered great." Buyer Frank Tillman agreed. "He had a fine delivery and a wonderful voice; he took bids quickly, with no exertion at all. He was what we call a natural auctioneer." Buck Hall added that Baker dressed "as nice as any professor you ever saw, everything neat and starched, and he'd have a fresh straw hat going around like that while he'd call the bids twenty-two twenty three and a half Liggett and Myers and all the time spinning that straw hat. He was something to see and hear." [49]

The warehouse owner would usually start the bidding after moving ahead and taking a sample hand of tobacco. The auctioneer would then pick up the bid. "In my selling I fill in, use a little bit of everything to keep from getting monotonous," Earl Brady explained. "I make the syllable or sound; I don't sound out the whole word. Seven, seven, and a quarter, half, three, eight and make the eight plain. I'm baritone and at times you can hear me clear across the warehouse—when I'm feeling good or coming in about through."[50]

Occasionally an auctioneer would "step out." Buck Hall, who carried the book behind auctioneers, recalled that Roy Daniel had first sale at the Big Bull warehouse one Monday morning. "Roy said, 'I'm going to step out this morning,' so they got him an extra ticket marker, an extra bookman, and an extra clipman. He was supposed to come out at three fifteen— that's what the Bull takes from wall to wall—and he came out at twelve fifteen. We were going about seven or eight hundred piles an hour and no single crew could have kept up with him." Earl Brady remembered one day when he stepped out. "One Monday morning I sold 320,000 pounds on the Carolina floor by 12:30, a house that's supposed to take 5 1/2 hours from wall to wall."[51]

By the mid-1930s, local tobacco boards set the speed of sales, and the major companies instructed their buyers not to proceed if sales passed that limit. Thus auctioneers would not be able to step out again. "We don't sell that fast any more," Earl Brady admitted; "the tendency is to slow down the sales." The Durham tobacco board set the rate at 360 piles an hour. Brady argued that fast sales discriminated against farmers and buyers. "Fast sales are to the interest of the warehouse and the auctioneer. The more tobacco that's sold the more the warehouse makes, and auctioneers get a percent of all over a certain amount they sell."[52]

As they went from warehouse to warehouse in the course of a day, auctioneers would stop off at local taverns to soothe their throats. Earl Brady, who had auctioned for thirty years by 1939, reported that one auctioneer named Sullivan told him, "Earl, you know when I get hold of that stuff it makes me wish I had a neck a yard long and a taster all the way down." Although drinking had allegedly slowed down by the late 1930s, auctioneers preserved a reputation for hard drinking. Arthur Rawls, a warehouse operator, said, "It looks like auctioneers just will drink." They would leave the auction floor and start drinking, and after a few seasons they ruined their voices. "But on the other hand I never saw an auctioneer who didn't drink who was any 'count."[53]

Although the auction still persisted as an extravaganza, it had changed drastically since the days when Herbert Baker dressed like a professor and his cohorts drank like sailors. Auctioneer Earl Brady spent several hours posing for pictures to promote Lucky Strikes. "I got $500 for my endorsement, and they've been sending me a carton of Luckies a week for 14 months now," he bragged.[54]

Auctioneers were the aristocrats of the tobacco warehouse culture. Possessing gifted voices and the ability to think and calculate quickly, they strode through the saleshouses as local gods. They moved in another world from that of the farmers who hung on their every unintelligible syllable. Unlike the buyers who did the bidding, the auctioneers were independent in the exchange of tobacco. Their job demanded the ability to order the sales. Besides with their voice, the other way they could excel was in speed of selling. By 1939 the constant complaints and new selling regulations had ended that path to glory.[55]

Like many other people who worked in warehouses, buyers often came from the farms of the flue-cured area. Many of them had started out working in warehouses when they left the farm, then had done work for redrying plants, and finally became buyers after learning the intricacies of grades. There was a great deal to learn about tobacco, and Frank Tillman insisted that "a very important factor is light." It was better to have "the light over the buyer's shoulder instead of in his face." A buyer would often turn around with a hand of tobacco to get the light over his shoulder. "Whitewashing will make tobacco show more color and give it a deceitful appearance," and farmers knew how color and light in a warehouse might fool buyers. "Putting pale tobacco up against a red brick wall will tend to soften it and make it look ripe and spongy." Green tobacco could be disguised by placing it against a solid wall. Speculators usually put their tobacco in the middle of the house to get a better light. "Sometimes, of course," he joked, "the truest light is not, for a speculator, the best light." Most buyers were even in their judgment, he said. "A buyer shouldn't play favorites among the farmers; the fact that I raised tobacco might make me feel kindlier toward the men whose tobacco I'm buying, but I've only a certain amount to pay and a set average to keep to."[56]

Warehouse people drew a sharp distinction between pinhookers and leaf buyers. "If I was to buy tobacco direct from the farmer before he put it on the floor, that would be pinhooking," explained Dixon Kavanaugh. "But if I buy on the floor for sale I'm what you call a leaf dealer;

some calls it a speculator." Bill Jordan agreed. "Way back yonder they used to even buy tobacco green in the field. That's when a farmer would say, 'I've pinhooked my crop.'" D. W. Daniels had heard the term all his life, and his understanding was that it originated "from the idea of a man being a small buyer—fishing with a pinhook." Isaac Carter, who had been an auctioneer for thirty-five years, remembered that "in the old days the farmer used to give speculators some money, pin money, to get them to bid up their tobacco against the regular buyers. Later, when they bought tobacco directly from the farmer to resell it on the floor, the name stuck to them."[57]

Behind the auctioneer and buyers trailed a small army of men who translated the chant and bid into dollars and cents. Buck Hall, who grew up on a Virginia fire-cured tobacco farm and worked throughout the tobacco belt as a bookman, described his job. "The clipman and the bookman follow along behind the auctioneer and ticket marker. The bookman puts down who buys the pile, the grade, and the price, and the clipman has the same thing, and they figure each pile separately and check." They rounded off the numbers and gave the benefit to the farmers. "We have to figure the prices in our head as fast as the auctioneer sells. You pick up short cuts in figuring," he revealed, and gave some examples. "Math is something that just came to me; that's the way it is with a book or clipman; it either just comes to you or it doesn't—I don't know why it is."

The fast calculations were only part of the job, Hall continued. "He's got to go to work then and make out bills for American, say eighteen thousand pounds, Liggett and Myers, twenty thousand, for everybody who's bought as much as one pile of tobacco." Such work took as much time as the sales. "Everybody works at it, the clipman, bookman, ticket marker, and the weigh man." They tried to get it all to come out to the penny. "It used to be that we might get through in the office at midnight and I'd go home, set the clock for three o'clock, and never close my eyes before it would ring and I'd come on at four and weigh tobacco with thirty-five trucks rolling." Hall boasted that he had once followed auctioneer Roy Daniel in the Big Bull warehouse when he stepped out. Like the auctioneer, his train of followers also prided themselves in doing fast work. Buck Hall realized the difference between his station in life and that of the auctioneers. "And I smoke Luckies," he said, "but I don't get five hundred dollars and the carton a week for a year."[58]

The warehouse was a man's world, and in many cases it was almost exclusively a white man's world. Black growers received the same reception as whites, but there were no black auctioneers, no black buyers, no black bookmen or clipmen, no black warehouse owners. Only the wagehands who unloaded the tobacco and then moved it after sales were black. Some women and children attended the sales, enjoying a vacation from the farm routine. A grower would occasionally sit an attractive daughter on top of his tobacco, hoping to tempt buyers to bid higher. But women, by and large, stood in the wings as the procession of buyers marched through the house.

There was no sentiment in buying tobacco; it was a cash transaction. A farmer took his tag and cashed it in at the warehouse window. For a few months the warehouse district of the tobacco belt thrived on the infusion of cash, and then it slowed down during the spring and summer months. While the farmer worked his next crop, the warehouse people drifted to other jobs or played setback and dominoes with friends in the empty warehouse. They too had a culture, but it did not operate thirteen months a year. Still, it was part of the larger culture; it was tobacco.

The Carolina-Canada Link

The flue-cured culture not only spread from Granville County southeast; it also reached to Canada. F. R. Gregory grew up in Granville County, moved to Leamington, Ontario, in 1911, and, he boasted, began the flue-cured tobacco culture there. He contracted with the Empire Tobacco Company and then lured curing experts from his native county to Ontario. By 1928 he had seventeen farms under his control, and each year he returned to his North Carolina home and contracted neighbors to cure tobacco in Ontario. Gregory had more applications than he could fill, for farmers who went north returned with happy memories and cash. "I engage curers, only," he explained, "and no primers or laborers, although one old man without our knowledge or consent, and very much to our disgust brought his wife along."[59]

By 1930 the Canadian tobacco culture had grown in no small part because of the influx of North Carolinians. Sid Williams, who worked as a floorman in Durham, first went to Canada in 1930 with two carloads of Tarheels. He did not take his wife or small children, he said, because Canadians were "the roughest-talking and wickedest people in the world. They never think about such a thing as Jesus Christ, they don't give Him a thought." Still, he admitted, they had good land. "I think they call that part of Canada Ontario," he mused. "I once bought a hat up there and it had it in it." He took one of his sons there on his first trip in 1930. "When we got ready to come back that fall, well sir he'd got to going round with a Canadian girl and he just decided to stay and help her people raise a crop next year." The couple got married, and the groom went into the barbering business, a trade he had learned at home. After three years, however, he got homesick and returned to Person County with his wife. "She and my boy didn't get along together and she couldn't get on around my wife. She was too rough-talking; Canadians are the roughest-talking people in the world and the women are as bad as the men." When Williams returned the next year, he took his son's wife with him and left her there. "They'll never get back together," he concluded.

The first man Williams worked for in Canada was from North Carolina. "There are a lot of North Carolina people there, curing and raising," he noted. Most of the people who raised tobacco in the section where he worked were Belgians, and they used "those big Belgian horses that leave a track the size of a cuspidor and then some; the ice wagon horses they used to have here are ponies beside those Belgian horses." Most of the tobacco growers, like those in the Carolinas and Virginia, were sharecroppers, but there were no blacks, he observed.[60]

Danny Kelly's son-in-law spent several seasons in Canada curing tobacco. "He worked for a Belgian who married a Granville County girl." The Belgian, Paul Dufour, visited the home place, and he was a big man with a great appetite. "Eat—that fellow liked to eat about as well as I do myself," Kelly admitted. "And they use beer for water up there; they make their own and have it setting in barrels in their basements. Dufour wanted to know what sort of beer this was we had here in tin cans; not fit to drink, he said. He was an awful nice fellow."[61]

Clyde Roberts had traveled to Canada in 1928 and worked for a Granville County man. He cured that year, and the next he raised a crop for himself. Drought, flood, and an early freeze ruined his crop. "I'd taken two Southerners to help me and at curing time I hired another, all from Durham." He was impressed with the Belgian horses and considered them better than tractors. The landlord also furnished "an automatic planter, a fertilizer distributor that opened and sowed two rows at the time; and a very good house." Evidently the Canadians were adapting new technology more quickly than were North Carolinians. There was no auction system in Canada. Roberts noted that company buyers came around and bought in the barns, but he preferred the American auction system. Unlike in the southern culture, Canadians planted not in hills but on flat land. Farmers there made about a thousand pounds per acre, about two hundred pounds more than in Granville County.[62]

Flue-cured imperialism carried the culture to virgin growing areas in Georgia and Florida and north to Ontario. This expansion opened a wider world for even the most isolated tobacco growers, for they heard tales in the warehouses, perhaps had friends or relatives who had cured in Canada, and possessed a general knowledge about tobacco's international travels. The spread of flue-cured tobacco satisfied the growing international demand, but it also held down the price. Not all farmers shared in mobility, for from all accounts only white farmers transferred the cultural secrets. There was also a steady stream of growers who took jobs at warehouses, and while blacks were imprisoned at hand-labor tasks, whites moved up through the ranks of the warehouse structure.

Yet the New Deal ended the dynamic expansion of bright tobacco even as it ended the option of an auctioneer to "step out." The government regulated tobacco growers, just as it had begun regulating other industries during the Progressive Era. Many tobacco farmers were no doubt better off, for they had dependable incomes. By confining them with acreage allotments, however, the AAA enclosed the culture. Small growers fought to survive for another quarter-century before other forces drove them off the land and, as in the cotton culture, consolidated the property and mechanized the work.

10

*It is getting to be just as natural
for a farmer to tell one of his
boys to go out and steam up the
engine as it is to tell him to go to
the barn and hitch up the team.*
—*Frank Foley, 1904*

Islands of Progress:
The Rice Culture

When the railroad opened the southwestern Louisiana prairie in the 1880s, there were already two distinct rice-growing cultures in the state. Cajun farmers grew Providence rice in the prairie, and farmers along the Mississippi cultivated river rice using river water to flood the fields. While river growers persisted with traditional cultivation and harvesting methods, the Providence culture evolved into highly mechanized and irrigated farming that quickly dominated the United States market. Farmers invested in plows, binders, and later in steam traction engines, threshers, pumping plants, tractors, and combines. Unlike tobacco and cotton farmers, who used primitive tools until the mid-twentieth century, rice growers, many transplanted from the midwestern wheat-growing area, epitomized the ideal of the progressive American farmer. Rice farming left time for growing other crops and for keeping up houses, barns, and fences. Wives, freed from fieldwork, concentrated on family, gardens, flowers, and community functions. Indeed, the prairie rice culture seemed misplaced—in Louisiana, a Cajun island shared with Midwesterners; in Texas, a checkerboard of oil derricks, cattle herds, and rice irrigation pumps; in Arkansas, a four-county refuge surrounded by cotton sharecroppers and their lords.[1]

By the turn of the century most prairie rice farmers looked back to the Providence days as old-fashioned and backward. Yet that method of cultivation had its own work routine and—as with so many crops that rely on rainfall—a serious element of risk. Cajun farmers built small ponds to capture rainwater, and, using the slope of the land to their advantage, planted rice and then released water to flood it. This got the rice started, but for the remainder of the season the farmers depended on Providence for irrigation. William Maher, who moved to Acadia Parish in 1874, recalled that "in the early days we had no artificial irrigation, except such as we obtained by damming up small coulees, and this was a very unsatisfactory method of irrigation." They raised some good crops but had frequent failures. The local population consumed most of the crop, but farmers hauled some to Opelousas, at that time a marketing center. "Crowley had not been even thought of, and the present sites of Rayne, Jennings, Gueydan, Morse, Estherwood, Iota, Eunice and the dozen or more other smaller rice towns of this section were open prairie," he recalled.

Maher plowed his 1875 crop with oxen and with "an old fashioned Hall plow." The work proved to be labor intensive. "I sowed the rice by hand, broadcast, as the sower in the Bible sowed wheat," he remembered. After broadcasting the seed, he used a homemade harrow to cover it. The 1875 crop received plenty of rainfall; using "the old fashioned sickle" to harvest it, he made about twenty barrels to the acre. After standing the grain in shocks until dry, "We threshed with flails and by tamping out the grain with animals, as they did in the days of Abraham." There were no mills in the prairie then, so Maher used the mortar and pestle, "such as druggists use, only larger. The mortar was made from a section of log hollowed out, and the pestle was a stick of oak or cypress about four feet long." By 1905, when Maher wrote his account of the early days, he raised not only rice but also twenty-five bales of cotton, vegetables, meat, horse feed, and even his own mules.[2]

While Maher had migrated to the prairie, Rouseb Soileau's grandfather, Gerard Miller, had roots in the area near present-day Eunice. Remembering what his grandfather had passed down, Soileau recalled that they planted rice in a low field and flooded it with water that had been dammed up. At harvest time they cut the rice with a sickle and, after shocking, hauled it to the fenced hog lot. After turning out the hogs to fatten in the harvested fields, they piled the rice into two long ten- to twelve-foot-high stacks called melons. The separator sat between the rows and, as oxen or mules turned a shaft that through a rope set gears in motion, they threshed the rice. This labor-intensive threshing sometimes lasted from October until Christmas. About the time farmers started using steam threshers, Miller went to church and met a recent German immigrant. The man explained how the steam thresher worked and asked if Miller wanted to use it. "Hell no, I don't want any fire around my melon of rice," he replied, envisioning a spark

setting the entire crop afire. Most of the Providence crop was marketed in the nearby town of Washington, Soileau recalled, and farmers
received silver dollars in payment.

Soileau also explained the origin of the barrel measure. Rice fell
from the thresher into a barrel, and laborers then dumped the barrel
into a sack. This insured that each sack contained approximately 162
pounds of rice. With faster threshing, farmers discarded the barrel,
and the rice fell directly into sacks. While Arkansas farmers use bushels as their measure and most other states use the hundredweight,
Louisiana farmers still insist that the measure be converted to barrels.[3]

The immigrant population, familiar with the midwestern wheat
culture, quickly learned the Cajun rituals and then added their own
innovations. While William Maher used biblical analogies to describe
rice growing in the 1870s, a decade later a new vocabulary took root in
the prairie, one that relied on science and technology. As in other commodity cultures, the special needs of the rice plant dictated the farmer's yearly cycle. After harvest most farmers turned the soil with gang
plows. Seaman Knapp warned that deep plowing just before planting
could bring "too much alkali to the surface." In the spring they plowed
again and followed quickly with a disc harrow and then a smoothing
harrow and a roller. "The roller," Knapp observed, "will crush the
lumps, make the soil more compact, and conserve the moisture for
germinating the grain, rendering it unnecessary to flood for 'sprout-
ing.'" Before planting, the farmer constructed small levees around the
fields with a road grader or a specially constructed plow. Knapp preferred drilling to broadcasting seed and suggested having a roller pack
the earth so that birds could not steal the seed.[4]

If the soil possessed enough moisture, flooding could wait until the
rice grew six or eight inches high, or to where it shaded the ground.
The field then remained under water until several weeks before harvest. A constant flow of water discouraged weeds. "The water should
stand at uniform depth all over the field," Knapp suggested. "Unequal
depths of water will cause the crop to ripen at different times." Rice
was planted from April through May and harvested from late July into
mid-September. William Carter Stubbs, the director of Louisiana experiment stations, revealed in 1901 that rice farmers had far more leisure time than did sugar planters. "The rice planter only needs men to
break the land. Keeping the crop between the planting and the harvest
requires only about 1 man to three or four hundred acres; whereas the
sugar planter has to have a large gang of hands all the while."[5] He

could have extended the comparison to cotton and tobacco farmers, who worked intensively during the spring and summer months.

As the rice matured, farmers looked for signs of ripening. Several weeks before harvest they drained the fields to allow the soil to harden so that mechanical binders could operate. The rice grain binder cut the stalks and automatically tied them into bundles. Workers followed, collecting the bundles and then shocking them. Knapp warned that shocking should not be left "to some boy who can do nothing else." Rather, he gave explicit directions: "First, shock on dry ground; second, brace the bundles carefully against each other, so as to resist wind or storm; third, let the shock be longest east and west and cap carefully with bundles, allowing the heads of the capping bundles to fall on the north side of the shock to avoid the sun." Rice should stand in the shock "till the straw is cured and the kernel hard."[6]

After the rice had ripened properly in shocks, the threshing operation began. "Then," William Carter Stubbs revealed, "the threshing is done whenever we can get those traveling threshers that pass through the country. They are numerous, and probably one man will thresh today, another tomorrow, and so on, in passing through a community. Large rice planters have their own thresher, and they commence as soon as the rice is cut, and continue until it is finished." Stubbs insisted that the cane and rice section of Louisina was, "perhaps, more intelligently cultivated, and there is more economy in methods, than in any other portion of the world."[7]

The report of the Industrial Commission added some information on the labor system at the turn of the century. In southwest Louisiana, it observed, "the labor is divided between the whites and the blacks. Many small white planters do their own field work, while the more extensive ones hire both white and negro labor." Seaman Knapp calculated that in Texas and Louisiana "the labor of a man two days and the use of a team one and one-half days form the maximum expenditure of effort on one acre of rice." He contrasted this with 80 days of labor per acre in Bengal and 120 days in Japan. Except in the southern prairies, rice cultivation throughout the world resembled the tobacco culture in its labor requirement.[8]

The rice prairies resembled the Midwest wheat plains and differed remarkably from other commodity areas in the South. Using oxen, mules, and horses, farmers turned the land with gang plows, harvested with binders, and threshed with modern steam equipment. A farmer and his family, with perhaps a few hired hands, could break the land, sow the seed, and care for several hundred acres of rice. As in the Midwest wheat culture, at harvest time an influx of laborers handled the labor-intensive tasks. Cotton sharecroppers supplied the bulk of this seasonal labor. It took two men to handle each binder, one to operate it and one to drive the team. Two or three men followed and shocked. After the rice had dried in shocks for several weeks, threshing began, and cotton sharecroppers returned with teams and wagons. One man pitched the bundles up on the wagon to another worker who stacked them. The wagon then moved to the thresher. Stalks blew out one pipe and threshed rice fell into a sack that a worker sewed shut. It took three men to handle and sew the sacks and three or four wagons to keep the thresher busy, so the labor force sometimes reached several dozen. For cotton sharecroppers, it meant needed cash during layby time or after picking.[9]

The machine-intensive culture evolved quickly. Frank Foley recalled in 1904 that, when the rice culture had first started on the prairie in the mid-1880s, plowing had been done with walking plows, and a man could only turn a few acres a day. With gang plows and discs, one man could till ten acres a day. By 1904 some farmers used steam traction engines and could handle fifteen to twenty acres. Before binders arrived, cut rice had to be tied into bundles by hand, and a machine could cut only ten acres a day. It took four horses and two men to handle the machine, a half-dozen to bind the grain, and two more to shock it. By 1904 a modern rice binder handled by two men could cut fifteen acres, and because the grain was tied when it fell from the binder, shocking required fewer workers. Whereas the old stock-propelled threshers of Gerard Miller's day could only separate six or seven hundred bushels of grain a day, modern steam threshers could separate thousands of bushels. Before threshers became commonplace, farmers exchanged work. By 1904, Foley observed, nearly every farmer owned his own threshing rig, and "its capacity is only limited by the amount of help he had to run it with." The gigantic machines were no longer curiosities. "It is getting to be just as natural for a farmer to tell one of his boys to go out and steam up the engine," Foley wrote, "as it is to tell him to go to the barn and hitch up the team." Foley and other farmers complained about harvest workers. He hoped that railroads would give preferential rates to workers to lure Midwesterners to travel south: "The very best young men would come here, and one of those boys who are familiar with machinery, and all kinds of farming, would be worth more than three colored men." He feared that, because of the large cotton crop in 1904, laborers would be scarce "at any price." [10]

In the fall of 1910, even as growers condemned crop estimates and formed cooperatives, a gasoline engine appeared on the market that could drive the binder mechanism. Until this time binders had operated on mechanical power generated by a bull wheel, a master wheel located under the machine. In the marshy riceland the bull wheel had to be fitted with large "lugs" instead of with the cleats used in wheat fields. It took five or six mules or horses to pull the binder through a dry field, but when the ground was soggy it took seven or eight. Farmers became impatient with bull wheel power, for under poor conditions the machine would stall or choke. [11]

As harvest approached in 1910, the Cushman Motor Works demonstrated a binder engine on the Jay Freeland farm in Acadia Parish near Crowley. The three-horsepower four-cycle engine drove the machinery; horses or mules still pulled it through the fields. "In the test," *The Rice Journal* reported, "the engine was tried out in all kinds of grain, ripe, green, straight and tangled, and it worked perfectly under all conditions." Freeland explained that it took only three mules to pull the binder with the Cushman engine attached, while it had taken twice as many using the bull wheel. Freeland purchased the engine "on the spot;" other farmers also placed orders. He reported later that farmers near Crowley used the Cushman and International Harvester brand engines to harvest the Honduras variety, but that the engines were not satisfactory in cutting Japanese rice. From Orange, Texas, A. F. Burns reported that farmers were using the Gilson binder engine. Arkansas farmers were experimenting with the same engines in 1910 and by 1911 used them regularly. Despite mechanization, rice farmers put in long and tiring days during harvest season. "The farmers have worked day and night, and Sundays since the 20th of August to secure the crop," W. M. Morris reported from Rice, Louisiana, in the December 1911 issue of *The Rice Journal*, "even hauling it to the warehouse by moonlight." [12]

J. M. Spicer, who wrote *Beginnings of the Rice Industry in Arkansas* (1964), moved from Ohio to the Arkansas prairie in 1914 at the age of twenty-five. Recalling the old days of the rice culture in 1982, the ninety-three-year-old Spicer furnished some insights into the harvest routine using binders. He ran three binders and recalled that it took four men to shock for one binder and a crew of twenty to keep a thresher running. During harvest he delighted in operating a binder. "I had a fine team of long-legged horses," he remembered, "and the one that worked next to the grain, what we call the grain horse, he would just hug that grain all day long. You didn't have to drive him; he just put his side up against that grain." On the outside the other horse, called the swing horse, learned how to move in harmony with the binder engine. "And he'd go along, see, and cock his ear back to that engine and if that engine starts to drag he started dragging his feet. And when the engine would pick up, well, he'd pick up and go on." When the binder reached a corner, the grain horse, Buck, would stop and back up while the swing horse, Bob, would "come around on a trot." Since the crew was competing, Spicer bragged that he always got ahead on the corners because his team worked so well together.[13]

Spicer in his book concluded that gasoline engines were "far from an unmixed blessing." The engines required water to cool them, hoses to circulate the water, tanks to hold it, gas tanks, and batteries. "Needless to say, with all the pulling and hauling and twisting and all the vibration," he explained, "many things could—and did—happen to such a bunglesome assembly as this; hoses were often pulled loose as the binder was hauled over the levees or through the mud. Holes were worn through them by coming in contact with moving chains, resulting in loss of cooling water with, many times, none at hand or no way of getting it into the tank." Many farmers had no idea how to repair their engines. Spicer related one story of a mechanic who drove fifteen miles to repair a gasoline engine "only to find that the farmer had replaced a lost gas tank cap with a sweet potato, wedged in so tightly that the gas could not flow into the carburetor." While some farmers threw up their hands and went back to bull wheel power, others tinkered with the machines. "Many of the improvements and adaptions in the various farm machines originated here in the rice fields, often being the ideas and innovations of these young rice growers," Spicer wrote.[14]

While cotton and tobacco farmers continued to use mules for power, rice farmers turned to tractors by 1914. Despite frequent problems with the giant machines, farmers bought the Avery, Twin City, Aultman-Taylor, Pioneer, Rumley, Russell, and other brands. In Arkansas, G. I. Dill invented one of the more remarkable implements. Upset after losing his 1913 crop to a wet harvest season that mired his binders, Dill mounted a binder mechanism on a tractor. In 1914 he demonstrated his invention to farmers and began taking orders at $4,000 each. He built four machines in 1914. Orders increased, and in 1919 he bought land in Little Rock to expand operations. He refused to sell his patent to a large implement company, and in 1920 the agricultural depression ruined his business. Yet Dill had attracted buyers from as far away as California and Japan.[15]

In 1919 the newly marketed Fordson tractor, a light machine possessing features that delighted farmers, swept the rice area. Unlike the expensive Dill tractor, the Fordson sold for $450. Spicer reported that in 1919 a Stuttgart tractor salesman, Thad McCullum, "was able to sell, in a twenty-four month period, a total of 1400 Fordsons." The Stuttgart dealership sold more tractors in 1919 than any dealer in the world, Spicer claimed. Rice farmers extended wheel rims and experimented with different lugs to obtain better traction in the soggy fields. A promotional article stressed that a mule or a horse would eat the product of five acres of land per year and "must be fed nearly as high when resting as when working." A tractor, on the other hand, "uses fuel only when in use and is always ready to perform the work at rush seasons when every day's delay means a big loss." Even tractors with gasoline-driven binders did not satisfy rice farmers. In Arkansas, George and W. C. Carlson of Stuttgart developed a power takeoff to couple tractor power to rice binders, and by 1925 two companies were marketing sophisticated power takeoffs. In 1926 the Farmall general-purpose tractor arrived on the prairie and proved more versatile than the Fordson.[16]

The highly mechanized state of rice production separated it from other southern crop cultures. Sharecroppers who arrived to harvest rice spent most of the year tending small cotton farms, limited by the labor-intensive plowing, hoeing, and picking tasks. A thousand miles away, tobacco farmers worked even harder in an exhausting thirteen-month routine. Rice farming was not labor intensive except at harvest time, and then huge machines eased and sped up the work. Still, rice farmers were tied to the soil and to farming as a way of life. No matter how mechanized farming became, farmers always separated themselves from other workers. They were husbandmen in an annual routine, a natural cycle of land preparation, planting, cultivation, and harvest that turned year after year. They were seldom alienated from their work, even though they utilized machines to ease the workload.

The Louisiana prairie became transformed from a Cajun preserve to an area that, with rice warehouses, mills, and broad fields, resembled the midwestern prairie. Sylvester L. Cary, one of the great boosters of the area, made a significant observation about the change. When he had first arrived on a railroad car in the early 1880s, no houses were visible along the tracks. Cajuns settled along the bayous and rivers which they used for transportation, fishing, hunting, and trapping. The new culture that Cary personified relied on both water and steel; farmers captured water for their thirsty fields and built houses and towns along the rails. The rice frontier altered the existing way of life, and the clash of cultures continued as Cajuns and midwestern immigrants coexisted, each culture giving, taking, and synthesizing.[17]

When the land boom began on the prairies, many Northerners and Midwesterners evaluated the area and then invested in land. Canal companies often owned extensive tracts and leased land and water to tenants for a share of the crop. Cary commented on the tenure system in 1909, first pointing out that a tenant shared his crop with the land-lord 50–50. "The tenant furnishes half or all the sacks, pays all threshing expenses (except some owners pay machine charges) and half the sacks and deliver to warehouses in town." They also furnished the teams and machinery to do all the work, "seeding, levying, ditching, watching and repairing levees, harvesting and threshing." The owner furnished the water for two-tenths of the crop, the seed for one-tenth, the land for two-tenths, and the tenant took five-tenths of the crop. Cary noted that the system had worked well. The tenants, he claimed, "are always white and from the north, generally from Iowa or Illinois." According to Cary, these tenants often became owners, and he pointed to ten of his own former tenants as examples. With ample land available and tenants making from $10,000 to $20,000 a year, Cary argued that tenancy was indeed a good route to landownership.[18]

Paul Chaudron of Crowley, angry at an article in which a historian named Goldwin Smith asserted that whites could not perform farm work, wrote in 1903 that in the prairie white farmers did all the work. "The sight of a negro at the plow or in the field is a novelty, so much so that a lot of about a dozen of them recently imported from Alabama as an experiment are looked upon rather as curiosities." Rice, he pointed out, is "cultivated by two classes of whites." Cajuns, "many of them being unable to speak or understand a word of English," composed one class. "The other is a set of sturdy Western farmers, mostly from Illinois and Indiana, who have moved and are still moving here in numbers." It did not surprise Chaudron that many people made "misstatements regarding negro conditions, basing them on impressions derived from a sporadic and exceptional individual, such as the one recently entertained at the White House." His reference was to Booker T. Washington's recent dinner with President Theodore Roosevelt that had caused consternation throughout the South. Despite Chaudron's comments, photographs of rice harvesting, pumping plants, and even millers' workforces usually contained blacks. They were, it seems, an invisible but crucial component of the rice culture. Still, most tenants were white.[19]

In the early years of the prairie rice culture, sharing a crop with a landlord provided a viable way of entering the owning class. A colony of German immigrants, for example, settled in the Robert's Cove section of Acadia Parish between Crowley and Rayne. Some arrived with enough money to buy land immediately, but others started off by sharecropping. Carl Hetzel arrived in the prairie in 1887 with $300. He farmed on shares for three years, then bought a 325-acre rice farm, paid it off in two years, added 40 more acres, and by 1907 owned 680 acres. The Dischler family, Xavier and his two sons, Charles and Joseph, arrived in the Robert's Cove community in 1886. Lacking capital, they sharecropped for two years and then bought 320 acres of riceland. In addition to the land that Charles Dischler owned, he rented 170 acres near Eunice in 1907, which made him both an owner and a tenant. Stories of such successful steps up the agricultural ladder were common, but little evidence has survived of tenants who continued in that status.[20]

J. M. Spicer started as a hired hand in 1914, when he arrived in Arkansas from Ohio. By 1916 he had become a foreman, and during World War I he managed over a thousand acres. He bought equipment in 1920 and began sharecropping, furnishing half the seed and all the labor while the landlord furnished water. He, his brother, and two hired hands managed the rice until harvest time, when he hired some twenty laborers. His cousin, on the other hand, arrived from Ohio in 1917 with $3,000 and managed to buy mules and farm equipment and to feed his wife and three children until harvest time without running out of money.[21]

Until World War I tenancy offered a way to climb the agricultural ladder, but after the postwar collapse in 1920 even owners found it difficult to continue profitable operations. Indeed, tenancy increasingly became a refuge for those who had lost their farms. With banks and life insurance companies foreclosing, renting or sharecropping allowed rice farmers to continue working land that no longer belonged to them. J. M. Spicer managed to survive despite the 1920 depression. "Right at harvest time," he recalled of 1920, "just like that, everything

just drops out. The banks quit loaning us money, prices went down."
At the time he had 26,000 bushels of unsold rice "and could not give it
away." He got no offers to sell at a fair price until the next spring. "We
like to starved to death." (Of course, Spicer could have eaten his stored
rice; tobacco and cotton growers, for their part, could find little such
nourishment.) But since so many other farmers were also broke,
Spicer did not feel so bad about the hard times. As pointed out above,
by 1930 tenants tilled some 44 percent of the irrigated farms in the
Grand Prairie of Arkansas.[22]

Land tenure in the rice area of Louisiana differed radically from that
in other areas of the state and from other commodity cultures throughout the South. Using census records, questionnaires, AAA records,
farm management surveys, and tax records, agricultural specialists in
Louisiana in 1935 charted 147 tenancy areas in the state and distilled
these into eleven primary tenancy areas. In one of the areas, five parishes grew rice, but only Calcasieu and Jefferson Davis parishes devoted most of the farmland to that crop. In Calcasieu Parish farmers
rented nearly 66 percent of their farm land, and of the 15 percent of
landlords who rented additional land, 38 percent rented over 1,250
acres. Nearly 13 percent of the 976 owner-operated farms were held by
blacks, and the 1930 tax records showed that 70 percent of black-
owned farms were mortgaged. Jefferson Davis farmers rented 50 percent of their land. Twice as many rented additional land as in Calcasieu, but only 13 percent rented over 1,250 acres. Half as many blacks
owned farms in Jefferson Davis Parish, but 47 percent of them carried
mortgages. Unlike the state at large, with its sharecropper average of
46 percent, the rice area ran mostly on rental arrangements. Only 17
percent of Jefferson Davis tenants were croppers and 2 percent cash
renters; Calcasieu had 9 percent croppers and 12 percent cash renters.
Both parishes had a large number of wagehands, 932 in Calcasieu and
1,403 in Jefferson Davis, but the report did not indicate the relationship to landlords or the relative standard of living compared to that of
wagehands in other tenure areas.

The rice parishes stood in stark contrast to other tenure areas in
Louisiana. "The area has more tractors and large machinery than any
of the other areas," the report concluded. Tenant farms were as large
as owner-operated farms. "Many tenants rent land for cotton and work
for wages in the production of rice and the caring for beef cattle," it
added. Instead of the close supervision that characterized other areas,
most tenants only received occasional direction from canal companies

and other landlords, and they had written leases. Almost 87 percent of the parish landlords had one or two tenants per farm. Calcasieu and Jefferson Davis farms averaged 114 acres, while the state at large only averaged 39.5 acres. Thus the rice area differed in significant ways from other commodity areas—in size of farms, machinery, written leases, and rental patterns.[23]

Even the 1920s agricultural depression did not completely dismantle the agricultural ladder. When Theodore Cormier moved to Welsh with his family, his only possession was a mule. In 1931 he bought the 383-acre farm that he had formerly rented, and he leased another 350 acres. He employed four tenants and four to seven wagehands by the month "during the busy seasons." In addition to 600 acres of rice, Cormier planted 40 acres of corn and 60 of cotton; he had 140 head of cattle, chickens, and a garden. He even traded Missouri mules in the area and made a tidy profit on the transactions.[24]

A more specific account in 1931 revealed that, on his 425-acre farm near Welsh, Rufus A. Estes had two tenant families and "three farmers employed by the month to furnish a sufficient labor supply." Estes grew rice but supplemented it with seventy-five acres planted in cotton, corn, and sweet potatoes. Each family had a garden and milk cows and shared pork raised on the place. The Estes family and the tenants "lived at home," meaning that they seldom purchased food. The milk, butter, and eggs came from the farm, along with the pork and poultry, and a peach orchard of 140 trees furnished additional income. Estes also kept a close rein on his tenants. He enforced a rule that each was to finish the year with a credit balance, getting rid of those who did not live up to his high standards.[25]

When Mrs. Edward Martin's husband died in 1926, she managed three rice farms that had six tenant familes. She owned a floral business in town, but she quickly made time to run the farm. "She had to make daily trips to the farm twelve miles from Lake Charles," *The Rice Journal* reported, "do all the buying for her tenants, even their personal shopping; attend to all the selling; make improvements and plan for the next season." After sorting out the problems, Martin only made a weekly trip to the farms, and "the tenants are making money and the farms themselves are in better condition than they have ever been." She read all she could on raising rice, but she admitted that, in addition to advice from friends, she learned a lot "from one of my tenants who had been with my husband for some years." In 1930 her son, a Broadway actor, visited the farm at harvest time. "Can you imagine a

Broadway actor working fourteen hours a day on a rice farm and liking it?" she asked. "But then, that is what rice farming is—a fascinating game," she concluded.[26]

Considering the number of tenants in the rice area, little historical documentation survives revealing their culture and work habits. Works Progress Administration writers did not stray into the prairie to record the tenants' lives. Living a little below the status of owners and yet far above tenants and sharecroppers in other areas of the South, these workers attracted little attention from magazines such as *The Rice Journal* or from historians interested in explaining traditional sharecropping. Even as sharecroppers and tenants in other areas were being tossed off the land, rice tenants were vested with producer allotments, giving them a bargaining tool that allowed them to continue farm work. The dearth of writing on tenure relationships in the rice culture invites historical investigation.

Hired hands, even more than sharecroppers and tenants, remained faceless. Indeed, photographs furnish as much tangible information as do written records. Farm organization and size largely determined labor needs. Small family-operated farms, whether tilled by owners or tenants, could get by with very little hired help except at harvest and threshing season. Farmers hired wagehands, tenants, or sharecroppers to do chores, walk levees, repair fences, and keep machinery operable. The traditional hired hand, so common in the Northeast and Midwest, became part of the rice culture also. Harvest and threshing attracted many workers from outside the immediate rice-growing area. *The Rice Journal* reported in October 1907, however, that farmers in Acadia Parish were not standing on street corners waiting for laborers to arrive but were "clubbing together, 'changing work,' as done in the farming communities of the North."[27]

Trading harvest work may have helped ease the labor problem, but farmers still needed wagehands. "Labor is very plentiful—ours cost one dollar per day to harvest and one dollar and twenty-five cents now," T. J. Mock reported from Jennings in October 1910. A year later *The Rice Journal* noted that workers "are scarce, so the threshing will likely be prolonged beyond the usual time, even if good weather prevails from now on." During the 1931 harvest season the journal reported that workers were more plentiful than ever, some from other sections of the state, others from out of state, and many cotton sharecroppers who refused to pick at the prevailing wages. During each harvest season workers flocked to the rice area, hoping to pick up extra

Harvest scene on P. S. Lovell Plantation. Crowley, Louisiana. 1894. E. K. Sturdivant. (Rice, Miscellaneous, Box 1, USL*)*

Threshing scene. Wagons shown at right are hauling to machine, shown in center, the grain on the stalk. The thresher flails the grain from the stalk and sacks it, as shown at the left. This threshing scene taken about 1923. Near Crowley, Louisiana. Barnett. (RMA Papers, Box 15, USL*)*

Threshing scene, 1934–35. Lunch break. (Rice, Miscellaneous, Box 1,
USL). *[Writing on truck door: Pierre Trahan, Farmer, Morse, La.]*

cash. No doubt most of them came from the immediate vicinity, from
the cotton farms and sugar plantations.[28]

J. M. Spicer observed that sharecroppers from the cotton area that
surrounded the Arkansas rice prairie would "come out here just in
droves" during the layby season or after picking. He would see "four or
five of 'em walking down the road looking for work. You could get some
mighty good men." Many were black, he recalled, "good responsible
men, good workers, and intelligent too." He hired one man, and the
next year that man returned with almost a dozen of his friends. "And
we had a bunk house there where they could stay overnight and we
fed 'em there too." If they worked the entire harvest and threshing season, Spicer paid a twenty-five-cent per day bonus. After the first year
the hands no longer called it a bonus but a holdback. During the war
Spicer took over the operation of a large farm that used white laborers,
only to discover that they were bootleggers and had dismantled some
engines in order to fashion fuel lines for a still. "They were pretty sorry,
usually," he said of these white workers.[29]

Photographs illustrate work organization and the racial composition
of the workforce. During rice harvest in 1894 on the P. S. Lovell plantation near Crowley workers posed on four binders, each pulled by five
mules. The crews on at least three of the binders were black, obviously
men familiar enough with the machines and mules to do efficient

work. One man, perhaps Lovell, is seated on a horse, and another is standing alongside. The photographer, E. K. Sturdivant, posed P. S. Lovell for another exposure showing the crew from the rear and revealing that Lovell owned Deering binders. Another photograph taken near Crowley on the A. Kaplan farm shows a threshing crew of eighteen men posed in front of hundreds of rice bags.[30]

A 1923 photograph taken near Crowley gives a more dynamic view of the threshing operation. As two couples, probably the owners of the farm and their wives, posed, the threshing operation progressed. One man pitched the unthreshed rice off the wagon into the thresher. Another driver waited in line. Two men held a sack to catch the threshed rice while the stalks and chaff were blown into a pile. By this time trucks hauled threshed rice to the mills, and a Case tractor provided power to drive the thresher. Another photograph taken about 1934 or 1935 shows the crew taking a break for lunch on the Pierre Trahan farm near Morse. Eighteen men appear along with a Case tractor, two trucks, and three teams used to haul the shocked rice to the thresher. Although the photograph bears no caption, Trahan's name and his location appear on the door of the truck.[31]

Such photographs give an indication of the size of the workforce and an insight into their tasks, but they do not reveal the origins of the workers. Rouseb Soileau remembered that many drove their teams to the area from surrounding cotton farms. Photographs from Arkansas reveal much the same routine as do those from Louisiana. Black workers appear in some of the scenes, although most of the machinery was handled by whites. Mrs. Bennie F. Burkett remembered that some harvest labor came from cotton plantations a few counties away in the Arkansas Delta. The Arkansas, Louisiana, and Texas prairies, located near more labor-intensive crop areas, could attract cash-hungry workers for harvest.[32]

Not only did rice tenants have machinery and allotments, but their tenant status also varied from traditional tenancy in cotton and tobacco areas. A meeting in Little Rock, Arkansas, regarding landlord-tenant relations revealed that rice tenants fought for their share of the crop. "We found the rice tenant farmers in general do not have many problems as far as their legal status is concerned," the rural economist J. G. McNeeley said, "because they have sufficient funds and can carry any case to court. They usually have written leases." Such was not the case in the nearby cotton culture. Even with a large membership and national publicity, the Southern Tenant Farmers Union operating just east of the Grand Prairie in the Arkansas Delta could not successfully fight cotton landlords over tenure disputes. A rice tenant or sharecropper and his cotton-growing counterpart varied so radically that the terms hardly fit both categories. Rice sharecroppers, taking implements and other capital into the arrangement, transcended the legal designation that in many southern states equated them with wagehands. A careful study of court cases arising from landlord-tenant conflicts in the rice area would no doubt add an important chapter to southern labor history.[33]

Despite the huge amount of land owned by banks, insurance companies, and canal companies and farmed by tenants, owners who tilled or managed their own land personified the rice culture. Newspapers and journals delighted in carrying stories of successful owners. Since the early days of the rice culture, when railroad brochures boasted of the prospects on the prairies, such stories painted a bright picture of the lives and fortunes of rice growers. In 1920 the Carlisle *Independent*, for example, ran a special issue devoted to the rice culture in the Arkansas prairie and reported some local success stories. Frank C. Bennett had started farming rice in 1906 on his farm near Carlisle. By 1920 he owned a large farm, planted 100 acres of rice, and rented 200 acres on an adjoining farm. Douglas and Frank Brass moved to the Arkansas prairie from Michigan in 1879 and purchased a 320-acre farm near Carlisle. They planted 120 acres to rice, owned a tractor, twenty horses and mules, fifty head of stock, and some hogs. H. A. Cyrier moved from Kankakee, Illinois, in 1911 and ran a 480-acre farm near Lonoke. He owned four tractors and eight horses and mules. Mrs. C. L. Gonter managed a 420-acre farm near Carlisle that she had taken over when her husband died. She planted 120 acres to rice and had a Reave and a Case tractor, a Freze thresher, and her own irrigation works.[34]

The accounts of rice growers that appeared in *The Rice Journal* fell into a pattern—the farmer's background, the avenue to success, and the scale of operation. Taken together, such episodes furnish additional pieces of the rice culture puzzle. I. M. Bennett of Almyra, Arkansas, personified the rise of a rice farmer. He arrived from Iowa with his parents in the days when oxen pulled wagons and hay was the principal crop. In 1900 he took a job as clerk in Jefferson County and then went to business school. Bennett became a partner in the store, later managed a cotton plantation, served as postmaster, and held other positions before a flood in 1906 wiped him out. Moving back home to take advantage of the rice boom, he bought 240 acres adjoining his father's farm and quickly became a leader of the community and president of the Rice Planter's Bank in Almyra. Bennett, the journal observed in 1933, "is a type of the progressive, enterprising wide-awake farmer who keeps on learning all the time." He rotated his rice with soybeans and also planted cowpeas, cotton, corn, and oats. His wife became interested in club work and kept neat accounts of her poultry and dairy products. The outbuildings and house appeared spotless, and the family owned a radio, a good library, a vacuum cleaner, washer, and refrigerator.[35]

The journal often neglected aspects of the work culture, but obviously fieldwork required stamina. In the summer of 1930 a parching drought and heat wave hit the South. Two rice farmers in Ulm, Arkansas, "succumbed to the excessive heat of July 13." There had been no rain since May 18, and the temperature during July hung at 110 degrees.[36] Yet feature articles in *The Rice Journal* concentrated upon success and material surroundings, largely ignoring the work routine. The journal also concentrated upon immigrants into the rice area and seldom identified Cajuns as successful farmers.

Not far from Houston, Texas, Bill Gardner owned a 4,000-acre farm near the Spindletop oil field. He had formerly farmed in Liberty, Chambers, and Jefferson counties. He bought some of his irrigation water from the Texas Public Service Company and used his own pump for additional water. "Rice is the easiest crop to grow," Gardner admitted, "and there is less hazard involved." He only worried about it during harvest season. He owned a large herd of cattle, "four model L Case tractors; a T-40 Trac-Tractor; International's caterpillar type tractor; rubber-tired harvesting equipment, including two-wheel dump-cars to haul the bundles of rice to the thresher." A 110-volt generator ran a pump that furnished water for the house and drove the lights, refrigerator, vacuum cleaner, and washing machine. Each May, Gardner took his wife and two children to the Indianapolis 500 automobile race, continuing an interest that had started in his youth, when he had raced cars at a dirt track near Beaumont.[37]

W. M. Fenton arrived in Louisiana in 1888, when his father left upstate New York for health reasons. The town of Fenton, Louisiana, took its name from the senior Fenton, who ran a general store there for fourteen years. After going to school the son took a job as agent and telegraph operator for the railroad, and then he spent two years working in Beaumont. He returned home, bought a rice farm, and installed

Harvesting rice, Arkansas County (Stuttgart), Arkansas. September 1927. (s-9502-c, Box 196, National Archives)

the first irrigation well in that part of the prairie. "The railroad was putting down a well for the engines and for the use of the station," he recalled, "and I thought it would be a good time to put down a similar one to help out with the irrigation of my rice farm." His neighbors, he mused, "thought I was crazy," but when the rains failed that year "I wasn't so crazy after all, it seems." In 1930 he farmed with his father-in-law; together they owned 2,100 acres and planted 950 of them to rice. Like other successful farmers, Fenton owned cattle, mules, poultry, and had modern conveniences in his house.[38]

Alcee Benoit, one of the few Cajun-named farmers to appear in *The Rice Journal* features, grew up on a rice farm near Welsh and for nineteen years farmed rice in the community. In 1920 he moved to Vinton to take advantage of water supplied by the Sabine Canal. For four years he rented land in Gum Cove and planted from 300 to 450 acres of rice a year. In 1929 he bought a farm east of Vinton, planted 175 acres, and made $2,000. Benoit diversified while living at Gum Cove, planting cucumbers and mustard. He doubted that he could turn completely to truck farming, but he hoped that a market would develop in Orange, Texas, the site of a large canning factory. Benoit's tenants also practiced living at home, and diversified crops gave work the year around. At harvest time he hired from thirty to forty laborers, and his wife cooked for the entire crew.[39]

Such stories appeared regularly in *The Rice Journal* and provided recurring testimony of the profits from rice. Many of these stories ran during the first years of the Depression, giving encouragement to growers who despaired. Yet these accounts and others seldom raised questions about underlying farm problems. Features discussed the export market, ways to increase domestic consumption, reports from growing areas, and the business of millers and growers' cooperatives; rarely, however, did they deal with labor problems. From such accounts the world of rice growers seemed like the promised land, full of healthy crops and livestock and peopled by an energetic breed of farmers who never experienced failure. In many ways the prairie rice culture was exceptional and stood in stark contrast to other areas of the South, but rice farmers also had problems.

In addition to the confusion in the AAA program, dissatisfaction with producer allotments among large landowners, and a guerrilla war launched by millers, the New Deal introduced other aggravations, especially government intrusion into traditional relationships. In 1935, as the processing tax went into effect, many rice growers objected to a tax on the rice that they milled for tenants. "It has been the practice and custom throughout the history of rice production in the State," extension agent R. A. Wasson wrote to Rice Section chief Charles G. Miller, "for landlords to furnish their tenants rice in payment for their services and the attitude of the Internal Revenue Division which is breaking down this practice has created severe hardships and intense antagonism to the program." Such rice, Wasson pointed out, did not enter commercial channels. He enclosed a letter from W. E. Lawson, a Crowley Ford dealer who also owned land and a rice mill. "My situation is just this," Lawson wrote, "I have about fifty negro families working on my different farms that I supply during the season with rice." His small mill at Midland did custom milling and also milled rice for his laborers. "I am perfectly willing to sell this rice at the market price to these darkies, who certainly need it, without additional revenue tax," Lawson argued. The tax would "work a hardship on them without benefitting me materially" if they had to pay an additional two cents per pound for it. Across the bottom of the page, Lawson wrote sarcastically that perhaps he should sell the rough rice to the laborers and let them pound it out by mortar and pestle. He doubted that the government would prosecute him for that.[40]

Although the National Recovery Administration exempted agricultural labor from minimum wages, the proliferation of government programs threatened rice farmers' rural labor supply. Charles R. Houssiere, who controlled some rice land near Jennings, wrote to A. J. S. Weaver in August 1933, pointing out that farm laborers had started moving to town to obtain jobs that paid twenty-five to thirty cents an hour. "The common laborers are already asserting themselves that they will not work on the farms at farmer's prices," he complained. Even in the rice area, which had a higher wage scale than cotton or tobacco regions, the New Deal threatened the old structure by offering better wages.[41]

Rice growers, like their fellow farmers in the cotton and tobacco areas, bought radios for entertainment and news. By 1930 station KFDM in Beaumont carried regular broadcasts pertaining to rice farming. Sponsored by the Magnolia Petroleum Company and produced by the National Rice Association, the programs discussed rice farming, promoted rice dishes, explained the uses of rice byproducts, and gave sketches of the rice culture in other countries. Most programs were derived from articles in *The Rice Journal*. Farmers increasingly listened to their radios for weather reports and commodity prices. By 1934 WWL in New Orleans featured regular weather reports, and farm programs discussed soil erosion, care of livestock, and crop estimates. The station also carried features by agricultural experts and music aimed at the farm population. In 1935 KPLC in Lake Charles, KVOL in Lafayette, and KALB in Alexandria went on the air.[42]

Yet New Deal agricultural programs had no more influence on farming practices in the rice prairies than they did in the flue-cured tobacco area. Unlike the cotton culture, where tractors and acreage reduction in the mid-1930s diminished the farm population, the number of rice farmers remained stable. Tractors pulled gang plows, discs, and land levelers to prepare the fields, and irrigation practices changed little over the years. Binders pulled by tractors instead of by mules still cut the rice, though power came not from bull wheels or even from gasoline engines but from tractor power takeoffs. Mules still pulled wagons filled with cured rice to the thresher, and sacked rice traveled to the mills in farm trucks. As early as 1927 the J. I. Case and McCormick-

Deering companies successfully demonstrated tractor-drawn combines in Vinton, Louisiana. Despite the successful demonstration, farmers did not adapt combines for another fifteen years. Combined rice had a moisture content of from 18 to 21 percent, so the grain required drying to reduce its moisture to 12.5 percent or lower for milling. Rice growers seldom hesitated in adapting the latest technology, but few turned to combines and driers before World War II.[43]

In 1909 Sylvester L. Cary recalled the changes he had seen in the quarter-century since he moved to Louisiana. The prairie had evolved from a poor area to one of the state's richest. Over the years the sickle and cradle gave way to binders, and rice mills made from tree stumps and logs yielded to modern rice mills. "I have seen a fertile prairie surrounded by timber with a pastoral people changed into the highest class of machine using farmers of the intensive type," he boasted. People who in 1880 "cultivated gambling on a 5-cent ante" were by 1909 "taking chances on 1000 acres of rice." He had also seen the postage rate fall from "25 cents, 10 cents, 5 cents, 2 cents."[44] As the century moved forward, rice farmers continued to change the prairie, using capital to bring forth the land's riches. Indeed, Cary was correct in pointing to the changes in the prairies and connecting them to technology, for the rice prairies of Louisiana, Texas, and Arkansas varied radically from other southern rural areas.

The prairie culture no longer centered along the bayous but instead nestled along the Southern Pacific Railroad tracks and, later, along Interstate 10. Just as the postage rate climbed back toward a quarter, the price of maintaining a rice farm escalated. Yet rice farming had a magnetic pull. Roger Crum, whose father moved from Indiana to Arkansas in 1911, completed a college education and during the Depression worked as a county agent implementing the AAA program. When an interviewer asked him why he gave up government work to return to rice farming, Crum put into a simple statement the sentiment of many farmers: "There's something about the farming life."[45]

Book Four: The Triumph of Capitalist Agriculture

I will overturn, overturn, overturn, it: and it shall be no more. . . .

—*Ezekiel 21 : 27*

Cotton harvesting by machine. Stoneville, Mississippi. October 1946.
Forsythe. (16-N-11980, National Archives)

11

I knowed as much about mule farmin as ary man in this country. But when they brought in tractors, that lost me.

—Ned Cobb

The Reconfiguration of the Cotton Culture

When H. L. Mitchell, who helped found the Southern Tenant Farmers Union in the 1930s, returned to the Arkansas Delta in 1960, he observed that "conditions on the cotton plantations had radically changed in the twelve years since I had left the area for Washington." Mostly old people remained in the rural communities, and tractor drivers held the only remaining agricultural jobs. Fieldwork customarily done by women and children had ended, except for occasional chopping tasks and picking the leavings of cotton-harvesting machines.[1] In the space of a decade the changes that Mitchell observed in Arkansas had swept through the old cotton-growing areas of the South. The need for hand labor that had motivated antebellum trading in slaves and postwar sharecropping had ended. After World War II millions of rural folk who had served in the military or labored in defense industries abandoned, either from choice or from necessity, the farming life. A work culture that utilized hoes, mule-drawn implements, and family-operated farms yielded to machines, chemicals, and large units of production. Agriculture, as a refuge for those who liked fieldwork and abhorred cities, factories, and complexity, had become reconfigured into a machine culture that relied upon federal programs to maintain its structure. The change in the mode of production, in social organization, and in the nature of rural life proved the most revolutionary in southern history.

As in other segments of the economy, agricultural planners and scientists accepted the idea that mechanization was inevitable. The push for better machines, effective chemicals, and improved seeds came from many directions, but most planners were interested in making farm life less labor intensive (thus more attractive) and in ending the need for hired labor (thus lowering the cost of production). Since intense labor was needed only at plowing, planting, hoeing, and harvest times, each of these disparate tasks had to be mechanized before the need for hand labor would end. So long as even one hand task remained, planters would need a cheap source of seasonal labor. The new structure would, of course, require fewer rural workers, and some USDA agencies studied what could be done with millions of excess farmers.

Even as these ideas developed in the mid-1930s, the southern sharecropping system increasingly entered the national consciousness as an evil akin to slavery, an embarrassment that should be ended. Articles, books, and photographs revealed a life of hardship and poverty. From the fiction of William Faulkner, who showed how Mississippi rural folk survived in poverty, to the dramatic 1939 Missouri roadside demonstration by displaced sharecroppers, Americans were led to face the grim truth about southern rural life. Anything, it seemed, would be preferable to the eviscerating poverty of the sharecropping system. Public awareness of the ills of the South briefly made the political atmosphere conducive to remedial legislation, but before new programs could become effective the transformation of the rural South was well under way. Machine-intensive agriculture would end both the sharecropping system and the shame that it engendered, and the rural labor force fled into urban exile. Ironically, the forces that changed the system derived not from protest against the rural labor system or the relief agencies but from the AAA, mechanization, science, and war.[2]

The groundwork for this transformation had been laid in the 1930s with AAA programs and increasing mechanization in the cotton culture. The USDA never resolved the contradictions inherent in its policies, especially the problem of whether to preserve or destroy the sharecropping system. In 1941 Undersecretary of Agriculture Paul Appleby perceived that many sharecroppers would have no choice but to leave the land because of the changing structure of farming. "At best," he admitted, "the results can not be too good." A year earlier M. L. Wilson, who had been one of the primary shapers of agricultural policy, recalled that prior to the New Deal agricultural planners "did not bother much about people whose circumstances were such that they could not get into the good income group." He added that "agricultural institutions of research and education were practically unaware of the extent and nature of poverty in rural areas." This attitude changed in the 1930s as some government programs aided poorer farmers, but such efforts were largely offset by mechanization. Lewis Cecil Grey, a USDA economist who wrote a massive history of antebellum southern agriculture, admitted that most farm policy was aimed at the middle and upper classes and helped only a fraction of rural people: "Although some of the benefits of these programs have tended to seep down to the disadvantaged groups, this process has not been extensive."[3]

The irony of federal intrusion lay not in the fact that the government entered agriculture or that in the 1930s it took control of much of its planning. Rather, it created conflicting programs that largely ignored not only its own role and that of poor farmers but also that of technology.[4] The painstaking studies of tenure, of moving people to more fertile land, and of aiding a small percentage of marginal farmers largely ignored the emerging structure of the cotton culture. The science arm of the USDA worked to create a new mode of production while its social agencies sifted through plans to prop up the old structure. Such contradictions barely touched the rice or tobacco cultures until later. From the 1930s to the 1950s, however, the cotton South metamorphosed from a labor-intensive culture to one that increasingly used machines and chemicals, and the production of cotton moved ever westward.[5]

By 1939 the changing structure of the cotton culture was apparent in the western growing areas. D. C. Baker, a small farmowner from Tahoka, Texas, complained that when he had arrived in the area fifteen years earlier a man could successfully farm 100 to 125 acres with four head of work stock and a few implements. AAA payments had changed that, for "land owners take these checks and buy tractors and hire a man for 75¢ or $1.00 per day and rent the tenants out and work the land themselves with this cheap labor." The new farm units contained 320 to 2,000 acres, six to twelve tractors, and hired hands. Baker complained that it was unfair for "some men to work the whole country and others to be put out in the road without a place to make an honest living on."[6]

Baker gave an excellent description of what the geographer Merle Prunty, Jr., labeled a neo-plantation, where an owner or manager ran the entire operation utilizing hired labor. Such units resembled antebellum plantations, in that many existed in the old plantation areas of the South and that housing and barns were usually centralized. Although the spatial elements of plantations changed from antebellum centralized slave quarters to postbellum fragmented sharecropper shacks to neo-plantation centralized houses and barns, the work culture and human relations changed more dramatically. Both under slavery and under sharecropping, paternalism mediated the relations between workers and owners or managers; in exchange for labor, tenants received not only a share of the crop but also housing, fuel, food, and other perquisites. The new plantation system utilized hired laborers and machines, and, after decades of coaching from extension agents and agricultural schools, a new plantation resembled a factory or business operation. Only large-scale farmers could take advantage of this scale of operation, and in many cases small owners in the old cotton-producing areas east of the Mississippi River never adjusted their operations to such a scale. Rather, they turned to other crops as cotton became less profitable because of high wages and the competition from more efficient and mechanized farms farther west. World War II stimulated soybean production throughout the South, and ultimately beans became more important than cotton in the old growing areas.[7]

The change in plantation organization was well under way by the beginning of World War II, but most southern farms still needed seasonal labor. In May 1941 a South Carolina farm labor committee expressed alarm that many agricultural workers had moved to towns and cities, and it theorized that "it is doubtful that their families will return to seasonal farm work at the wage now being paid." Mechanization caused part of the rural exodus, but, as so many studies reiterated, it was not clear whether people were pushed off the land by machines, fled in anticipation of them, or were lured away by factory jobs. No matter what the cause, farmers who needed labor feared that they would not find it.[8]

World War II accelerated the changes already under way due to depression, mechanization, and government programs. Marginal farmworkers flocked to cities searching for well-paying employment. Coastal cities such as Savannah, Charleston, Norfolk, and Mobile swelled with defense workers. The southern farm population dropped by 3.4 million, but those left behind enjoyed the higher prices generated by wartime demand. Cotton prices jumped from around 10 cents per pound in 1939 to over 22 cents in 1945. Despite grumpy observations from the USDA that the South still produced too much cotton, plantings decreased by 5 million acres during the war. Urban demand for food accomplished what the Extension Service could not with its earlier entreaties, and farmers increasingly turned to truck farming and dairying.[9]

P. O. Davis, the director of extension work in Alabama, complained in 1942 that the war was siphoning off farm laborers, primarily because of the pay differential. He gave what he admitted was an extreme example of a black worker who asked for a raise in his $1 a day wages. When the planter refused, the man went "to a war plant and for his first week his check was above $80.00." As much as the USDA wanted to clear excess farmers from nonproductive land, it feared that a mass exodus from rural areas would dry up the labor supply.[10]

The Farm Security Administration furnished one of the last hopes of reconciling the forces of change and the old structure. In many ways it served as a brake on the rapidly changing rural South; it represented the old culture, not the new. What Wilhelm Anderson, who worked in the BAE's division of State and Local Planning, discovered in Alabama would ultimately be true of the entire South: "The Farm Bureau, the State Extension Service, and the AAA seem to be aligning themselves against the FSA," he reported in May 1941. Local agents had not responded to planning tasks, and Anderson argued that this was not because they were overworked, as they claimed, but because of "the continuous mending of political fences and in attempts to satisfy the ever increasing demands of the Farm Bureau."[11]

Increasingly the FSA came under attack not for its attempts to resettle traditional farmers but for its cooperative ventures in the 1930s and for its management of farm labor during the war. By 1942 critics charged that the FSA was a leftist organizaton that threatened traditional farm policy—an ironic charge for an agency that attempted to stabilize rural change and clean up some of the human refuse left by other USDA programs. The Farm Bureau–FSA struggle epitomized the contrast between the 1930s and the 1940s that C. Vann Woodward observed in "The Irony of Southern History." The permissive and experimental atmosphere that tolerated the FSA changed, as the agricultural establishment castigated the FSA at congressional hearings with a host of criticisms ranging from mismanagement to communism. In 1946, with its program stunted, it became the Farmers Home Administration.[12] With the one agency that hoped to reduce the human costs of rural change crippled, the armed forces and defense work became the resettlement administration for rural southerners. In this respect the war proved providential.

World War II furnished an opportunity to reorder southern agriculture and eliminate the embarrassing problem of rural overpopulation and misery. It would present an interesting counterfactual exercise to speculate on the fate of the rural South had there been no war. In this sense, the war solved many of the human problems generated by the Great Depression, government policies, and mechanization. The old society filled with racism and one-crop one-mule agriculture, one-party politics, and numerous forms of discrimination faded. And, as C. Vann Woodward has reminded us, "It would take a blind sentimentalist to mourn their passing." [13]

As sharecroppers left the Cotton South, farmers planted less cotton. The AAA set the cotton allotment at roughly 27 million acres during the war years, but farmers harvested far less than that. For example, in 1940 the nationwide cotton allotment was 27.5 million acres, but only 23.7 million were harvested; by 1943 the harvested acreage dropped to 21.4 million. In 1944, when Congress lifted controls on the amount of cotton that could be planted, southern farmers in the old cotton areas showed that, for the first time since the late eighteenth century, they had broken the bonds of King Cotton. Instead of planting cotton, many farmers grew other crops or raised cattle. This marked the most drastic change in southern agriculture since the invention of the cotton gin. While farmers in the eastern Cotton Belt planted less cotton, production shifted to the west even more dramatically, especially to Texas and Oklahoma. Whether this change resulted from the crippling cost of production or from the expense and shortage of labor, it proved a fortuitous decision. Thus much of the disorganization that characterized the upper South in the 1930s and 1940s came not from the perfection of the spindle cotton picker but from the initial stages of mechanization, war demands, and government policy. The war reconfigured the southern rural labor system, phasing out sharecropping and utilizing wage labor, and many people who did not fit into the new scheme fled the land—and often the South—forever. [14]

Those familiar with the old system that had taken such a tremendous human toll often viewed capital-intensive agriculture with ambivalence. As H. L. Mitchell suggested, many old people remained in the same communities, but, except for tractor drivers and others who found jobs in the nearby towns, the younger generation left for distant cities. Many cotton farmers either were too proud to change their work habits or did not understand how to apply new techniques. Ned Cobb, the Alabama cotton farmer who had served a prison sentence for union activity, returned to his Alabama farm in April 1945. He continued farming with mules and fighting the boll weevil as he had earlier, but after another decade he observed that farming as he knew it was ending. One son left for Ohio; another bought a tractor and quickly paid off all his debts. "But I was a mule farmin man to the last," Cobb insisted, "never did make a crop with a tractor." He also summed up the burden of his generation. "I was caught between two opinions: new rulins is takin place and old ones is bein done away with." He continued to farm with mules until his health was too poor for him to learn to drive a tractor. "I knowed as much about mule farmin as ary man in this country," he boasted. "But when they brought in tractors, that lost me." [15] Obviously Cobb linked cotton farming to mule power, and he had no inclination to make the change. Mules died off and were not replaced, and farmers like Ned Cobb watched the changes pass them by, proud of their children's ability to prosper under the new ways but ambivalent about whether people were better off.

To many rural Southerners farming would be forever connected to the dream of a small farm that involved the entire family. Agricultural planners, on the other hand, grappled with the problem of excess farm population and the forces of change unleashed by government programs and mechanization. The AAA reduced crop acreage—the Extension Service taught farmers how to grow more on fewer acres. Reduced acreage drove people from the land—the FSA attempted to resettle marginal farmers. Planters looked eagerly to government payments and diminished labor needs—the USDA tried to reform the tenure system in the South. Ned Cobb's generation retired, farmers unable to adjust left the land, and those who remained in the cotton South increasingly used chemicals and machines.

Several historians have explained the mechanization of the cotton culture, and all emphasize that change came about gradually. As Gilbert C. Fite explained, "before full mechanization of the cotton crop could be achieved the combined contributions of engineers, chemists, and fertilizer specialists, plant breeders, entomologists, agronomists, and other scientists were necessary." This host of experts rarely considered the small farm units that characterized the old cotton-growing areas. The central engine of transformation, of course, was the spindle cotton picker. Although the Rust brothers (who had worked since the 1920s on a spindle-type machine) and others had pondered the impact on sharecroppers and tenants, few scientists within the USDA agricultural complex paused to consider the human cost of mechanization. After all, mechanization had been their consuming dream since

The Rust cotton picker in a cotton field on Cloverdale Plantation.
Clarksdale (vicinity), Mississippi, in the Delta area. October 1939.
Marion Post Wolcott. (LC USF 33 30619-M5, *Library of Congress*)

the turn of the century. By World War II, International Harvester developed a practical picking machine. Already in the western growing
areas cotton-stripping machines that simply pulled off the boll and the
lint had cut production costs. During the war International Harvester
marketed about 100 spindle pickers, and by 1948 it had sold 1,500 of
the machines, mostly to farmers in California and in the Mississippi
Delta.[16]

The picking machine did not immediately end the need for hired labor, for no way to thin and chop cotton had been perfected. With the
millennium at hand, and armed with special congressional appropriations and backing from the Cotton Council of America, researchers at
agricultural colleges and experiment stations worked to forge the final
links in the chain of mechanization. By the 1960s scientists taught
chemicals to kill weeds and spare cotton stalks. To prevent trash from
ruining the quality of lint, defoliants could be used to strip the leaves
before harvest, and cleaning machinery could be installed on cotton gins to improve quality. This oversimplifies the process of mechanization, for along the way many stages of improvement evolved
simultaneously.[17]

Immediately after World War II agricultural planners acknowledged

Four-row flame weeder that uses bottled gas for fuel. As the machine is pulled along the cotton rows, the burners—much like a plumber's blowtorch—sear the young weeds in the rows with killing flame. The cotton plants have tougher stems so are unharmed. October 1946. Forsythe. (N 8695, Box 120, National Archives)

that a revolution was under way in the cotton-growing areas of the country. "The cotton farmers' implements have been a one-horse seed planter, a one-horse fertilizer distributor, and scales to 'weigh up' the cotton at picking time in the fall," Arthur F. Raper told a meeting of sociologists in Atlanta in May 1946. After reviewing old cultivation methods, Raper observed that, in Texas and Oklahoma, cotton farmers were making "extensive use of farm machinery." These states most closely approximated the national average of farmers owning tractors, while the rest of the South lagged far behind. They also had the largest decrease in the number of sharecroppers and tenants. While farm-owners increased slightly in both states during the 1930s, the number of sharecroppers in Texas decreased by 62 percent and in Oklahoma by 77 percent, and the number of other tenants by 16 and 11 percent respectively.[18]

By 1946 many of the elements of mechanization were apparent. On the Mississippi Experiment Station at Stoneville, flame weeders burned off weeds and mechanical pickers harvested the crop. The flame weeder could cover twenty-five acres a day and burn only $3.50

to $5.00 of fuel. Airplanes sprayed calcium cyanamide to defoliate. Picking machines cleaned 95 percent of the cotton from the stalks, and the quality was as good as that of hand pickers. One machine could do the work of forty people. Using chemicals, flame weeders, and the picking machine, the Stoneville station had eliminated the need for hand workers. The implications were enormous.[19]

In the 1950s the adoption of cotton harvesters dramatically reduced the number of tenants on many Arkansas Delta plantations. By 1959 Crittenden County farmers had 295 mechanical cotton pickers, and during the decade the number of tenants decreased from 5,192 to 1,365. Phillips County had 197 mechanical pickers, and the tenant population fell from 2,994 to 1,060. The relationship of mechanization to human displacement was ominous. Once the trend toward mechanization started, it ground on ruthlessly. In 1958 Mississippi Delta planters harvested 27 percent of the crop with machines; by 1964 the percentage increased to 81.[20]

The new plantation system that emerged from the collapse of the old sharecropping system retained elements of the old culture while turning to a more scientific system of management and cultivation. The Delta and Pine Land Company, for example, had once planted 16,000 acres to cotton and utilized 1,200 tenant families. By 1969 the corporation planted only 7,200 acres to cotton and diversified with soybeans, rice, silage corn, green beans, pasture, and other crops. Instead of mules, the company had 3,200 head of cattle, 150 tractors, 9 combines, 31 mechanical cotton pickers, and other implements. The workforce consisted of 510 hired hands; there were no tenants.[21]

The changing structure of southern agriculture can be illustrated in statistics, which only suggest the human dimensions of the problem. Few historians who write of technological change discuss the government policy that first began scattering the rural population, nor do they give proper credit to government-sponsored research that continued federal intrusion into the rural South. In the census South during the war, the number of white sharecroppers fell from 242,172 to 176,290, and blacks from 299,118 to 270,296. At the same time the number of tenants of all classes fell from 942,655 to 689,540 and from 506,638 to 475,739 respectively. The decline in both groups continued until 1959, the last year in which sharecroppers were counted, when there were but 73,387 black and 47,650 white croppers left. By 1969 the number of tenants of all classes had fallen to 18,235 blacks and 118,153 whites.[22]

These refugees from mechanization left the dilapidated housing, low wages, and poor schools of the rural South. At the same time, such uneducated and dependent workers had little to recommend them to urban employers, except at the most menial level. They were thus caught in a cycle that tossed them off the land, where each day and year was tied to weather and the cultivation of crops, and placed them in an environment where urban and factory time dictated their daily and yearly routines.[23]

That millions of Southerners, black and white, moved from their native section is well documented in census data. Yet the direction of the movement and its inner dynamics remain hidden, although the primary routes of migration seem clear. Migrants from the states directly south of the Potomac River moved to the Northeast. The Mississippi River led migrants from that area north to Chicago, Detroit, and the Midwest, while those west of the Mississippi often headed to the West Coast. Some migrants left the rural South and headed directly to northern cities, while others paused in southern towns before moving on. The migration from south to north is better charted than the intrastate migration from farm to city, and that of black migrants is more precisely understood than that of whites. The historian Jack Temple Kirby, after exhausting census possibilities and the literature of migrants produced by scholars, has concluded, "The ideal history of the great southern exodus—especially of the whites—may not be possible."[24]

Along with other changes in the South, cotton gins adjusted to handle machine-harvested cotton. Despite the central role of the gin in cotton's move from field to factory, there is no definitive study of ginners or buyers in the twentieth century. From the invention of the cotton gin in 1793 until the Civil War, most plantations set up gins to separate seeds from lint. Following the war, the ginning operation moved from the farm to commercial gins; the scale of operation increased, as did the quality of equipment. During the post–Civil War years, byproducts of cottonseeds became increasingly important, and oil mills crushed the seed for fertilizer and vegetable oil. By 1869 there were 26 cottonseed mills operating in the South, and by 1914 882 mills were employing some 22,000 workers and generating $212 million worth of products.

Cottonseeds proved extremely versatile and lucrative. The linters, the fuzzy fibers clinging to the seed, were cut off and at first used for stuffing or wadding. Linters eventually found use in rayon production, dresses, stockings, underwear, paint, film, airplane dope, and other products. During World War I the nitrocellulose in linters yielded smokeless powder. The seed hull could be burned for fuel or used as livestock feed. Mills crushed the unhulled seed to obtain oil used in the manufacture of lard, soap, and margarine. The meal left over after crushing, called cottonseed cake and meal, yielded fertilizer and cattle feed.[25]

Cotton gins and seed crushers established strong ties as the crushing industry gained economic importance. Throughout the South most gins remained in the hands of local businessmen, but the crushing business became divided into two parts. As M. R. Jones of Clarksdale, Mississippi, explained in 1929, the crushing industry was divided into "the mills owned or operated by the refining interests, or commonly called big companies, and those engaged only in the crude-mill business, or referred to as independents." Both groups competed intensely for seeds during the short ginning season. In 1915 crushing mills reached a peak number of 885, but by 1930 only 510 mills were operating, reflecting the overexpansion of the industry and its contraction and consolidation. The drive for rationalization among leading seed crushers attracted a Federal Trade Commission investigation in 1929, a massive study that offers invaluable insight into the dynamics of the industry and its relationship with ginners. The largest (and, by many accounts, the most ruthless) of the big companies was the Buckeye Cotton Oil Company, a subsidiary of Procter and Gamble Company. The Southern Cotton Oil Company was part of the Wesson Oil and Snowdrift Company. Swift and Company operated under its own name and through the Consumers Cotton Oil Company.[26]

Although some of the large seed crushers owned their own gins, the practice was not common. To secure seeds each mill sent out agents, and it became a general practice for crushers to lend money to gins. Many of the loans were never repaid. One cottonseed oil mill owner, in a statement that could have applied to much of the South, estimated that in 1928 "70 per cent of the ginners in the State of Arkansas are obligated to some oil mill, either by securing a loan or by having been furnished bagging and ties, or by past experiences in which they were protected in high prices." The fierce competition for seeds during the ginning season led to price fluctuations that prevented any industrywide collaboration. The Buckeye, for instance, would suddenly increase prices in order to get the seed it needed, causing consternation among other crushers. At the same time, ginners and farmers profited from the competition.[27]

Before the mule culture disappeared, farmers received their first money of the year from selling seed. For each 500-pound bale of lint cotton there were about 890 pounds of cottonseed. In October 1929 the price of cotton was about 17 cents a pound, so a 500-pound bale would bring $85. At $33 per ton, 890 pounds of cottonseed would bring about $14.25. If the gin charged 90 cents per hundred pounds for ginning, the farmer would subtract $4.50 from his seed account and take his bale of cotton and almost $10 of seed money.[28]

By 1945 the number of oil mills had fallen to 382, and a similar contraction of gins progressed. Because of higher moisture content and more trash in the cotton, gins had to invest in drying and cleaning equipment. Mechanical harvesters worked so quickly that the three-month picking season telescoped to six weeks, so gins had to expand capacity. The financial investment required for a modern cotton gin led to contraction in the ginning industry, much as the surrounding farming community became concentrated in larger units. At the turn of the century the country had boasted almost 32,000 gins, but by 1973 the number had fallen to 2,880.[29]

As the structure of American agriculture changed, cotton became less important to southern farmers east of the Mississippi River. Unable to compete with western cotton growers, southern farmers turned to other crops. By 1978 cotton farmers in North and South Carolina, Georgia, Alabama, and Tennessee tended less than 8 percent of the nation's 13.3 million acres. Instead of the one cash crop that had characterized southern production until the 1930s, these farmers diversified into soybeans, peanuts, poultry, hogs, and cattle. Mississippi, Louisiana, Arkansas, Texas, Missouri, and Oklahoma farmers grew 10.3 million acres of cotton, and the remainder of the acreage shifted to Arizona, New Mexico, and California. Texas led all other states in acreage harvested with 6.9 million; the nearest competitor was California, with 1.5 million, followed by Mississippi, with 1.2 million. Of course, western farmers also diversified their crops.[30]

To farmers in the old cotton-producing areas of the South, soybeans came to rival the central role that had formerly belonged to cotton. Prior to the war, beans had been grown mostly for hay or plowed back into the land as fertilizer. By 1940 chemists had deleted the unappetizing taste from soybean oil, making it acceptable for oil food products. Southern states grasped at this crop, and production increased rapidly. In Alabama, where the boll weevil had caused so much damage, farmers harvested 770,000 bales of cotton in 1940 but only 291,000 in

1978. Over the same years soybean production rose from 72,000 to 42.9 million bushels. The shift in other southern states proved as significant. Georgia, for example, grew 1 million bales of cotton in 1940 and only 111,000 in 1975, while soybean production during the same years rose from 91,000 to 29.4 million bushels. As much as any other crop, soybeans made diversification attractive to southern farmers. This change took place not just in the old cotton-growing areas but throughout the South—and, indeed, throughout the nation.[31]

Soybeans epitomized only one of many dramatic production shifts in southern agriculture. Peanut growers, who had taken over large areas of North Carolina, Georgia, and Alabama, expanded production. In 1978 Georgia farmers planted 530,000 acres to peanuts and only 120,000 to cotton. The state's farmers earned $32 million from cotton, $363.4 million from peanuts, and $188.1 million from beans. Georgia livestock producers earned $264.7 million in 1978, and 61,000 acres of tobacco brought an income of approximately $16.6 million. Other southern states offered a similar profile of diversity. The old one-crop hand operation had disappeared. Instead of buying chemicals to kill grass, many southern farmers fed that grass to cattle.[32]

Along with other aspects of diversification, the South grew poultry and hogs. In 1977 Georgia raised 35.9 million chickens that returned $66.3 million, and the city of Gainesville features a monument topped by a chicken as a testimonial to poultry's importance. North Carolina farmers received $40.3 million from poultry, while Alabama farmers earned $33.9 million, South Carolina $12.4 million, and Mississippi $21.1 million. North Carolina hog farmers in 1977 received $173.9 million, followed by Georgia with $133.2 million, Alabama with $50.4 million, South Carolina with $38.8 million, and Mississippi with $29.9 million.[33]

At last the agricultural scientific community located in the USDA, the agricultural schools, and the Extension Service had an attentive audience in the rural South. Farmers, Gilbert Fite concluded, "responded by planting better breeds of crops and livestock, by applying the correct kinds and amounts of fertilizer and insecticides, by keeping accurate business records, by adopting the most efficient machines, and by accepting advice on how to control plant and animal diseases." Yet the expertise only went to large farmers, and the USDA, according to Fite, "insisted that they had neither the know-how nor the resources to save the small farmer." In that sense the policies of the

USDA had remained consistent during the years of change in the rural South.[34]

By 1980 southern cotton farmers no longer used the same vocabulary that had sufficed for a mule culture. At the 1980 Beltwide Cotton Production-Mechanization Conference, Mark A. Shelton III, who managed the World Farming Company operation in Altheimer, Arkansas, described his 2,000-acre cotton plantation that was supplemented by rice and soybean production. "We start," he began, "with shredding our stalks and subsoiling in the fall." In the spring he applied potash and phosphate sparingly in fields where soil tests indicated a need. "We disc once, then row our land and apply anhydrous ammonia at the same time, then we knock down the rows and plant and apply pre-emergence herbicides." After planting, "we cultivate and apply directed postemergence herbicides approximately three times. This is followed with a layby herbicide application and insect control treatments." The tasks connected with producing cotton had changed little, but they were performed quite differently. Tractors did the field-work, chemicals did most of the weeding (though Shelton had one itemized expense of hand chopping), and airplanes sprayed insecticides, defoliants, and fertilizer over the crop. The World Farming Company, attempting to make a better return, had gone into ginning, compressing, storage, and cottonseed processing. In one sense Shelton's operation seemed a return to the self-contained antebellum plantation, but in other respects it more nearly resembled a factory. Instead of managing slaves, Shelton stressed the management of land, chemicals, implements, and ledger books. To prosper, he concluded, a farmer "must keep himself current on new methods and materials and be flexible and adaptable to meet the challenge of a crop that has changed so much over the years."[35]

Yet fuel-hungry implements and expensive chemicals drained profits and raised questions about the blessings of scientific and mechanized farming. Allen Bragg, who grew cotton in Toney, Alabama, experimented with no-till cotton. He had good implements with which to farm in the traditional manner, he stressed, but the high cost of machinery and fuel "has made us look further for more economical methods of producing cotton." Having experimented successfully with no-till soybeans, he experimented for three years with no-till cotton. He gave a detailed description of the implements used, the quality of seed, and chemicals that retarded weed growth. He used strippers to harvest the crop and reported that yields had been "equal to or better than that of conventional cotton on our farms."[36]

Clifford Hoelscher of Garden City, Texas, irrigated his crop and produced two bales per acre. In the 1960s, he stated, cotton farmers were trying to produce maximum yields, but by the 1970s the Texas Extension Service stressed "maximizing profits." He described the irrigation process in his area and stressed that irrigating at the right time discouraged bollworms and budworms. If rain ruined this strategy, he was ready to use chemicals to kill insects. To cut his fertilizer expenses, he rotated crops scientifically. Like many other farmers facing higher interest, fuel, and machinery expenses, Hoelscher used any strategy to keep on farming. "We are talking about methods of survival in cotton production as much as anything," he concluded.[37]

Despite the scientific vocabulary, by the 1980s farmers were more interested in how to save money formerly spent on chemicals, fuel, implements, and land preparation. For a time after World War II it seemed that science would produce a chemical or implement that would replace nature, but as oil-based chemicals rose in price and implements and the fuel to run them became more expensive, farmers thought more in terms of allying with nature, rather than attacking it. Farmers, as Clifford Hoelscher put it, were trying to survive. Diversification and mechanization were no longer enough to insure success.

North Carolina cotton farmers and entomologists conducted one of the more significant, and ironic, experiments. In 1975 state farmers harvested only 53,000 acres of cotton, but by 1982 they planted 72,000 acres. This increase came primarily because of a $5 million boll weevil eradication plan in the northern cotton-growing counties that was jointly funded by cotton farmers and state and federal agencies. A cotton farmer named J. Clarence Leary, Jr., revealed that by killing off boll weevils the cost of production had dropped by $100 to $150 per acre, while production increased. Farmers in the southern part of the state were contributing to a fund to eradicate their weevils. By using a buffer zone in the middle of the state, primarily tobacco country, the USDA and local farmers had finally achieved what farmers in Texas had failed to manage at the turn of the century.

North Carolina farmers increased cotton acreage not because cotton was more profitable and highly mechanized but because they needed a crop other than soybeans to rotate after peanuts. The North Carolina experiment fits the pattern of the modern southern farmer. Government scientists furnished the expertise to fight the weevil, farmers and the government financed it, and crop rotation practices made it feasible. As a result, the westward shift in cotton production may reverse to some extent. This demonstrates the resilience of the southern farmer, who, after all the years of dispossession, allotments, government programs, and inventions that changed the nature of farming, still has the initiative to turn back to the old staple. But it will never be the same, for cotton is only part of the modern southern farm. Its status has been reduced from that of king to commoner.[38]

12

Entropy and Transformation in the Tobacco Culture

Black people have also migrated to the North from eastern North Carolina, to be sure, but in far smaller numbers, because the massive labor requirements of flue-cured tobacco production kept many black workers in the area until jobs began to open up in integrated factories.
—John Fraser Hart and Ennis L. Chestang, 1978

The allotment system ended expansion of the flue-cured tobacco kingdom. Unlike the westward-tilting cotton culture and the often expanding rice culture, tobacco growers after 1933 voted for a closed system. With no possibility of new land, tobacco farmers tilled their tobacco patches more intensively. During World War II the yield reached nearly 1,000 pounds per acre, compared to 710 pounds in 1918. Scientific application of fertilizer and plant disease control contributed to improved yields. Except for purchasing a few tractors that prepared the land and hauled tobacco to the scaffold, tobacco farmers paid scant attention to machines until the 1960s.

The dynamics of World War II strengthened the position of tobacco growers and manufacturers. Cigarette smoking seemed to fit the wartime mood, whether as a nervous habit or a sophisticated affectation. Roosevelt had his Camels, Churchill his cigar, and Stalin his pipe. Who could doubt the central place of tobacco in the war? Cigarettes were part of soldiers' rations, which introduced American brands around the world. Indeed, cigarettes became a form of currency in postwar Europe. Movies and advertisements, invariably showing people smoking stylishly, demanded emulation. Per capita cigarette consumption increased from 1,551 in 1941 to 2,027 by the end of the war. When women could not obtain cigarettes, they turned to pipes.[1]

Logically, with the rural labor force reduced by military and defense industries and tobacco being a luxury item not vital to the war effort, tobacco growers and production should have declined during the war.

Instead, production and the number of farms increased. Franklin County, North Carolina, for example, had 3,368 tobacco farms in 1940 and 246 more five years later. During the war reduced allotments trimmed off 5,000 acres, but, due to more intense cultivation, production only fell from 18.4 million pounds to 16.2 million. Ten years after the war the county still had 3,448 farms, planted 16,078 acres (down from 21,724 acres in 1940), and produced 15.8 million pounds of tobacco. Other counties in the heart of the North Carolina bright tobacco area showed a similar trend. The number of Nash County farms increased by 525 during the war, and in 1954 there were still 106 more farms than there had been in 1940. Although acreage planted from 1940 to 1954 decreased by over 5,400, production increased by 1.2 million pounds. The increased yield came about primarily by using more productive land and better fertilizer, but the AAA's emphasis on conservation and cover crops also contributed.[2]

The cigarette industry had prospered during the Depression, and it also turned out to be warproof. The industry consumed about 75 percent of all tobacco manufactured in the United States, and flue-cured composed 60 percent of that amount. By 1947 the war boom ended, but flue-cured prices held at 41 cents per pound, and the Korean War pushed the price to 55 cents in 1950. In 1947 supply finally outran demand, and the Commodity Credit Corporation (CCC) purchased about 20 percent of the crop; the USDA reduced allotments the next year. Agricultural legislation in 1948 and 1949 supported tobacco at 90 percent of parity, as had been the case in the two previous years. The CCC program had not affected flue-cured tobacco until the 1939 marketing year, when the British buyers left the market, and during the war prices were so high that loans were unnecessary. From 1933 to 1955 the CCC actually experienced a $188,000 net gain. Murray R. Benedict and Oscar C. Stine concluded, in *The Agricultural Commodity Programs: Two Decades of Experience*, that, "On the whole, the tobacco program, if its general objectives are accepted, has been one of the most manageable and successful of the farm programs." They explained this by observing that production controls were strictly enforced, and that the adjustments made did not affect farm organization.[3]

The government aided the tobacco industry in many ways. The Commodity Credit Corporation sold to the Lend-Lease Administration the tobacco bought for the Imperial Tobacco Company and shipped it to the British Empire, netting a bookkeeping gain of over $1 million in the transaction. Small farmers took advantage of the new grower provisions, which explains the increase in the number of farms reported in the census. The price for flue-cured tobacco rose from 16 cents per pound in 1940 to 44 cents in 1945.[4]

The tobacco culture thus endured the war and prospered, although the geographical boundary of the tobacco-growing area remained largely frozen. In 1937 and 1939, when controls were lax, Florida growers had expanded acreage. Within the flue-cured belt, the number of allotments rose from 191,857 in 1941 to 210,735 in 1951, the acreage planted increased from 761,591 to 1,119,309, and the average size of tobacco allotments increased from 4 to 5.3 acres. At the same time, allotments increased land value.[5]

The war increased the tempo of change in the rural United States. During the 1930s many farmers went broke, and others were displaced by AAA acreage reduction policies, especially in the cotton-growing areas. The war, to reiterate, absorbed many of these people into the military or defense industries. According to a 1945 BAE report, "nearly 2 million farm people went into the armed forces and another 9 million either moved off farms or quit farming, while 4 million moved to farms." Snatched from the countryside, trained, transported, and shot at, southern servicemen saw another world and shared stories with their comrades in arms from all over the country. For many, wartime experiences broke the gravitational pull of the land. They would never return.[6]

The exodus from rural areas created a manpower shortage. To make the best use of available workers, the FSA and the Extension Service managed the movement of farm labor throughout the country. In addition to those who stayed on the farms, there were nearly 75,000 prisoners of war who worked in agriculture and over 85,000 foreign workers, mostly from Barbados, Jamaica, and the Bahamas. In North Dakota 4,500 Mexicans and 700 Mexican-Americans helped harvest wheat and sugar beets. City folks, youngsters, and senior citizens helped bring in the harvests. Some farmers were partial to prisoners of war and foreign workers and lobbied to keep the prisoners long after the war had ended. Florida cane growers secured permission to continue using workers from Jamaica, Barbados, and the Bahamas.[7]

The tremendous domestic migration of farm workers affected the tobacco culture in a quite different manner. By the war years, Canada had institutionalized the practice of importing curers from the South, and there was a large demand not only for curers but also for primers. In 1944, for example, 1,575 tobacco workers traveled to Canada during harvest season. Thus, at the same time that many American farmers were requesting foreign laborers and prisoners of war, southern tobacco farmers were traveling to Canada to cure tobacco—hardly a strategic crop. North Carolina sent 907 workers to Ontario and 29 to Quebec in 1944, and Virginia followed, with 369 to Ontario and 12 to Quebec. Other southern states, as well as the District of Columbia, Ohio, and Maryland, contributed to the northward stream of tobacco workers. "We were able to save the biggest crop in our history, and the men from the United States played an important part in obtaining this result," an administrator in Canada wrote to the United States Department of Agriculture.[8] Thus the flue-cured tobacco culture seemed in many ways completely outside the regular channels of farm labor, just as tobacco legislators bypassed most congressional procedures in setting up the tobacco program.

At the same time that some tobacco workers departed for Canada, others needed additional laborers to house their crops. In other crop areas women, children, and senior citizens were being utilized for the first time, but since the tobacco culture had customarily relied on these workers, growers looked for new sources of labor. Although the number used in harvesting tobacco is not available, in June 1945 there were 841 prisoners of war in North Carolina, 1,009 in South Carolina, and 1,767 in Georgia.[9]

In 1944 the government set up a prisoner-of-war camp on the banks of the Roanoke River near Williamston, North Carolina. The camp first held Italian prisoners, but soon Germans replaced them. By conducting interviews, a group of high school students in Martin County discovered in 1978 that prisoners "were used to cut wood for curing tobacco, to prepare seed beds, and to prime the tobacco leaves at harvest." Hilton Forbes of Williamston recalled for the students that he was drafted in the summer of 1944, and that at the same time his father became ill. He asked a German prisoner of war to care for the crop. "Many people in the county said that no one could have done it better!" he remembered. Germans soon learned about the tobacco culture, even about the morning breaks. They chose Dr. Pepper as their favorite drink and learned that the advertising slogan "10−2−4" meant the time of day for a Dr. Pepper break. They ate at growers' tables and became friends with Martin County farmers. The friendships endured after the Germans returned home, and some came back with their families to visit, while county residents looked up former prisoners when visiting Germany.[10]

Thus World War II pushed tobacco growers into contact with the wider world. At the same time, the culture stabilized, as tobacco farms and demand for flue-cured tobacco increased. Tobacco legislators protected the federal program and made it work extremely well for those who had managed to obtain allotments. Returning veterans found the tobacco culture much as they had left it. An occasional tractor replaced mules, and oil burners had been supplanting wood furnaces since the late 1930s.[11] While rice growers turned to combines and cotton growers were on the verge of utilizing mechanical harvesters, tobacco farmers (except for scientific fertilizer application) made few bows to the modern world. Radios and automobiles seemed their only concessions to modern technology.

The old culture still had two decades to linger before the modern invasion began in earnest, for it remained relatively stable until the mid-1950s and largely unmechanized through the 1960s. When the structural changes that had been eviscerating the old cotton culture since the 1930s appeared in the flue-cured tobacco area in the 1960s, the familiar pattern of dispossession and concentration followed. The revolution in the bright tobacco culture dramatizes the close interrelationship between government programs and mechanization. The cost-price squeeze in the 1950s, the Soil Bank Program, inflation—particularly more expensive labor, fertilizer, fuel, and chemicals—urbanization, industrialization, the civil rights movement, and many other factors altered the old culture. Increasingly medical researchers linked cigarettes, manufactured primarily from flue-cured tobacco, to cancer. Manufacturers turned to low-tar and low-nicotine filter cigarettes, recycled floor sweepings and dust, bought less expensive foreign tobacco, updated their machinery, and diversified. Small allotment holders found other jobs and used their tobacco crops as a hobby to bring in extra cash, or later leased their allotments. With better roads, TV, and supermarkets, farmers no longer felt tied to the crossroads store and the community. With consolidated and integrated schools, children no longer felt constrained by the old customs. The old tobacco culture at last faltered, and tobacco farming became more a business and less a way of life.[12]

The first major structural change appeared in the mid-1950s. Census figures show an abrupt decline in the number of tobacco farms between 1954 and 1959. Again using Franklin County, North Carolina, as an example, tobacco farms declined from 3,448 in 1954 to almost a thousand fewer in 1959, and acreage declined from 16,078 to 11,231.

Three beauties wearing bathing suits made of tobacco leaves pose for a photograph at the Tobacco Festival. Moultrie, Georgia. 1950s. Earl Murray. (Vanishing Georgia Collection, CLQ-92, Courtesy of Georgia Department of Archives and History)

Nash, Wilson, and Pitt counties showed similar declines. During the same years Nash County lost 1,404 farms and 8,303 acres, Wilson County had 1,108 fewer farms and 8,122 fewer acres, and Pitt County lost 2,595 farms and 11,601 acres. Because allotments were based on acreage, production did not decline proportionately, for farmers cultivated the land more intensively. The average yield per acre increased from 922 pounds in 1939 to 2,200 in 1964.[13]

Historians have not analyzed the dynamics of this decline in the number of tobacco farms. Since it preceded major steps in mechanization, the decrease probably came partly from landowners putting their land in the Soil Bank Program established by the Republican administration in 1956. Also, caught in the cost-price squeeze, small farmers sold out to larger growers. At the same time, many growers dismissed their sharecroppers, used tractors to prepare the land and to plow, and hired seasonal labor at harvest time. Thus the landowner could consolidate several tenant farms.[14] In those five years North Carolina lost 37,440 flue-cured tobacco farms, planted 218,311 fewer acres, and harvested 141.6 million fewer pounds. The impact of the reduction in farms changed the traditional relationship between landlords and tenants, especially black tenants. White outmigration from the bright tobacco area declined during the 1960s, but black outmigration increased.[15]

Until the 1960s the tractor remained the major element of mechanization. Tractors tilled the land and saved time and labor costs; they also pulled the sleds from the fields to the scaffold. Harvest remained as labor intensive as in the past, as primers walked through the fields, scaffold help handed each leaf, and the crew passed the sticks into the barns. Small farms did not lend themselves to huge, expensive machinery, and few farmers would have had enough capital or credit to invest in such machinery even if it had been available.

When the old labor-intensive tobacco culture finally yielded to the more modern structure, the causes for the transformation stood out clearly. The legal structure established by Congress to deal with small allotments, family farmers, and tenants discouraged attempts to mechanize tobacco on as large a scale as rice or cotton. Tobacco could not migrate west, as cotton had throughout its history; nor could it expand geographically, as rice had. Frozen into a small area and broken into small allotments, tobacco seemed to belong to another century.

Still, inventors unleashed their genius upon the problem of modernizing the tobacco culture. Some of the first attempts to mechanize flue-cured tobacco resulted in labor savings, but others were dead ends. No machine so awesome as a rice combine or cotton picker seemed feasible. In the 1950s a device eliminated the labor-intensive handing and stringing operation by mechanically sewing the leaves to the stick. In the same decade a machine appeared in the fields that resembled a spindly-legged bird rearing above the tobacco stalks. Primers rode on seats on the lower part, priming leaves in the old fashion. They attached each bundle of leaves to a pulley that carried it up to stringers on the top level. Racks held the full sticks. Periodically the machine traveled to the barn to unload. Thus the scaffold moved to the field and through the field. This awkward machine, a study concluded, saved no money and little effort. Many farmers did adopt and simplify the lower part of the machine, for sitting down and riding through a field proved preferable to stoop labor. A tractor pulled a frame with four seats, and primers stacked the tobacco on large attached shelves. At the end of the row they transferred it to a large trailer, and another tractor or pickup truck pulled it to the scaffold. None of these operations taken separately or together promised a unified harvesting system.[16]

Small farms provided the perfect scale of operation for a family, but, as labor costs increased and young adults moved to urban areas, a family often could not provide sufficient labor even for a small farm. Many growers rented their land to larger farmers, but because the law required that tobacco be grown on the land where the allotment resided, a farmer who rented land had to move his workforce and machines from farm to farm—an uneconomical and tiresome chore. The tobacco culture gradually became less labor intensive, though. In addition to tractors, a mechanical topper that came into use in the late 1960s covered twenty acres a day, not only removing the flowery tops, but at the same time spraying for suckers and hornworms.[17] Farmers no longer had to spend endless hours hiking through tobacco patches throughout the summer. Harvest and grading still required an enormous amount of seasonal labor.

The demand for a larger-scale operation, dramatized by a petition signed by 75,000 farmers, led to a lease and transfer program in 1961. Under this law a grower could lease five acres from another farmer within the county. Six years later an amendment permitted unlimited leasing within a county. Thus a farmer with tractors and toppers could expand and concentrate his operation, while small farmers could collect rent from their allotments and work off the farm, or retire.[18] This structural change in the allotment program had dramatic results in the flue-cured area, and it coincided with another legislative change.

In 1968, two years after permitting unlimited intracounty leasing, Congress extended loose-leaf marketing to all sales areas. Farmers in Georgia and Florida had customarily marketed their crops this way, and, with better transportation, farmers from the Carolinas and Virginia trucked their tobacco to southern warehouses to obtain cash as soon as they took the cured tobacco out of the barns. Faced with smaller sales, warehouse owners in the Carolinas and Virginia lobbied for relief, and in 1974 the USDA required farmers to designate sales warehouses within one hundred miles of their county seats; otherwise they would not be eligible for price support.[19] Because efficient use of machinery required a different field layout, farmers lobbied for changes in the acreage allotment program, and in 1965 Congress changed the allotment to a poundage quota. This change met no resistance from farmers, despite the unhappy experience in 1938.[20]

Prior to these changes tobacco had been handled very carefully. Nearly every operation fit into a person's hand, from priming in the fields, to handing, to stringing, to finally tying tobacco into hands for marketing. With loose-leaf marketing, the hand scale began to disappear from the tobacco culture. The most obvious change came when farmers discarded their old barns and sticks and turned to bulk curers. Resembling a house trailer, a bulk barn handles tobacco in large lots, not in hand-sized dribbles. A farmer could stuff tobacco into the bulk barn in large trays, turn on the heat, and let an automatic thermostat regulate the curing cycle. The curing skills previously passed from generation to generation could thus be supplanted by dials and gears. In 1972 only 8 percent of flue-cured farmers used bulk barns, but seven year later over 61 percent had adopted them. This change saved tremendous labor costs during harvest, and there was no longer any grading and preparation for market; farmers took the cured tobacco from bulks barns, dumped it into burlap sheets, and hauled it to market.

As more farmers leased their allotments, the number of tobacco farms in North Carolina declined rapidly, and the labor-intensive nature of the culture also changed. All these changes meant that sharecroppers disappeared, for land that had been tilled by croppers and their families could be leased more efficiently. Still, the number of allotments far exceeded the number of active farms.[21]

Even before these structural shifts took place, researchers began drafting blueprints for a harvester that could perform all the fieldwork and dispense with primers altogether. Early efforts to utilize these principles failed, but in the mid-1960s R. J. Reynolds Tobacco Company encouraged further development with a grant to North Carolina State University. By 1969 the collaboration led to a successful har-

Johnny Finch using a mechanical tobacco harvester near Floods Chapel, North Carolina. July 18, 1983. Pete Daniel.

vester, and the Harrington Manufacturing Company put the machine into production. Although most allotments remained small, the harvester had been designed for a break-even capacity of forty to fifty acres. Like so many development projects, the structure of the old ways did not seem to matter. Only large-scale farmers could afford such expensive machines. Small farmers, faced with inflation and stagnant allotments, had to expand, lease, mechanize, or sell out. A single machine threatened to end one of the last vestiges of the traditional family farm. The savings in field labor proved immense. Instead of the 370 manhours per acre that an all-hand-labor operation required, machinery for plowing and topping and the harvester could perform the task in a mere 58 hours. One estimate concluded that by 1979 harvesters primed 20 percent of the flue-cured crop, while a 1980 study estimated that 46 percent of North Carolina's crop was being mechanically primed.[22]

Despite mechanization, there were significant differences between rural displacement in eastern North Carolina and that in the old cotton-growing areas of the South. Because the tobacco culture became mechanized so recently, major changes had taken place in eastern North Carolina before technological displacement began. By the 1960s the impact of the civil rights movement led to consolidated and integrated schools, the franchise for blacks, and a more open society. Every North Carolina governor since Luther Hodges took office in 1954 attempted to attract industry to North Carolina, and Governor James Hunt, inaugurated in 1977, proved especially successful in that pursuit.[23] The advent of increasing numbers of factory jobs coincided with the displacement of agricultural workers. Unlike cotton farmers displaced in the 1930s by the AAA and later by picking machines, tobacco farmers could remain and work in the same communities where they had farmed. The factories came to them. Better educated than the croppers who fled the cotton area, mobile with autos, and more accustomed to the modern world, displaced tobacco farmers could make the transition to factory life with much less trauma than could earlier generations of rural folk.

In the heart of the North Carolina tobacco belt—Edgecombe, Green, Lenoir, Pitt, Nash, Wayne, and Wilson counties—the number of workers employed in manufacturing rose from 24,700 in 1963 to 59,606 in 1976, while agricultural workers declined from 45,020 to 22,950, an almost perfect exchange. Whether former sharecroppers and small farmers composed the new factory workforce cannot be determined, but certainly the options open in the 1970s had not been present thirty or forty years before. The lateness of mechanization thus eased the transition of these farmworkers to factory life. "Black people have also migrated to the North from eastern North Carolina, to be sure," a study concluded, "but in far smaller numbers, because the massive labor requirements of flue-cured tobacco production kept many black workers in the area until jobs began to open up in integrated factories." While many blacks moved North in search of equal opportunity, those who stayed behind in the Tobacco Belt discovered that the civil rights movement ultimately caught up with them at home, allowing many to remain in the same communities that they had called home for generations. Although they drove to work in nearby factories, they returned home; the neighbors, churches, stores, and schools were part of the old community.[24]

The impact of these changes appears clearly in census statistics. In Nash County the number of tobacco farms dropped from 2,653 in 1964 to 1,084 ten years later, and the number of tenants fell from

1,834 to 361. Still, in 1982 county residents held 2,895 allotments. Wilson County lost 1,067 farms and Pitt County lost 1,355 during the same years. In 1980 the state had 34,200 tobacco farms and 82,000 allotment holders. Leasing and mechanization accounted for most of the decline in the number of farms.[25] The state lost 32,546 tobacco farms in the decade. The number of tobacco farms in North Carolina dropped from 52,000 in 1977 to 46,000 in 1978—a 12 percent decline in one year. At the other end of the scale, the size of allotments increased from 5.2 acres in 1964 to 12.2 acres in 1978.[26]

Changes in the allotment system and mechanization have pushed tobacco along the same road taken by cotton and other crops that have mechanized. The "family farm," in the traditional sense of the term, has been transformed into a capital-intensive operation. Some farmers still employ youngsters and women to pack tobacco into racks that are hung in bulk barns. As priming, handing, stringing, and grading operations fell from use, the workforce dwindled. It takes only five workers to run the harvest operation with a mechanical harvester and bulk barns.[27]

The changing farm structure in the flue-cured tobacco area produced problems that, along with the smoking-and-health controversy, focused attention on the federal tobacco support program. Tight production controls and high support prices undermined the farmers' competitive position in world trade and threatened them with cheaper imported leaf. After the approval of leasing in 1961, many marginal farmers retired and leased their acreages, as did corporations, banks, townships, and even educational institutions that owned allotments. Leasing and mechanization led to a demise of small units of production and a move to large-scale operations on a single farm. Even as a new farm structure evolved, public pressure increased to end all federal connection with the tobacco program. Through the years tobacco-state politicians have carefully hidden tobacco bills in congressional byways, seldom allowing the issue to reach the floor for debate. After the 1980 election the protective screen was pushed aside—partly because of the health issue, but also because of the new Republican majority in the Senate. Jesse Helms of North Carolina assumed chairmanship of the Senate Agriculture, Forestry, and Nutrition Committee; this tobacco state senator offered a tempting target, both to those who detested cigarettes and to those who opposed his conservative politics. During the debate on the 1981 farm bill, tobacco senators avoided by only one vote an amendment that would have changed the support program. Ultimately a bargain emerged that would result in a year-long study culminating in a plan to remove the tobacco support program from the federal budget.[28] Faced with the program's extinction, politicians and farm leaders conducted hearings and drafted a "no net cost program."

In addition to hearings in several tobacco states, the Government Accounting Office conducted a study of the burley and flue-cured tobacco programs. Thirty farms from each of the sixteen counties in two USDA flue-cured regions composed the flue-cured sample; the burley program had a parallel study. The report revealed that many of the original allotment owners no longer farmed, if they ever had. "Retired farmers, widows of farmers, and nonfarming owners such as doctors, teachers, realtors, truck drivers, and construction workers made up the majority of the owners." In the flue-cured sample, only 12 percent of the leaseowners actually grew tobacco, while 57 percent leased out their allotments. That is, 68,000 out of the 83,941 farms in the area leased out allotments. Only 21 percent of the leaseholders were full-time farmers, and another 3 percent were parttime farmers. Retired farmers and widows made up 25 percent, while the remaining allotment holders were either nonfarmers or unknown. Leasing rates varied from area to area, depending on yield and other factors. For example, the Pitt County government amassed an allotment of 42,331 pounds and leased it for 65 to 67 cents a pound, while in Rocky Mount the city auctioned off its 19,000-pound quota for 66 cents a pound.

Lease rates increased dramatically over the years. "In 1979," the report observed, "lease rates amounted to 29 percent of the average sale price of flue-cured tobacco—the highest of any year." Predictably, leasing increased in direct proportion to mechanization. From 1972 to 1980 leasing increased 55 percent in flue-cured areas. The report acknowledged that increasing mechanization required larger units of production, at least fifteen acres or 30,000 pounds of quota. Large-scale farmers could buy additional land to secure larger allotments, but since the allotment went with the land, a farmer might be forced to buy an extensive farm in order to obtain a small additional allotment. Even as farmers sought to increase their allotments, the USDA reduced the total flue-cured quota. From 1975 to 1981 allotments dropped by 32.1 percent.[29]

As leasing drove up the price of tobacco and the cost of production, foreign sales declined and imports of foreign tobacco increased. Historically, American tobacco had been popular because of its quality, but with improving quality in other countries, and lower prices, the competitive position of American tobacco declined. Between 1966 (the first year of unlimited intracounty leasing) and 1981, the U.S. share of world tobacco exports dropped from 60 percent to 28 percent.[30] Meanwhile, imports increased from 10 million pounds in 1970 to 84 million in 1980. Obviously lower-priced foreign tobacco appealed to manufacturers. Due to the federal allotment system and production control, the price of U.S. tobacco was sometimes double that of foreign leaf.[31]

In effect, the tobacco program forced flue-cured farmers into a dilemma. Only those who mechanized could remain in production, but to mechanize meant leasing out larger allotments. Leasing pushed up production costs and required higher support levels. This, in turn, pushed prices beyond the world level, causing a decline in exports and an increase in imports of cheaper tobacco. In the short term, farmers have still managed to profit, but at some point the entire structure could collapse under the strain of such contradictions. Meanwhile, the CCC, which funded the Flue-Cured Cooperative Stabilization Corporation, accumulated large stocks of low-grade tobacco that manufacturers refused to buy. Despite these and other problems, there seemed no motivation to change the tobacco program until the 1981 Senate debates resulted in an ultimatum to force the tobacco program to operate without federal funds.

After passing in the House without debate, the no net cost tobacco bill arrived in the Senate in early July 1982 and faced a deadline imposed by market openings. On July 14 the Senate took up the proposed bill, drafted primarily by Democratic Congressman Charles Rose and Republican Senator Jesse Helms. To remove the Commodity Credit Corporation from the support program, tobacco growers throughout the country would contribute to a "No Net Cost Tobacco Fund" utilized by the various cooperative associations that purchased tobacco. This, in effect, forced farmers to pay for their own price-support program. To discourage overproduction, the bill gave the secretary of agriculture power to reduce the support level on grades of tobacco that were in excess supply.

By far the most significant part of the bill concerned allotments. In addition to prohibiting speculative fall leasing, the bill permitted farmers to sell their allotments from farms where they historically resided. Only active tobacco farmers in the same county could buy them. While farmers could sell their allotments, nonfarmers who held allotments, such as public utilities, banks, educational or religious institutions, and local government units, had to sell all their allotments by December 1, 1983, or forfeit them. For farmers who had survived the transition period of mechanization, this opened up a startling allotment bonanza in the tobacco area. Obviously farmers engaged in large-scale operations eagerly sought such allotments to expand their operations. Neither the GAO report nor floor debates revealed exactly who the nonfarm owners were. As industrialism and urbanization increased, some farmland had become part of towns or factory sites and was no longer part of rural America—but it still had a tobacco allotment attached to it. The provisions only aided current tobacco farmers, not prospective growers or young farmers who might want to become tobacco farmers, for in order to obtain an allotment, one had to be actively engaged in farming. The reason given for this provision was that it cut out speculation in allotments. It also preserved the old network of farmers who had survived since the 1930s. After extensive debate and amendments, the bill passed, 77 to 17.[32]

It was somehow fitting that a host of southern Republicans presided over the demise of a federal program that originated during the New Deal, especially since they shifted the cost of the program to producers. Southern Republican political power epitomized many changes in the area, especially the rural-to-urban shift and the influx of Northerners. A new set of priorities had developed, and tobacco no longer dominated the political arena.[33] The structure has changed to the point that the tobacco culture has been transformed from family farm units to agribusiness. While some small allotment holders continue to lease their quotas, the thousands of sharecroppers and wagehands who left the culture received few of the tobacco program's cash benefits. Like such tenure groups in other commodity cultures, they had only their labor to sell, and when that labor was no longer needed, the mechanical enclosure disposed of them.[34]

13

It burns one up when he realizes he had brought his children up to love the farm, only to learn there is no future in it for them.
—*Henry Unkel, Kinder, Louisiana, 1955*

Readjustment and Remechanization in the Rice Culture

The history of rice farming in the southern prairies revolves around the theme of mechanization and remechanization. Rising labor costs and scarcity during World War II encouraged rice farmers to adopt combines in order to reduce the demand for harvest labor. Combines, driers, gigantic tractors, and airplanes epitomized the remechanization of the rice culture. More efficient machines, improved fertilizer and seed, and no acreage controls led to overproduction, and by 1955 rice farmers experienced federal-mandated acreage reductions similar to those that had contributed to the reconfiguration of the cotton culture twenty years before. To reduce the growing surplus (which had been encouraged in part by its policies) the USDA intervened in 1955 to cut acreage. This move, coupled with revisions in the producer allotment program, drove many rice farmers from the land. After almost twenty years of retrenchment and quotas, the rice culture expanded dramatically in the 1970s. By 1980, however, rice farmers again produced more than could be marketed, so the federal government paid them in surplus rice to idle their land. The seesaw policies of the USDA reflected both the free market policies of Herbert Hoover and the federal intrusion advocated by Franklin D. Roosevelt. The rice program, like so many aspects of the economy, tilted from one ideology to the other.[1]

As war spread across Europe and Asia during the late 1930s, it disrupted the usual channels of rice supply. After the attack on Pearl Harbor in December 1941, United States rice became a key commodity to alleviate the worldwide food shortage. In 1942 the USDA urged rice farmers to increase production and even penalized growers who planted less than their allotments. Rice farmers responded to the emergency and exceeded the 1.3-million-acre goal by planting 1.4 million acres, a 20 percent increase over the previous year.[2]

Because of a shortage of harvest labor, farmers found it difficult to expand acreage. To solve this problem they turned to combines, driers, and bulk storage. Despite wartime shortages, rice farmers quickly adopted combine technology. Hired labor costs rose from $.20 per hour in 1940 to $.70 by 1946. Farmers in Texas and California employed combines first, but by 1946 44.6 percent of Louisiana rice farmers also used them. A year later an Arkansas study revealed that half the farmers in the sample had shifted to combines. Using binders, it took two men to cut the rice and four to shock. The threshing operation took fourteen men, eight teams and wagons, and two additional men to haul the rice to an elevator. With a combine, a farmer and one hired hand could harvest a 250-acre crop and deliver it to the elevator. The combine reduced labor per acre from eleven to three hours. The number of driers increased proportionally, and commercial driers charged $.50 per barrel. Using hand labor and binders, it cost Louisiana farmers $1.50 per barrel to harvest, but with combines the price dropped to $1.05. The combine revolution began during the war and rapidly ran its course. Young rice farmers returning from the war witnessed a different work culture, much as cotton farmers did when they viewed the new mechanical cotton pickers.[3]

Converting to combines and driers involved a high risk for both farmers and millers. With combines, farmers could expand acreage, but at the same time they went into debt to finance the new machines. Millers, to accept the combined rice, financed expensive driers. As long as demand remained high, both groups could pay off their loans, but a postwar depression could put them in serious financial trouble. The quick conversion to combines and driers also led to waste when the new technology did not function properly. In 1945, for example, the War Food Administration rejected 24 million pounds of rice because driers did not reduce moisture enough to prevent kernel damage. In some cases millers found it difficult to finance drying equipment and appealed to the government for help.[4]

The government set a ceiling on rice prices early in 1942, and though it allowed a 10 percent increase that August, the ceiling remained in place until 1946. After jumping from $1.80 per hundred pounds in 1940 to $3.01 in 1941, prices increased only to $3.98 by 1945. Rice farmers prospered even with a price ceiling, for they could take advantage of expanded acreage and the savings realized by using combines. The value of the rice crop rose from $69 million in 1941 to $122 million in 1945. Millers, on the other hand, objected to government setasides for the military and for export, for they had painstakingly developed the domestic market. With from 40 to 80 percent reserved for government use, rice disappeared from grocers' shelves, and millers feared that ultimately Americans would lose their already paltry appetite for the product. These problems plagued the rice industry during the war, and, looking ahead to normal world production, both growers and millers feared a collapse similar to that of 1920. The government, having disrupted the domestic market, in the opinion of millers and farmers, had a responsibility to stabilize the rice industry when peace returned.[5]

During the summer of 1945 the worldwide rice shortage became so critical that the government set aside most of the U.S. rice supply for its programs. U.S. commitments for the 1945–46 fiscal year called for 28 million bags of rice, but domestic production only yielded 20.5 million. Since not all claimants could be satisfied, the government set up a formula, but growers and millers continually protested the low priority assigned to the domestic market. By October 1945 the Production and Marketing Administration (PMA) eased the setaside to 40 percent, 15 percent lower than the August figure.[6]

By early 1946 the domestic supply dwindled further. As Louisiana Congressmen James Domengeaux and Harry D. Larcade, Jr., pointed out, "there will be practically no rice available for civilian consumption over a seven month period, or until the next crop." They feared "the occurrence of what happened following World War I when due precisely to circumstances as we have now, a great deal of rice was channeled to offshore areas and the domestic rate of consumption showed a sharp decline which required a number of years to build up to its present figure of approximately six pounds per capita." The present policy, they argued, defeated the expensive advertising campaign conducted by the rice industry. The United States should not turn its back on starving people, they admitted, but it should prepare for the resumption of rice competition from Asia. After World War I, they revealed, the British government had embargoed rice supplies in Burma until the spring of 1920; then it had flooded the market, sending prices down. They suggested that the British had again cornered vast supplies of rice that portended a repeat of the 1920 disaster. On a much lighter note, H. C. Denturk, a photographer in Huntington, New York, suggested that thousands of tons of rice could be saved each year—if people would not waste it at weddings.[7]

Frank A. Godchaux, Jr., impatient with government indecision, lashed out at the uncoordinated federal programs. Growers and millers had invested millions of dollars during the war to increase production at the government's request, he wrote to the Rice Section. The Louisiana State Rice Milling Company, which he headed, had spent more than $1 million updating its equipment. He argued that government "vacillation first one way and then another is ample evidence of a lack of clear policy, and a lack of understanding of what they are doing to the industry and the country."[8]

By harvest season in 1946 farmers were holding their rice off the market, hoping for a price increase of a dollar a barrel. Some millers bought at higher prices in anticipation. The director of the Grain Branch requested a price increase, arguing that rice prices had been controlled since 1942. Given those circumstances, the USDA feared that without a price increase there would be a "chaotic condition in the industry and it is questionable whether price ceilings on rice could be effectively maintained." Ultimately the goverment granted the increase.[9]

Fortunately, the expected collapse did not follow the war, nor did prices fall when controls were removed in July 1947. In that year the average price per hundred pounds rose to $5.97, and farmers received a record $210 million for the crop, almost five times the 1940 figure. The next year, however, prices fell to $4.88. For the first time since 1941, when CCC loans became available for rice, farmers put their rice under loan. As the harvest season began in 1950, the CCC owned 459,000 bags of rice. Homer L. Brinkley, the spokesman for the American Rice Growers' Cooperative Association, wrote to Secretary of Agriculture Charles F. Brannan, charging that the oversupply came primarily from California expansion. "California," he charged, "has increased its production two million barrels over last year, which is at least two million barrels in excess of any commercial market they have ever had." If the government imposed quotas, he argued, it would be "unjust to the South to permit this situation to tip the scale as to whether quotas should be imposed on the entire United States industry, including the South." He reasoned that California growers were producing for the CCC market and that acreage allotments would stop their reckless expansion. He also feared that a 20 percent decrease in production would harm small growers, and he calculated that even a 50 percent penalty on overproduction would not deter "those highly efficient producers raising rice on good land with the most modern and efficient machinery known to agriculture."[10]

In December 1949 the USDA instituted acreage allotments to reduce the oversupply. Because acreage had expanded so rapidly since the war, the department used a weighted formula to arrive at each state's allotment. Under this formula it cut Louisiana acreage by 7.8 percent, Texas by 14.9 percent, Arkansas by 16.1 percent, and California by 19.2 percent. Acreage planted in excess of allotments did not qualify for price supports, but if prices remained high due to market conditions, those who overplanted stood to reap a windfall. "Only when marketing quotas have been proclaimed and approved by a two-thirds majority of eligible rice growers," the department explained, "is the excess production on an overplanted farm subject to penalty." The announcement set off a wave of protest from rice growers, many of whom did not understand that they only risked loss of price support on rice that exceeded allotments.[11]

E. L. Boston, a banker in Angleton, Texas, complained to Senator Tom Connally that the 1949 hurricane had ruined the rice crop in Brazoria and Galveston counties, and he asked that farmers there be exempt from allotments. He also doubted that the Production and Marketing Administration, the predecessor of the Agricultural Stabilization and Conservation program (ASC), understood how to set allotments. The PMA had held meetings behind closed doors, he complained, and none of them "knows one thing about the production of rice or the mechanics of financing or securing the financing of a production loan." By the time the local committee had made its decision and the bureaucracy had ruled on it, Boston feared that it would be too late to plant. "In addition to the red tape and regimentation that is being inflicted upon the farmers," he added, "the local PMA office never opens its doors on Saturday." Even during the week the local PMA manager was out of his office three out of five days. "For your information," he concluded, "the people in this part of these United States are fed up on the trend toward socialism."[12]

The bureaucracy, acreage allotments, mechanization, and the usual risks of farming weighed heavily on rice farmers. T. L. Drawhorn had farmed rice near Dayton, Texas, for two years and averaged 155 acres.

He owned $11,000 in machinery and rented or sharecropped his land. A hurricane destroyed 30 percent of his 1949 crop, leaving him $3,000 in debt. For the 1950 crop he arranged to farm 300 acres on half-shares. He calculated that he needed production from 150 acres to pay off his debts. The PMA awarded him 45 acres. Since planting time was at hand, he hoped to avoid the lengthy local and state appeal process with a direct appeal to the USDA. The department answered that his small allotment no doubt came from his brief production history (only two years) and, ignoring his request for speedy action, referred him to the local and state appeal channels.[13] Such officious replies increasingly appeared in farmers' mailboxes.

In Arkansas the allotment program threatened small farmers and tenants. H. B. Brown wrote from Harrisburg, asking his congressman "if you could inform me what the renters with machinery for the purpose of raising rice can do now, after the land owner is holding all the allotment for himself." Brown had $7,000 invested in machinery and knew that he could not sell it for half that price; other farmers in the area faced similar conditions. "The average man just figures it a waste of time to write you or any one else," he lamented. John Garrich of Stuttgart only received a 49-acre allotment but had counted on supporting his family of seven and various relatives on 80 acres. He had already invested $4,500 in a new well, $500 for seed rice, and prepared his land. Carl Pohlner wrote from Fisher that he had farmed rice for twenty years, "except for the four years spent with the army in the South Pacific." He returned from the military, "brushed the rust off my farming equipment and added some new until I now own over ten thousand dollars worth of rice producing machinery." He rented all his land, but the allotment reduction threatened to end his farming career. "I have always been able to earn a normal existence but have now been forced to my row's end," he despaired. Pohlner survived, however, and by 1956 had a base allotment of 187 acres, which the ASC cut to 115. The records do not make clear whether or not he owned the farm that he operated.[14]

Almost unnoticed in the turmoil over allotment reduction in 1949, the Louisiana PMA state committee ended producer allotments. The Agricultural Adjustment Act of 1938, as amended, provided that the secretary of agriculture could set rice allotments, basing them either on each grower's production history or, if the state PMA committee decided, "he may provide for the apportionment of the State acreage allotment to farms on the basis of past production of rice on the farm in lieu of past production of rice by producers." The change did not require a vote of rice producers, but only a decision by the six-member state PMA committee.[15] The full significance of this shift would not become apparent for six years.

After the protest over allotments receded, rice farmers in all four major rice-producing states overplanted allotments in 1950. Whether the world situation aggravated by the Korean War eased the allotment policy or whether farmers simply risked low prices and lack of price support on excess production, Louisiana farmers overplanted by 11,000 acres, Texas by almost 34,000, Arkansas by 9,000, and California by 279 acres. Still, farmers planted some 231,000 fewer acres in 1950 than the year before. Due to increased demand, prices rose from $4.10 in 1949 to $5.09, and the farm value of the rice crop increased by $24 million. The Korean war postponed the day of reckoning for U.S. rice farmers. Unfortunately, records do not reveal the impact of the 1950 program on individual farmers. Census figures indicate that between 1945 and 1954 the number of rice farms in Louisiana decreased from 6,390 to 4,748, while in Arkansas they increased from 2,212 to 3,588. Production in both states rose dramatically, in Louisiana from 5.5 million barrels to 10 million, and in Arkansas from 2.2 million to 3.6 million.[16]

The new machinery that emerged during and after World War II changed the work culture dramatically. Instead of using grain drills, many farmers turned to airplanes for seeding. They applied liquid fertilizer and in some cases also sprayed from airplanes. Combines cut so rapidly that they kept several grain trucks busy delivering rice to driers, and in the fields grain carts that could manuever over the levees took the grain from the combines and augered it into the larger grain trucks. J. M. Spicer retired from farming in 1949, and a few years later, when his son was sick, he and his brother again managed a rice farm. "It was just amazing the change in equipment when we left the farm in '49. In those few years the equipment had changed so that we were almost like raw hands."[17]

Women, like hired hands, seldom appeared in accounts of the rice work culture, but in Mississippi, which began growing rice commercially in the late 1940s, L. E. Grant's daughters helped during harvest. Grant began growing rice in 1950, and by 1954 he and his son Charles planted 700 acres to rice. Olga, his twenty-one-year-old daughter, attended college for a year but left to help out on the farm. She and her younger sister Frances drove rice trucks at harvest. "People in the nearby towns have grown quite accustomed by now to seeing them roar by in their big green truck," *The Rice Journal* reported, "giving an occasional blare from the huge air horns their Dad gave them."[18]

Mrs. Bennie Burkett, a historian of Arkansas County, revealed that in Arkansas German farmers often put their daughters behind the wheels of grain trucks. Other farmers in the Arkansas prairie did not use women in the harvest, but Germans often did. Of course, women cooked for the harvest crews, but the coming of the combine meant that labor needs diminished, as did the volume of cooking. Ernest Frey, farming near Eunice, Louisiana, surmises that many farmers will utilize women to drive trucks as the rice culture adjusts to surplus supplies, low prices, and expensive labor.[19]

Not only did the work routine change, but rice also continued to expand into new areas. Because cotton allotments were falling in 1954, cotton farmers in Arkansas and Mississippi were turning to rice production. A. W. Lenius of Stuttgart complained to Secretary of Agriculture Ezra Taft Benson that rice production should be curtailed in 1954. The USDA reply admitted that "it is expected that a substantial acreage of rice will be planted on diverted cotton land in Arkansas as well as in the other rice-producing states." Yet the department saw no need to call for a referendum on rice quotas.[20]

Increasingly farmers encountered government regulations that prevented them from making commonsense adjustments. Dr. W. T. Champion, a resident of Stuttgart, Arkansas, owned farms in two counties, Lonoke and Lee. In 1955, due to floods in Lonoke County, he could not plant his rice in time; instead he planted fifty-six of his seventy-four-acre allotment in Lee County. After he had "worked night and day" to get the crop planted, he discovered that "there were no provisions in the county or state regulations that would allow such a transfer." He appealed to the Grain Section of the USDA for aid. Arkansas had a farm allotment system, and the USDA responded that it could not help Champion. "Only in States where rice acreage allotments are established on a producer basis can a farmer plant his allotted rice acreage on a farm of his own choosing," Marvin McLain replied. Texas and California had producer allotments at that time, but the Arkansan Champion suffered due to an inconsistent allotment policy.[21]

Although allotments did not reappear until 1955, by 1953 increasing supplies and lower prices caused farmers to turn to the loan program. The CCC took 3 million bags that year. Two years later the CCC owned nearly 25 million bags. Facing oversupply and dwindling markets, 90 percent of eligible rice farmers in January 1955 approved quotas for that growing season. The USDA cut allotments by 24.7 percent—a decision that set off another wave of complaints from rice farmers, especially the tenants and small farmers who were most vulnerable. According to George Blair, the general manager of the American Rice Growers' Association, who testified before the House Agriculture Committee in 1955, many Louisiana growers voted for the program at the insistence of bankers who advertised in newspapers urging farmers to support the program. When asked if the government had aggravated the oversupply problem that led to allotments, R. C. Laan, the president of a New Orleans rice milling company, stated in a Senate hearing, "The present law did, and the Korean demand, and the Army purchases, and everything that went with it." [22]

Allotment cuts drove many farmers off the land. B. D. White from Craighead County, Arkansas, related that in 1954 there were 326 growers in his county, but only 234 remained after allotments were cut. "A big percentage of those farmers quit and folded up, and moved their families north in order to obtain work in the factories," he revealed. White gave his personal example of the expense of production in the mid-1950s. "I have two wells on the farm which cost around $5,000 each to put down. I am down to an 80-acre allotment on my farm of 350 acres in cultivation. I have around $20,000 invested in rolling equipment for the production of rice, which includes one heavy rice field tractor which costs $3,500; a combine which costs $6,500; a grain buggy which costs $1,000; and a cultivator tractor which costs $3,300—a tractor, cultivator and planter combined." Neither he nor his neighbors could pay off implement loans with income from such small allotments. [23]

In November 1955, Louis Richard wrote from Welsh, Louisiana, to Senator Russell B. Long claiming that his landlord, Theodore Cormier, "has taken my rice acreage history away from me and I am unable to find land with acres." In 1931 *The Rice Journal* had featured Cormier as a young and promising farmer who traded in mules, bought land, and energetically made his way. By 1955 the opportunities that had been open to Cormer a quarter-century earlier were not available to his tenant Louis Richard, and Richard resented it. "Although I am a tenant," he wrote, "I believe I have as much right to plant rice as anyone else." He had worked on the same farm for twelve years and obviously thought he had a right to continue. "The present law was made by only a few men," he wrote. "Why is it that we cannot vote on such an important matter?" He hoped that Senator Long would intercede.[24]

By the fall of 1955 numerous Louisiana tenants realized that the shift from producer to farm allotments threatened to alter the farm structure. Wilson Mott wrote to Senator Russell Long from Welsh, charging that the Farm Bureau representative, "who is unfriendly towards our way of thinking," failed to arrange for farmers to make a statement at an Alexandria hearing. Mott complained that federal policies favored landowners: "Most landowners plant their own land and possibly rent a small piece of land from a landlord on a tenant basis." Such landowners lost their allotment on rented acreage but kept the allotment used on their own land. "The landowners who plant their own land cannot be affected either way this situation is handled however they want justice for the tenant many have relatives who are tenants in many cases one or more sons," he explained. Obviously landowners who faced acreage cuts chose to consolidate allotments on one farm, and tenants, many of whom owned production machinery, were left with no land to farm.[25]

The change in assigning allotments ignored the traditions of the Louisiana rice prairie that had led to producer allotments in 1933. Finest J. Pitre wrote from Kinder to Congressman Allen J. Ellender outlining the problem. Pitre served on the Allen Parish ASC allotment board and argued that tenants should have protection. "We have tenant farmers who have farmed all their life and who were ejected from the land they farmed last year, leaving them to gaze into a dark future because of no acreage assurance to lean towards," he wrote. The USDA informed Pitre that the 1955 and 1956 provisions allowed the ASC county committee "to reduce, prior to planting, the original allotment determined for any farm if it finds that tenant rice farmers are being forced to vacate because the owner decides to operate the farm." The ASC committees should also aid tenants who lost their allotments and award them new producer acreage, the reply added.[26]

Yet rules did not always operate judiciously in the rice prairies, any more than they did in the cotton or tobacco areas. Nor were all ASC committeemen as concerned about tenants as Pitre was. In November 1955 Herman Talley complained to Congressman Ellender that he had been evicted. "I am a tenant farmer I have been planting around 240 acres and now I have none," he wrote. Ellender's reply offered no help, and in January 1956 Talley wrote again, protesting that "there is no law to protect the tenant at all." He asked if there was something Ellender could do. The congressman replied that the ASC committee had power to penalize landowners "who were found to be treating their tenant farmers unfairly." In February Talley received a reply from a state administrative officer named C. E. Slack, informing him that his landlord "was entitled to farm the rice allotment for the farm owned by him." Slack informed Ellender that the Jefferson Davis Parish ASC committee had investigated the case and, "based on the facts in the situation, determined that Mr. Talley was not evicted by the landlord for the purpose of diverting acreage to the landlord's benefit."

Talley disagreed and refused to give up. In March 1956 he again wrote to Ellender, admitting that "I cannot get this matter complete." All he wanted, he wrote, "is what is justly mine and I think that I am not getting that because I took that farm over in 1950 and it was being rented then." He farmed it through 1955, and even an ASC committeeman had told him that he could not be evicted. He had his marketing cards to prove his tie to the land. "I have some prominent men here in our community to sign this petition that I was evicted," he disclosed. He again asked for Ellender's aid. As planting season arrived, the USDA again ruled against Talley, explaining to Ellender that the landlord had a better story.[27]

Farmowners also resented allotment cuts. From Stuttgart, Jimmie Hanson wrote to Secretary of Agriculture Ezra Taft Benson complaining of a 40 percent acreage reduction. He owned a Packard dealership and a 640-acre farm that he had planted to rice for forty years, but in 1955 higher machinery costs, drought, insects, rain, and wind had hurt him financially. "I voted my first G.O.P ticket for the President & a lot of other Boys around me Did the Same thing But if things Dont change never again," he warned. He asked Benson to "admit you made a mistake." Landowner Ray Folkland, who lived near Welsh, Louisiana, owned a 360-acre farm and planted 118 acres of it to rice. "I am still in debt having to borrow money for taxes and insurance," he wrote. Folkland wanted to continue farming but did not see how he could manage. "Machinery, fertilizer and labor higher than ever and rice prices at average then you cut us down to nothing on acreage," he complained to Benson.[28]

Henry Unkel, in a letter to Congressman T. A. Thompson, hit another nerve that went to the center of the agricultural education complex and the future of family farms. The new structure of agriculture increasingly froze out prospective young farmers. Unkel had a son who was finishing college in the spring of 1956, a boy who had been president of the Future Farmers of America in high school and who was majoring in agriculture. "How disappointing it was during his Christmas vacation at home when he asked me what he was going to do. It burns one up when he realizes he has brought his children up to love the farm, only to learn there is no future in it for them." Acreage reduction threatened the family tradition. "Many a farm boy looked forward to the day when they could follow in the foot steps of their father, tilling the soil," he lamented. Unkel asked an end to the USDA paradox that encouraged agricultural education but reduced the amount of acreage available for farming.[29]

Six years later August Cihal of Ganado, Texas, voiced the frustration of a father who wanted to see his children in rice farming. "Now, I have got these children, and I have got to keep them living," he told a congressional committee. "I have got to give my history to my children to keep them living. If I didn't, they would be out on the streets somewhere." He added that there were many such young men who didn't know anything but rice farming, but they could not get a start with "those 3 to 6 acre allotments" that new producers received. "This may be a pretty good program," he conceded, "but what about the kids?"[30]

Dennie D. Tilbury wrote from Bonita, Louisiana, urging Secretary Benson to give young men a chance to begin farming. He had been growing rice since 1907 in three Arkansas counties and two Louisiana parishes. Several men in the area, including his son Albert, made applications for new allotments but received "oooo zero." Albert Tilbury had 400 acres of good rice land, and the ruling that he could not farm rice would be "comical" except that he would have to "seek public work in order to sustain his family." The government reply offered no hope for an allotment for his son.[31] In other words, to employ an Irish bull, the only way a farmer could get an allotment was to already have one.

Some farmers thought through their problems and suggested practical solutions. Hubert C. Wirtz wrote from Houston, Texas, in December 1955, suggesting to Allen Ellender that small farmers bore the brunt of acreage contraction. He, like other farmers, resented "individuals farming large allotments that derive but a small portion of their income from the rice produced on this allotment." He had suggested earlier that allotments be placed on a progressive scale. "There could be a base acreage below which no individual could be reduced; then a sliding scale upward through the large acreages to form the final allotments," he explained. Such a plan would protect small farmers and also cut the oversupply of rice.[32]

By 1956 allotment reductions were strangling many small farmers and tenants, and these families resented large landlords who controlled much of the rice land in the prairie. A Texan named Gene R. Andrew, like Henry Wirtz, called for progressive allotments based on a scale similar to the income tax. The idea resembled W. J. Lowe's 1935 plan to cut large growers and build up small ones. "In the past few years," Andrew wrote in January 1956, "there has been an ever increasing number of individuals who entered the rice farming business from various other occupations where they were millionaires or near-millionaires, who had never farmed before, who obviously do not make a living from farming and do not intend to but for the sole purpose of income tax evasion." Such wealthy men "are depriving the bonafide farmers of their acreages and income, their very living." Andrew realized that no law could drive such wealthy men from agriculture; still, he thought something should be done. "It would be no more unconstitutional to enforce such a limitation as it is to actually deprive another group of their profession, their livelihood, and their freedom of choice of it." The Department of Agriculture replied that "the law does not provide for taking into consideration a producer's financial status in determining rice acreage allotments for producers who produced rice during the base period."[33]

The idea of a progressive acreage reduction continued to spread. In January 1956, Isaac Guillory wrote to Senator Long: "I wonder why the acreage basis couldn't be fixed like the income tax system, give a farmer a certain amount of acres and then anything above that start cutting by percentage." First of all, Marvin L. McLain replied, such a program "would create many administrative problems which would be difficult to handle." In addition, the law did not provide for such a system. He also explained that "it would be neither practical nor desirable" to have minimum allotments. McLain wrote that minimum-allotment experiments with other commodities showed "that it is impossible to allocate a minimum acreage to every grower sufficient to give each grower an efficient operations unit." Yet the tobacco program had guaranteed growers at least a three-acre allotment, and that program had saved many small tobacco farmers.[34]

The dynamics of acreage reduction, high prices for fuel and implements, and the Soil Bank program threatened the future of small farmers. A case from Texas revealed the problem facing a mother and her veteran sons. Grace Sykes wrote to Secretary Benson and explained that, after her two sons entered the service during the Korean War, her husband died, yet she did not ask for her sons' release from military service. After the war her oldest son returned home first, received a 25-acre allotment which would not support his family, and left farming for a position as an airline copilot. Lowell, the younger son, returned home in February 1953, immediately secured rice machinery, and planted 63 acres of rice; a tenant farmed the other land. In 1954 Lowell took over the entire farm and planted 297 acres, yet when allotments were awarded in 1955 he received only 82 acres and his mother 65. She unsuccessfully requested additional acreage from the county ASC office and became disillusioned. "Do I have to continue seeing America as I do at present," she queried. "A government which took my son into service and after giving him an honorable discharge will not let him farm his widowed mother's land?" She did not want to put the land in the Soil Bank, she explained, for that program was fine for large farmers "but a little farmer like Lowell and myself would not receive the aid needed to have a decent living and pay any toward a big machinery debt." Lowell added a separate letter to Secretary Benson: "I feel that as United States Secretary of Agriculture you would not intend for this allotment program to completely wipe out a farmer who is fully set up with farm equipment and whose sole source of income is from the farm." The reply from the Grain Branch assured the Sykeses that their appeal would be heard if it had merit.[35]

To focus entirely upon farmers would distort the problem of acreage reduction, for it had a domino effect. Farmers had fixed costs in rice production, and it took as much financing to grow 30 acres as to grow 100. As Marcus Mauritz, president of the Rice Promotional Association, explained to a congressional committee, water companies contracted in advance for power (either electricity or gas) to run pumping stations, and water companies had minimum cost scales whether a farmer irrigated 100 or 500 acres. When acreage fell in 1955, implement dealers in Texas saw their sales fall 30 percent. Less rice meant fewer jobs for people who customarily worked in the culture. Since millers had expanded drier capacity, with less volume they could not pay off their loans. Bankers calculated fixed costs and wondered if less acreage would threaten loan repayments. Texas landowners worried that allotment cuts would cripple tenants, for they could not secure enough land. Producers who had signed long-term contracts faced paying rent for land that they could not farm to capacity. In short, reduced allotments threatened the entire farm structure and supporting institutions.[36]

The Soil Bank further eroded the position of tenants. This program paid a landowner for taking land out of production, and rice farmers put 242,000 acres into it in 1957. Ewell Moore wrote from Datto, Arkansas, complaining to the ASC office that he had received a 0.6 acre allotment. The landowner from whom Moore had previously rented planted part of his allotment and put the remainder in the Soil Bank. "So you can see that the soil bank has put me out of business unless I can get a larger allotment on the ground I now have rented," he explained. Moore only asked for enough allotment "to finish paying out my equipment."[37]

In April 1958, as farmers throughout the prairie grappled with smaller allotments and bureaucratic tangles, the Louisiana ASC State Committee recommended that ten rice-growing parishes in the river district form a separate administrative area and revert to producer allotments. It justified the request by noting that most rice in this area was grown "on one-producer units, the operators of which follow a process of rotating from one tract to another without regard to parish lines." Clarence Slack, who wrote the memorandum to Washington, personified the myopia that increasingly afflicted USDA officials. "The use of the producer allotment provision in western Louisiana is not applicable because on most farms there are at least three interested producers and it would be almost impossible administratively to establish allotments on a producer basis," Slack explained. Until eight years before, of course, all of Louisiana had producer allotments. Moreover, since Texas and California had producer allotments that worked well, Slack's logic was as faulty as his understanding of past allotment programs. Congress passed the enabling legislation, and with producer allotments in the river districts the Louisiana rice culture became as divided in allotment policy as it had always been in cultural methods.[38]

The different allotment systems in rice-producing states confused the Northwestern Mutual Life Insurance Company. Glenn W. Buzzard, who managed farm loans, asked the USDA to explain why in Arkansas allotments went with the land but in California they went with producers. "Our main concern, however, is the ability to hold intact the rice acreage on any tract which might be acquired by the Company by foreclosure or voluntary conveyance," he wrote. Raymond J. Pollock replied for the government that indeed the two states had different allotment systems, and he sent along an explanation.

Texas and California farmers used producer allotments, and Louisiana, Arkansas, and Mississippi had farm allotments.[39]

The allotment cuts in the 1950s had severe implications for the rice culture in southwestern Louisiana. In Acadia Parish, for example, the number of rice farms decreased from 1,007 in 1954 to 771 by 1959, and the number of tenants fell from 1,524 to 931. In neighboring Calcasieu Parish, the number of farms fell from 261 to 211, and tenants decreased from 255 to 132 over the same years. The complaints that arrived in Washington revealed the changing tenure pattern in the Louisiana prairie as farmowners consolidated their allotments and expelled tenants. So rice tenant families joined the exodus from the land, in a movement that continued in the cotton area and that increasingly threatened tobacco growers. The farm programs in rice and tobacco that emerged in the 1950s set in motion another enclosure movement similar to the one that had started in cotton in 1935, this one also fed both by mechanization and by government programs. Even highly mechanized Louisiana, Arkansas, and Mississippi tenant farmers had little security once rice allotments went to landowners. The government gave all rice producers allotments in the 1930s, and in the 1950s the government, through the PMA and later ASC state committees, took allotments from tenants. The contraction in acreage worked itself out during the 1960s as rice production decreased.[40]

In a congressional hearing in 1961, J. M. Spicer, who had written extensively on the rice culture and who had farmed since 1914, summarized why farmers were leaving the rice culture in Arkansas. "I think that is just natural," he said, "partly due to increased mechanization, and partly due to the fact a great many I know of have quit farming, not because they were crowded out, but because they felt like the operations were not commensurate with the returns from it." Other farmers testified that they wanted larger allotments, but most farmers could not reconcile the contradictions between supply and demand. They only knew that smaller allotments threatened their livelihoods— but so would lower prices.[41]

From 1955 through 1973 the USDA issued annual allotments and quotas on rice production. In most years the allotments remained stable, but in 1962 and 1966 allotments were increased by 10 percent and 20 percent respectively. Rice farmers, like tobacco growers, evaded acreage restrictions by intensifying cultivation, and each year from 1950 to 1970 they increased acreage yield by 3 percent. Between 1948 and 1973 the government support price largely determined the domes-

Dennis Fortune leads Marvin Scroggins on combines, as Gary Lawson maneuvers a grain cart to take rice from the moving combine. Stuttgart, Arkansas. August 31, 1982. Pete Daniel.

tic price for rice, and it swung between the $4.08 support price in 1948 and $4.86 per hundred pounds in 1970. Only in 1954 did the average price to farmers drop below the support price. Still, the CCC took in larger percentages of the crop—as high as 48 percent in 1954, and a low of 11 percent in 1964. If farmers stayed within their allotted acreages, they received a guaranteed support price for their crops. The CCC meanwhile accumulated large supplies of rice, and in 1954 Congress passed the Agricultural Trade and Development Assistance Act (or PL 480), a program that authorized the export of surplus commodities to friendly countries for foreign currency rather than for dollars, as a grant, or on concessional terms. Due to pressure from growers, the Agricultural Act of 1956 set a minimum national allotment of 1.61 million acres. Since farmers grew more rice per acre and thus reduced costs, they agreed to lower parity rates, which fell progressively from 91 percent in 1954 to 65 percent in 1974.[42]

The proliferation of programs set up more contradictions. Acadia Parish produced 1.9 million barrels of rice on 119,120 acres in 1954 and 4.4 million barrels on 111,430 acreas twenty years later. Even as the government reduced allotments to keep down production, it promoted research to produce higher yields per acre. It disposed of surplus rice through the PL 480 program, preached a free market economy, promoted research for costly implements, and advocated a modest family farm operation. The USDA bureaucracy grew larger and set up new programs that ultimately multiplied the contradictions and complexity.[43]

In the early 1970s worldwide grain shortages led to increased rice production, and in 1974 the USDA removed acreage quotas. Production quickly increased by 25 percent as growers in traditional rice areas and new producers, such as those in the Mississippi Delta, planted more rice. Mississippi producers, many of whom did not have allotments, gambled that demand would remain high, and they invested in expensive machinery and irrigation systems that would be jeopardized if quotas were resumed. The USDA hoped that market forces would rule rice production, but as demand dropped, rice farmers again faced large surpluses. Between 1972 and 1978 harvested acreage increased from 1.8 million to 3 million acres, and the returns to farmers rose from $575 million in 1972 to $1.2 billion a year later. In 1978, with the price down to $7.72 from the record $13.80 per hundredweight of four years earlier, the value of production still remained over $1 billion. Arkansas, meanwhile, expanded its acreage from 837,000 acres in 1976 to over 1 million in 1978, while Mississippi increased production from 144,000 to 215,000 acres over the same years. Louisiana and Texas also expanded, but not as dramatically. Despite increased demand, farmers still put rice under CCC loans. Though in 1974 the rate dropped to 8.3 percent of the crop, by 1978 it rose to 21.7 percent. As with other expansions of the rice culture, farmers invested in additional land and implements, and when demand and prices dropped, they were overextended. At present, rice farmers, like other farmers throughout the country, are worried about survival.[44]

Boom and bust in the rice culture had become a cycle. During World Wars I and II and in the mid-1970s production expanded, only to glut the market and threaten bankruptcy as prices fell. Increased demand set off expansion, investment, mortgages, and optimism; then recession brought curtailment, desperation, and bankruptcy. Modern rice farmers operate almost like poker players. Some have good hands and gamble for high stakes, while others call until their chips disappear. But they are all addicted to the farming game. Like desperate poker players who know they can win a big pot, farmers scrape up another ante, hoping for good cards. Yet the federal government, international trade, inflation, and the weather constantly shuffle the deck. The fraternity of husbandmen has dwindled as the ante increases each year, and an uneasiness pervades the hinterland as farmers wait for the next cards to fall.

14

*Tedium is the worst pain. The
dull victim, staring, vague-eyed,
at seasons that never were
meant to be observed.*
—John Gardner, Grendel

"Tedium Is
the Worst Pain"

Until a century and a half ago, the pace of change in agricultural so-
cieties moved with agonizing slowness as farmers gradually improved
implements and methods of cultivation. Rural people looked to the sky
for rain, for sunshine, and for signs from the moon and stars. They explored the soil to find what pleased and stimulated it to produce abundant crops. They moved, insofar as they were able, in cycle with
heaven and earth and in harmony with nature. Farmers in the southern United States were part of the slowly evolving world pattern, and,
under slavery and later post–Civil War sharecropping, implements and
cultivation practices changed little into the twentieth century. Within
forty years after the turn of the century, however, southern rural society
and work habits passed through a process that transformed tenure,
credit, implements, and community organization. Traditional rural life
yielded to the seemingly irresistible forces of mechanization and government policy that created a different rural structure.

The disparate work routines that had characterized cotton, tobacco,
and rice cultures became increasingly alike, for mechanization erased
distinctiveness. The federal government not only continues to encourage mechanization and increased production, but also ignores any
contradictions that its conflicting programs generate. Implement companies confront a dwindling market, in part because there are fewer
farmers, but also because farmers buy used machinery from their
bankrupt neighbors. A Payment in Kind program pays farmers to produce but a fraction of their capacity, while other government programs
continue to explore the limits of production and mechanization. In
some respects, mechanized agriculture is following heavy industry. It

took large farmers a generation longer than businessmen to ask the government to rationalize production and stabilize prices, but, despite a half-century of government programs, there is the constant threat that farmers will follow heavy industry into oblivion. The U.S. Department of Agriculture has discovered no solution to farm failures and a declining farm population. The process of dispossession began with the eviction of sharecroppers, and it continues with the failure of millionaire farmers. The government's promised land of agriculture has produced contradictions that grow even as the farm population dwindles. The singleminded pursuit of higher production has warped agriculture and alienated it from tradition.

The sources of the present agricultural structure date to the nineteenth-century notion that American farms should utilize labor-saving implements and that science should rule every sphere of rural life. Agriculture schools, the USDA, and state and local agriculture programs all stressed modernization and science. This program was but the cutting edge of a larger plan to force all farmers into commercial agriculture. Liberty Hyde Bailey in *The Country-Life-Movement*, published in 1918, set forth his dream: "There will be established out in the open country plant doctors, plant-breeders, soil experts, health experts, pruning and spraying experts, forest experts, recreation experts, market experts, and many others," he accurately prophesied. "There will be housekeeping experts or supervisors."[1]

Bailey had an expert for every rural factor—except the southern tenure system. His grand scheme hardly mentioned the South, nor did he acknowledge the presence of blacks in the garden of experts, or ask how to improve the caliber of southern rural life by lifting sharecroppers of both races out of the annual cycle of advances, unjust settlements, and yearly moves. Because they ignored the reality of southern tenancy, such expert answers regarding rural life had little relevance to the masses of southern farmers. Indeed, most rural experts had a difficult time comprehending that sharecroppers or lower-class farmers of any tenure had a place in their plans. In essence, the USDA rarely addressed the central problems that affected southern farming, instead seeking to change the structure of farming to fit its preconceptions. It never paused to consider whether its model fit the South. Ideas on reforming the southern tenure system did emerge in the mid-1930s, a generation too late; by then the transformation had already moved too far. By sweeping off lower-tenure farmers, the way was cleared for increasing mechanization and the realm of experts.

Robert Anderson operating a mechanical cotton picker on the farm of A. B. Crawford. Grand Junction, Tennessee. October 14, 1983. Pete Daniel.

An ambivalence has endured over the final figures in the ledger book of change, over the gains and losses involved in abandoning small-unit farming and driving off the refugees to cities. Those who left were offered no choice, and to many it must have appeared irrational to struggle to remain sharecroppers. In a larger sense, in the

Johnny Finch harvesting tobacco mechanically. Floods Chapel, North Carolina. July 18, 1983. Pete Daniel.

1930s and 1940s an enclosure movement spread across the Cotton South, as landlords evicted tenants or cut off the traditional shelter, food, and right to hunt and fish. A similar revolution swept through the tobacco and rice cultures after the mid-1950s. The federal government filled the vacuum left by planters, mediating between landlord and tenant and offering relief programs. Even as rural workers who fled the land were largely the victims of government programs, they switched their allegiance from their rural landlords and benefactors to President Franklin D. Roosevelt and his heirs. The customs and work that they had followed for generations was left behind, and the often demeaning welfare programs and menial jobs offered in an urban environment provided little aid in building a new culture. Perhaps the simmering resentment of centuries of oppression or neglect contributed to the urban riots of the 1960s.

Unlike English rural workers who broke threshing machines under the banner of Captain Swing in the early nineteenth century, southern sharecroppers left the land peacefully. New Deal spokesmen promised hope for the dispossesed and downtrodden through agencies of the federal government. Even illiterate farmers heard Roosevelt, his cabi-

Combine in the Scroggins brothers' rice field. Stuttgart, Arkansas.
August 31, 1982. Pete Daniel.

net members, and agency officials express concern and explain programs on the radio. Indeed, the media helped mold a consensus about
government activity and its benefits, just as it pacified listeners with
soap operas and other programs. Even those who were evicted from
their farms by AAA programs, removed from family holdings by TVA,
ineligible for CWA, FERA, or WPA work, or denied subsistence housing, loans, or relief trusted that the New Deal would ultimately re-
spond to their individual needs. No longer looking to a local landlord
for furnish or to the community for emergency support, tenants and
other victims of the Depression looked to Washington, to the bureaucracy, to Roosevelt. The more desperate the circumstances, the more
likely a farmer was to believe that the New Deal cared for him. But in
reality the most unfortunate farmers had less chance to qualify for
such programs as FSA or subsistence homes. As the 1930s ground on
and Congress enacted its programs and the bureaucracy carried them
out and President Roosevelt explained how all were benefiting, many
Southerners seemed transfixed, expectant, waiting. Surely, they
thought, the promise of justice and prosperity would prevail. The con-

stant doses of hope numbed the spirit of protest; many sharecroppers continued to think that the New Deal would save them. On another level, landlords restructured their operations and used AAA payments to invest in labor-saving machinery. They were implementing the dream of progress so long advocated by agricultural planners, and now they face the same fate as did sharecroppers.

Was this the most beneficial farm structure for the South? The basic question lingers unanswered. Time has not been kind to goverment programs. Current problems question whether machines and chemicals are a substitute for husbandry, for understanding the land, for a way of life. Instead of visionary programs, USDA policy is trapped in the original nineteenth-century premise of modernization. The complexity of modern agriculture with its intricate financing, gigantic implements, prescription fertilizer and chemicals, numerous federal programs, and frequent bankruptcies calls into question the notion of progress. Are farmers today any more secure than were their ancestors at the turn of the century? Like so many Americans, farmers search for something that was lost as rural life became transformed.

Nostalgia is easily stirred in the United States, for there is something mystical about the past with its frontier, its challenges, and orderly family life. The imperative to recapture a bit of the past drew millions of people to the shores of Manhattan Island on Independence Day 1976 to witness the passing of the tall ships, a turnout that no number of steamships could generate. It was more than just that sailboats combined aesthetics and motion; it was that sails relied on wind, on nature, and were vulnerable and beautiful. Herman Melville in *Moby-Dick* explored vulnerability as he explained how men were lowered in fragile boats and confronted their prey with harpoons. He deified the leviathan and its spirit, carefully studied it, and plumbed both the strengths and weaknesses of the hunter and the hunted. Something was lost when whales became targets for cannons on steamships. During the same years of transition, craftsmen lost the pride and coherence that had united the process of production as they came to serve machines that required monotonous and repetitive tasks. Some farsighted workers broke their machines and called for a respite in the mechanical restructuring of their work routine, but the Luddites have generally been viewed as at least irrational, if not mad.

It is far too easy to see technological change as inevitable, as part of some cosmic predestination. Luddites, however, stopped the clock and posed their question dramatically.[2] Following the logic that changes had to move in a certain direction, the options offered by Populists, by reformers, or even by such a plan as producer allotments, or the idea that allotments should be reduced on a progressive scale, were doomed. Occasional southern voices harkened back to some mystical yeoman paradise, but even those voices were muffled by government policy.

Despite the numbing aspects of the old tenure system, it existed in the context of a community life and culture that rural people built to protect and sustain themselves. The South contained one of the richest folk cultures in the nation—or, rather, contained some of the richest folk cultures, for the South was as diverse culturally as it was in other ways. Whether one looks to the pages of fiction, where William Faulkner, Flannery O'Connor, and Eudora Welty come to mind, or to autobiography, where William Alexander Percy, Ned Cobb, and Harry Crews provide compelling evidence, or to interviews and historical documents, the South was alive with tradition and creativity. Storytelling reached almost perfection. Gospel singing, mountain music, Cajun culture in Louisiana, country music, Delta blues, and much more flavored the South with distinctiveness.

In addition to ample jest and fun, the culture possessed a theme of suffering and defeat, as C. Vann Woodward and William Faulkner have so poignantly explained, and a warning against pride and other sins, a plaintive cry for movements that never came to fruition, against diseases and feuds that struck people down in their prime, economic cycles that extracted whatever money one hoped to put aside for dreams, and illiteracy that robbed generation after generation of a chance to break free from the cycle. Ironically, without such suffering and distress, southern culture would have resembled more the mainstream—which is to say that the suffering created a strength, an endurance, and an almost indifference to the grotesque that has continually amazed and often disturbed people from other sections of the country. Building on the strengths of the old culture and reforming its abuses, there were options that could have kept people farming and preserved the culture and community that gave a deeper meaning to life in the rural South. Larger farms, mammoth implements, killer chemicals, and government intrusion were not inevitable.

Even as the USDA and machines restructured southern rural life, a hundred miles from the department's headquarters in Washington some Amish farmers continued to cultivate their land in much the same way as had their ancestors who settled in Pennsylvania centuries ago. Fueled by the Anabaptist heritage that made them pariahs in Europe, determined to live a simple life, using few modern implements, and repudiating federal aid, they prosper even as mechanized farmers surrounding them go bankrupt. When younger farmers experimented with tractors, the Amish elders watched and made their judgment: "They don't make manure."[3] The strict Amish repudiated tractors and remain an island of stasis in a world of flux, a reminder that, despite the USDA promised land of modern farming, there were options, possibilities. In a larger sense, the Amish are a repudiation of the notion of progress. They have resisted the pressure of modernization and government planning; they stand as a reminder of the potential inherent in looking to the heavens and the earth for harmony with nature.

Although Booker T. Whatley is neither Luddite nor Amishman, he has recently undermined the USDA idea that only large agricultural units can succeed. Reared on a farm near Anniston and holding a doctorate in horticulture, he worked in several southern states before returning to his native Alabama to teach at Tuskegee Institute. In 1974 he began working on the problems of small farmers and developed a plan that matured into a way for a farmer with twenty-five acres to gross $100,000 a year. While the USDA and state experiment stations studied how to produce traditional cash crops, Whatley demonstrated that farmers within forty miles of a metropolitan area could grow a sequence of crops for urban customers. Sweet potatoes, fish, rabbits, game birds, berries, fruit, grapes, and vegetables allow a farmer to have a constant market. Whatley never forgot his farm background, nor did he turn his ear from small farmers who had motivation and ability. "The land grant system hasn't addressed the problems of the small farmer," he complained. "They weren't even doing research that related to small farmers."[4] Many farmers turn to Whatley's newsletter for sound advice, knowing that the USDA has few such offerings.

Whatley avoided the preconception that land concentration and large-scale agriculture were inevitable. He paused to reconsider the forces that had not only driven millions of farmers from the land but also endangered those who remained. Whatley and the Amish offer alternatives to the USDA model of large-scale agriculture. The transformations of cotton, tobacco, and rice cultures over the past century offer three lenses for focusing upon other options. The modernization of the rural South ended an oppressive sharecropping system, on the one hand, but on the other hand it offered few alternatives for evicted farmers. Mechanization has reduced farm drudgery, but it has also driven farmers into debt and bankruptcy. Chemicals have been trained to kill weeds, but they have not been disciplined to leave other forms of life intact. Productivity has risen so dramatically that quotas are necessary for control. With the premise that science, mechanization, and large-scale farming provide the only model for U.S. agriculture, the USDA will continually attempt to restructure rural life into its updated fantasy of giant machines, robots, experts, computers, and chemicals that leaves no place for farmers who move in relation to natural cycles. The vigorous work cultures that thrived at the turn of the century have withered. Farm work, like factory work, has become specialized, mechanized, and sapped of the human relations that blessed and cursed the rural South. Could farming, like much factory work, become just another boring occupation? "Tedium is the worst pain," the monster Grendel warned. "The dull victim, staring, vague-eyed, at seasons that never were meant to be observed."[5]

Notes

Chapter 1

1. On the reaction of blacks and whites to freedom, see James L. Roark, *Masters without Slaves: Southern Planters in the Civil War and Reconstruction* (New York, 1977), 68–108; U.S. Congress, Senate, "Report of Carl Schurz on the States of South Carolina, Georgia, Alabama, Mississippi, and Louisiana," Senate Exec. Doc. 2, 39 Cong., 1 Sess., 1866; Whitelaw Reid, *A Tour of the Southern States, 1865–1866* (New York, 1965); Albion W. Tourgee, *A Fool's Errand: A Novel of the South during Reconstruction* (New York, 1961); Sidney Andrews, *The South since the War: As Shown by Fourteen Weeks of Travel and Observation in Georgia and the Carolinas* (Boston, 1866); Thomas W. Knox, *Camp-fire and Cotton Fields: Southern Adventure in Time of War* (New York, 1865); Eric Foner, "Reconstruction and the Crisis of Free Labor," in *Politics and Ideology in the Age of the Civil War* (New York, 1980), 97–127. Steven Hahn has studied the transformation of yeomen farmers to sharecroppers in *The Roots of Southern Populism: Yeoman Farmers and the Transformation of the Georgia Upcountry, 1850–1890* (New York, 1983).

2. See Stephen J. DeCanio, *Agriculture in the Postbellum South: The Economics of Production and Supply* (Cambridge, 1974); Robert Higgs, *Competition and Coercion: Blacks in the American Economy, 1865–1914* (New York, 1977); Robert L. Ransom and Richard Sutch, *One Kind of Freedom: The Economic Consequences of Emancipation* (Cambridge, 1977); Jonathan M. Wiener, *Social Origins of the New South: Alabama, 1860–1885* (Baton Rouge, 1978); Harold Woodman, "Sequel to Slavery: The New History Views the Postbellum South," *Journal of Southern History* 43 (Nov. 1977), 523–44; C. Vann Woodward, *Origins of the New South* (Baton Rouge, 1951).

3. Woodward, *Origins of the New South*, 350–68; Lawrence Goodwyn, *Democratic Promise: The Populist Moment in America* (New York, 1976); Louis R. Harlan, *Booker T. Washington: The Making of a Black Leader, 1856–1901* (New York, 1972), 204–28.

4. Pete Daniel, "The Metamorphosis of Slavery, 1865–1900," *Journal of American History* 66 (June 1979), 92–95.

5. William Cohen, "Negro Involuntary Servitude in the South, 1865–1940: A Preliminary Analysis," *Journal of Southern History* 42 (Feb. 1976), 33–35; Woodman, "Sequel to Slavery"; Harold Woodman, "Post–Civil War Southern Agriculture and the Law," *Agricultural History* 53 (Jan. 1979), 319–37; Pete Daniel, *The Shadow of Slavery: Peonage in the South, 1901–1969* (Urbana, 1972), 3–81.

6. Douglas Helms, "Just Lookin' for a Home: The Cotton Boll Weevil and the South" (Ph.D. diss., Florida State University, 1977).

7. Marvanna S. Smith, comp., *Chronological Landmarks in American Agriculture*, USDA, ESCS, Agricultural Information Bulletin no. 425 (Washington, 1979), 33; James H. Street, *The New Revolution in the Cotton Economy: Mechanization and Its Consequences* (Chapel Hill, 1957), 117–18.

8. Pete Daniel, *Deep'n as It Come: The 1927 Mississippi River Flood* (New York, 1977); Nan E. Woodruff, "The Failure of Relief during the Arkansas Drought of 1930–1931," *Arkansas Historical Quarterly* 39 (Winter 1980), 301–13.

9. Helms, "Just Lookin' for a Home," 27, 34.

10. Ibid., 49–55; Joseph Cannon Bailey, *Seaman A. Knapp: Schoolmaster of American Agriculture* (New York, 1971), 1–132; Roy V. Scott, *The Reluctant Farmer: The Rise of Agricultural Extension to 1914* (Urbana, 1970), 206–27.

11. Helms, "Just Lookin' for a Home," 166–68. Helms gave the example of the Andrew Querles plantation near Shreveport, Louisiana. Querles usually harvested 500 bales of cotton from his 1,100-acre operation. After the boll weevil hit in 1907, he harvested 63 bales, and the next year only 25 bales. See also Bradford Knapp to L. E. Perrin, St. Landry, La., Apr. 27, 1911; M. B. Mercier to Knapp, Apr. 28, 1911; Knapp to B. H. Hibbard, May 16, 1911, Records of the Federal Extension Service, Record Group 33, National Archives (hereafter cited as Extension Service, RG 33, NA).

12. Helms, "Just Lookin' for a Home," 193, 223–26, 231–57, 274, 277–80. Production increased from 376,042 to 452,064 bales (see Appendix A, 404).

13. Booker T. Washington and Seaman A. Knapp, "A Memorandum of Agreement between Tuskegee Institute and the General Education Board," Tuskegee, Ala., Nov. 9, 1906, in Louis R. Harlan and Raymond W. Smock, eds., *The Booker T. Washington Papers*, vol. 9 (Urbana, 1980), 121–22. For an excellent account of Tuskegee's role in this endeavor, see Louis R. Harlan, *Booker T. Washington: The Wizard of Tuskegee, 1901–1915* (New York, 1983), 206–16.

14. Allen W. Jones, "The South's First Black Farm Agents," *Agricultural History* 50 (Oct. 1976), 636–44; Earl W. Crosby, "Limited Success against Long Odds: The Black County Agent," *Agricultural History* 57 (July 1983), 277–88; Scott, *Reluctant Farmer*, 232–36, 288–313.

15. W. W. Long to H. E. Savely, Jan. 13, 1915; Savely to Long, Jan. 19, 1915, Extension Service, RG 33, NA. See also J. Luke Burdette, Washington, Ga., to J. Phil Campbell, Athens, Ga., May 29, 1916; George B. Eunice, Douglas, Ga., to Campbell, May 29, 1916; Thomas M. Campbell to J. F. Dugger, Oct. 2, 1915; Bradford Knapp to Long, Nov. 23, 1915, ibid.

16. Eugene A. Williams to Thomas M. Campbell, June 4, 1916, ibid.

17. E. R. Lloyd to Bradford Knapp, Mar. 30, 1917; H. E. Savely to Knapp, June 15, 1917, ibid. See also Lloyd to Knapp, Apr. 22, 1918; W. C. Lewis, Eudora, Ark., to David F. Houston, Feb. 19, 1918; Knapp to C. A. Keffer, Feb. 25, 1918, ibid.

18. "Negro Extension Work," USDA circular 355 (Washington, 1923), 5, 7, 24.

19. Seaman A. Knapp to James Wilson, Mar. 4, 1911, Extension Service, RG 33, NA.

20. W. A. L. to S. T. Newton, Apr. 16, 1918; R. S. Wilson to Bradford Knapp, Jan. 8, 1914, ibid. See also George M. Goolsby, Wauchula, Fla., to H. J. Drane, July 8, 1917; C. K. McQuarrie to Goolsby, July 5, 1917; David F. Houston to Drane, July 28, 1917, ibid.

21. G. T. McElderry to Bradford Knapp, Mar. 3, 1914, ibid.

22. L. M. Calhoon to Bradford Knapp, Feb. 13, 1914, ibid.

23. Theodore Rosengarten, *All God's Dangers: The Life of Nate Shaw* (New York, 1974), 144, 221–26.

24. Helms, "Just Lookin' for a Home," 392–93.

25. George B. Tindall, *The Emergence of the New South, 1913–1945* (Baton Rouge, 1967), 15; Christiana McFadyen Campbell, *The Farm Bureau: A Study of the Making of National Farm Policy, 1933–40* (Urbana, 1962), 5.

26. Bruce Kennedy to C. J. Haden, July 9, 1915, Extension Service, RG 33, NA.

27. Bradford Knapp to A. M. Smith, July 16, 1915; Knapp to J. A. Evans, Oct. 31, 1915, ibid. See also Charles Keffer, Knoxville, Tenn., to Knapp, Oct. 12, 1915; Keffer to Charles J. Hasse, Oct. 13, 1915; Knapp to J. A. Evans, Oct. 26, 1915, ibid.

28. Bradford Knapp to Andrew M. Soule, Athens, Ga., Dec. 11, 1915, ibid. For other Extension Service problems connected with private enterprise, see Knapp to W. W. Long, Apr. 21, 1916; J. T. Watt to Knapp, Oct. 9, 1916, ibid.

29. Bradford Knapp to Andrew W. Soule, Feb. 13, 1916; Mary Feminear, Auburn, Ala., to Mary E. Creswell, May 15, 1918; O. B. Martin to Feminear, May 20, 1918, ibid. For an overview of the role of business in extension work, see Scott, *Reluctant Farmer*, 190–205.

30. Gilbert C. Fite, "Voluntary Attempts to Reduce Cotton Acreage in the South, 1914–1933," *Journal of Southern History* 14 (Nov. 1948), 484–85.

31. Ibid., 487–89.

32. Ibid., 492, 495–97.

33. T. Harry Williams, *Huey Long* (New York, 1969), 531–32.

34. Robert E. Snyder, "The Cotton Holiday Movement in Mississippi, 1931," *Journal of Mississippi History* 40 (Feb. 1978), 14–16.

35. Ibid., 18, 21–29; Williams, *Huey Long*, 533.

36. Fite, "Voluntary Attempts to Reduce Cotton Acreage," 499.

37. Henry I. Richards, *Cotton and the AAA* (Washington, 1936), 25–26.

Chapter 2

1. Harold B. Rowe, *Tobacco under the AAA* (Washington, 1935), 27–47; Paul G. E. Clemens, *The Atlantic Economy and Colonial Maryland's Eastern Shore: From Tobacco to Grain* (Ithaca, 1980), 41–79; Susan Gibbs and Becky Harrison, "The Old vs. the New in the Culture of Tobacco," in *Smoke to Gold: The Story of Tobacco in Martin County* (Greenville, N.C., 1978), 24. This book evolved from an eighth-grade project directed by Elizabeth Roberson. The his-

torical research is sound, and the interviews and illustrations show imagination and are revealing of the bright-tobacco culture.

2. Nannie May Tilley, *The Bright-Tobacco Industry, 1860–1929* (Chapel Hill, 1948), 6, 24–25; Bob Peele, "An Accident in Caswell County Really Changed Things!," in *Smoke to Gold*, 24–25; Joseph C. Robert, *The Story of Tobacco in America* (Chapel Hill, 1949), 183; Leonard Rapport, "History of Tobacco in North Carolina," manuscript in possession of Rapport. Rapport worked for the Works Progress Administration Federal Writers' Project and directed the interviews on the tobacco culture. He conducted the interviews of the warehouse culture and has written several unpublished pieces on the history of tobacco in North Carolina.

3. See the account of the old culture in Mary Brumfield Garnett, *Bright Leaf: An Account of a Virginia Farm* (privately printed; loaned by William Dunn); Tilley, *Bright-Tobacco Industry*, 72–73, 78; "'Parson' Barnes, Negro Warehouse Laborer," 88, "Dixon Kavanaugh, Speculator," 107, "D. W. Daniels, Veteran Tobacco Man," 116, all WPA interviews by Leonard Rapport, in his possession (hereafter cited as Rapport WPA interviews).

4. Tilley, *Bright-Tobacco Industry*, 80; Mariann Moore, "The First Growers of Tobacco in Martin County," 12–13, and Gibbs and Harrison, "The Old vs. the New," 22, in *Smoke to Gold*.

5. Tilley, *Bright-Tobacco Industry*, 37–43.

6. Interview with Luther Harris, in *Smoke to Gold*, 54.

7. See Robert Byron Lamb, *The Mule in Southern Agriculture* (Berkeley and Los Angeles, 1963); Harry Crews, *A Childhood: The Biography of a Place* (New York, 1978), 51–53.

8. Interview with Henry and Sadie Williams, Georgia, in Pamela Barefoot and Burt Kornegay, *Mules & Memories: A Photo Documentary of the Tobacco Farmer* (Winston-Salem, 1978), 64; Bob Peele, "The Cussed Mule," in *Smoke to Gold*, 62.

9. "'Parson' Barnes," 79, in Rapport WPA interviews; Moore, "First Growers of Tobacco," in *Smoke to Gold*, 11–13; Tilley, *Bright-Tobacco Industry*, 157–84. For an overview of fertilizer use in the tobacco area of the country, see A. L. Mehring, "Consumption and Composition of Tobacco Fertilizers," *Agronomy Journal* 41 (June 1940), 240–46.

10. Moore, "First Growers of Tobacco," in *Smoke to Gold*, 12–13.

11. Tilley, *Bright-Tobacco Industry*, 50–51; "Tobacco Share-cropper," 2, in Rapport WPA interviews.

12. Tilley, *Bright-Tobacco Industry*, 176; "'Mister Danny' Kelly, Operator," 67, in Rapport WPA interviews.

13. Interview with W. O. Peele, Sr., 56–57, Gibbs and Harrison, "The Old vs. the New," 23, both in *Smoke to Gold*; Tilley, *Bright-Tobacco Industry*, 68, 70; "D. W. Daniels, Veteran Tobaccoman," 116, and "Sam Hobgood, Factory Manager," 5, in Rapport WPA interviews; interview with Simon Collie, Seven Paths, N.C., Feb. 20, 1982. See also Anthony Badger, *Prosperity Road: The New Deal, Tobacco, and North Carolina* (Chapel Hill, 1980), 8. The account of the tobacco culture is derived from numerous sources and from personal observation.

14. Leonard Rapport, "Tobacco Comes to Town," 25, 34, manuscript in possession of Rapport; Tilley, *Bright-Tobacco Industry*, 85–87.

15. Tilley, *Bright-Tobacco Industry*, 199; Charles E. Gage, "Historical Factors Affecting American Tobacco Types and Uses and the Evolution of the Auction Market," *Agricultural History* 2 (Jan. 1937), 51–57.

16. Tilley, *Bright-Tobacco Industry*, 106, 143, 152–53, 346, 373; Charles Kellogg Mann, *Tobacco: The Ants and the Elephants* (Salt Lake City, 1975), 30. Mann argued that the allotment system begun in 1933 stopped the shift southeastward of the bright tobacco culture.

17. Tilley, *Bright-Tobacco Industry*, 95. See also Dolores Janiewski, "Women and the Making of a Rural Proletariat in the Bright Tobacco Belt, 1880–1930," *Insurgent Sociologist* 10 (Summer 1980), 16–17.

18. Tilley, *Bright-Tobacco Industry*, 102–3.

19. "'Parson' Barnes," 80–81, "'Mister Danny' Kelly, Operator," 70, "Sam Hobgood, Factory Manager," 4, and "Tobacco Share-cropper," 1, all in Rapport WPA interviews; Thomas J. Woofter, *The Plight of Cigarette Tobacco* (Chapel Hill, 1931), 13.

20. Tilley, *Bright-Tobacco Industry*, 397–405.

21. Ibid., 409–17. See also Dwight B. Billings, Jr., *Planters and the Making of a "New South": Class, Politics, and Development in North Carolina, 1865–1900* (Chapel Hill, 1979), 120; Helen G. Edmonds, *The Negro and Fusion Politics in North Carolina, 1894–1901* (Chapel Hill, 1951).

22. Tilley, *Bright-Tobacco Industry*, 387–90, 393, 451.

23. Ibid., 451–59. At the National Agricultural Conference held in Washington, D.C., Jan. 23–27, 1922, delegates recommended production statistics, research on soil and disease, grading, and warehouse reform ("National Agricultural Conference," Statistics and History File, H. C. Taylor Papers, Records of the Bureau of Agricultural Economics, Record Group 83, National Archives). For an account of Poe's career, see Joseph A. Cote, "Clarence Hamilton Poe: The Farmer's Voice, 1899–1964," *Agricultural History* 53 (Jan. 1979), 30–41.

24. Tilley, *Bright-Tobacco Industry*, 460–63; Badger, *Prosperity Road*, 23–26.

25. Tilley, *Bright-Tobacco Industry*, 464–85. For an insider's view of the cooperative's failure, see Clarence Poe to Robert W. Bingham, Apr. 26, 1927; Poe to G. A. Norwood, Mar. 12, 1926, Clarence Poe Papers, Coooperative Marketing, North Carolina Department of Archives and History, Raleigh.

26. Badger, *Prosperity Road*, 28–37; H. L. Hough to Duncan Fletcher, Aug. 31, 1931; William Collins to Hough, Sept. 24, 1931, Records of the Secretary of Agriculture, Tobacco, Record Group 16, National Archives.

27. Badger, *Prosperity Road*, 23.

28. Raleigh *News and Observer*, Feb. 21, 1930.

29. Roland B. Eustler, "Agricultural Credit and the Negro Farmer, I," *Social Forces* 8 (Mar. 1930), 416–25. "When distributed by sources, 84 per cent of the users of bank credit, 63 per cent of the users of merchant credit, and 70 per cent of the users of individual credit were owners. The tenants, therefore, were primarily dependent upon landlords for their short time cash needs, although

a few loans were secured through the other agencies. Of the total number of tenants using short time cash loans, 65 per cent received their credit from landlords, 16 per cent from banks, 11 per cent from merchants, and 8 per cent from individuals" (425).

30. Eustler, "Agricultural Credit and the Negro Farmer, II," *Social Forces* 8 (June 1930), 565–73.

31. Clipping in J. Y. Floyd to F. W. Hancock, Jr., Sept. 28, 1933; Biscoe Davis to Henry A. Wallace, Sept. 20, 1933, Records of the Agricultural Stabilization and Conservation Service, Agricultural Adjustment Administration, Tobacco, Record Group 145, National Archives. Woofter, *Plight of Cigarette Tobacco*, (20–21), cited a S.C. Department of Agriculture study done in 1923 that set the cost of production at $100.37 per acre.

Chapter 3

1. James M. Clifton, "Twilight Comes to the Rice Kingdom: Postbellum Rice Culture on the South Atlantic Coast," *Georgia Historical Quarterly* 62 (Summer 1978), 146–54; Thomas F. Armstrong, "From Task Labor to Free Labor: The Transition along Georgia's Rice Coast, 1820–1880," *Georgia Historical Quarterly* 64 (Winter 1980), 432–47; Eric Foner, *Nothing but Freedom: Emancipation and Its Legacy* (Baton Rouge, 1983); Edward Hake Phillips, "The Gulf Coast Rice Industry," *Agricultural History* 25 (Apr. 1951), 91–92; Seaman A. Knapp, "The Present Status of Rice Culture in the United States," USDA bulletin no. 22 (Washington, 1899), 12–21; Arthur H. Cole, "The American Rice-Growing Industry: A Study of Comparative Advantage," *Quarterly Journal of Economics* 41 (Aug. 1927), 595–604.

2. Henry C. Dethloff, "Rice Revolution in the Southwest, 1880–1910," *Arkansas Historical Quarterly* 29 (Spring 1970), 66–68.

3. "Jennings, La.," in *Louisiana Rice Book* (Omaha, 1901), 202; Sylvester L. Cary Scrapbook, Department of Archives and Manuscripts, Louisiana State University, Baton Rouge (hereafter cited as Sylvester L. Cary Scrapbook, LSU); "Father Cary, Rice Missionary," *The Rice Journal* 12 (July 1909), 137–38. *The Rice Journal and Gulf Coast Farmer* changed its title to *The Rice Journal and Southern Farmer* in the May 1905 issue and later changed to simply *The Rice Journal*. The latter title will be cited throughout.

4. Joseph Cannon Bailey, *Seaman A. Knapp: Schoolmaster of American Agriculture* (New York, 1971), 109–11.

5. Ibid., 113–16.

6. Ibid., 114–20; Phillips, "Gulf Coast Rice Industry," 93.

7. Sylvester L. Cary, "The Present Outlook of Agriculture in Southwest Louisiana," 15, and "Jennings, La.," 102, in *Louisiana Rice Book*; Bailey, *Seaman A. Knapp*, 120–23; *The Rice Journal* 33 (Nov. 1930), 10.

8. Phillips, "Gulf Coast Rice Industry," 94; Bailey, *Seaman A. Knapp*, 117–23.

9. Sylvester L. Cary, "Wonderful Developments in Recent Years," 13, and

"The Present Outlook of Agriculture in Southwest Louisiana," 15–21, "Rice," 22, J. F. Wellington, "A Model Plantation," 31, all in *Louisiana Rice Book*; Sylvester L. Cary, "Immigration," Sylvester L. Cary Scrapbook, LSU.

10. Knapp, "Present Status of Rice Culture," 23; Dethloff, "Rice Revolution," 70–71; Phillips, "Gulf Coast Rice Industry," 95; Mildred Kelly Ginn, ed., "A History of Rice Production in Louisiana to 1896," *Louisiana Historical Quarterly* 23 (Apr. 1940), 3–47; Crowley *Signal*, May 1898, Crowley *Daily Signal*, Oct. 4, 1937, clippings in Paul B. Freeland Papers, Southwestern Archives, University of Southwestern Louisiana, Lafayette; Miron Abbott, "Irrigation from Streams," 32–33; Frank Randolph, "Rice Fact and Fancy," 17–18; "Canals Distributing Water," 42–51, all three in *The Rice Journal* 6 (Jan. 1903).

11. Seaman A. Knapp, "Rice Culture in the South," 41–42, in *Louisiana Rice Book*; Ginn, ed., "History of Rice Production," 29.

12. Wellington, "Model Plantation," 30–31.

13. "Jennings, La.," 101, "Rice," 21, Cary, "Wonderful Developments in Recent Years," 10, all three in *Louisiana Rice Book*; Dethloff, "Rice Revolution," 70–72; Lawson P. Babineaux, "A History of the Rice Industry of Southwestern Louisiana" (M.A. thesis, University of Southwestern Louisiana, 1967), 28.

14. Bailey, *Seaman A. Knapp*, 123–27; Phillips, "Gulf Coast Rice Industry," 95.

15. Sister Francis Assisi Scanlon, "The Rice Industry in Texas" (M.A. thesis, University of Texas, 1954), 35–38; Dethloff, "Rice Revolution," 71; Thomas U. Taylor, *Rice Irrigation in Texas*, Bulletin of the University of Texas, no. 16, 1902, 10–12; Work Projects Administration, *Texas: A Guide to the Lone Star State* (reprint ed., New York, 1974), 195–96, 411.

16. Taylor, *Rice Irrigation in Texas*, 12, 16; Le Grand Powers and R. P. Teele, "Irrigation for Rice Growing: Louisiana, Texas, and Arkansas," *Thirteenth Census of the United States*, bulletin (Washington, 1910), 5; Scanlon, "Rice Industry in Texas," 51–52. See also "Rice-Growing Is a Recent Development in American Agriculture," St. Louis *Republic*, May 1899, reprinted in *Louisiana Rice Book*, 33, 37–38. The Texas rice counties were Austin, Brazoria, Calhoun, Chambers, Colorado, Fort Bend, Galveston, Hardin, Harris, Jackson, Lavaca, Liberty, Matagorda, Orange, Polk, Victoria, Waller, and Wharton.

17. "History of Rice Development in Arkansas," supplement in Carlisle *Independent*, June 24, 1920, 7–9; "Early Rice Farming on the Grand Prairie," affidavit of W. H. Fuller and H. H. Puryear, Dec. 13, 1909, in *Arkansas Historical Quarterly* 14 (Spring 1955), 72–74; George Sibley, "Rice in Arkansas," *The Rice Journal* 7 (Aug. 1904), 13; Florence L. Rosencrantz, "The Rice Industry in Arkansas," *Arkansas Historical Quarterly* 5 (Summer 1946), 123–24; Ernest E. Sampson, "Half Century on Grand Prairie," *Arkansas Historical Quarterly* 14 (Spring 1955), 32–37.

18. Walter L. Brown, ed., "Notes on Early Rice Culture in Arkansas," *Arkansas Historical Quarterly* 29 (Winter 1970), 76–79; Sibley, "Rice in Arkansas," 13.

19. *The Rice Journal* 10 (Jan. 1907), 35; "The New Rice Eldorado," ibid. 13 (Apr. 1910), 5.

20. A. A. Kaiser, "Rice Growing in Arkansas," ibid. 12 (Aug. 1909), 162; G. W. Fagan, "The Truth about Arkansas," 1–4, and A. A. Kaiser, "What Goeth on in Arkansas?" 4–5, both ibid. 13 (Aug. 1910).

21. Fagan, "Truth about Arkansas," 1–4; Rosencrantz, "Rice Industry in Arkansas," 123–25. See also "Lonoke, Ark.," 26, and "Arkansas Co.," 27, both in *The Rice Journal* 13 (Feb. 1910).

22. *The Rice Journal* 13 (Dec. 1910), 23. For an overview of the early development of the prairie rice culture, see John Norman Efferson, *The Production and Marketing of Rice* (New Orleans, 1952), 408–16.

23. Dethloff, "Rice Revolution," 70; Bailey, *Seaman A. Knapp*, 126; Ginn, ed., "History of Rice Production," 32. For a description of rice milling, see Knapp, "Present Status of Rice Culture," 34–35; Cole, "American Rice-Growing Industry," 626–27.

24. "That Rice Crop Estimate," *The Rice Journal* 6 (Oct. 1903), 11; "James Ellis, Welsh," ibid. 11 (Apr. 1908), 72.

25. "Studying Rice Conditions," ibid. (Oct. 1908), 13.

26. Powers and Teele, "Irrigation for Rice Growing," 1, 4, 6; James Ellis, "The Water Rent Question," *The Rice Journal* 12 (Dec. 1909), 257; "The Rent Question," ibid. 14 (Feb. 1911), 19.

27. "Texas Rice Farmers' Association," *The Rice Journal* 11 (Feb. 1908), 24; ibid. (Dec. 1908), 262–63.

28. "Louisiana Rice Growers' Association," ibid. 12 (Feb. 1909), 26–27, quoting the Crowley *Signal.*

29. "President Winn on Market Letters," ibid. (Apr. 1909), 69.

30. Charles E. Burkhead, John W. Kirkbride, and William B. Hudson, comps., "Rice, Popcorn, and Buckwheat: Acreage, Yield, Production, Price, and Value by States, 1906–1953," Statistical Bulletin no. 238, USDA, Agricultural Marketing Service (Washington, 1958), 6–8.

31. "The Farmer Movement," *The Rice Journal* 12 (Apr. 1909), 66; "Mr. Orme's Opinion," ibid. 13 (Jan. 1910), 4; "Southern Rice Growers' Association," ibid. (Nov. 1910), 3–10.

32. S. Locke Breaux, "New Orleans, La.," ibid. 14 (Mar. 1911), 14; ibid. 13 (Mar. 1910), 34.

33. J. A. Kinney, "Arkansas Rice Association," *Farm and Ranch*, reprinted in *The Rice Journal* 14 (July 1911), 10. See John S. Collier, "Report of Investigation Concerning Rice" (Stuttgart, 1910), 41.

34. Babineaux, "History of the Rice Industry," 46–63; "Beaumont Headquarters Southern Rice Growers," 35, and A. R. Krieshbaum, "History of the Rice Millers Association," 32, both in *The Rice Journal* 20 (May 1917); "Our First Fifty Years," address by William M. Reid, Rice Millers' Association Convention, Hot Springs, Ark., 1949, Box 1, Rice Millers' Papers, Southwestern Archives and Manuscripts Collection, University of Southwestern Louisiana, Lafayette (hereafter cited as RMA Papers, USL); Carlisle *Independent*, June 24, 1920, 23.

35. "Louisiana State Rice Mills," *The Rice Journal* 14 (Oct. 1911), 23. See also "Modern Abbeville," ibid. 11 (May 1908), 83.

36. Krieshbaum, "History of the Rice Millers Association," 32–33; Cordelia W.

Wise, "A History of the Rice Millers' Association," Box 1, RMA Papers, USL; *The Rice Journal* 11 (Nov. 1908), 222–23.

37. Burkhead, Kirkbride, and Hudson, "Rice, Popcorn, and Buckwheat," 2, 6–9; Babineaux, "History of the Rice Industry," 68–69; "Government Regulations for Handling 1918 Rice Crop," *The Rice Journal* 21 (Aug. 1918), 31.

38. Edward Hake Phillips, "The Historical Significance of the Tariff on Rice," *Agricultural History* 26 (July 1952), 89–92; Cole, "American Rice-Growing Industry," 619–23; Babineaux, "History of the Rice Industry," 71.

39. "The Rice Situation," *The Rice Journal* 30 (Mar. 1927), 11–13; Burkhead, Kirkbride, and Hudson, "Rice, Popcorn, and Buckwheat," 2.

40. Babineaux, "History of the Rice Industry," 72–75; "American Rice Export Corporation," *The Rice Journal* 30 (Feb. 1927), 14; F. B. Wise to Members of Rice Millers' Association, Oct. 30, 1925, RMA Papers, USL; Burkhead, Kirkbride, and Hudson, "Rice, Popcorn, and Buckwheat," 2, 7–8.

41. "Rice Farmers Now Largest Millers in Arkansas," *The Rice Journal* 29 (Mar. 1926), 16; "Arkansas Rice Growers' Co-Operative Association: Its History in Brief, and Its Method of Operation," ibid. 33 (June 1930), 16–17; J. David Morrisy, *Riceland Foods: Innovative Cooperation in the International Market*, Farmer Cooperative Service, USDA, FCS, Information, 101 (Washington, 1975), 17–26.

42. "Development of Rice Cultivation in Missouri," *The Rice Journal* 29 (Nov. 1926), 11–12; "The Northern Missouri Rice Crop," ibid. 30 (Feb. 1927), 13–14; "North Missouri Rice," ibid. (Apr. 1927), 20–23.

43. S. Locke Breaux, "The Rice Crop along the Mississippi River," ibid. 6 (Jan. 1903), 25; W. D. Smith, "Handling the River Rice Crop," ibid. 30 (July 1927), 12–14.

44. S. H. McCroy, "Investigations in the Grand Prairie Rice Region, Arkansas," Farm Credit Administration, BAE (Washington, 1934), 26.

45. Ibid., 30, 33, 35, 37.

46. Ibid., 37, 39.

47. Ibid., 51–61.

48. "Rice Farmers Have Weathered the Storm," *The Rice Journal* 34 (May 1931), 20; Efferson, *Production and Marketing of Rice*, 427.

Chapter 4

1. Virginius Dabney, *Below the Potomac: A Book about the New South* (New York, 1942), 59.

2. William Faulkner, *The Town* (New York, 1957), 245.

3. Harry Crews, *A Childhood: The Biography of a Place* (New York, 1978), 133. For an account of how poor relief worked in the late nineteenth century, see Crandall A. Shifflett, *Patronage and Poverty in the Tobacco South: Louisa County, Virginia, 1860–1900* (Knoxville, 1982), 70–80.

4. Crews, *Childhood*, 119.

5. Theodore Rosengarten, *All God's Dangers: The Life of Nate Shaw* (New York, 1974), 39–41, 84–91.

6. Crews, *Childhood*, 40.

7. Pete Daniel, *Deep'n as It Come: The 1927 Mississippi River Flood* (New York, 1977), 10.

8. Ibid., 94–109.

9. Ibid., 84–123. The Red Cross did not help in all natural disasters. In 1929 overflows covered Desha County, Arkansas, and no outside relief was available. Dr. J. C. Miller, a field agent of the U.S. Public Health Service, complained in May 1929 that the county was in as serious a condition as it had been during the 1927 flood. "In 1927," he observed, "they had so much outside help, money and supplies were sent here from every part of the United States. . . . Now they are not receiving any outside help at all, and are worse demoralized over the situation than ever before" (Miller to C. W. Garrison, May 21, 1929, State Boards of Health, Arkansas, Box 7, Records of the Public Health Service, Record Group 90, National Archives).

10. Nan Woodruff, *As Rare as Rain* (Urbana, forthcoming), 33 (page numbers refer to typescript). For Hoover's ideas on the drought relief, see David E. Hamilton, "Herbert Hoover and the Great Drought of 1930," *Journal of American History*, 68 (Mar. 1982), 854–58.

11. Woodruff, *As Rare as Rain*, 43–44, 52. Hamilton, in "Hoover and the Great Drought," does not deal with local pressures on Red Cross relief policy. One reason why the Red Cross wanted to proceed quietly was because of its reluctance to upset the traditional landlord-tenant situation.

12. Woodruff, *As Rare as Rain*, 35–36, 41.

13. Seymour Jones to Arthur M. Hyde, Aug. 9, 1930, Drought file, Records of the Secretary of Agriculture, Record Group 16, National Archives.

14. Woodruff, *As Rare as Rain*, 42–43, 126.

15. Ibid., 68–70, 76–77. While Hoover continued to press the Red Cross to furnish aid, John Barton Payne, head of the organization, testified before a congressional committee on January 6, 1931. "The Red Cross cannot provide a complete insurance against all the hazards of agriculture and industry," Payne argued. When asked if the Red Cross could distribute federal money, he observed that its charter prohibited it from taking money directly from the government (112–13). For victims' reactions to relief, see ibid., 50, 169, 173; and for Red Cross rationale on waiting to start relief, 67, and Hamilton, "Hoover and the Great Drought," 859–62.

16. Woodruff, *As Rare as Rain*, 117, 134, 139, 148, 222–25; Hamilton, "Hoover and the Great Drought," 868.

17. George B. Tindall, *The Emergence of the New South, 1913–1945* (Baton Rouge, 1967), 473–76.

18. Philip G. Beck and M. C. Foster, *Six Rural Problem Areas: Relief— Resources—Rehabilitation: An Analysis of the Human and Material Resources in Six Rural Areas with High Relief Rates*, Research Monograph 1 (Washington, 1935), Federal Relief Administration (reprint ed., New York, 1971), 1-3. For an excellent account of the role of the FERA, see John A. Salmond, *A Southern Rebel: The Life and Times of Aubrey Willis Williams, 1890– 1965* (Chapel Hill, 1983), 43–104.

19. Nannie May Tilley, *The Bright-Tobacco Industry, 1860–1929* (Chapel Hill, 1948), 143–52; U.S. Dept. of Commerce, Bureau of the Census, *U.S. Census of Agriculture*, 1934, Franklin County, N.C.

20. FERA, Division of Research and Statistics, Harold Hoffsommer, Survey of Rural Problem Areas, Cotton Growing Region of the Old South: Franklin County, N.C., "Service Agencies and Industries: Present and Recently Discontinued, of Population Centers in Franklin County, N.C., 1934," x-xiv, Bureau of Agricultural Economics, Record Group 83, National Archives (hereafter cited by author, title, and county, BAE, RG 83, NA). The pagination in the reports varies; generally each report begins with upper-case Roman numerals, shifts to Arabic numerals, and ends with lower-case Roman numerals. Other variations will be explained.

21. U.S. *Census of Agriculture*, 1934, Franklin County, N.C.; Hoffsommer, Survey, Franklin County, N.C., I, 18, BAE, RG 83, NA.

22. "Color and Tenure of Farm Operators in Franklin County, N.C., 1900–1930," Hoffsommer, Survey, Franklin County, N.C., xx, BAE, RG 83, NA.

23. "Persons Ten Years of Age and Over in Gainful Occupations by Industry Groups and Race in Franklin County, N.C., 1930," vii, 20–21, ibid.

24. Hoffsommer, Survey, Franklin County, N.C., 61, 63–64, xxvii-xxx, xxxii, ibid. Charles S. Johnson, *Statistical Atlas of Southern Counties: Listing and Analysis of Socio-Economic Indices of 1104 Southern Counties* (Chapel Hill, 1941), 182.

25. Hoffsommer, Survey, Franklin County, N.C., 61–62, BAE, RG 83, NA; Johnson, *Statistical Atlas*, 182.

26. FERA, Division of Research and Statistics, "Rural Problem Areas Survey Report No. 52, The Cotton Growing Areas of the Old South," Franklin County, N.C., Dec. 27, 1934, 4–5, BAE, RG 83, NA (hereafter cited as "Rural Problem Areas Survey Report," number, BAE, RG 83, NA). This series constitutes a synopsis of the manuscript reports.

27. Hoffsommer, Survey, Franklin County, N.C., Table Forms, "Survey of Rural Problem Areas as of June, 1934," appendix, ibid.

28. Hickok to Hopkins, Apr. 2, 1934, in Richard Lowitt and Maurine Beasley, eds., *One Third of a Nation: Lorena Hickok Reports on the Great Depression* (Urbana, 1981), 206.

29. Hoffsommer, Survey, Franklin County, N.C., 55–59, BAE, RG 83, NA.

30. "Rural Problem Areas Survey Report No. 52," Franklin County, N.C., 5, ibid.

31. Hoffsommer, Survey, Franklin County, N.C., 28–35, 58–59, ibid.

32. Pete Bobbitt, case history, unnumbered appendix following xxxii, ibid.

33. FERA, Division of Research and Statistics, "Rural Problem Areas Survey Report No. 29, The Cotton Growing Areas of the Old South," Meriwether County, Ga., Nov. 24, 1934, I, ibid.

34. FERA, Division of Research and Statistics, Harold Hoffsommer, Survey of Rural Problem Areas, Cotton Growing Region of the Old South: Meriwether County, Ga., vii-viii, ibid.; Frank Freidel, *F.D.R. and the South* (Baton Rouge, 1965), 10–14.

35. "Rural Problem Areas Survey Report No. 29," Meriwether County, Ga., 1-2, ibid.

36. Hoffsommer, Survey, Meriwether County, Ga., V-VII, 86–87, ibid.

37. "Rural Problem Areas Survey Report No. 29," Meriwether County, Ga., 5–6, ibid.

38. Hoffsommer, Survey, Meriwether County, Ga., "Color and Tenure of Farm Operators in Meriwether County, Georgia, 1930," 46, ibid.

39. Hoffsommer, Survey, Meriwether County, Ga., 41–50, ibid.

40. Hoffsommer, Survey, Meriwether County, Ga., "Farm Expenditure for Feed, Fertilizer and Labor, Meriwether County, Georgia, 1909–1929," 49; and "Rural Problem Areas Survey Report No. 29," Meriwether County, Ga., 9, ibid.

41. Hoffsommer, Survey, Meriwether County, Ga., "Farms Reporting Certain Machinery and Facilities, Meriwether County, Georgia, 1930," 49, ibid. The report noted that the farm machinery that did exist had fallen into disrepair in recent years (ibid., 50).

42. "Rural Problem Areas Survey Report No. 29," Meriwether County, Ga., 7–8, ibid. On the mortgage rate, see Hoffsommer, Survey, Meriwether County, Ga., 50–51, ibid.

43. Johnson, *Statistical Atlas*, 103; Hoffsommer, Survey, Meriwether County, Ga., 92–93, BAE, RG 83, NA.

44. Hoffsommer, Survey, Meriwether County, Ga., 92–96, ibid.

45. "Rural Problem Areas Survey Report No. 29," Meriwether County, Ga., 8, ibid.

46. Ibid., 9. See also J. Crawford King, Jr., "Closing the Southern Range: An Exploratory Study," *Journal of Southern History* 48 (Feb. 1982), 54, 60; Forrest McDonald and Grady McWhiney, "The South from Self-Sufficiency to Peonage: An Interpretation," *American Historical Review*, 85 (Dec. 1980), 1095–1118; Steven Hahn, "Common Right and Commonwealth: The Stock-Law Struggle and the Roots of Southern Populism," in J. Morgan Kousser and James McPherson, *Region, Race, and Reconstruction: Essays in Honor of C. Vann Woodward* (New York, 1982), 51–58.

47. FERA, Division of Research and Statistics, "Rural Problem Areas Survey Report No. 2, The Cotton Growing Areas of the Old South," Dallas County, Ala., 1, BAE, RG 83, NA.

48. FERA, Division of Research and Statistics, Harold Hoffsommer, Survey of Rural Problem Areas, Cotton Growing Region of the Old South: Dallas County, Ala., 12–17, 26, 29, 32, 49, 52–53 (1); 40 (2), ibid. This report is divided into two parts, both numbered in Arabic numerals. The division is indicated by (1) and (2).

49. Ibid., 52–53 (1); 40 (2).

50. "Rural Problem Areas Survey Report No. 2," Dallas County, Ala., 4; Hoffsommer, Survey, Dallas County, Ala., 26 (2). In 1934 the county also received $203,900 from the AAA contracts, and it expected $58,300 more in parity payments for cotton. Corn and hog contracts brought $4,800, and $25,100 in surplus commodities had been dispensed. The county received $329,147.78 in CWA funds, but, as the report noted, the program was filled with corrup-

tion. The PWA employed 936 people, and the CCC took 155 whites and 69 blacks. Hoffsommer, Survey, Dallas County, Ala., 49–53 (2), ibid.

51. FERA, Division of Research and Statistics, "Rural Problem Areas Survey Report No. 17, The Cotton Growing Areas of the Old South," Leflore County, Miss., Nov. 9, 1934, 1, ibid; Daniel, *Deep'n as It Come*, 14–51.

52. FERA, Division of Research and Statistics, Harold Hoffsommer, Survey of Rural Problem Areas, Cotton Growing Region of the Old South: Leflore County, Miss., II, 67–69; "Rural Problem Areas Survey Report No. 17," Leflore County, Miss., 6, BAE, RG 83, NA.

53. Hoffsommer, Survey, Leflore County, Miss., 69, xii, ibid.

54. Ibid., 20, 45, xix-xxi; "Rural Problem Areas Survey Report No. 17," Leflore County, Miss., 6, ibid. John Faulkner, in *Men Working* (New York, 1941), gives a fictional account of a Mississippi family that gave up sharecropping for WPA work.

55. Anonymous to Gov. M. S. Connor, Aug. 23, 1933, in Hoffsommer, Survey, Leflore County, Miss., 47–50, BAE, RG 83, NA. See also Conrad Eric Grabowski, "The New Deal Agricultural Relief Program in Leflore County" (M.A. thesis, Mississippi State University, 1971).

56. Hickok to Hopkins, Apr. 8, 1934, New Orleans, in Lowitt and Beasley, eds., *One Third of a Nation*, 215.

Chapter 5

1. Paul A. Porter, Information Division, AAA, to Marvin McIntyre, July 20, 1933, Records of the Agricultural Stabilization and Conservation Service, Agricultural Adjustment Administration, Cotton, Record Group 145, National Archives (hereafter cited as AAA, RG 145, NA). Henry I. Richards, *Cotton and the AAA* (Washington, 1936), 1-99; Murray R. Benedict and Oscar C. Stine, *The Agricultural Commodity Programs: Two Decades of Experience* (New York, 1956), 3–10; Roy V. Scott and James G. Shoalmire, *The Public Career of Cully A. Cobb: A Study in Agricultural Leadership* (Jackson, Miss., 1973); David Eugene Conrad, *The Forgotten Farmers: The Story of Sharecroppers in the New Deal* (Urbana, 1965), 37–49. For an excellent account of the cotton program, see Paul W. Bruton, "Cotton Acreage Reduction and the Tenant Farmer," *Law and Contemporary Problems* 1 (June 1934), 275–79. For an assessment of conditions in the cotton area, see J. F. March to Henry A. Wallace, June 2, 1933; J. S. Wannamaker to Cully Cobb, June 19, 1933, Cotton, AAA, RG 145, NA.

2. Richards, *Cotton and the AAA*, 120.

3. S. Peirson to Henry A. Wallace, July 8, 1933, Cotton, AAA, RG 145, NA. R. E. Wood, president of Sears, Roebuck and Company, wrote to W. I. Westervelt complaining that farmers were "beginning to hang back" on signups. He enclosed a copy of *Sears News* that contained the line: "Sears-Roebuck Believes Acreage Cut Salvation" (Wood to Westervelt, July 7, 1933, ibid.). The 1934 and 1935 program included the Bankhead legislation that penalized

farmers who did not cooperate with the government program. Cotton farmers in a referendum overwhelmingly approved the plan (Richards, *Cotton and the AAA*, 163–93). For landlord-tenant disputes over cooperation with the AAA, see William Barrington to Henry A. Wallace, July 14, 1933; G. C. McKenzie to Cully Cobb, July 25, 1933, Cotton, AAA, RG 145, NA.

4. See Irvin O. Pitts, Carrollton, Ga., to Franklin D. Roosevelt, July 13, 1933; H. C. Robinson, Bowdon, Ga., to Henry A. Wallace, July 20, 1933, Cotton, AAA, RG 145, NA. For a different view, see Marcel J. Voorhies, Baton Rouge, La., to Cully Cobb, Aug. 29, 1933, ibid.

5. C. H. Mauk to Henry A. Wallace, July 10, 1933; Jno. H. Johnston to Wallace, June 20, 1933; G. W. Pearrow to AAA, Sept. 19, 1933, ibid.

6. Nick Tosches, *Hellfire: The Jerry Lee Lewis Story* (New York, 1982), 21–22.

7. Richards, *Cotton and the AAA*, 138–40; Donald H. Grubbs, *Cry from the Cotton: The Southern Tenant Farmers' Union and the New Deal* (Chapel Hill, 1971), 19. Much of the confusion over government payments occurred because state laws defined tenure status differently. See Bruton, "Cotton Acreage Reduction," 280–86.

8. FERA, Division of Research and Statistics, Harold Hoffsommer, Survey of Rural Problem Areas, Cotton Growing Region of the Old South, Marlboro County, S.C. xxx; "Rural Problem Areas Survey Report No. 13, The Cotton Growing Areas of the Old South," Limestone County, Ala., Oct. 29, 1934, 5, both in Bureau of Agricultural Economics, Record Group 83, National Archives (hereafter cited as BAE, RG 83, NA); Arthur F. Raper and Ira De A. Reid, *Sharecroppers All* (Chapel Hill, 1941), 43.

9. E. D. Hartsell to Henry A. Wallace, July 1933; Cully Cobb to Hartsell, July 24, 1933, Cotton, AAA, RG 145, NA. See also John Land, Osceola, Ark., to Wallace, July 24, 1933; Cobb to Land, July 27, 1933; E. W. Moore, Tyronza, Ark., to J. E. Rankin, July 10, 1933, ibid., and Conrad, *Forgotten Farmers*, 52–53, 64–67. For an account of how the 1934 contract affected each tenure group, see Bruton, "Cotton Acreage Reduction," 286–91. Lorena Hickok reported that "hardly any tenants ever got any of the cotton reduction money. The landlords always could present bills for the entire amount, and the tenants, being illiterate and never knowing exactly what they did owe the landlords, were just out of luck" (Hickok to Harry Hopkins, Apr. 17, 1934, in Richard Lowitt and Maurine Beasley, eds., *One Third of a Nation: Lorena Hickok Reports on the Great Depression* [Urbana, 1981], 212).

10. Dawson Kea to Henry A. Wallace, June 22, 1933; Cully Cobb to Kea, June 27, 1933; C. O. Maddox to Cobb, June 24, 1933, Cotton, AAA, RG 145, NA.

11. Whitaker & Whitaker, attorneys, to Henry A. Wallace, June 27, 1933; Cully Cobb to Whitaker & Whitaker, June 29, 1933, ibid.

12. W. D. Hass to Henry A. Wallace, June 27, 1933, ibid.

13. R. V. Kerr to Eleanor Roosevelt, Aug. 5, 1933, ibid.

14. J. R. Lowery to Henry A. Wallace, July 13, 1933; Cully Cobb to Lowery, July 18, 1933; L. C. Reid, Cheraw, S.C., to Wallace, June 24, 1933; Cobb to Reid, June 28, 1933, ibid.

15. O. L. Warr to Secretary of Agriculture, Aug. 28, 1933; Cully Cobb to Warr, Sept. 22, 1933, ibid.

16. D. S. Wheatley to Henry A. Wallace, Nov. 21, 1933; Paul Appleby to Wheatley, Dec. 6, 1933, ibid. For the complete ruling, see Richards, *Cotton and the AAA*, 140–41.

17. Richards, *Cotton and the AAA*, 140–41. For a discussion of the 1934 contract, see Conrad, *Forgotten Farmers*, 54–57.

18. Fred C. Frey and T. Lynn Smith, "The Influence of the AAA Cotton Program upon the Tenant, Cropper, and Laborer," *Rural Sociology* 1 (Dec. 1936), 489.

19. Conrad, *Forgotten Farmers*, 120–35; J. Phil Campbell, "Summary Reports Received to Date by Adjustment Committee on Investigation of Complaints Relating to Landlord-Tenant Relationships under Cotton Contract," Cotton, AAA, RG 145, NA; Theodore Saloutos, *The American Farmer and the New Deal* (Ames, 1982), 110–11.

20. Campbell, "Summary of Reports," Cotton, AAA, RG 145, NA; H. L. Mitchell, *Mean Things Happening in This Land: The Life and Times of H. L. Mitchell, Cofounder of the Southern Tenant Farmers Union* (Montclair, N.J., 1979), 60–74.

21. Frey and Smith, "Influence of the AAA Cotton Program," 497, 500–501.

22. Chester C. Davis, "Statement of Policy in Connection with Landlord-Tenant Relations under Cotton Adjustment Contract," n.d., Cotton, AAA, RG 145, NA; Richards, *Cotton and the AAA*, 135–62; Calvin B. Hoover, "Human Problems in Acreage Reduction in the South," n.d. [1934], Cotton, AAA, RG 145, NA; Conrad, *Forgotten Farmers*, 68–82. Cully Cobb attempted to explain the difference between a sharecropper and a wagehand and concluded that each case had to be decided "on the basis of the facts found by the local representatives as to the relationship intended by the parties themselves, under the terms of their expressed agreements" (Cobb to J. W. Bateman, Sept. 27, 1935, Cotton, AAA, RG 145, NA).

23. Davis, "Statement of Policy," Cotton, AAA, RG 145, NA.

24. W. J. Green, "Report on a Survey to Determine What Relationship, If Any, Existed between the Cotton Acreage Reduction Program and the Number of Tenants and Former Tenants Enrolled as Emergency Relief Clients in the Period January 1, 1934 to March 15, 1935," Sept. 1, 1935, Cotton, AAA, RG 145, NA.

25. William T. Ham, "Memorandum re: 'Report on a Survey to Determine . . . ,'" n.d., ibid. See also Conrad, *Forgotten Farmers*, 188–97.

26. D. P. Trent to Jerome Frank, Sept. 18, 1934, Cotton, AAA, RG 145, NA.

27. D. P. Trent to C. C. Davis, Dec. 28, 1934, ibid. See also J. Phil Campbell, E. A. Miller, and W. J. Green, "Report of Adjustment Committee on Investigation of Landlord-Tenant Complaints under the Cotton and Tobacco Adjustment Contracts," Sept. 1, 1934; "Statement of the Results of Cotton Program and Its Effect upon Tenant Farmer Situation in the South," May 27, 1935, ibid.; Conrad, *Forgotten Farmers*, 120–35.

28. H. R. Jackson, "Arkansas Plantation Survey, 1935," Table 2, "Distri-

bution of Tenants According to Status and Race, and Annual Amount of Land in Crops, 1930–1935," Cotton, AAA, RG 145, NA.

29. Table 7, "Comparative Types of Gross Income of Landlord in Relation to Tenant, on Nine Items in 1932 Compared to 1934 on Plantation One," ibid.

30. For a complete analysis of the investigations and the purge, see Grubbs, *Cry from the Cotton*, 30–61; Saloutos, *American Farmer and the New Deal*, 110–23; Lawrence J. Nelson, "The Art of the Possible: Another Look at the 'Purge' of the AAA Liberals in 1935," *Agricultural History* 57 (Oct. 1983), 416–35.

31. Marshall Harris in the Bureau of Agricultural Economics collected material on how to reform the southern tenure system. See his "Compensation as a Means of Improving the Farm Tenancy System," Nov. 1936; "Compensation for Improvement, Deterioration, and Disturbance in Landlord-Tenant Relations," July 1935, Land Tenure Section, BAE, RG 83, NA. For the background of the Bureau of Agricultural Economics, see Harry C. McDean, "Professionalism, Policy, and Farm Economists in the Early Bureau of Agricultural Economics," *Agricultural History* 57 (Jan. 1983), 64–82.

32. Interview with Paul Appleby, 1952–53, Columbia University Oral History Project, 97–98, copy in Library of Congress; Calvin Hoover, memorandum to the Secretary of Agriculture, Jan. 8, 1935, Landlord-Tenant file, AAA, RG 145, NA.

33. Mordecai Ezekiel, memorandum to Henry A. Wallace, Feb. 5, 1936, Tenancy, Records of the Secretary of Agriculture, Record Group 16, National Archives (hereafter cited as SOA, RG 16, NA). In May 1936 the Washington *Herald* broke a story that the AAA program had not benefited tenants at all. Quoting from a study done by the BAE, which it reported had been suppressed, it charged, "In 1934 the net incomes received by sharecroppers and ordinary share tenants probably averaged slightly less than they would have without an adjustment program." It also pointed out that landlords profited from the program and displaced tenants (Washington *Herald*, May 17, 18, 19, 1936; clipping in History and Statistics, BAE, RG 83, NA). On the role of the Farm Bureau during the New Deal, see Clifford V. Gregory, "The American Farm Bureau Federation and the AAA," *Annals of the American Academy of Political and Social Science* 79 (1935), 152–57; Theodore Saloutos, "Edward A. O'Neal: The Farm Bureau and the New Deal," *Current History* 28 (1955), 356–61; Christiana McFadyen Campell, *The Farm Bureau: A Study of the Making of National Farm Policy, 1933–40* (Urbana, 1962).

34. Will Alexander to James L. McCamy, assistant to the secretary, Dec. 26, 1939; Henry A. Wallace to Hattie Caraway, Feb. 10, 1940, SOA, RG 16, NA. For a discussion of the FSA role in meeting such problems, see "Statement of Dr. Will Alexander," May 24, 1939, Temporary National Economic Committee Hearings, Statements and Reports, Records of the Temporary National Economic Committee, Record Group 144, National Archives.

35. "Concentration of Control of Agricultural Land," n.d., Land Tenure Section, BAE, RG 83, NA.

36. Solicitor to Paul Appleby, June 6, 1941; Appleby to Lucy Randolph Mason, June 18, 1941, ibid.

Chapter 6

1. U.S. *Statutes at Large*, 48, pt. 1, 32; J. C. Williamson, Jr., and W. D. Toussaint, "Parity and Support Prices for Flue-Cured Tobacco," *Journal of Farm Economics* 48 (1961), 13–15; Anthony Badger, *Prosperity Road: The New Deal, Tobacco, and North Carolina* (Chapel Hill, 1980), 40. For the background of the parity concept and acreage allotments and their implementation in the Agricultural Adjustment Act, see Gilbert Fite, *American Farmers: The New Minority* (Bloomington, Ind., 1981), 42–65; George B. Tindall, *The Emergence of the New South, 1913–1945* (Baton Rouge, 1967), 391–93; and Harold B. Rowe, *Tobacco under the AAA* (Washington, 1935), 12–20, 87–88.

2. Badger, *Prosperity Road*, 39; Pete Daniel, "The Formative Period of Flue-Cured Tobacco Acreage Control in North Carolina" (M.A. thesis, Wake Forest University, 1962), 12–16.

3. Mrs. Gatewood to Franklin D. Roosevelt, May 12, 1933, Records of the Secretary of Agriculture, Record Group 16, National Archives (hereafter cited as SOA, RG 16, NA). See also J. Hurt Whitehead to Gus W. Dyer, July 22, 1933, ibid.

4. *Progressive Farmer*, June 1933, 32.

5. Badger, *Prosperity Road*, 45; *Who Was Who in America*, 4 (Chicago, 1968), 479; Raleigh *News and Observer*, July 29, 1933.

6. Petition from the County Organization of the Men's Clubs of Halifax County, Va., signed by C. L. Hall, July 29, 1933, Records of the Agricultural Stabilization and Conservation Service, Agricultural Adjustment Administration, Tobacco, Record Group 145, National Archives (hereafter cited as AAA, RG 145, NA).

7. Raleigh *News and Observer*, Aug. 4, 6, 1933; petition from M. D. Dickerson et al. to Franklin D. Roosevelt, Aug. 3, 1933, Tobacco, AAA, RG 145, NA.

8. Raleigh *News and Observer*, Aug. 6, 1933; petition from Coffee County, Ga., Aug. 7, 1933, signed by J. W. Quincey and J. H. Williams, Tobacco, AAA, RG 145, NA.

9. Raleigh *News and Observer*, Aug. 10, 1933; T. E. Person to Chester Davis, Aug. 10, 1933, Tobacco, AAA, RG 145, NA. See also petition from Franklin County, N.C., Aug. 10, and petition from Granville County, N.C., Aug. 12, ibid.

10. Jonathan Daniels to Henry A. Wallace, Aug. 10, 25, 1933, Tobacco, AAA, RG 145, NA; Raleigh *News and Observer*, Aug. 22, 1933.

11. L. T. Townsend to J. Con Lanier, Aug. 26, 1933, Tobacco, AAA, RG 145, NA; Raleigh *News and Observer*, Aug. 30, 1933.

12. J. Y. Joyner to John C. B. Ehringhaus, Aug. 31, 1933, in John Christoph Blucher Ehringhaus Papers, State Department of Archives and History, Raleigh, N.C. (hereafter cited as Ehringhaus Papers); David Leroy Corbitt, ed., *Addresses, Letters and Papers of John Christoph Blucher Ehringhaus, Governor of North Carolina, 1933–1937* (Raleigh, 1950), 70–72.

13. Raleigh *News and Observer*, Sept. 3, 7, 1933; Winston-Salem *Journal*, Sept. 14, 1933.

14. Winston-Salem *Journal*, Sept. 16, 17, 23, 1933. For a biographical

sketch of Williams, see Winston-Salem *Journal and Sentinel*, Apr. 24, 1938.

15. H. Kemper Cooke to Henry A. Wallace, clipping from Horry *Herald*, Sept. 14, 1933, Tobacco, AAA, RG 145, NA. See also Biscoe Davis to Wallace, Sept. 20, 1933, ibid.

16. Raleigh *News and Observer*, Sept. 26, 1933.

17. Winston-Salem *Journal*, Oct. 12, 1933. See also Van L. Perkins, *Crisis in Agriculture: The Agricultural Adjustment Administration and the New Deal, 1933* (Berkeley and Los Angeles, 1969), 147–62.

18. Badger, *Prosperity Road*, 65, 73. See also Murray R. Benedict and Oscar C. Stine, *The Agricultural Commodity Programs: Two Decades of Experience* (New York, 1956), 95.

19. Maynard P. West to Thomas G. Burch, Sept. 13, 1933, Tobacco, AAA, RG 145, NA. West's spelling is faithfully reproduced, as are other misspellings throughout. For details of acreage reduction, see J. B. Hutson to C. G. Merchant, Dec. 6, 1933, ibid.; Rowe, *Tobacco under the AAA*, 294–97; Badger, *Prosperity Road*, 112.

20. J. B. Hutson to Maynard P. West, Sept. 26, 1933, Tobacco, AAA, RG 145, NA.

21. Thomas R. Buckman to U.S. Department of Agriculture, Sept. 15, 1933; J. B. Hutson to Buckman, Sept. 19, 1933; Hutson to Farmer H. Jones, Sept. 18, 1933, Tobacco, AAA, RG 145, NA. See also L. B. Mitchell, Rocky Mount, N.C., to USDA, Jan. 26, 1934, and Henry A. Wallace to W. L. Winters, Jonesville, N.C., Apr. 7, 1934, ibid.; Alonzo F. Harrison, Robersonville, N.C., to Ehringhaus, May 3, 1934; E. L. Currin to John C. B. Ehringhaus, Mar. 1, 1934, Box 12, Ehringhaus Papers.

22. R. S. Hazelwood to Secretary of Agriculture, Sept. 28, 1933, Tobacco, AAA, RG 145, NA. See also Walter D. Thompson, Whiteville, N.C., to C. L. Cobb, Jan. 24, 1934; Marvin Gaskin to Henry A. Wallace, Dec. 19, 1933; Wallace to Gaskin, Dec. 27, 1933, ibid.

23. Selma A. Katzenstein to Henry A. Wallace, Feb. 5, 1934, ibid. See also L. E. Newsome to Wallace, Dec. 6, 1933, ibid.

24. Lorena Hickok to Harry Hopkins, Feb. 14, 1934, in Richard Lowitt and Maurine Beasley, eds., *One Third of a Nation: Lorena Hickok Reports on the Great Depression* (Urbana, 1981), 188–90.

25. Gordon W. Blackwell, "The Displaced Tenant Farm Family in North Carolina," *Social Forces* 13 (Oct. 1934), 67–68, 72–73. See also "The Problem of the Displaced Tenant Farm Family," a cooperative study by the North Carolina FERA and the Institute for Research in Social Science, Landlord-Tenant file, AAA, RG 145, NA; David W. Pettus, "Farm Rental Agreements in Caswell County, North Carolina," Oct. 1940, Manuscripts, 1940–46, Box 988, Bureau of Agricultural Economics, Record Group 83, National Archives (hereafter cited as BAE, RG 83, NA). See also C. Horace Hamilton, "Rural-Urban Migration in North Carolina, 1920–1930" (Raleigh: N.C. Agricultural Experiment Station, 1933).

26. Badger, *Prosperity Road*, 73–74, 205.

27. Arthur M. Collens to J. B. Hutson, Sept. 25, 1933, Tobacco, AAA, RG 145, NA.

28. Glen E. Rogers to J. B. Hutson, Jan. 19, 1934; Hutson to Rogers, Jan. 22, 1934, ibid.

29. *Progressive Farmer*, 48 (Dec. 1933), 18; Winston-Salem *Journal and Sentinel*, Jan. 21, 1934.

30. U.S. *Statutes at Large*, 43, pt. 1, 1276–77; Winston-Salem *Journal*, June 29, 1934. For an explanation of the special provisions of the Kerr Tobacco Act, see J. B. Hutson to L. R. Richardson, July 18, 1934, Tobacco, AAA, RG 145, NA.

31. J. Con Lanier to John R. Watson, July 12, 1934; Lanier to R. B. Mallard, Tabor, N.C., June 27, 1934, AAA, RG 145, NA. See also J. R. McCarl to Henry A. Wallace, Jan. 7, 1936, SOA, RG 16, NA; Winston-Salem *Journal*, Oct. 10, 1934; USDA, *Agricultural Adjustment, 1933 to 1935: A Report of Administration of the Agricultural Adjustment Act, May 13, 1933, to December 31, 1935*, (Washington, 1936), 207. Only thirty-three complaints regarding tobacco contracts reached the AAA—nine from Georgia, twenty-two from North Carolina, and two from South Carolina. One North Carolina contract was cancelled ("Summary of Reports Received to Date by Adjustment Committee from Field Representatives Investigating and Adjusting Landlord Tenant Complaints, Cotton and Tobacco," Landlord-Tenant File, AAA, RG 145, NA).

32. Winston-Salem *Journal*, July 7, 25, 28, 1934; Corbitt, *Addresses, Letters and Papers of Ehringhaus*, 380; Ben Kilgore, "Farmers Have 'Set Stage' for Higher Tobacco Prices," *Progressive Farmer* 49 (Aug. 1934), 5.

33. Winston-Salem *Journal*, Aug. 3, 10, 11, 1934; Winston-Salem *Journal and Sentinel*, Aug. 26, 1934.

34. Badger, *Prosperity Road*, 95.

35. Winston-Salem *Journal*, Sept. 6, Nov. 1, 1934; Dean I. O. Schaub to John C. B. Ehringhaus, Sept. 17, 1934, Box 109, Ehringhaus Papers.

36. Badger, *Prosperity Road*, 105; *Biographical Directory of the American Congress, 1774–1971* (Washington, 1971), 943; *Who Was Who in America*, 3 (Chicago, 1968), 287.

37. Badger, *Prosperity Road*, 106.

38. Ibid., 107–11. See also Charles Kellog Mann, *Tobacco: The Ants and the Elephants* (Salt Lake City, 1975), 38.

39. Memorandum, 1938, Tobacco, AAA, RG 145, NA.

40. Badger, *Prosperity Road*, 117–18.

41. "An Analysis of the Effects of the Processing Tax Levied under the Agricultural Adjustment Act," Confidential Report, May 1937, 58–74, in Manuscripts, 1940–46, Box 966, BAE, RG 83, NA; Joseph C. Robert, *The Story of Tobacco in America* (Chapel Hill, 1949), 257–58. Robert argued that the ten-cent brands did extremely well during the 1930s, which contradicts the BAE report. Van L. Perkins, in *Crisis in Agriculture*, argued that manufacturers "absorbed the entire burden of the increased prices and of the processing tax as well" (155–56).

42. Badger, *Prosperity Road*, 111–18.

43. See John C. B. Ehringhaus to Franklin D. Roosevelt, Mar. 13, 1936, SOA, RG 16, NA.

44. Benedict and Stine, *Agricultural Commodity Programs*, 62.

45. Badger, *Prosperity Road*, 144–47.

46. Ibid., 149–50.

47. Ibid., 153–54, 158.

48. W. A. Minor to Eugenia Boone, May 25, 1938, Tobacco, AAA, RG 145, NA. For complaints about allotments, see H. A. Ray to Harry S. Brown, Mar. 26, 1938; W. J. Hooten to Claude Pepper, June 30, 1938; R. R. Jordan, Smithfield, N.C., to Dear Sir, July 5, 1938, Tobacco, AAA, RG 145, NA.

49. Warren R. Mixon to Richard B. Russell, June 30, 1938, ibid. Badger observed the results of the Georgia complaints: "The protest from Georgia growers and politicians was so great that the AAA basically gave Georgia farmers all the quota they needed" (*Prosperity Road*, 162).

50. I. W. Duggan to R. R. Moore, July 7, 1938, Tobacco, AAA, RG 145, NA; Badger, *Prosperity Road*, 161. See also Wade H. Watson to Richard Russell, July 16, 1938, Tobacco, AAA, RG 145, NA.

51. Newton Watkins to Homer S. Durden, Aug. 3, 1938; J. E. Thigpen to Watkins, Aug. 12, 1938, Tobacco, AAA, RG 145, NA. See also Jerome Crawley, Waycross, Ga., to Henry A. Wallace, Aug. 23, 1938, ibid.

52. B. B. Sugg to J. B. Hutson, July 28, 1938; Hutson to Sugg, Aug. 8, 1938; Newton H. Eildon to Robert R. Reynolds, Sept. 16, 1938, ibid. See also William Collins to H. B. Johnson, Wilson, N.C., Sept. 23, 1938; H. J. Beasley to J. Edgar Hoover, Oct. 6, 1938; Collins to J. Mott Robertson, Lynchburg, Va., Dec. 13, 1938, ibid.

53. Badger, *Prosperity Road*, 166–74.

54. Ibid., 176–77.

55. Leonard Rapport, "Tobacco Comes to Town," 27, manuscript in possession of Rapport. The average price was $15.03 per hundred pounds compared to $22.35 a year before. For the reaction of Georgia growers, see Leonard Rapport, "Georgia Sells a Crop," *Georgia Historical Quarterly* (Winter 1978), 316–21.

56. Badger, *Prosperity Road*, 175–83; Rapport, "Tobacco Comes to Town," 27–29.

57. Badger, *Prosperity Road*, 183–88. On the government program, see Henry A. Wallace to Flue-cured Tobacco Farmers, Sept. 16, 1939, Foreign Trade, SOA, RG 16, NA.

58. Badger, *Prosperity Road*, 190–93; Mann, *Tobacco*, 54; Williamson and Toussaint, "Parity and Support Prices for Flue-Cured Tobacco," 15–16.

Chapter 7

1. See Rice Millers' Association Newsletters, Mar. 27, Apr. 10, 17, 24, 26, 1933, Box 2, William M. Reid Papers, Southwestern Archives and Manuscripts Collection, University of Southwestern Louisiana, Lafayette (hereafter cited as Reid Papers, USL).

2. Frank A. Godchaux to Henry A. Wallace, May 30, 1933, Rice, Records of the Agricultural Stabilization and Conservation Service, Agricultural Adjustment Administration, Record Group 145, National Archives (hereafter cited as

AAA, RG 145, NA). See also RMA Newsletter, Apr. 24, 1933, Box 2, Reid Papers, USL.

3. "Rice," in Bureau of Agricultural Economics, "An Analysis of the Effects of the Processing Taxes Levied under the Agricultural Adjustment Act" (Washington, 1937), Manuscripts, 1940–46, Bureau of Agricultural Economics, Record Group 83, National Archives (hereafter cited as BAE, RG 83, NA); unsigned memorandum for the Secretary, Mar. 19, 1935, Rice, Records of the Secretary of Agriculture, Record Group 16, National Archives (hereafter cited as SOA, RG 16, NA); RMA Newsletter, Oct. 2, 1933, Box 2, Reid Papers, USL; Murray R. Benedict and Oscar C. Stine, *The Agricultural Commodity Programs: Two Decades of Experience* (New York, 1956), 139n; Rudolph Carrol Hammack, "The New Deal and Louisiana Agriculture" (Ph.D. diss., Tulane University, 1973), 111–14; Charles E. Burkhead, John W. Kirkbride, and William B. Hudson, comps., "Rice, Popcorn, and Buckwheat: Acreage, Yield, Production, Price, and Value by States, 1906–1953," Statistical Bulletin no. 238, USDA, Agricultural Marketing Service (Washington, 1958), 2; "Frank A. Godchaux Issues Letter to Rice Trade Explaining Operation of the New Set-up," *The Rice Journal* 36 (Nov. 1933), 29. The varieties were set at the following prices: Blue Rose, $3.15; Fortuna, $3.45; Rexora, $3.50; Early Prolific, $2.75; Lady Wright, $3.15; Japan, $2.85.

4. Minutes, Control Committee, Southern Rice Milling Industry, Oct. 27, 29, Nov. 11, 12, 1933, Box 3, Reid Papers, USL.

5. Minutes, Control Committee, Dec. 4, 1933; Frank A. Godchaux, Jr., to A. J. Weaver and Control Committee, Dec. 12, 1933, ibid.

6. Report by William M. Reid, Apr. 5, 1934, Box 1, ibid.

7. Hammack, "New Deal and Louisiana Agriculture," 117–20; Administrative Work and Statistical Reports of Director of Extension of Louisiana, 1933, 4–7, Department of Archives and Manuscripts, Louisiana State University, Baton Rouge; USDA, *Agricultural Adjustment: A Report of Administration of the Agricultural Adjustment Act, May 1933-February 1934* (Washington, 1934), 173–79.

8. Unsigned memorandum for the Secretary, Mar. 19, 1935, Rice, SOA, RG 16, NA; Hammack, "New Deal and Louisiana Agriculture," 121.

9. A. J. Weaver, memorandum to Chester C. Davis, Aug. 16, 1933, Rice, AAA, RG 145, NA; "The Amended Crop Control Agreement for the Southern Rice Milling Industry," *The Rice Journal* 37 (July 1934), 8; "The Rice Marketing Agreement," ibid. (Sept. 1934), 12.

10. Minutes, Control Committee, May 18, 1934; Minutes, Millers' Advisory Council, Aug. 15, 1934, Box 3, Reid Papers, USL.

11. Minutes, Millers' Advisory Council, Oct. 4, 1934, ibid.

12. Charles G. Miller to LaVerne Swim, Stuttgart, Ark., Dec. 3, 1934; J. W. Bateman to Henry A. Wallace, Jan. 8, 1935; Charles B. Howe, memorandum to William E. Byrd, Mar. 12, 1936, Rice, AAA, RG 145, NA; Minutes, Millers' Advisory Council, Aug. 15, 1934, Reid Papers, Box 3, USL; "Rice—as Agricultural Guinea Pig," Rice Millers' Papers, Box 1, Southwestern Archives and Manuscripts Collection, University of Southwestern Louisiana, Lafayette (hereafter cited as RMA Papers, USL). See also Henry A. Wallace to W. I.

Myers, governor of the Farm Credit Administration, Apr. 20, 1934, Rice AAA, RG 145, NA. For an account of Bateman's life, see *Memoirs of J. W. Bateman, 1884–1969* (Louisiana State University Extension Service, n.d.).

13. J. W. Bateman to Henry A. Wallace, Jan. 8, 1935; Charles B. Howe, memorandum to William E. Byrd, Mar. 12, 1936, Rice, AAA, RG 145, NA; Hammack, "New Deal and Louisiana Agriculture," 121–25; "Excerpts from the Report of the Secretary of Agriculture Issued December 12, 1934," *The Rice Journal* 37 (Dec. 1934), 7–8. See also Minutes, Millers' Committee, Southern Rice Milling Industry, Nov. 17, 1934, Box 3, Reid Papers, USL.

14. Allen Dezauche to Henry A. Wallace, Feb. 5, 1934, Rice, AAA, RG 145, NA.

15. C. N. Taylor to A. J. Weaver, Jan. 27, 1934, ibid.

16. R. A. Wasson to A. J. Weaver, Feb. 9, 1934; Carol M. Rosenquist to Wasson, Mar. 13, 1934, ibid.; Hammack, "New Deal and Louisiana Agriculture," 118–21.

17. W. J. Lowe to Henry A. Wallace and Charles G. Miller, Apr. 29, 1935; Lowe to Wallace, May 7, 1935, Rice, SOA, RG 16, NA. For a similar argument on redistributing allotments, see Charles C. Bellar, Anahuac, Tex., to James Miller, Nov. 22, 1933, Rice AAA, RG 145, NA.

18. Carl M. Rosenquist to Frank G. Middleton, Mar. 23, 1934; Rosenquist to J. G. McDaniel, Mar. 12, 1934, Rice, AAA, RG 145, NA.

19. J. W. Bateman to Henry A. Wallace, Jan. 8, 1935, ibid. See also Robert H. Shields, memorandum of conference re: Rice, Jan. 16, 1935, ibid.

20. "Legislative History of De Rouen Amendment," RMA Papers, Box 1, USL; Hammack, "New Deal and Louisiana Agriculture," 129–30; Charles Howe, memorandum to William E. Byrd, Mar. 12, 1936; R. A. Wasson to Charles G. Miller, Feb. 25, 1935, Rice, AAA, RG 145, NA. See also Chester C. Davis, memorandum to the Secretary, Feb. 15, 1935, ibid. For a complaint about lax enforcement of accused millers, see L. M. Simon to Charles G. Miller, Mar. 26, 1935, ibid.

21. Announcement, 1935 Adjustment Program for Southern Rice, Mar. 19, 1935, Petition folder, 1935, Rice, AAA, RG 145, NA; Edwin G. Nourse, Joseph S. Davis, and John D. Black, *Three Years of the Agricultural Adjustment Administration* (Washington, 1937), 112; Benedict and Stine, *Agricultural Commodity Programs*, 140–42. "For example," the announcement explained, "a grower with an acreage allotment of 100 acres and a production quota of 1,000 barrels will receive payment on 850 barrels, provided he plants as much as 85 acres and not more than 100 acres. If he plants 80 acres, his payments will be based on 800 barrels, and if he plants 50 acres, his payments will be based on 500 barrels." Acreage was measured, and if a grower overplanted he could "retire the excess acreage from production in order to comply with his contract."

22. Charles Howe, memorandum to William E. Byrd, Mar. 12, 1936, Rice, AAA, RG 145, NA; Burkhead, Kirkbride, and Hudson, "Rice, Popcorn, and Buckwheat," 7.

23. Charles Howe, memorandum to William E. Byrd, Mar. 12, 1936, Rice, AAA, RG 145, NA.

24. U.S. Congress, Senate, *Payments Under Agricultural Adjustment Program*, Senate Doc. 274, 74 Cong., 2 Sess., 1936, 68–71.

25. "An Analysis of the Effects of the Processing Tax Levied under the Agricultural Adjustment Act," Confidential Report, May 1937, 89, Manuscripts, 1940–46, Box 966, BAE, RG 83, NA; John Norman Efferson, *The Production and Marketing of Rice* (New Orleans, 1952) 428.

26. Report of William M. Reid to the Rice Millers' Association, May 30, 1936, Box 1, Reid Papers, USL; Hammack, "New Deal and Louisiana Agriculture," 136.

27. C. H. Alvord, acting director, southern division, memorandum to Sam Bledsoe, Oct. 26, 1937, Rice, AAA, RG 145, NA; Benedict and Stine, *Agricultural Commodity Programs*, 140.

28. Lawrence Myers, chief, marketing section, to John L. McClellan, May 7, 1937, Rice, AAA, RG 145, NA; Nourse, Davis, and Black, *Three Years of the Agricultural Adjustment Administration*, 111, 131, 320; "Rice, Parity Report," Manuscripts, 1940–46, Box 1004, BAE, RG 83, NA.

29. I. W. Duggan to E. J. Broussard, Lake Arthur, La., Mar. 9, 1938, Rice, AAA, RG 145, NA.

30. T. B. King to W. A. Mayfield, Mar. 22, 1938, ibid.

31. Burkhead, Kirkbride, and Hudson, "Rice, Popcorn, and Buckwheat," 6–8; Benedict and Stine, *Agricultural Commodity Programs*, 140–41; Leon A. Mears, *The Political Economy of Rice in the United States*, Food Research Institute Studies, 14 (Stanford, 1976), 339–40.

Chapter 8

1. John Crowe Ransom, "Reconstructed but Unregenerate," in Twelve Southerners, *I'll Take My Stand* (reprint ed., New York, 1962), 19–20.

2. Theodore Rosengarten, *All God's Dangers: The Life of Nate Shaw* (New York, 1974), 177–82.

3. William Faulkner, *The Hamlet* (New York, 1940), 148–49.

4. Rosengarten, *All God's Dangers*, 108, 118, 183–90.

5. "A Speech before the Boston Unitarian Club," 1888, in Louis R. Harlan, ed., *The Booker T. Washington Papers*, vol. 2 (Urbana, 1972), 503–4; Booker T. Washington to George Washington Cable, Oct. 8, 1889, ibid., vol. 3 (Urbana, 1974), 7–8.

6. Testimony of O. B. Stevens, Mar. 15, 1901, *Report of the Industrial Commission on Agriculture and Agricultural Labor*, vol. 10 (Washington, 1901), 907–9.

7. Testimony of Robert Ransom Poole, Mar. 23, 1901, 921–25; testimony of Pitt Dillingham, Apr. 8, 1898, 166–68, ibid. J. Pope Brown testified that Southerners were not mechanically minded: "We have not been educated on that line. We are deficient in mechanical education" (testimony of J. Pope Brown, June 20, 1899, ibid., 80). W. L. Peek claimed that "the South is rapidly going into industrial slavery and our lands are going into the hands of a few men."

He predicted that the country would ultimately become "a nation of tenants." The only remedy, he suggested, was "Government ownership" (testimony of W. L. Peek, Mar. 19, 1900, ibid., 462–63).

8. Testimony of L. W. Youmans, June 22, 1899, ibid., 199–222.

9. Benson H. Wiley to Henry Wallace, Dec. 21, 1936, President's Committee on Tenancy, Box 31, Bureau of Agricultural Economics, Record Group 83, National Archives (hereafter cited as BAE, RG 83, NA).

10. Brooks Hays to Mr. Porter, Apr. 15, 1935, Land Tenure, Records of the Agricultural Stabilization and Conservation Service, Agricultural Adjustment Administration, Record Group 145, National Archives (hereafter cited as AAA, RG 145, NA).

11. Kenneth D. Yielding and Paul H. Carlson, comps., *Ah That Voice: The Fireside Chats of Franklin Delano Roosevelt* (Odessa, Tex., 1974), 22.

12. Frank Mullen to Niles Trammell, Oct. 14, 1933, Confidential, NBC Papers, Box 31, folder 19, "DS 9–12/33," Mass Communications History Center, State Historical Society of Wisconsin (citation furnished by Susan Smulyan); Charles Grant Curtis, Jr., "Franklin D. Roosevelt and the Commonwealth of Broadcasting" (honors thesis, Harvard College, 1978), 71–78. For a fictional account of the impact of radio on a relief family, see John Faulkner, *Men Working* (New York, 1941), 85ff.

13. James Agee and Walker Evans, *Let Us Now Praise Famous Men* (Boston, 1941), 115–16, 314, 327, 429.

14. Charles S. Johnson, Edwin R. Embree, and Will W. Alexander, *The Collapse of Cotton Tenancy,* quoted in Arthur F. Raper and Ira De A. Reid, *Sharecroppers All* (Chapel Hill, 1941), 35; "Land Ownership and Farm Tenancy," n.d., Tenure Section, BAE, RG 83, NA. On rural land ownership, see C. Vann Woodward, *Origins of the New South* (Baton Rouge, 1951), 118–20; "Foreign Investment in U.S. Agricultural Land—How It Shapes Up," Report by the Comptroller of the United States, July 30, 1979; "Who Owns the Land? A Preliminary Report of a U.S. Landownership Survey," USDA, Economics, Statistics and Cooperatives Service (Washington, 1979); "Concentration of Control of Agricultural Land," BAE, RG 83, NA.

15. "Concentration of Control of Agricultural Land," BAE, RG 83, NA. See also Thomas J. Woofter, Jr., *Landlord and Tenant on the Cotton Plantation* (New York, 1969), xxi-xxii, 15–24, table 24, 211.

16. Lawrence J. Nelson, "Oscar Johnston, the New Deal, and the Cotton Subsidy Payments Controversy, 1936–1937," *Journal of Southern History* 40 (Aug. 1974), 399–416; U.S. Congress, Senate, *Payments under Agricultural Adjustment Program,* Senate Doc. 274, 74 Cong., 2 Sess., 1936.

17. *Payments under Agricultural Adjustment Program,* 33; FERA, Division of Research and Statistics, "Rural Problem Areas Survey Report No. 17, The Cotton Growing Areas of the Old South," Leflore County, Mississippi, Nov. 9, 1934, 6, BAE, RG 83, NA; Oscar F. Bledsoe to Sam B. Bledsoe, Dec. 4, 1941, Agricultural Labor, Records of the Secretary of Agriculture, Record Group 16, National Archives (hereafter cited as SOA, RG 16, NA).

18. *Payments under Agricultural Adjustment Program,* 11-12, 33–35, 47–49, 55–56.

19. Arthur F. Raper, *Preface to Peasantry: A Tale of Two Black Belt Counties* (New York, 1968), 232.

20. *Payments under Agricultural Adjustment Program*, 47; C. G. Wosham to Cully Cobb, July 1, 1933; Kenyon B. Zahner to Cobb, June 24, 1933; Zahner to J. Olin Horne, n.d., Cotton, AAA, RG 145, NA. See also Mississippi Delta History, Land Tenure Section, BAE RG 83, NA.

21. "New Data on Farm Mortgages and Farm Real Estate of Life Insurance Companies," *Agricultural Finance Review* 3 (May 1940), 35, copy in Government Competition with Private Enterprise, Credit, Box 16, Temporary National Economic Committee, Record Group 144, National Archives (hereafter cited as TNEC, RG 144, NA). See also Richard S. Kirkendall, *Social Scientists and Farm Politics in the Age of Roosevelt* (Columbia, Mo., 1966), 35–37.

22. *Payments under Agricultural Adjustment Program*, 32–57.

23. Ibid., 10–58; "Concentration of Control of Agricultural Land," BAE, RG 83, NA; Nelson, "Oscar Johnston," 413, 414n.

24. "An Analysis of the Effects of the Processing Tax Levied under the Agricultural Adjustment Act," Confidential Report, May 1937, 55–56, Manuscripts, 1940–46, Box 966, BAE, RG 83, NA. See also Theodore Saloutos, *The American Farmer and the New Deal* (Ames, 1982), 124–36.

25. Harold T. Lingard, "Lender Distribution of Farm-Mortgage Recordings," *Agricultural Finance Review* 3 (May 1940), 25, copy in BAE, RG 83, NA. Until World War I most mortgages in the South were held by local merchants and private sources. In 1913, however, the National Banking Act was amended to permit national banks to lend on real estate security, and in 1916 the Federal Farm Loan Act created two federal lending agencies.

26. "Farm Credit Administration," typescript in TNEC, RG 144, NA.

27. Lingard, "Lender Distribution," 25. See also Harold C. Larsen, "Farm-Mortgage Investments of Life Insurance Companies," Dec. 1943, Box 986, Manuscripts, 1940–46, BAE, RG 83, NA; Larsen, "Distribution by Lender Groups on Farm-Mortgage and Real Estate Holdings, Jan. 1, 1930–1945," Aug. 1945, Box 980, ibid; J. G. Evans, Chapel Hill, N.C., to Rexford Tugwell, June 2, 1934, Tenancy, SOA, RG 16, NA. Evans wrote that the Federal Land Bank in Columbia, S.C., "has deliberately followed a policy of strengthening land lordism in its district by making it difficult for owners of small farms to get loans while breaking the spirit of the law, at least, to make loans to owners of very large farms."

28. "Concentration of Control of Agricultural Land," BAE, RG 83, NA. This report shows that in 1933 "93.6 farms per 1,000 changed ownership for one reason or another, the number changing in satisfaction of debt and for taxes representing 54.1 per thousand farms." William A. Bristol of Statesville, N.C., wrote on January 4, 1934, that nine years earlier he had been worth $300,000. "Today," he wrote, "I am worth nothing. My lands are all gone, in the hands of insurance companies, my money is all gone" (Bristol to Henry A. Wallace, Jan. 4, 1934, Farm Security Administration, Subsistence Homestead Division, General Correspondence, 1933–35, Records of the Farmers Home Administration, Record Group 96, National Archives [hereafter cited as SHD, FHA, RG 96, NA]).

29. Moses Senkumba Musoke, "Technical Change in Cotton Production in the United States, 1925–1960" (Ph.D. diss., University of Wisconsin-Madison, 1976), 95, 111; David Wayne Ganger, "The Impact of Mechanization and the New Deal's Acreage Reduction Programs on Cotton Farmers during the 1930s" (Ph.D. diss., University of California–Los Angeles, 1973), 335, 345; interview with Gordon Cotton, director of the Old Courthouse Museum, Vicksburg, Miss., Mar. 30, 1979.

30. Ganger, "Impact of Mechanization," 360–61, 401–2, 405–6.

31. Arthur Raper, "The Role of Agricultural Technology in Southern Social Change," 5, Table, 6, Box 1032, Manuscripts, 1940–46, BAE, RG 83, NA.

32. J. C. Elrod, D. E. Young, and W. T. Fullilove, "Farm Rental Arrangements in Georgia," ibid. See also J. C. Elrod, "Types of Tenancy Areas in Georgia," Land Tenure Section, ibid.

33. Glen T. Barton and J. G. McNeely, "Recent Changes in Labor Organization on Arkansas Plantations," Box 1030, Manuscripts, 1940–46, ibid. Due to a large 1937 harvest, the AAA cut allotments from 34.5 million acres to 27.5 million acres in 1938 (Murray R. Benedict and Oscar C. Stine, *The Agricultural Commodity Programs: Two Decades of Experience* [New York, 1956], 17–19).

34. Barton and McNeely, "Recent Changes in Labor Organization."

35. Donald C. Alexander, *The Arkansas Plantation, 1920–1942* (New Haven, 1943), 79, 86–87; *Payments under the Agricultural Adjustment Program,* 38.

36. Raper, "Role of Agricultural Technology," Table 6. See also Albert A. Thornbrough, "Tractor Operation on 62 Virginia Tractor Farms in 1938," n.d., Manuscripts, 1940–46, Box 1044, BAE, RG 83, NA.

37. John L. Fulmer, *Agricultural Progress in the Cotton Belt since 1920* (Chapel Hill, 1950), 62–75.

38. Herman B. James, "The Effects of the Mechanization of Agriculture in the Northern Tidewater Area of North Carolina" (Ph.D. diss., Duke University, 1949), 98, 114, 191, 204. The study included Currituck, Camden, Pasquotank, Tyrell, Dare, Hyde, Beaufort, and Pamlico counties.

39. Charles B. Ratchford, "Rental Arrangements in a Developing Economy" (Ph.D. diss., Duke University, 1951), 91–92; Appendix G, Table V, "Number of Workstock and Tractors in Coastal Plain, North Carolina, 1890–1945," 515.

40. Ibid., Preface, 1, 123, 171, 417–18, 426.

41. U.S. Congress, Senate, "Special Committee to Investigate Unemployment and Relief," Feb. 28-Apr. 8, 1938, Testimony of Paul S. Taylor, 1158, 1161, 75 Cong., 3 Sess., copy in Statistics and History, BAE, RG 83, NA.

42. Ibid., 1162–63. See also "Testimony before the TNEC on Human and Socio-Economic Effects of Displacement in Agriculture," testimony of Paul S. Taylor, Box 34, TNEC, RG 144, NA; "Plan for Cooperation between Rural Rehabilitation Division of the FERA and the AAA in Handling Cases of Eviction of Tenants and Sharecroppers on Account of Inability of Landlords to Finance Them," May 27, 1935, Cotton, AAA, RG 145, NA; Citizen of Desha County to Franklin D. Roosevelt, May 6, 1935, SHD, FHA, RG 96, NA; Richard H. Day, "The Economics of Technological Change and the Demise of the Sharecrop-

per," *American Economic Review* 57 (June 1967), 427–49; Carroll W. Pursell, Jr., "Government and Technology in the Great Depression," *Technology and Culture* 20 (Jan. 1979), 162–74.

43. "Message from the President Transmitting 'The Report of the Special Committee on Farm Tenancy,'" Feb. 16, 1937 (Washington, 1937), copy in project files, Land Tenure Section, BAE, RG 83, NA; Donald H. Grubbs, *Cry from the Cotton: The Southern Tenant Farmers' Union and the New Deal* (Chapel Hill, 1971), 140–61.

44. Daniel M. Johnson and Rex R. Campbell, *Black Migration in America: A Social Demographic History* (Durham, 1981), 90–100; Jay R. Mandle, *The Roots of Black Poverty: The Southern Plantation Economy after the Civil War* (Durham, 1978), 71–83; Jack Temple Kirby, "The Southern Exodus, 1910–1960: A Primer for Historians," *Journal of Southern History* 49 (Nov. 1983), 585–600.

Chapter 9

1. "You're Gonna Have Lace Curtains," in *These Are Our Lives* (1939; reprint ed., New York, 1975), 4–17. The novelist Harry Crews related a similar game of escape. When a neighboring black woman and her son looked after him while grownups were working in the fields, Crews took a Sears, Roebuck catalog and made up stories about the models. The perfect people in the catalog contrasted with the bruised and scarred people he knew. In the course of an afternoon, he related, he, the black woman, and her son would have the entire catalog in conflict, living out the realities of the country and at the same time taking the models down a notch. "Since where we lived and how we lived was almost hermetically sealed from everything and everybody else, fabrication became a way of life. Making up stories, it seems to me now, was not only a way for us to understand the way we lived but also a defense against it" (Crews, *A Childhood: The Biography of a Place* [New York, 1978], 55–58).

2. See Reynold M. Wik, "The Radio in Rural America during the 1920s," *Agricultural History* 55 (Oct. 1981), 339–50; John C. Baker, *Farm Broadcasting: The First Sixty Years* (Ames, 1981).

3. "I Has a Garden," in *These Are Our Lives*, 46, 51–52.

4. "We Makes Plenty," ibid., 70; Margaret Jarman Hagood, *Mothers of the South: Portraiture of the White Tenant Farm Woman* (1939; reprint ed., New York, 1977), 15.

5. "Staying Right Here," in John L. Robinson, *Living Hard: Southern Americans in the Great Depression* (Washington, 1981), 102–3; Mary A. Hicks and Edwin Massengill, "'Backer Barning," 201, North Carolina Folklore, USWPA, Manuscripts Division, Library of Congress, Washington (hereafter cited as N.C. Folklore, USWPA, LC).

6. Hagood, *Mothers of the South*, 22.

7. Crews, *Childhood*, 128–29.

8. "I Saved My Money," in *These Are Our Lives*, 98.

9. "I Has a Garden," 49–50, ibid. See also "I Saved My Money," 91; "We Makes Plenty," 71–73; "Marsh Taylor, Landlord," 123, ibid.

10. Hicks and Massengill, "'Backer Barning," 202. For an excellent discussion of childbearing among white tenant women, see Hagood, *Mothers of the South*, 108–27.

11. Hagood, *Mothers of the South*, 15. On pellagra, see Elizabeth W. Etheridge, *The Butterfly Caste: A Social History of Pellagra in the South* (Westport, 1972).

12. Crews, *Childhood*, 156–58.

13. Clarence Poe, *My First 80 Years* (Chapel Hill, 1963), 46; Crews, *Childhood*, 114.

14. "I Saved My Money," in *These Are Our Lives*, 96; Hicks and Massengill, "'Backer Barning," 201.

15. T. Pat Matthews and Claude V. Dunnagan, "Lived Hard but Still Got My Dogs," 193, N.C. Folklore, USWPA, LC. See also Crews, *Childhood*, 124–27.

16. Matthews and Dunnagan, "Lived Hard but Still Got My Dogs," 190, N.C. Folklore, USWPA, LC; "We Makes Plenty," in *These Are Our Lives*, 75; Poe, *My First 80 Years*, 52.

17. "You're Gonna Have Lace Curtains," in *These Are Our Lives*, 16.

18. "I Has a Garden," 47, 53; "We Makes Plenty," 71, ibid.

19. "I Saved My Money," 94, ibid.; Hagood, *Mothers of the South*, 18.

20. Mary A. Hicks, "Tobacco's in My Blood," 155, 158–59, 161, N.C. Folklore, USWPA, LC. See also Crews, *Childhood*, 119–20.

21. "I Has a Garden," in *These Are Our Lives* 52; "We Makes Plenty," ibid., 74–75; Hicks and Massengill, "'Backer Barning," 202; Hicks, "Tobacco's in My Blood," 162; Hagood, *Mothers of the South*, 239.

22. "Get Out and Hoe," in *These Are Our Lives*, 31.

23. Kenneth D. Yielding and Paul H. Carlson, comps., *Ah That Voice: The Fireside Chats of Franklin D. Roosevelt* (Odessa, Tex., 1974), 26; "I Saved My Money," in *These Are Our Lives*, 95.

24. Baker, *Farm Broadcasting*, 29–30.

25. "Things Are Changin'," in Robinson, *Living Hard*, 141–42.

26. "Staying Right Here," in *These Are Our Lives*, 102–3; "We Makes Plenty," 75, ibid.

27. "Things Are Changin'," 141, "A Pretty Hard Life," 107, 109, both in Robinson, *Living Hard*.

28. Hagood, *Mothers of the South*, 84–85; Hicks, "Tobacco's in My Blood," 162.

29. Hagood, *Mothers of the South*, 77, 87, 89.

30. Ibid., 91, 239.

31. Pamela Barefoot and Burt Kornegay, *Mules & Memories: A Photo Documentary of the Tobacco Farmer* (Winston-Salem, 1978), 102.

32. Hicks and Massengill, "'Backer Barning," 197–202. Italics in original. See also Hagood, *Mothers of the South*, 23; Dolores Janiewski, "Women and the Making of a Rural Proletariat in the Bright Tobacco Belt, 1880–1930," *Insurgent Sociologist* 10 (Summer 1980), 24–25. "When that economy lost the male labor necessary to operate a tobacco farm, its members, especially its fe-

male members, became likely candidates for migration," Janiewski wrote. Although the city (Durham, in this case) drew young women from the farms, she concluded that they were, "at the same time, driven from the land by the combined force of class, racial, and sexual subordination."

33. Poe, *My First 80 Years*, 53; "I Has a Garden," in *These Are Our Lives*, 52–53.

34. "I Saved My Money," *These Are Our Lives*, 100.

35. Matthews and Dunnagan, "Lived Hard but Still Got My Dogs," 195.

36. "I Has a Garden," in *These Are Our Lives*, 54; "Get Out and Hoe," 37, ibid.

37. "Staying Right Here," 105, ibid.

38. Nannie May Tilley, *The Bright-Tobacco Industry, 1860–1929* (Chapel Hill, 1948), 213.

39. "Dixon Kavanaugh, Speculator," 111; "Clyde Singleton, Doorman," 153; "Otis Rucker, Tobacco Auctioneer," 3, all in Leonard Rapport, WPA interviews, copies in his possession.

40. Interview with Roy Pearce, in Barefoot and Kornegay, *Mules & Memories*, 82; interview with Leonard Rapport, Washington, D.C., Dec. 11, 1981; Rapport, "Tobacco Comes to Town," 6, 13–14, 63, unpublished MS in his possession; "Clyde Singleton, Doorman," 153, and "Otis Rucker, Tobacco Auctioneer," 3, both in Rapport WPA interviews.

41. Tilley, *Bright-Tobacco Industry*, 226; Rapport, "Tobacco Comes to Town," 6–8; "Bill Jordan, Speculator," 1; "Sam Hobgood, Factory Manager," 3, all in Rapport WPA interviews.

42. Interview with Leonard Rapport, Washington, D.C., Dec. 11, 1981.

43. "'Parson' Barnes, Negro Warehouse Laborer," 79, 84–85; "D. W. Daniels, Veteran Tobaccoman," 116; "'Mister Danny' Kelly, Operator," 67; "Claude King, Cafe Operator," 1; "Clyde Roberts, Policeman," 6; all in Rapport WPA interviews.

44. "Frank Tillman, Buyer," 122–23, ibid.

45. "Sam Hobgood, Factory Manager," 1–4, ibid. See also "Sid Williams, Floorman," 138; "Clyde Singleton, Doorman," 151; "Wilson Broadwell, Leaf Dealer," 141–43, ibid.

46. "Clyde Roberts, Policeman," 6, ibid.

47. Rapport, "Tobacco Comes to Town," 41–42; "'Parson' Arthur Barnes, Negro Warehouse Laborer," 84, ibid.

48. "Josiah Roberts, Peddler," 175–76, ibid.

49. Tilley, *Bright-Tobacco Industry*, 239–40; "Earl Brady, Auctioneer," 95; "Frank Tillman, Buyer," 128; "Buck Hall, Bookman," 7, all in Rapport WPA interviews.

50. "Earl Brady, Auctioneer," 98, in Rapport WPA interviews.

51. "Buck Hall, Bookman," 6–7; "Earl Brady, Auctioneer," 98–99, ibid.

52. Anthony Badger, *Prosperity Road: The New Deal, Tobacco, and North Carolina* (Chapel Hill, 1980), 210; "Earl Brady, Auctioneer," 99, and "Frank Tillman, Buyer," 127–28, both in Rapport WPA interviews.

53. Rapport, "Tobacco Comes to Town," 59, 64.

54. "Earl Brady, Auctioneer," 102, in Rapport WPA interviews.

55. For an excellent description of a tobacco auctioneer in action, see Leonard Rapport, "Tobacco Auctioneer," in Benjamin A. Botkin, ed., *A Treasury of Southern Folklore: Stories, Ballads, Traditions, and Folkways of the People of the South* (New York, 1949), 652–54. See also Thomas J. Woofter, *The Plight of Cigarette Tobacco* (Chapel Hill, 1931), 42–55.

56. "Frank Tillman, Buyer," 128–33, in Rapport WPA interviews.

57. "Dixon Kavanaugh, Speculator," 111, and "Bill Jordan, Speculator," 3, both in Rapport WPA interviews; Rapport, "Tobacco Comes to Town," 59–60.

58. "Buck Hall, Bookman," 1–8, in Rapport WPA interviews.

59. F. R. Gregory to A. MacNamara, Deputy Minister of Labour, Ottawa, Sept. 6, 1945, Extension Service, Farm Labor Program, Records of the Federal Extension Service, Record Group 33, National Archives.

60. "Sid Williams, Floorman," 134–38, in Rapport WPA interviews.

61. "'Mister Danny' Kelly, Operator," 74–75, ibid.

62. "Clyde Roberts, Policeman," 1–3, ibid. Simon Collie related that farmers in Franklin County also went to Canada to cure tobacco (interview with Simon Collie, Seven Paths, N.C., Feb. 20, 1982).

Chapter 10

1. On river rice, see S. Locke Breaux, "The Rice Crop along the Mississippi River," *The Rice Journal* 6 (Jan. 1903), 25; Frellsen Plantation Diary, 1878–84, Department of Archives and Manuscripts, Louisiana State University, Baton Rouge; Jenkin W. Jones, "Rice Production in the Southern States," Farmers Bulletin no. 2043, USDA, 31–32.

2. William Maher, "Early Rice Growing," *The Rice Journal* 8 (Mar. 1905), 19.

3. Interview with Rouseb Soileau, Sept. 4, 1982, Eunice, La. For a history of threshing, see Leo Rogin, *The Introduction of Farm Machinery in Its Relation to the Productivity of Labor in the Agriculture of the United States during the Nineteenth Century*, University of California Publications in Economics, vol. 9 (Berkeley, 1931), 154–91.

4. Seaman A. Knapp, "The Present Status of Rice Culture in the United States," USDA bulletin no. 22 (Washington, 1899), 16–27.

5. Ibid., 28; Testimony of William Carter Stubbs, Jan. 29, 1901, in *Report of the Industrial Commission on Agriculture and Agricultural Labor*, vol. 10 (Washington, 1901), 760–77.

6. Knapp, "Present Status of Rice Culture," 29; "Farmers' Institute by Mail," *The Rice Journal* 6 (Aug. 1903), 6–7, 14.

7. Testimony of William Carter Stubbs, in *Report of the Industrial Commission*, 769–70.

8. Ibid., vol. 11 (Washington, 1901), 96; Seaman A. Knapp, "Rice," *Papers and Proceedings of the Sixteenth Annual Meeting of the American Economic Association*, pt. 1, (New York, 1904), 108; John Norman Efferson, *The Production and Marketing of Rice* (New Orleans, 1952), 2–29.

9. See Efferson, *Production and Marketing of Rice*, 463; interview with

J. M. Spicer, Aug. 31, 1982, Stuttgart, Ark.; J. M. Spicer, *Beginnings of the Rice Industry in Arkansas* (Stuttgart, 1964), 71–96.

10. Frank Foley, "Harvesting and Threshing," *The Rice Journal* 7 (June 1904), 19.

11. Spicer, *Beginnings of the Rice Industry*, 71–72.

12. "Harvester Gasoline Engine," *The Rice Journal* 13 (Sept. 1910), 15; ibid. (Oct. 1910), 14, 19; ibid., 14 (Dec. 1911), 16–17; Spicer, *Beginnings of the Rice Industry*, 71–75; Carlisle *Independent*, June 24, 1920, 22.

13. Interview with J. M. Spicer, Aug. 31, 1982.

14. Spicer, *Beginnings of the Rice Industry*, 74.

15. Ibid., 46–47, 50–52.

16. Ibid., 52–54, 77–81; "Farmall General Purpose Tractor Removes Bottle Neck from Farm Operations," *The Rice Journal* 29 (June 1926), 32–33; "Rice Belt Farmers Must Have Tractors," ibid., 21 (Nov. 1921), 36–40.

17. Sylvester L. Cary Scrapbook, Department of Archives and Manuscripts, LSU.

18. "Tenants in Rice," *The Rice Journal* 12 (Aug. 1909), 161.

19. "A Misstatement Corrected," ibid., 6 (June 1903), 30.

20. "The Thrifty German Farmer," ibid., 10 (Mar. 1907), 78–79.

21. Interview with J. M. Spicer, Aug. 31, 1982.

22. Ibid.; S. H. McCroy, "Investigations in the Grand Prairie Rice Region, Arkansas," Farm Credit Administration, Bureau of Agricultural Economics (Washington, 1934), 37, 39.

23. Ralph J. Ramsey and Harold Hoffsommer, "Farm Tenancy in Louisiana" (1940), Manuscripts, 1940–46, Box 989, Records of the Bureau of Agricultural Economics, Record Group 83, National Archives (hereafter cited as BAE, RG 83, NA).

24. *The Rice Journal* 34 (May 1931), 12–13.

25. "Adherence to Budgets Is Big Aid to Rufus A. Estes, Rice Farmer, Welsh, Louisiana," ibid. (June 1931), 17.

26. "Prominent Louisiana Woman Makes Success of Rice Farming," ibid., 33 (Mar. 1930), 26.

27. "Solving Labor Question," ibid., 10 (Oct. 1907), 259.

28. Ibid., 13 (Oct. 1910), 17; ibid., 14 (Nov. 1911), 16; ibid., 34 (Oct. 1931), 39; interview with Rouseb Soileau, Sept. 4, 1982.

29. Interview with J. M. Spicer, Aug. 31, 1982.

30. Harvest Scenes on P. S. Lovell Plantation, Crowley, La., photograph by E. K. Sturdivant, Rice Miscellaneous, Box 1, Southwestern Archives and Manuscripts Collection, University of Southwestern Louisiana, Lafayette.

31. Threshing scene, 1934–35, ibid.

32. Bennie Frownfelter Burkett, *Stuttgart, Arkansas: One Hundred Years on the Grand Prairie* (Stuttgart, 1980); interview with J. M. Spicer, Aug. 31, 1982; interview with Bennie Frownfelter Burkett, Aug. 31, 1982, Stuttgart, Ark.

33. "Minutes of Conference Held at Little Rock on October 20, 1938, Relative to the Legal Aspects of the Landlord-Tenant Relationships in Arkansas," Land Tenure Section, BAE, RG 83, NA. See also Harold Woodman, "Post–

Civil War Southern Agriculture and the Law," *Agricultural History* 53 (Jan. 1979), 319–37.

34. Carlisle *Independent*, Sept. 24, 1920, 103, 106–8.

35. Florence March Rosencrantz, "I. M. Bennett, Almyra, Arkansas Rice Grower Raises Poultry for Weekly Cash Income," *The Rice Journal* 36 (Apr. 1933), 9.

36. Ibid., 33 (Aug. 1930), 35.

37. Eugenia Henry, "In the Shadow of Spindletop," ibid., 42 (Apr. 1939), 10–11.

38. "Mr. W. M. Fenton, Pioneer Rice Grower, Is a Valuable Citizen to His Community and the American Rice Growers' Association," ibid., 33 (July 1930), 23–25.

39. "Alcee Benoit Makes Rice Farming Pay," ibid., 34 (Feb. 1931), 9–10.

40. R. A. Wasson to Charles G. Miller, Sept. 23, 1935; W. E. Lawson to Wasson, Sept. 20, 1935, Rice, Records of the Agricultural Stabilization and Conservation Service, Agricultural Adjustment Administration, Record Group 145, National Archives.

41. Charles R. Houssiere to A. J. S. Weaver, Aug. 19, 1933, Ibid.

42. "Flashes from the Rice Belt—Programs over KFDM through the Courtesy of the Magnolia Petroleum Company," *The Rice Journal* 33 (Oct. 1930), 12; A. C. Pritchard, "What Radio Has Done for Farmers," ibid., 37 (Nov. 1934), 9; C. Joseph Pusateri, *Enterprise in Radio: WWL and the Business of Broadcasting in America* (Washington, 1980), 157. See also John C. Baker, *Farm Broadcasting: The First Sixty Years* (Ames, 1981), 149.

43. "New Combine to Harvest and Thresh Rice in One Operation," *The Rice Journal* 30 (Nov. 1927), 16; "Rice Cut with Combine Can Be Dried with the Ellis Drier," ibid., 17, 28; T. H. Johnston and M. D. Miller, "Culture," in *Rice in the United States: Varieties and Production*, Agriculture Handbook No. 289, Agriculture Research Service, USDA (June 1973), 120–21; Efferson, *Production and Marketing of Rice*, 462–68; C. Roy Adair and Kyle Engler, "The Irrigation and Culture of Rice," in *The Yearbook of Agriculture, 1955, Water* (Washington, 1955), 389–94.

44. "Father Cary, Rice Missionary," *The Rice Journal* 12 (July 1909), 137.

45. Roger Crum interview, Arkansas County Agricultural Museum, Stuttgart, Ark.

Chapter 11

1. H. L. Mitchell, *Mean Things Happening in This Land: The Life and Times of H. L. Mitchell, Cofounder of the Southern Tenant Farmers Union* (Montclair, N.J., 1979), 296–97.

2. See, for example, Louis Cantor, *A Prologue to the Protest Movement: The Missouri Sharecropper Roadside Demonstrations of 1939* (Durham, 1969); Arthur F. Raper, *Preface to Peasantry: A Tale of Two Black Belt Counties* (Chapel Hill, 1936); Arthur F. Raper and Ira De A. Reid, *Sharecroppers All*

(Chapel Hill, 1941); James Agee and Walker Evans, *Let Us Now Praise Famous Men* (Boston, 1941); Erskine Caldwell and Margaret Bourke-White, *You Have Seen Their Faces* (New York, 1937); F. Jack Hurley, *Portrait of a Decade: Roy Stryker and the Development of Documentary Photography in the Thirties* (Baton Rouge, 1972); Dorothea Lange and Paul S. Taylor, *An American Exodus: A Record of Human Erosion* (New York, 1939); Arthur F. Raper and Jack Delano, *Tenants of the Almighty* (New York, 1943); Rupert Vance, *How the Other Half Is Housed: A Pictorial Record of Sub-Minimum Farm Housing in the South* (Chapel Hill, 1936).

3. Paul Appleby to Paul de Kruif, Jan. 17, 1941, Records of the Secretary of Agriculture, Record Group 16, National Archives (hereafter cited as SOA, RG 16, NA); M. L. Wilson, "Problem of Poverty in Agriculture," *Journal of Farm Economics* 22 (Feb. 1940), 10–11; Lewis C. Gray, "Disadvantaged Rural Classes," ibid. 20 (Feb. 1938), 71–85. See Lewis C. Gray, *History of Agriculture in the Southern United States to 1860* (Washington, 1933). See also Paul Appleby to Lucy Randolph Mason, June 18, 1941, SOA, RG 16, NA; Murray R. Benedict, "Farm People and the Land after the War," confidential memorandum, Sept. 17, 1943, Land Tenure Section, Project Files, Bureau of Agricultural Economics, Record Group 83, National Archives (hereafter cited as BAE, RG 83, NA).

4. On this theme see Carroll W. Pursell, Jr., "Government and Technology in the Great Depression," *Technology and Culture* 20 (Jan. 1979), 162–74.

5. By the mid-1930s the USDA began investigating southern tenancy and made several reports. A massive study of the legal underpinnings of the sharecropper system can be found in "Cotton," Landlord-Tenant file, SOA, RG 16, NA. See also "Farm Tenure Improvement," ibid.; Marshall Harris, "Compensation as a Means of Improving the Farm Tenancy System," Nov. 1936; "Compensation for Improvement, Deterioration, and Disturbance in Landlord-Tenant Relations," July 1935; Murray Benedict, "Farm People and the Land after the War," Sept. 1943, confidential memorandum, Land Tenure Section, all three in BAE, RG 83, NA; Secretary to members of State Agricultural Planning Committees re: *Department Policy on Family-Size Farms*, Nov. 18, 1941, Wilhelm Anderson Papers, Box 3, ibid. The major suggestions were written leases, tenant ownership of implements, compensation for improvements, credit for repairs, landlord claim for tenant damage and erosion, no termination of leases without six months' notice, boards of arbitration, and that "farming shall be regarded as a way of life rather than a profit making enterprise" (Report on County Land Use Planning, Land Tenure Section, ibid.) See also Wilhelm Anderson, "County Land-Use Planning," Dec. 1939, strictly confidential, ibid.

6. D. C. Baker to Texas Farm and Home Program, Dec. 28, 1939, Farm Security, Tenancy, SOA, RG 16, NA.

7. Merle C. Prunty, Jr., "Renaissance of the Southern Plantation," *Geographic Review* 45 (Oct. 1955), 459–91; Jack Temple Kirby, "From Fragmented to Neo-Plantations, 1920–60," draft of article in Kirby's possession; Sam B. Hillard, "The Dynamics of Power: Recent Trends in Mechanization on

the American Farm," *Technology and Culture* 13 (Jan. 1972), 10–11; Harry D. Fornari, "The Big Change: Cotton to Soybeans," *Agricultural History* 53 (Jan. 1979), 245–53.

8. William T. Hicks, Farm Labor Subcommittee Report, May 19, 1941, Wilhelm Anderson Papers, Box 5, BAE, RG 83, NA.

9. George B. Tindall, *The Emergence of the New South, 1913–1945*, (Baton Rouge, 1967), 703–4.

10. P. O. Davis to Claude A. Wickard, Aug. 29, 1942, Cost of Living File, SOA, RG 16, NA. See also "Race Tension and Farm Wages in the Rural South," Sept. 22, 1943, for confidential use, Manuscripts, 1940–46, Box 1029, BAE, RG 83, NA.

11. Wilhelm Anderson to D. A. FitzGerald, May 12, 1941, Wilhelm Anderson Papers, Box 2, BAE, RG 83, NA.

12. "The Irony of Southern History," in C. Vann Woodward, *The Burden of Southern History* (New York, 1960), 176–77; Tindall, *Emergence of the New South*, 708–10; Sidney Baldwin, *Poverty and Politics: The Rise and Decline of the Farm Security Administration* (Chapel Hill, 1968), 325–404; Edward C. Banfield, "Ten Years of the Farm Tenant Purchase Program," *Journal of Farm Economics* 31 (Aug. 1949), 469–86; Rexford G. Tugwell, "The Resettlement Idea," *Agricultural History* 33 (Oct. 1959), 159–64; Donald Holley, *Uncle Sam's Farmers: The New Deal Communities in the Lower Mississippi Valley* (Urbana, 1975).

13. Woodward, "Irony of Southern History," 5.

14. Murray R. Benedict and Oscar C. Stine, *The Agricultural Commodity Programs: Two Decades of Experience* (New York, 1956), 27, 41; Dabney S. Wellford, "Cotton Programs of the Federal Government: 1929–1967," Table 3, National Cotton Council of America (July 1968); James H. Street, in *The New Revolution in the Cotton Economy: Mechanization and Its Consequences* (Chapel Hill, 1957), reported that farm wages in the South "nearly tripled from 1940 to 1945, and by 1948 were at least three and a half times what they had been before the war" (203).

15. Theodore Rosengarten, *All God's Dangers: The Life of Nate Shaw* (New York, 1974), 419, 466, 493. For an account of the decline of a black community from 1930 to 1950, see W. S. M. Banks II, "Beasley Community: A Study of the Response of a Local Community to Observed Trends among the Rural Negro Population of the State of Georgia" (ca. 1950), Farming, SOA, RG 16, NA.

16. Richard H. Day, "The Economics of Technological Change and the Demise of the Sharecropper," *American Economic Review* 57 (June 1967), 427–49; G. F. Donaldson and J. P. McInerney, "Changing Machinery and Agricultural Adjustment," *American Journal of Agricultural Economics* 55 (Dec. 1973), 829–39; Gilbert C. Fite, "Mechanization of Cotton Production since World War II," *Agricultural History* 54 (Jan. 1980), 190–207; Charles R. Sayre, "Cotton Mechanization since World War II," ibid., 53 (Jan. 1979), 105–24; Street, *New Revolution*, 136–56. On early problems with machine harvest, see Ralph A. Rusca and Charles A. Bennett, "Problems of Machine Picking," in *Crops in Peace and War: The Yearbook of Agriculture, 1950–1951* (Washington, 1951), 441–44.

17. Fite, "Mechanization of Cotton Production," 190–207. For a chart showing the various stages of mechanization in the 1950s, 1960s, and 1970s, see Sayre, "Cotton Mechanization since World War II," 112–13.

18. In 1945 the percentage of U.S. farm operators reporting tractors was 30.5. In Texas the percentage was 29.1; in Oklahoma, 30.3; in Louisiana, 6.9; in Arkansas, 6.6; in Mississippi, 4.1; in Alabama, 4.5; in Georgia, 5.9; in South Carolina, 5.4; and in North Carolina, 6.4. During the 1930s South Carolina lost 31.6 percent of its sharecroppers; Georgia, 39.6; Alabama, 36.5; Mississippi, 7.3 (25.5 percent of other tenants); Arkansas, 36.5; and Louisiana, 19.8. See Arthur F. Raper, "The Role of Agricultural Technology in Southern Social Change," Box 1032, Manuscripts, 1940–46, BAE, RG 83, NA.

19. Ibid. See also Street, *The New Revolultion*, 130.

20. Harry C. Dillingham and David F. Sly, "The Mechanical Cotton-Picker, Negro Migration, and the Integration Movement," *Human Organization* 25 (Winter 1966), 347–48. For an account of how the forces of government and mechanization affected cotton farmers in the 1950s, see Max M. Tharp and E. Lee Langsford, "Where Our Cotton Comes From," in *Land: The Yearbook of Agriculture, 1958* (Washington, 1958), 129–35. On diversification in the old cotton-growing area, see G. H. Aull, "Changes in the Land of Cotton," ibid., 136–41.

21. Francis Butler Simkins and Charles Pierce Roland, *A History of the South*, 4th ed. (New York, 1972), 580. For an account of cotton cultivation practices in the 1960s, see Vernon L. Harness and Horace G. Porter, "Cotton, King of Fibers," in *Farmer's World: The Yearbook of Agriculture, 1964* (Washington, 1964), 222–24. For a review of cotton mechanization and ginning changes, see Rex F. Colwick and Vernon P. Moore, "King Cotton Blasts Off," in *Contours of Change: The Yearbook of Agriculture, 1970* (Washington, 1970), 39–46.

22. *Historical Statistics of the United States: Colonial Times to 1970*, pt. 1, Series K 109–53, "Farms, by Race and Tenure of Operator, and Acreage and Value, by Tenure of Operator: 1880–1969," 465. For an overview of the government's role in agricultural research, see Bob Bergland, "The Federal Role in Agricultural Research," address before the USDA Science and Educational Administration, Reston, Va., Jan. 31, 1980.

23. Raper, "Role of Agricultural Technology." See also Frank J. Welch and D. Gray Miley, "Mechanization of the Cotton Harvest," *Journal of Farm Economics* 27 (Nov. 1945), 928–46; John R. Skates, Jr., "World War II as a Watershed in Mississippi History," *Journal of Mississippi History* 37 (May 1975), 131–42.

24. Jack Temple Kirby, "The Southern Exodus, 1910–1960: A Primer for Historians," *Journal of Southern History* 49 (Nov. 1983), 600.

25. Maurice R. Cooper, "History of Cotton and the United States Cottonseed Industry," in Alton E. Bailey, ed., *Cottonseed and Cottonseed Products: Their Chemistry and Chemical Technology* (New York, 1948), 17–23 and Table 3, "Cottonseed Oil Mills: Number of Mills, Number of Wage Earners, Quantity of Seed Crushed, and Value of Products in the United States in Specified Years, 1859–1939"; Luther A. Ransom, *The Great Cottonseed Industry of the South*

(New York, 1911), 21–22; H. C. Nixon, "The Rise of the American Cottonseed Oil Industry," *Journal of Political Economy* 38 (Feb. 1930), 73–85.

26. M. R. Jones to Christie Benet, Feb. 21, 1929, in *Investigation of the Cottonseed Industry*, Senate Docs., 71 Cong., 2 Sess., pt. 7, Mississippi, 7894–95; D. A. Blanton to W. F. Bridewell, Jan. 4, 1929, in pt. 11, Arkansas, 13985; testimony of D. A. Blanton, ibid., 13395; Federal Trade Commission letter of submittal, May 19, 1933, ibid., vol. 19, ix.

27. J. E. Doherty to C. D. Jordan, Sept. 25, 1929, ibid., pt. 11, Arkansas, 13968–75; D. B. Brown to J. R. Whitthorne, Oct. 3, 1928, ibid., 13857; H. M. Evans to S. G. Sample,·Nov. 12, 1928, pt. 7, Mississippi, 7927–28. For a summary of the findings of the FTC investigation, see Summary Report, ibid., vol. 19, vii–xv.

28. Temple Cotton Oil Co. to F. T. Mitchell, Oct. 9, 1929, ibid., pt. 11, Arkansas, 13915; John F. Moloney, "Economics of Cottonseed Crushing," in Bailey, ed., *Cottonseed and Cottonseed Products*, 656; Benedict and Stine, *Agricultural Commodity Programs*, 7–8.

29. Moloney, "Economics of Cottonseed Crushing," 651; Charles S. Aiken, "Cotton Ginning," in David C. Roller and Robert W. Twyman, eds., *The Encyclopedia of Southern History* (Baton Rouge, 1979), 302–3.

30. Table 83, "Cotton: Area, Yield, and Production, by States, 1976–78," in USDA, *Agricultural Statistics, 1979* (Washington, 1979), 62; Sayre, "Cotton Mechanization since World War II," 117.

31. Fornari, "Big Change"; Table 1, "Cotton and Soybean Production," 247; Table 85, "Cotton: Production, Season Average Price per Pound, and Value, by States, 1976–78," 63; Table 181, "Soybeans: Area, Yield, and Production, by States, 1976–78," 131, all tables in *Agricultural Statistics, 1979*.

32. Table 85, "Cotton: Production, Season Average Price per Pound, and Value, by States, 1976–78," 63; Table 172, "Peanuts: Area, Yield, and Production, by States, 1976–78," 126; Table 183, "Soybeans for Beans: Production, Disposition, and Value, by States, Crop of 1978 (Preliminary)," 132; Table 458, "Cattle and Calves: Production, Disposition, Cash Receipts, and Gross Income, by States, 1978 (Preliminary)," 308–9; Table 138, "Tobacco: Area, Yield, Production, and Value, United States, 1964–78," 99; Table 139, "Tobacco, Area, Yield, and Production, by States, 1976–78," 99, all in *Agricultural Statistics, 1979*; Gilbert C. Fite, "Southern Agriculture since the Civil War: An Overview," *Agricultural History* 53 (Jan. 1979), 19.

33. Table 569, "Chickens: Number, Value per Head, and Total Value, by States, Dec. 1976–78," 396; Table 466, "Hogs and Pigs: Number and Value, by States, Dec. 1, 1976–78," 314, in *Agricultural Statistics, 1979*.

34. Fite, "Southern Agriculture since the Civil War," 20. On the increased use of fertilizer in the South, see Richard C. Sheridan, "Chemical Fertilizers in Southern Agriculture," *Agricultural History* 53 (Jan. 1979), 308–18.

35. Mark A. Shelton III, "Cotton Production Systems: Yields, Cost and Returns: A Mid-Southern Farmer's Systems Approach and Views," in *Proceedings of the 1980 Beltwide Cotton Production-Mechanization Conference*, St. Louis, Mo., Jan 9–10, 1980, 46.

36. Allen Bragg, "Cotton Production Systems: Yields, Cost and Returns: A Southeastern Farmer's Systems Approach and Views," ibid., 45.

37. Clifford Hoelscher, "Cotton Production Systems: Yields, Costs and Returns: A Southwestern Farmer's Systems Approach and Views," ibid., 46–47.

38. Raleigh *News and Observer*, Dec. 12, 1982. "Cotton: Acres, Yield, Production and Value by Counties, 1975–76," in *North Carolina Agricultural Statistics* (Raleigh, 1978), 28–29.

Chapter 12

1. Joseph C. Robert, *The Story of Tobacco in America* (Chapel Hill, 1949), 269–72; J. R. Ferrell, "Wartime Changes in Farming and Their Peacetime Implications: Tobacco," in Manuscripts, 1940–46, Box 1048, Bureau of Agricultural Economics, Record Group 83, National Archives (hereafter cited as BAE, RG 83, NA).

2. U.S. Department of Commerce, Bureau of the Census, *United States Census of Agriculture*, N.C., Tobacco, 1940–54 vols.; Murray R. Benedict and Oscar C. Stine, *The Agricultural Commodity Programs: Two Decades of Experience* (New York, 1956), 69–70. For an analysis of the political dimensions of tobacco during the war era, see Charles M. Hardin, "The Tobacco Program: Exception or Portent?" *Journal of Farm Economics* 28 (Nov. 1946), 920–37.

3. Benedict and Stine, *Agricultural Commodity Programs*, 71–72, 78–79, 95.

4. Ibid., 67; Ferrell, "Wartime Changes in Farming."

5. Benedict and Stine, *Agricultural Commodity Programs*, 85–87. See also John E. Mason, "Acreage Allotments and Land Prices," *Journal of Land and Public Utility Economics* (May 1946), 176–81; Calvin B. Hoover and B. U. Ratchford, *Economic Resources and Policies of the South* (New York, 1951), 357.

6. "Report to the Chief, 1945," Manuscripts, 1940–46, Box 966, BAE, RG 83, NA.

7. Meredith C. Wilson, deputy director, Extension Farm Labor Program, to J. B. Hutson, Aug. 8, 1945; E. J. Overby, assistant to the secretary, to Joseph O. Parker, House Agriculture Committee, Dec. 23, 1947, Employment, Records of the Secretary of Agriculture, Record Group 16, National Archives (hereafter cited as SOA, RG 16, NA). See also numerous requests for farm labor in the employment file, ibid., and Clinton P. Anderson to J. B. Hutson, Aug. 14, 1945, ibid.

8. W. Davidson, agricultural advisor, to C. W. E. Pittman, extension service, Dec. 22, 1944; Davidson to Pittman, July 18, 1945, Farm Labor Program, War Correspondence, Records of the Extension Service, Record Group 33, National Archives. See also W. S. Brown, director of Extension Service, Georgia, to Meredith C. Wilson, July 10, 1944, and H. S. McLendon, assistant state farm labor supervisor, to Pittman, June 20, 1946, ibid.

9. "Number of Prisoners of War Actually Working in Agriculture," June 21, 1945, Prisoners of War, ibid.

10. Susan Gibbs and Bob Peele, "German Prisoners of War in Martin County Help with Tobacco Harvest," in *Smoke to Gold: The Story of Tobacco in Martin County* (Greenville, N.C., 1978), 70–71.

11. Ferrell, "Wartime Changes in Farming"; "'Mister Danny' Kelly, Operator," 68, and "Sam Hobgood, Factory Manager," 5, both in WPA interviews by Leonard Rapport, in his possession; interview with Simon Collie, Seven Paths, N.C., Feb. 20, 1982.

12. For a discussion of the health issue, see pt. 5, "The Risks of Smoking: Rights and Ramifications," in William R. Finger, ed., *The Tobacco Industry in Transition: Policies for the 1980s* (Lexington, Mass., 1981), 235–85.

13. *U.S. Census of Agriculture*, N.C., 1954, 1959. Dale M. Hoover, in "The Structure of Tobacco Production Units," in Frank Bordeaux, Jr., and Russell H. Brannon, eds., *Social and Economic Issues Confronting the Tobacco Industry in the Seventies* (Lexington, Ky., 1972), 134, 136, reports that the number of flue-cured farms fell 53 percent over the 1949–64 period, but he does not explain why. Sumter County, S.C., showed a similar trend, as did Tift County, Ga. Sumter County farms between 1954 and 1959 declined from 1,124 to 648 in number, and the acreage dropped from 2,859 to 2,026. During the same years Tift County farms declined from 890 to 604 and acreage dropped from 3,810 to 2,608 (*U.S. Census of Agriculture*, S.C., Ga., 1954, 1959). See also S. H. Hobbs, Jr., "Tar Heel Farming: A Time of Sweeping Change," in Hugh Talmage Lefler, ed., *North Carolina History Told by Contemporaries* (Chapel Hill, 1965), 519–22.

14. John Fraser Hart and Ennis L. Chestang, "Rural Revolution in East Carolina," *Geographical Review* (1978), 453; Hoover, "Structure of Tobacco Production Units," 138. Tobacco prices continued to be supported at such a high percentage of parity that many agricultural leaders feared that export sales would drop drastically. A slight revision in the parity formula passed Congress in 1960. See J. C. Williamson, Jr., and W. D. Toussaint, "Parity and Support Prices for Flue-Cured Tobacco," *Journal of Farm Economics* 48 (1961), 16–26.

15. *U.S. Census of Agriculture*, N.C., 1954, 1959; Calvin L. Beale, "Impact of Changing Tobacco Demands and Technology on Population and Migration," in Bordeaux and Brannon, eds., *Social and Economic Issues Confronting the Tobacco Industry*, 248. See also C. B. Highfill, Randleman, N.C., to Ezra Taft Benson, Jan. 7, 1956, Economics 2, SOA, RG 16, NA.

16. W. D. Toussaint and P. S. Stone, "Evaluating a Farm Machine prior to Its Introduction," *Journal of Farm Economics* 42 (May 1969), 241–51; Hart and Chestang, "Rural Revolution in East Carolina," 446.

17. Hart and Chestang, "Rural Revolution in East Carolina," 443.

18. Charles K. Mann, "The Tobacco Franchise for Whom?," in Finger, ed., *Tobacco Industry in Transition*, 49, 51; Hart and Chestang, "Rural Revolution in East Carolina," 453.

19. Charles Pugh, "The Federal Tobacco Program: How It Works and Alternatives for Change," in Finger, ed., *Tobacco Industry in Transition*, 16–17.

20. Mann, "Tobacco Franchise for Whom?," 41.

21. Ibid., 42.

22. Gigi Berardi, "Can Tobacco Farmers Adjust to Mechanization? A Look at

Allotment Holders in Two North Carolina Counties," in Finger, ed., *Tobacco Industry in Transition*, 48–49. John C. Stovall, in "An Overview of Social and Economic Issues Confronting the Tobacco Industry in the Seventies," in Bordeaux and Brannon, eds., *Social and Economic Issues Confronting the Tobacco Industry*, pointed out that mechanization "would displace large numbers of workers and deprive them of their only means of livelihood." Unless the needs of such persons were cared for, "the results of mechanization could be worse than no mechanization at all," he concluded (6). See also Frederic L. Hoff, William D. Givan, Owen K. Shugars, and Verner M. Grise, "Flue-Cured Tobacco Mechanization and Labor: Impacts of Alternative Production Levels," USDA, Economic Research Service, Agricultural Economic Report No. 368, Apr. 1977; Hart and Chestang, "Rural Revolution in East Carolina," 46–47.

23. J. Barlow Herget, "Industrial Growth: An Alternative for North Carolina's Tobacco Farmers," in Finger, ed., *Tobacco Industry in Transition*, 103–8.

24. Hart and Chestang, "Rural Revolution in East Carolina," 456–57. See also Beale, "Impact of Changing Tobacco Demands," 248–49.

25. *U.S. Census of Agriculture*, N.C., 1964, 1969. Nathaniel Polster, "House Pressed to Eliminate Tobacco Supports," Oct. 27, 1981, MS in author's possession. In 1982 Wilson County had 2,096 allotments and Pitt County 2,456 (*Congressional Record*, July 14, 1982, S8285).

26. Herget, "Industrial Growth," 104; Robert Dalton, "Changes in the Structure of the Flue-Cured Tobacco Farm: A Compilation of Available Data Sources," in Finger, ed., *Tobacco Industry in Transition*, 64–65. The *Agricultural Census* shows 44,023 farms in North Carolina in 1974. Sumter County farms fell from 648 to 193 over the 1964–74 decade, and Tift County farms dropped from 428 to 191 (*U.S. Agricultural Census*, S.C., Ga., N.C., 1964, 1969, 1974).

27. Hart and Chestang, "Rural Revolution in East Carolina," 449–50. For a survey of the changes in the tobacco culture, see Philip L. Martin and Stanley S. Johnson, "Tobacco Technology and Agricultural Labor," *American Journal of Agricultural Economics* 60 (1978), 655–60.

28. Section 1109, Agriculture and Food Act of 1981, Public Law 97–98.

29. Quoted in *Congressional Record*, July 14, 1982, S8280–81, 8285. From USDA Flue-Cured Tobacco Region 17, the report included Edgecombe, Greene, Johnston, Pitt, Sampson, and Wake counties, N.C., and from Region 18, Caswell, Durham, Granville, Person, Rockingham, Surry, and Vance counties, N.C., and Luneburg, Mecklenburg, and Pittsylvania counties, Va. See also Berardi, "Can Tobacco Farmers Adjust?," 51–57.

30. *Congressional Record*, Sept. 17, 1981, S9891.

31. Ibid., July 14, 1982, S8282.

32. Ibid., S8190–93. The bill provided that a new grower could obtain an allotment if he shared in the risk of tobacco production for one year before purchase or through a new-grower provision. This hardly gave a prospective farmer time to organize resources before the December 1983 deadline for selling allotments (S8193). For a section-by-section analysis of the bill, see ibid., S8194–8200.

33. Ibid., S8188; Spring Hope *Enterprise*, July 29, 1982.

34. For an excellent critique of the tobacco program from 1933 to 1982, see Henry Ferrell, "'Moral Bankruptcy' in Tobacco," Raleigh *News and Observer*, Nov. 28, 1982.

Chapter 13

1. Charles E. Burkhead, John W. Kirkbride, and William B. Hudson, "Rice, Popcorn, and Buckwheat: Acreage, Yield, Production, Price, and Value by States, 1906–1953," Statistical Bulletin no. 238, USDA, Agricultural Marketing Service (Washington, 1958), 2–8; Murray R. Benedict and Oscar C. Stine, *The Agricultural Commodity Programs: Two Decades of Experience* (New York, 1956), 138–44; Leon A. Mears, *The Political Economy of Rice in the United States* (Stanford, 1976), 321–23, 335–54; Table 24, "Rice, Rough: Area, Yield, Production, Disposition, and Value, United States, 1964–78," *Agricultural Statistics, 1979* (Washington, 1979), 19.

2. Henry M. Bain, "Cooperative Marketing of Rice and Its Part in the War Emergency," USDA, Farm Credit Administration, Circular no. C-129 (June 1943), 10.

3. John Norman Efferson, "The Use of Combines on Louisiana Rice Farms in 1945," *Louisiana Rural Economist* 8 (Aug. 1946), 3–5; Efferson, "The Combining and Drying of Rice in the Louisiana Rice Area in 1945 and 1946," ibid., 9 (Aug. 1947), 2–3, 5–7; Efferson, *Production and Marketing of Rice*, (New Orleans, 1952), 462–76; Wilbur M. Hurst and W. R. Humphries, "Harvesting with Combines," Farmers Bulletin no. 1761, USDA (Washington, 1947), 30–31; M. W. Slusher and Troy Mullins, "Mechanization of the Rice Harvest," Arkansas Agricultural Experiment Station and the Bureau of Agricultural Economics, 1948. For an overview of the development of new varieties of rice and production methods, see Jenkin W. Jones, "New Rices; New Practices," in *Science in Farming: The Yearbook of Agriculture, 1943–1947* (Washington, 1947), 373–78.

4. Latham White to L. J. Cappleman, Apr. 12, 1945, Records of the Agricultural Stabilization and Conservation Service, Agricultural Adjustment Administration, Rice, Record Group 145, National Archives (hereafter cited as AAA, RG 145, NA); Efferson, *Production and Marketing of Rice*, 430–34.

5. Bain, "Cooperative Marketing of Rice," 1–10; Lawson P. Babineaux, "A History of the Rice Industry of Southwestern Louisiana" (M.A. thesis, University of Southwestern Louisiana, 1967), 85; Leroy K. Smith to the Administrator, Aug. 20, 1946, Rice, AAA, RG 145, NA.

6. M. L. Anderson to William H. Case and Jean E. Zeller, July 24, 1945; USDA press release, 1945, Rice, AAA, RG 145, NA.

7. James Domengeaux and Harry D. Larcade, Jr., to Clinton P. Anderson, Jan. 30, 1946; H. C. Denturk to U.S. Government, Feb. 20, 1946, ibid.

8. Frank A. Godchaux, Jr., to J. H. McLaurin, Feb. 22, 1946, ibid.

9. Leroy K. Smith to the Administrator, Aug. 20, 1946, ibid. See also Claude Holley to Clinton P. Anderson, Aug. 26, 1946, ibid.

10. Mears, *Political Economy of Rice*, 340; Benedict and Stine, *Agricultural*

Commodity Programs, 141; Efferson, *Production and Marketing of Rice*, 435; Homer L. Brinkley to Charles F. Brannan, Nov. 22, 1949, Rice, AAA, RG 145, NA. California production increased from 6.8 million bags in 1948 to 10.2 million in 1949 (Burkhead, Kirkbride, and Hudson, "Rice, Popcorn, and Buckwheat," 9). See also R. T. Briscoe to J. J. Mansfield, Oct. 17, 1946; R. H. Wilson to Clinton P. Anderson, Oct. 23, 1946, Rice, AAA, RG 145, NA.

11. A. J. Loveland to Henry D. Larcade, Jr., Feb. 20, 1950, Rice, AAA, RG 145, NA. "Such adjustment was made," Loveland explained, "by averaging the 2-year (1948–1949) average planted acreage with the 5-year (1945–1949) average planted acreage, by giving equal weight to each of such averages."

12. E. L. Boston to Tom Connally, Feb. 8, 1950, ibid.

13. T. L. Drawhorn to Charles F. Brannan, Mar. 16, 1950; William McArthur to Drawhorn, Mar. 28, 1950, ibid.

14. H. B. Brown to E. C. Gathings, Mar. 1, 1950; John Garrich to Charles F. Brannan, Mar. 17, 1950; Carl Pohlner to Gathings, Mar. 6, 1950, ibid.; U.S. Congress, House, Rice Subcommittee of the Committee on Agriculture, *Rice Quota Study*, 84 Cong., 2 Sess., 11. See also W. H. Vansandt to John L. McClellan, Feb. 6, 1950, and petition to McClellan, Feb. 6, 1950, Rice, AAA, RG 145, NA.

15. K. T. Hutchinson to James H. Morrison, Mar. 24, 1950; Thomas B. Walker to Everett L. Lehman, Feb. 24, 1950; Robert A. Hanson to J. R. Waggenspack & Sons, Feb. 4, 1957, Rice, AAA, RG 145, NA.

16. A. J. Loveland to Henry D. Larcade, Jr., Feb. 20, 1950, ibid.; Burkhead, Kirkbride, and Hudson, "Rice, Popcorn, and Buckwheat," 2, 6–9; U.S. Department of Commerce, Bureau of the Census, *United States Census of Agriculture*, La. and Ark., Rice, 1945, 1954 vols.

17. Interview with J. M. Spicer, Aug. 31, 1982, Stuttgart, Ark. See also Troy Mullins and M. W. Slusher, "Comparison of Farming Systems for Small Rice Farms in Arkansas," Arkansas Experiment Station and Bureau of Agricultural Economics, bulletin no. 498 (June 1950); Mullins and Slusher, "Comparison of Farming Systems on Large Rice Farms in Arkansas," Arkansas Experiment Station and Bureau of Agricultural Economics, bulletin no. 509 (June 1951); M. W. Slusher, "The Use of Airplanes on Rice Farms in Arkansas," Arkansas Experiment Station and USDA, bulletin no. 541 (Dec. 1953).

18. "Wife, Daughters Lend Willing Hands to Make This Rice Farm a Success," *The Rice Journal* 59 (May 1956), 8–10.

19. Interview with Mrs. Bennie Burkett, Aug. 31, 1982, Stuttgart, Ark.; interview with Ernest Frey, Sept. 4, 1982, Eunice, La.

20. A. W. Lenius to E. T. Benson, Jan. 25, 1954; Marvin L. McLain to Lenius, Feb. 4, 1954, Rice, AAA, RG 145, NA; Shelby H. Holder, Jr., and Warren R. Grant, *U.S. Rice Industry*, USDA, ESCS, Agricultural Economic Report no. 433 (Washington, 1979), 12.

21. W. T. Champion to Marvin McLain, Aug. 1, 1955; McLain to Champion, Aug. 12, 1955, Rice, AAA, RG 145, NA. In 1973 Congress enacted a provision to allow transfer of acreage due to natural disaster (Holder and Grant, *U.S. Rice Industry*, 39).

22. Benedict and Stine, *Agricultural Commodity Programs*, 141–44; U.S.

Congress, House, Subcommittee on Rice, Committee on Agriculture, *National Acreage Allotments—Rice, Hearing on H.R. 7367,* 84 Cong., 1 Sess., July 21, 25, 1955, 51; U.S. Congress, Senate, Committee on Agriculture and Forestry, *Various Two-Price Systems of Price Support and Marketing Which Could Be Made Applicable to Rice,* 84 Cong., 1 Sess., May 23, 24, 25, 26, 1955, 26.

23. U.S. Congress, House, *National Acreage Allotments—Rice, Hearings on H.R. 7367,* 42–43.

24. Louis Richard to Russell Long, Nov. 15, 1955; Lloyd N. Case to Long, Mar. 16, 1956, Rice, AAA, RG 145, NA; *The Rice Journal* 34 (May 1931), 12–13.

25. Wilson Mott to Russell Long, Nov. 14, 1955, Rice, AAA, RG 145, NA. See also Lloyd N. Case to Long, Mar. 16, 1956, ibid.

26. Finest J. Pitre to Allen J. Ellender, Nov. 3, 1955; Howard J. Doggett to Pitre, Dec. 5, 1955, ibid.

27. Herman Talley to Allen J. Ellender, Nov. 25, 1955; Talley to Ellender, Jan. 13, 1956; Ellender to Talley, Feb. 6, 1956; C. E. Slack to Talley, Feb. 20, 1956; Slack to Ellender, Feb. 27, 1956; Talley to Ellender, Mar. 9, 1956; True D. Morse to Ellender, Apr. 17, 1956, ibid. See also Lawrence Breaux to Ezra Taft Benson, Mar. 20, 1956; David Merritt to Benson, May 9, 1958; Raymond J. Pollock to Merritt, May 21, 1958; Eugene D. Kelly to Director, Grain Division, May 27, 1958; Pollock to Merritt, June 10, 1958, ibid.

28. Jimmie Hanson to Ezra Taft Benson, Dec. 8, 1955; Ray Folkland to Benson, Dec. 19, 1955, ibid.

29. Henry Unkel to T. A. Thompson, Dec. 29, 1955, ibid. See also Levy J. Foux to Dwight D. Eisenhower, Dec. 11, 1956, ibid.

30. U.S. Congress, House, Committee on Agriculture, *Hearings on Rice Acreage Allotments,* 87 Cong., 1 Sess., Nov. 7, 1961, El Campo, Tex., 46–47. See also August Cihal to Clark W. Thompson, Nov. 12, 1961, 60–61, ibid., and U.S. Congress, House, Committee on Agriculture, *Hearings on Rice Acreage Allotment,* 85 Cong., 1 Sess., July 1, 1957, 1–18.

31. Dennie D. Tilbury to Ezra Taft Benson, Mar. 3, 1956; John E. Trip to Tilbury, Mar. 20, 1956, ibid. It is not clear whether or not Albert Tilbury received an allotment in 1956, but in 1975 he was a ranger in a state park near Bastrop, La., where he eagerly shared his reminiscences of the 1927 Mississippi River flood. See Pete Daniel, *Deep'n as It Come: The 1927 Mississippi River Flood* (New York, 1977), 103–5.

32. Hubert C. Wirtz to Allen J. Ellender, Dec. 29, 1955, Rice, AAA, RG 145, NA.

33. Gene R. Andrew to Dwight D. Eisenhower, Feb. 20, 1954; Marvin L. McLain to Andrew, Mar. 22, 1954; Andrew to Ezra Taft Benson, Jan. 26, 1956; Lloyd Case to Andrew, Mar. 28, 1956, ibid.

34. Isaac Guillory to Russell Long, Jan. 30, 1956; Marvin L. McLain to Long, Mar. 14, 1956, ibid.

35. Grace E. Sykes to Ezra Taft Benson, Feb. 7, 1958; Raymond J. Pollock to Grace Sykes, Mar. 6, 1958; Lowell Vertrees Sykes to Ezra Taft Benson, Feb. 14, 1958, ibid.

36. U.S. Congress, House, *National Acreage Allotments—Rice, Hearings on H.R. 7367*, 20–21.

37. Ewell Moore to National ASC office, Apr. 22, 1957, Rice, AAA, RG 145, NA. See also Eldes Simon to Allen J. Ellender, ca. Mar. 20, 1957; Marvin L. McLain to Ellender, Apr. 29, 1957, ibid.; and *Rice Situation* (Dec. 1957), 9.

38. Clarence Slack to Raymond J. Pollock, Apr. 4, 1958; John E. Tripp to Chairman, Louisiana ASC state committee, Apr. 21, 1958; Slack to Director, Grain Division, July 21, 1958; John Sidney Caughey to Chairman, Louisiana ASC state committee, July 31, 1958, all in Rice, AAA, RG 145, NA. See also Marvin L. McLain to Allen J. Ellender, Aug. 4, 1958; F. S. Kelly, Jr., to Director, Grain Division, Oct. 15, 1958; Maurice L. Troxclair to Director, Grain Division, Sept. 26, 1958; D. Thibaut to Director, Grain Division, Sept. 29, 1958; Mason P. Gilfoil to J. Alton Satterfield, Sept. 29, 1958, ibid.

39. Glenn W. Buzzard to USDA, Oct. 29, 1958; Raymond J. Pollock to Buzzard, Nov. 10, 1958, ibid.

40. U.S. *Census of Agriculture*, La., Calcasieu and Acadia parishes, Rice, 1954, 1959 vols.

41. U.S. Congress, House, *Hearings on Rice Acreage Allotments*, 1961, 82.

42. Mears, *Political Economy of Rice*, 333, 340–44; U.S. Congress, House, *Rice Quota Study*, 1956, 18–19. See also Trudy Huskamp Peterson, *Agricultural Exports, Farm Income, and the Eisenhower Administration* (Lincoln, 1979).

43. U.S. *Census of Agriculture*, La., Calcasieu and Acadia parishes; Ark., Arkansas and Lonoke counties, Rice, 1954, 1974 vols.

44. Table 24, "Rice, Rough: Area, Yield, Production, Disposition, and Value, United States, 1964–78," 19; Table 34, "Rice, Rough: Price-Support Operations, United States, 1964–79," 24, *Agricultural Statistics, 1979*. Louisiana increased from 568,000 to 587,000, and Texas from 508,000 to 558,000. Table 30, "Rice: Area, Yield, and Production, by State, 1976–78," 21, ibid.

Chapter 14

1. Liberty Hyde Bailey, *The Country-Life Movement in the United States* (New York, 1918), 203. David B. Danbom, in *The Resisted Revolution: Urban America and the Industrialization of Agriculture, 1900–1930* (Ames, 1979), concludes: "The Country Life Movement, stripped of all pretensions, was nothing less than the demand of an ascendant urban-industrial America, backed by an increasingly activist state, for an organized and efficient agriculture that would adequately supplement it socially and economically" (74).

2. See David Noble, "Present Tense Technology," *Democracy* 3 (Spring 1983), 11.

3. John A. Hostetler, *Amish Society*, 3rd ed. (Baltimore, 1980), 127.

4. Ward Sinclair, "How to Make $100,000 from a 25-Acre Farm," *Washington Post*, Apr. 24, 1983; Krista Brewer, "The Good Life on a 25-Acre Farm," *Southern Exposure* 11 (Nov.-Dec. 1983), 27–29.

5. John Gardner, *Grendel* (New York, 1971), 121.

Index